The First European Agriculture

The First European Agriculture, a study of the Osteological and Botanical Evidence until 2000 BC, by Jacqueline Murray.

Edinburgh, at the University Press.

© *Jacqueline Murray 1970*

EDINBURGH UNIVERSITY PRESS

22 George Square, Edinburgh

ISBN 0 85224 182 8

North America

Aldine Publishing Company

529 South Wabash Avenue, Chicago 60605

Printed in Great Britain by

R. & R. Clark Ltd., Edinburgh

Contents

Preface

This book on the earliest agricultural societies of Europe derives from a thesis for the degree of PH.D. presented to Edinburgh University, and is a synopsis of the information from over a thousand excavations across Europe and the Near East, based upon the osteological and botanical remains that have been found at these sites. I have not undertaken new identifications or measurements at first hand on the extant material, but have felt that before new work of this kind is undertaken in detail and on a broad front, a digest of the information available up to the present is necessary as a point of departure. I have, therefore, endeavoured to set out the evidence, and draw conclusions, that mark the culmination of one stage of research, and provide the basis for the beginning of another. Where possible histograms have been constructed (often for the first time) to illustrate the relative importance of the different domestic animals. The information considered here includes both published and unpublished material known and accessible to me up until February 1968.

The result is an attempted synthesis of current views on the beginnings of European agriculture. The feeling that clarity is lost by the inclusion of too much detail may be inevitable, but a reference work of this nature cannot escape such detail, and it is hoped that the statistics and bibliographical apparatus here presented may have a permanent value. Doubtless time must modify many of the inferences made here, but a beginning has to be made. As on an excavation itself we must have a working hypothesis which is to be altered as new evidence comes to light, and this is the purpose of this book.

I must, in particular, thank Professor Stuart Piggott of Edinburgh University for his invaluable help and criticism, the result of which is this book in its present form. Professor and Mrs R. Braidwood helped greatly with valuable discussions, information and hospitality. I should also like to thank Professor C. Reed, Professor J. Boessneck, Professor M. Stenberger, Dr S. Bökönyi, Dr Maria Hopf and Mr E. Higgs for their correspondence and discussions. I must also thank Dr Ruth Tringham of Edinburgh University for her assistance in the collection of the Russian material, much of which was unavailable outside the Soviet Union, and also for her advice concerning the cultures of eastern Europe. To sketch my picture I have used the reports from numerous excavations, and I am indebted to all those responsible for these records.

JACQUELINE MURRAY

To Donald and Shelagh, Richard and Hester

       . . . . ; that which we are, we are;
One equal temper of heroic hearts,
Made weak by time and fate, but strong in will
To strive, to seek, to find, and not to yield.

    Tennyson

1. The Problems and the Background

The earliest concepts of a model of the prehistoric past were based upon technological divisions, which produced the idea of a Stone Age, Bronze Age and Iron Age. The Stone Age, that is the period in which stone cutting implements were manufactured but the use of metals was unknown, was first divided up by Lubbock into what he called the Old Stone Age, or Palaeolithic, and the New Stone Age, or Neolithic. These two epochs lay in different geological periods, with the earlier in the Pleistocene and the later in the Holocene. The basis of this new division was the method in which the stone tools were made, by chipping or by grinding, together with the absence or presence of pottery. With the work of certain eminent nineteenth and early twentieth century archaeologists a new criterion for distinguishing the Palaeolithic from the Neolithic became apparent, and this was based upon the method in which food was obtained by the communities involved. Their means of food production, or subsistence-economics, could be centred on hunting, fishing and gathering, or else on the breeding of their own animals and cultivation of the soil. As more information was amassed, it became clear that the stone-basis of differentiation was not valid, as polished stone occurred in the mesolithic as well as late palaeolithic periods, and also the pottery criterion was not sufficient since communities were discovered that bred animals and cultivated plants, polished their stone tools and constructed substantial settlements, but had no knowledge of the art of pottery making. So it became necessary to find a new distinguishing feature between the two prehistoric periods. At the present time the method of food production is probably the best dividing line between the pre-Neolithic and Neolithic societies, and it is therefore the subsistence-economics of these Neolithic people in Europe that are the subject of the study which has resulted in this book.

The evidence involved consists of the osteological and botanical remains that have been recovered during excavations. The greatest value clearly lies in those reports which provide descriptions, comparisons and a statistical analysis of both the bone and the plant remains that have been discovered, but unfortunately such reports are few in number. In the majority of cases only the species of animals and plants present are known, and in other instances it is stated that a certain animal was the basis of the economy, but the evidence upon which this statement is based is not provided. This is particularly unfortunate since the numbers upon which a conclusion is reached are all-important. The larger the number of bones or plants involved, the greater is the probability that the information derived will give an accurate representation of the economy. In many cases, both in the early part of this century, and occasionally up until the present day, the bones and plants found during excavations were regarded as being totally unimportant and irrelevant, and so were discarded without even being mentioned in the final publications. Such practice has made a coherent knowledge of the subsistence-economics in certain areas virtually impossible. So it is seen that the nature of the evidence is extremely variable, and certain areas are well documented whereas others are decidedly patchy or even devoid of information.

It is necessary at this stage to mention the method by which the various archaeological cultures have been dated in this book. The basis is that of isotopic dating by means of carbon 14, using the half-life of 5570 ± 30 years, and the Suess effect has been corrected for in the Gröningen dates. All dates mentioned appear in years BC. The recently discovered fluctuation between the carbon 14 content of wood whose age is known by means of dendrochronology, and the amount present in samples that were thought to be of the same age, has not been accounted for.

During the second half of the last century, some remarkable work was done by Rütimeyer and Heer on the domesticated animals and cultivated plants of the 'lake dwellings' in Switzerland. Rütimeyer found remains of small domestic animals which he termed 'turbary' (from their occurrence in peat deposits), and these were later found in many other areas of Europe. These include cattle (*Bos brachyceros*), sheep (*Ovis aries palustris*), goat (*Capra hircus palustris*), pig (*Sus scrofa palustris*) and dog (*Canis familiaris palustris*). Rütimeyer and Heer provided not only a description and identification of these remains, but also a statistical analysis so that an idea of the relative importance of the different animals could be obtained. This was the first time that archaeology and the natural sciences had worked together so successfully, and they provided, and still do provide, one of the best examples of how this work should be done. At a slightly later date equally vital work was being carried out in Scandinavia by Winge and Pira on the osteological refuse found in the coastal 'kitchen middens'. The first person to recognise the importance of the archaeological food remains in this country was Pitt-Rivers, and at about the same time Pumpelly and Duerst provided the first comprehensive report on the faunal remains in the Near East at a site in Turkmenia. This encouraging start was, however, soon forgotten, and in many areas of the Near East and of Europe very little information was obtained over the following thirty years. More recently the interest in this subject has been revived, and in most regions of Europe and the Near East the animal bones and plant remains have been preserved by the excavators and identified by experts in this field.

There are five main species of animals to be considered in the context of early domestication, namely cattle, sheep, goat, pig and dog. Of these cattle and pigs were found in most areas of Holocene Europe and the Near East, as they had been during the Pleistocene. The position of sheep and goat on the other hand is slightly different. They were known during the Pleistocene in both Europe and the Near East, but as their environment changed they became concentrated in the Near East, and the general opinion is that they became extinct in Europe as the climatic conditions became unfavourable. The accepted distribution of these four wild species during the period which in archaeological terms is the transitional mesolithic/neolithic phase is shown in Fig. 1. The question of the wild progenitor of the dog will be discussed shortly.

Wild cattle, or aurochs, which are found over most of Europe, are classified as *Bos primigenius*, and it is this species that occurs again in the Near East. The variant found in eastern Iran and India is referred to as *Bos namadicus*. It is basically the same animal as the aurochs, but has certain modifications as a result of its different environment. No small breed of wild cattle has been established, although there have been various claims for its existence. Hence it is from the large species *Bos primigenius* that all animals domesticated within the area under consideration must emerge.

The distribution of wild sheep and goat is confined to Asia and certain Mediterranean islands. The following species of sheep need to be considered as the prototypes for the domestic form: the European moufflon (*Ovis musimon*) which is confined to the islands of the Mediterranean, the urial or mountain sheep (*Ovis vignei*), the Asiatic moufflon or red sheep (*Ovis orientalis*) and the argali (*Ovis ammon*). The Asiatic moufflon and the urial have many similarities and it has been suggested that the latter could be included in the former group (Reed 1960). The main difference between the two lies in their areas of distribution, with the urial being found in the mountainous zones to the east of the moufflon, and extending from Iran, through India to Tibet. It would seem highly probable that the morphological differences that have been observed are purely the result of the differing environment. The argali is found to the north of this in the Altai mountains of China (see Fig. 1). The sheep relevant to the origins of domestication in the present context are the Asiatic moufflon and the urial.

There is only one species of wild goat, the bezoar or pasang (*Capra hircus aegagrus*), and it is from this animal that all the domestic forms arise. The bones of sheep and goat are virtually identical with only a few distinguishing features. For this reason it is often necessary to consider these animals together and they are then termed ovicaprids. The small domestic ovicaprids are called 'turbary', and the large sheep, similar to the moufflon, which were found during the late neolithic have been called 'Copper (Age) sheep' by Duerst.

All domestic pigs originate from the same wild species (*Sus scrofa ferus*). There is, however, a sub-species, *Sus vittatus*, which is found in south-east Asia, and is a slightly smaller animal. It has been suggested that pig domestication originated in this region of Asia and so spread to western Asia and Europe (Sauer 1952). The wild pig found in south-east Europe bears some similarity to this south-east Asian variety, and it is smaller than the usual boar found in other regions of Europe.

Various suggestions have been made for the wild ancestor of the dog. These include dingos, jackals, pariah dogs, unspecified wild dogs and the wolf. The idea of a wild dog as ancestor was first proposed by Dahr (1937), who thought that the difference between the domestic dogs and the wolves was too great for the former to have originated from the latter. The dingo and pariah dog are thought to be recent representatives of this extinct group of canids. However, it has been shown that domestication can reduce the size of the animals appreciably, so that Dahr's argument is no longer held to be valid. There has been no detailed study of the pariah dog, so that its role in the emergence of the dog cannot be established. It has also recently been shown that the jackal was not the ancestor of the dog (Clutton-Brock 1962, Reed 1960). There remains the wolf. There are two types to be considered, the large European wolf (*Canis lupus*) and the smaller Arabian wolf (*Canis lupus arabs*). Both of these are of importance to the evolution of the dog, and it is probable that both were domesticated independently.

Wild horses can be divided into an eastern and a western group. The former includes the Przewalski horse, which has recently been sighted again in Mongolia (Kaszab 1966), and the extinct tarpan, and of these the Przewalski horse has always been confined to Asia. The tarpan is known from various areas of the Near East, and it also extended into southern Russia and eastern Europe. The western group of horses were found in Europe and consist of the large *germanicus* horse of Scandinavia and Germany, and the smaller *miohip-*

pus horse which occurs to the south of this. Other equoids to be mentioned include the half-ass or onager and the donkey, both of which occur wild in the Near East. Of these various equoids, the tarpan is thought to be the most significant element in the evolution of the domestic horse (Lundholm 1949). In connection with the donkey, it should be mentioned that although this animal was thought to have been extinct in Europe after the Palaeolithic, it has recently been shown to be present during the early neolithic in eastern Europe as a wild animal.

The 'noble grasses', as the wild prototypes of the cultivated cereals are called, have a much more limited distribution. With the exception of millet they are confined to Asia, and their generalised distribution is shown in Fig. 2.

The wheat genus is divided into three groups. The first is the diploid group of which einkorn is the only representative, the second is tetraploid and includes emmer, hard wheat and other varieties which do not enter into this discussion. The final group is composed of the hexaploid wheats, namely bread wheat, club wheat and spelt. Einkorn originated from *Triticum aegilopoides* and emmer from *Triticum dicoccoides*, and of these einkorn has the widest Asiatic distribution and is also found in a small area of southern Greece. Both of these forms of wheat are also said to occur wild in Georgia and Armenia and to resemble the Near East species very closely (Zukovskiy 1962). There appear to be no wild prototypes for hexaploid wheats. Both bread wheat and club wheat are thought to have arisen as a result of chromosome aberration in emmer. The origin of spelt is more obscure. Hybridization between emmer and club wheat has been suggested as has chromosome aberration in club wheat. Spelt occurs in a few instances during the neolithic, but it is not until the Iron Age that it became of importance as a crop in its own right. Hard wheat is also derived from emmer (Helbaek 1960).

All cultivated barleys originate from a single wild form, *Hordeum spontaneum*, which has a wider distribution than either of the wild wheat forms (see Fig. 2). This wild form is two-rowed, and the earliest cultivated form is also two-rowed. From this species the six-rowed species emerged, and it has also been created artificially from the two-rowed form by radiation treatment. Four-rowed barley is also reported in Neolithic Europe, and it is probably derived from the two- and six-rowed types.

Millet occurs wild in both Europe and the Near East and may be divided into two cultivated species. The first is broomcorn millet (*Panicum miliaceum*) and its wild progenitor is unknown (Helbaek 1959b). The other subspecies is Italian millet (*Seteria italica*) which is derived from *Seteria viridis* and is found in southern Europe. Various legumes are found wild throughout Europe and the Near East, and those cultivated include peas, lentils, vetch and bean.

The other important plant to be grown was flax. This has been shown to be derived from *Linum bienne* by Helbaek (1959a), and it is found wild in the Near East. Another species is found in central Europe, *Linum austriaceum*, but the cultivated flax found in Europe is not derived from this sort.

The earliest attempts by man to domesticate animals and cultivate plants must necessarily have taken place within the area of distribution of the wild species. The primitive cereal crops contain a mixture of einkorn, emmer and barley, and these grasses are never found separately. Hence their cultivation must have been initiated within the area of their common distribution. It is seen from Fig. 2 that there are two such regions, one above the source of the Tigris in Kurdistan and the other in Palestine. The relevant wild animals ancestral to domestic forms are also found in these regions. There has been a certain amount of controversy as to where the origins of agriculture took place, and both of the above zones have strong supporters. Braidwood maintains that farming was first attempted in Kurdistan, in the crescent-shaped area that represents the region in which the wild wheats and barley occur together, and is referred to by Braidwood as the *Fertile Crescent*. In this hilly zone at the foothills of the Zagros mountains crops would seldom be lost because of lack of rain, and sheep and goat, which appear to have been the first animals to be domesticated, are often encountered in the surrounding countryside. Kenyon, however, thinks it is more probable that the change in subsistence economics took place in Palestine, and the site upon which her argument is based is Jericho, where domestic goats have been found. There has been no examination of the botanical remains as yet, but from the large size of the settlement it seems reasonable to assume that cereals were cultivated. There are, however, few further sites known to support this theory, whereas various primitive settlements have been found by Braidwood and his colleagues in the Fertile Crescent. The first to be found was that of Jarmo, but the date of this site is in some doubt since carbon 14 dates varying from 7000 to 5000 had been obtained, but a period around 6000 is thought to represent the likely date of settlement. Since the discovery of this site many others have been located, although obviously not all have yet been excavated, and one of these sites shows that sheep were in the process of being domesticated around 9000.

Braidwood has discussed the emergence of these food-producing societies in detail (1952–1962b). As he sees it, the evolution was a gradual one, starting with specialised food-gathering and the exploitation of a particular animal, and developing into a period of incipient agriculture from which the cultivation of wheat and barley emerged together with the domestication of ovicaprids. This resulted in the primary village farming communities, which gradually became more intensified and new animals and plants were added to the domestic stock. Eventually cattle were castrated and the ox-drawn plough constructed. Irrigation was invented to provide better crops and to extend the areas of their cultivation. Experiments were being made in the specialised breeding of animals, and sheep were reared for wool, cattle for milk, and different breeds of dogs emerged.

Before the evidence for European agriculture can be considered, it is necessary to examine the evidence from the Near East where the origins of agriculture took place, and from whence the impetus behind the spread of this new method of acquiring food must come. It is most unfortunate that this vital area was one of those to suffer most in earlier years from the lack of knowledge of the excavators, and in nearly all classical excavations the surviving ecological material was thrown on the refuse dumps and barely mentioned in the site publications. The evidence from this area may be divided into five sections. These consist of the Natufian sites of the mesolithic, and the Transitional, Aceramic, Neolithic and Chalcolithic sites.

The Natufian culture is centred in Palestine between 8500 and 7000 BC. In the late stages villages with circular or oval houses have been found as well as the traditional cave dwellings. Burials occur in the dwellings, be it house or cave. Microliths form the basis of the flint industry. Burins, scrapers, sickle blades, hoes all occur as well as ground stone vases, figurines, querns, mortars and pestles. The microlithic arrow heads take the form of lunate blades rather than the tanged shape. Many bone sickle hafts survive, and sometimes these have finely carved handles in the form of an animal's head, which are realistic and carefully executed. Other elements in the bone industry include needles, awls, harpoons and fish hooks. Food was obtained by the hunting of animals and the gathering of plants. The animals exploited include red deer, roe deer, fallow deer, aurochs, gazelle, goat, horse, boar, hyena, fox, small carnivores, hare and tortoise. Fruits and berries were gathered, wild grasses reaped and other vegetables and roots collected.

Claims for the domestication of cattle, goat and pig at this stage have been made by Neuville (1951) on the results of a site known as el-Khaim. In each case the evidence rests upon a single find, and after a careful examination both Reed and Zeuner came to the conclusion that the bones were morphologically identical to the wild species so

7

that there could be no grounds for assuming that domestication had taken place. Dogs are reported from two main sites, the Belt Cave which lies near the Caspian Sea, and from the caves of Mount Carmel in Palestine. According to Reed (1960) the necessary anatomical studies had not been carried out on the Belt Cave material (Coon 1951, Pohlhausen 1954). He thinks it probable that the bones belong to the wild jackal rather than the dog. The remains from Mount Carmel have recently been re-examined by Clutton-Brock (1962), with the following results. The canid reported from the pre-Natufian levels was not the jackal, as was earlier reported, but was in fact the small Arabian wolf. Also the 'Natufian dogs', said to be derived from the jackal, fall within the range of the small Arabian wolf and the pariah dogs. The only factor suggestive of domestication was one relatively wide jaw, and it is possible that this represents the initial stages of domestication of the small wolves, but this cannot be proven.

There is no evidence for plant cultivation at this stage. The wild grasses were probably reaped in quantity, as the presence of mortars, querns and pestles indicate, and the flint sickle blades were found to have a characteristic sheen which is only obtained from the cutting of reeds or wild or cultivated grasses. Intensified gathering was in all probability being practised. Hence it is seen that during the period of the Natufian culture there is no valid evidence for either the domestication of animals, or cultivation of plants, although it is possible that the dog was being domesticated from the small Arabian wolf.

There are two Transitional sites to be considered. These are Karim Shahir and Zawi-Chemi Shanidar, both of which lie in the Tigris-Euphrates region. This stage is approximately contemporary with the Natufian culture, although Zawi-Chemi Shanidar is slightly earlier, between 9000 and 8500. The oval and circular houses of the Natufian period are present and a large proportion of the flint industry is microlithic. Grinding stones, querns and hoes (ground or chipped) are all found, but sickle blades are not as common as in the Natufian culture. Well made ground stone objects include those used for personal decoration, such as rings, bracelets, pendants and beads. It is at this stage that the first evidence for domestication appears. Hunting was still widely practised, and the animals killed include red and roe deer, aurochs, pig, gazelle, sheep, goat, wolf, fox, bear, polecat, hare, tortoise, crab, rodents, birds and fish.

The only animal thought to have been domesticated is the sheep. Definite characteristics of domestication have been found at Zawi-Chemi Shanidar, and these sheep are clearly related to the local *Ovis orientalis* (Perkins 1960, Reed 1962). Throughout the 75,000 years of occupation at the nearby Shanidar cave, wild goats outnumber sheep

8

by three to one, but at this open site of Zawi-Chemi goats are relatively rare, indicating a distinct change in the economy. There is a possibility of sheep domestication at Karim Shahir, but the bones were too fragmentary to be certain of their status (Reed, personal communication). Ovicaprids were more numerous than any of the other animals (see Table No. 1). There is no indication of other domestic animals at these sites, and likewise no evidence for the cultivation of plants.

Agriculture was, however, well established in certain areas during the Aceramic period. The different stages of this phase are best illustrated by the finds made at Jericho, where three divisions have been observed. The earliest stage, known as 'Proto-Neolithic', is characterised by permanent settlements with a flint industry of Natufian type. It occurs immediately above the Natufian occupation, and at this stage there is no direct evidence for agriculture. This phase is placed between 7500 and 7000, although it may be slightly later at other sites. This is followed by the earliest known fortified town of 'Pre-pottery A', which developed out of the Proto-Neolithic phase and has been dated by radiocarbon to between 7000 and 6700. The houses still have an oval or circular plan, and are built with characteristic 'hog-backed' bricks. The flints are of Natufian derivation, and there is a rich bone industry.

Pre-pottery Neolithic B shows a complete break with the former occupation. The town was still walled, but the houses now have rectangular plans and consist of several rooms with plastered floors. Rush mats are found on these floors, and skulls with restored plaster features give an excellent impression of the appearance of these new people. The flint industry is entirely different from that of pre-pottery A, and finely worked stone bowls, vases and querns appear as well as stone axes. This stage occupied the period between 6500 and 5700.

The site of Jarmo in the Chemchemal valley of Iraqui-Kurdistan may be equated with the pre-pottery B phase at Jericho. The site is a village settlement of rectangular houses, and many fine stone vessels, microlithic flints and obsidian tools have been found. Unbaked clay figurines are common. These elements are also present in the Aceramic levels of Hacilar which lies on the Konya plain in Anatolia, and another settlement of this period was found at Khirokitia in Cyprus. It has a carbon 14 date of around 5500, and is best described as a small town, since the evidence indicates that several thousand people lived there. The domed houses were built on a circular plan and constructed of mud bricks and had a beehive-like appearance. Many polished stone bowls and dishes have been found and some have spouts. One such vessel was also present in the 'Amuq phase A (neolithic). Other elements in the culture include a flint industry reminiscent of the Upper Palaeolithic, obsidian, stone and bone personal ornaments, and bone awls, needles and pins.

The evidence from the central sites of Jarmo and Jericho shows that goats and probably dogs were being domesticated, but in neither case was there any evidence for sheep domestication (Kenyon 1960, Zeuner 1955, 1958). The material shows all the stages of initial domestication, and relates this goat to *Capra aegagrus*. Another site, this time in Jordan, that can be equated with pre-pottery B is Beidha, and here a preliminary analysis of the osteological material strongly suggests that goats were being domesticated, and that sheep were completely absent (Kirkbride 1966). Both sheep and goat are known from Hacilar, but there has been no detailed analysis of the material as yet although some of the remains are thought to be attributable to domestic animals (Mellaart, personal communication). There is a possibility of domestic ovicaprids at the Belt Cave, but as in the Natufian layers, no detailed examination of the material has been made, and the argument for their domesticity rests on their sudden appearance at this stage. Sheep and goat were the most common of the domestic animals at Khirokitia in Cyprus, and can be related to the wild species found on the island. A few bones thought to originate from domestic pigs were also found, but there was no indication of the dog. The dog is in fact only known from Jericho in Palestine. It has been found in the pre-pottery B stage and a considerable range in the size of the dogs was apparent. One animal is almost of wolf-size and another is close to the fox-terrier. Zeuner concluded that more than one breed was present, but according to Reed, at least some of these Jericho dogs lie within the range of the small Arabian wolf (Personal communication). In connection with this discussion on the dog, some figurines found at Jarmo are of interest. Models of very dog-like animals were found during the excavations, and although they are very small, the tails are clearly upturned and curled. This feature is unknown in wolves, and only occurs in domestic dogs. Clearly the inhabitants of Jarmo must have had some contact with dogs, if only indirectly.

The earliest indication of plant cultivation is found during this period, and there is evidence for the growing of both wheat and barley (see Table No. 2). The facts at present show that barley forms the bulk of the plant remains, and the two-rowed variety dominates at Jarmo (Helbaek 1960) and Beidha (Kirkbride 1966). At the last site tens of thousands of imprints were identified, and amongst these there were two which differ from the hulled two-rowed barley, and these are attributable to a naked barley. This can be assumed to be of the six-rowed species since there is no evidence for two-rowed naked types in antiquity (Helbaek 1966). The common two-rowed barley was also cultivated at Ali Kosh around 6500, to the east of the Tigris-Euphrates valley (Helbaek 1966). The cultivation of wheat includes that of einkorn and emmer, and this cereal has been found at Jarmo, Ali Kosh and Beidha; the absence of einkorn at Beidha is notable, since a large quantity of grain was involved. The situation on the Konya plain in Anatolia was different, and the main crop appears to be emmer, with hulled two-rowed barley more common than the naked six-rowed variety as at Beidha. There is no definite indication of einkorn cultivation. All the legumes that have been found in an Aceramic context are still in their wild state.

By the late Aceramic period the domestication of sheep and goat, together with dog, had been accomplished in certain areas within the distribution of the wild prototypes of these animals; in Cyprus the pig was added to this stock at a slightly later date. Wheat and barley were cultivated for the first time, and in the Fertile Crescent and Jordan two-rowed barley dominated the fields, with einkorn, emmer and six-rowed barley also present. To the north-west in Anatolia the main crop was emmer, with a smaller proportion of the two types of barley.

The sites now to be mentioned may be described as being truly 'Neolithic' since pottery, polished stone and evidence for agriculture all occur together. At some of the sites the pottery is still primitive and rough, and at later or more centralised sites it is much finer and may be burnished or have a cream slip. At the end of the neolithic painted ware occurs, and consists generally of a red design on a cream background. This became the common pattern during the early Chalcolithic. The neolithic may be placed between 6500 and 5500, except in some remote areas where this period persisted for longer. The importance of hunting relative to domestication is not known, but red and fallow deer, aurochs, pig, gazelle, donkey and possibly other equoids, antelope, sheep, goat, wolf, fox, leopard, cat, tortoise and birds were all hunted and probably formed a substantial part of the diet (see Table No. 3a).

During this period cattle and pigs were added to the range of domestic animals, and sheep, goat and dogs continued to be bred (see Table No. 3b). One of the best early excavations was carried out at Anau in Turkestan at the beginning of this century, and this is one of the first sites from which domestic cattle are known. The remains belong to the late neolithic, and other instances of cattle during this late phase have been observed in Anatolia. It must be remembered, that although no known instances occur within the central Mesopotamian area during the neolithic, the neolithic in these other regions was contemporary with the early Chalcolithic of Mesopotamia in which period domestic cattle are known to have been present.

The late neolithic culture found at Anau, known as Ia, contained many bones which illustrate the emergence of the domestic form of cattle from the local wild species *Bos namadicus* (Pumpelly 1904). Their domestication does not appear to have been fully accomplished until the following early Chalcolithic (Ib). Some of the bones show close agreement with those of the sacred bulls of Apis and so Duerst concluded that the inhabitants of Anau and those of Ancient Egypt were breeding the same type of cattle. Evidence from the 'Amuq (phases A and B) and the Konya plain also suggests that the domestication of cattle was being practised during the late neolithic (Braidwood & Braidwood 1959; Mellaart 1962).

The evolution of domestic sheep from the wild urial is illustrated at Anau (Pumpelly 1904). In the lower levels of the late neolithic the domestic sheep are still large and close to *Ovis vignei*, but in the upper levels the sheep become smaller until during the Chalcolithic some of them show great similarity to the turbary sheep of central Europe, *Ovis aries palustris*. This led Duerst to conclude that the turbary sheep of the Swiss lakes were descended from the urial. Sheep and goat were domesticated in the 'Amuq (Braidwood & Braidwood 1959, Garstang 1939), in the Tigris-Euphrates region (Braidwood & Reed, personal communication), and almost certainly in the Konya plain (Mellaart 1962, personal communication). Both the Asiatic moufflon and the urial were domesticated in their different regions.

There is very little evidence for pig domestication during the neolithic (see Table No. 3b). They are known to be absent at Anau, and are only known with certainty from the 'Amuq sequence (Braidwood & Braidwood 1959) and from Jarmo (Reed 1961). These pigs are still close to the wild species from which they were domesticated.

Dogs are also only known in two instances, the one from Jericho being very wolf-like. Nothing is known of the size of the dog present at the other site (Masson 1962), and there is a possibility of the dog being known in the Konya plain (see Table No. 3b).

The cultivation of wheat and barley continued during the neolithic and in addition legumes were added to the crops (see Table No. 6). Einkorn is known from the Konya plain as is emmer and bread wheat (Helbaek 1966), and emmer also occurs in the 'Amuq (Braidwood & Braidwood 1959) and bread wheat in Mesopotamia (Helbaek 1966). Hulled two-rowed barley was probably cultivated at Anau and also in the 'Amuq, and a fairly dense six-rowed naked barley was present at Çatal Hüyük in the Konya plain (Helbaek 1966). This six-rowed species is again the predominant type at the other Konya plain site of

Hacilar. This last site provides the only instance in which the relative importance of wheat and barley has been ascertained, and it is seen that barley is the largest single component in the field, followed fairly closely by wheat, of which emmer is the chief constituent. One deposit of grain revealed that wild grasses were still being collected (Helbaek, in press).

It is in this same area of Anatolia that the cultivation of legumes was being practised. Field peas, and probably also lentils and bitter vetch, were present amongst the field crops at Çatal Hüyük, but although many thousands of peas were found at Hacilar, they all appear to have been gathered. The only pulse which was cultivated was lentil which forms less than one per cent of the food plants (Helbaek, in press; Mellaart, personal communication).

During the late neolithic cattle and pigs were added to the domestic stock to the east and west of Mesopotamia, and sheep, goat and dog continued to be bred. Both wheat and barley were cultivated, and in one instance barley was the dominant crop. Both two-rowed hulled and six-rowed naked barley were known, and amongst the wheats was einkorn and emmer, and the presence of bread wheat and six-rowed hulled barley is first attested at this time. Legumes were also being cultivated in varying amounts.

The Chalcolithic period may be divided into three main cultures. The earliest is the Hassuna culture, dated to around 5500 to 5000, which originates in north Iran. This is followed by the Halaf culture of northern Mesopotamia (5000–4000) and the 'Ubaid culture of southern Mesopotamia (4000–3500). Red on cream painted pottery is common over most of the area, but in certain districts the black, grey or brown burnished ware of the neolithic continues. The Hassuna houses are built on a rectangular plan with several rooms, and both villages and fortified towns have been discovered. The designs on the pottery are usually rectilinear, although in the late stages some animal and human figures are represented. Obsidian and marble were worked as well as some semi-precious stones, and copper pins and awls appear. The only region in the Near East where copper is found is in the Highland zone of Iran and Anatolia, so that the Hassuna culture developed within this area.

The Halaf culture pottery is basically similar to that of the Hassuna culture, but more human and animal figures are present. This ware is extremely fine and resembles metal prototypes. Obsidian pendants, vessels and stamp seals were all finely worked, and copper becomes more common. This culture was superseded by the 'Ubaid culture which originated further south. The tholos-like shrines which were found during the Halaf period are replaced by an evolved form of rectilinear architecture which was to become the basis of later Meso-potamian religious buildings. Hunting and fishing were still prac-tised together with agriculture, and the animals exploited are similar to those of the Neolithic (see Table No. 7).

There is no definite instance of domestic cattle within the context of the Hassuna culture, although they may be present at the type-site, and the same applies to the sheep, goat and pig bones found at Has-suna (Reed 1960). These animals were, however, domesticated dur-ing the late neolithic in the 'Amuq (phase B), which does have some Hassuna characteristics.

Cattle, sheep, goat, probably pig and dog were kept during the following Halaf culture (see Table No. 8). This is the first non-con-troversial occurrence of domestic cattle in Mesopotamia, and the bones in question occur at the site of Gird Banahik (Reed 1961). All the bones found at Tell Halaf itself were discarded, as was the case at the other well-known site of Tell Arpachiyah. Some indirect evidence for cattle domestication was, however, found at this last site. A finely modelled head of a cow survived, and shows much similarity to the domestic cow of that area today. There are also various instances in which it is not certain if the bones found originate from wild or domestic cattle. Together with cattle, domestic goats were found at Gird Banahilk, and there is also a possibility that large domestic pigs were present (Reed 1960, 1961). During the period of Halafian in-fluence in the 'Amuq, phases c and D, cattle, sheep, pig and dog were domesticated (Braidwood & Braidwood 1959).

Domestic cattle were also present in an 'Ubaid context in Meso-potamia (Arne 1945), as were goats (Reed 1960) but there are no certain instances of pigs in this area. All three animals have, however, been found in the 'Amuq (phase E). At this stage Reed (1960) reports that a specialised breed of dog had emerged, namely the saluki, which was a little heavier than the modern examples of this race.

Domestic animals have been found at various other Chalcolithic sites of which two need to be mentioned (see Table No. 8). Two Chalcolithic periods are represented at Anau in Turkestan, known as ib and ii. The domestic cattle of ib are a continuation of the earlier late neolithic stock and are distinctly larger than the turbary animals known from Europe. During culture ii the cattle change, and al-though a few bones of large animals were found, the basic type is now the turbary breed. The turbary sheep, which began to evolve during ia, remain the chief breed until the middle of period ii, when they are superseded by a new hornless race which suddenly appear in large quantities. At this stage turbary goats also appear for the first time. The domestic pig was unknown until the latter stages of ib, and the

14

pigs of both this and the subsequent period are of the small turbary stock. The dog was not encountered until period II when a fairly large breed was present.

The camel also appears during the late Chalcolithic at Anau, and from historical considerations it is thought to be the Bactrian camel (*Camelus bactrianus*), and it was probably domesticated. Assyrian and Persian representations and sculptures prove that the camel was domesticated at a comparatively early date. A sherd was found at Tepe Siyalk III which bore the representation of a camel, and a single bone was recovered from Shah Tepe (Zeuner 1964, p. 359). In connection with these finds, it is interesting to note that the camel was also found in southern European Russia in a late Tripolye context (see p. 90).

The question of horse and donkey domestication first arises at this stage. At nearly all sites the equoid bones originate from wild animals, but the large collection from Anau reveals that their domestication had started during period Ib and was completed by period II. There has, however, been a certain amount of dispute over the type of equoid present. This animal was of medium height (mean of 1370mm. or between 13 and 14 hands) and had slender bones. Duerst could find no exact parallel to it and so he called it *Equus caballus Pumpellii*. Apart from its dental structure it has similarities to the Oriental group of equoids, and recently Hančar suggested that it could belong to the half-ass, *Equus hemionus*, which is a member of this group. Duerst himself noted many similarities between the half-ass and the Anau equoid, but did not assign it to this breed because of its tooth structure. An animal similar to that from Anau was also found at Tepe Siyalk in level III, and if the half-ass is present at Anau, it was probably domesticated here as well (Ghirshman 1939).

There is also a definite instance of the domestication of the donkey. This occurs at Bir-es-Safadi, the other important Chalcolithic site, where Josien (1956) found a few bones of this animal with evidence for domestication. The donkey is also known from the slightly later 'Amuq G phase. The information from this site is of much interest since a large quantity of bones were found and it is the only instance of a detailed statistical analysis in the Near East. The evidence shows that sheep farming was the basis of the economy, and that there were also a few goats, cattle, pigs and dogs (see Fig. 3 and Table No. 10). Nothing is known about the size of these animals.

There is no evidence for the cultivation of wheat during the Hassuna culture, but there is a single instance of barley (see Table No. 11). The Halafian site of Tell Arpachiyah provides evidence for the agricultural practice of that period. Both emmer wheat and barley were of importance, and it is interesting to note that the grains of emmer that were recovered had all been specially prepared and had their hulls removed (Mallowan & Rose 1935). During this period in the 'Amuq, at the site of Mersin, barley was the main crop with the two-rowed variety more common than the six-rowed. There was also a small proportion of emmer (Garstang 1953). Wheat and barley have been found at a few other Near Eastern sites, but the only case of a closer identification occurs at Anau where two-rowed barley was present.

The earliest evidence for the cultivation of flax comes from the Halaf culture. It has been found at two sites, both of which lie in the Kurdish foothills and are dated to around 5000 BC (see Table No. 11). *Linum bienne* is found to the north and east of the Tigris-Euphrates plain and so these sites lie within the distribution of the wild prototype.

Cattle, ovicaprids, pigs, dogs and equoids have all been identified at Chalcolithic sites, as has the camel. The first certain instance of cattle domestication occurs in the Halaf culture in Mesopotamia, and it is probable that pigs were also present at this time. Both animals occur during this period in the 'Amuq. The donkey and probably the half-ass were domesticated during the late Chalcolithic, and the camel also makes a rare appearance at this stage. Emmer is the only species of wheat known to have been cultivated, and two and six-rowed barley was grown and of importance. Flax was cultivated for the first time during the Halaf culture.

Such is the evidence for the earliest farming in the Near East. The first animals to be domesticated were the sheep and goat, and this was accomplished between 9000 and 7000 BC. At this stage crops were first cultivated, consisting of einkorn, emmer and barley, and the dog was domesticated. Cattle and pigs are not known until the late Neolithic and Chalcolithic periods. The first certain instance of cattle domestication in Mesopotamia occurs in the Halaf culture around or just after 5000, but these animals are known from the approximately contemporary late neolithic of Turkestan and Anatolia. As well as the earlier crops, legumes were now being cultivated, as was flax. During the late Chalcolithic the donkey and probably the half-ass were domesticated, and the camel makes a rare appearance as well. There is, however, no evidence for the domestication of the horse.

2. European Mesolithic and Aceramic Neolithic Economies

The evidence for agriculture in Europe may now be considered. The Mesolithic and Aceramic neolithic sites are investigated first, as was the case in the Near East, and included in the mesolithic period is the Ertebølle / Ellerbek culture. The exact status of this culture has been disputed, but it is usually regarded as mesolithic rather than neolithic and so is best considered at this stage rather than later.

Before the influence of the agricultural societies of the Near East reached Europe, there was in Mesolithic Europe, a single domestic animal, namely the dog. These dogs have been found at sites of the Tardenoisian, Azilian and Maglemose cultures. The Tardenoisian settlements have basically a coastal distribution and are found in most coastal areas of western Europe. These people lived on sandy soils, where some simple huts have been found, and they also sheltered in caves. This culture is characterised by geometric microliths which take the form of triangles, trapezes, rhomboids or crescents. Hunting and shell fish collecting form the basis of the economy. At present isotopic dating places this culture between 6000 and 3300 BC, so that in some areas it may be partially contemporary with neolithic communities.

The Azilian culture of western Europe is descended from the earlier Magdalenian culture, but much of the bone and flint-work is not as fine as that of the earlier culture. This applies to both bone harpoons and flint blades, which form the basis of the material that survives. Painted pebbles also occur. At one site Azilian harpoons are found together with a ground stone neolithic axe, and at others they are found in a Tardenoisian context (Childe 1957, 4). This implies that this culture belongs to the late mesolithic, and that, if the axe association is genuine, some sites must be contemporary with neolithic cultures. Also included in this cultural group are French sites of the late Magdalenian or Romanello-Azilian culture, and some Russian sites which have a similar although not identical culture.

The inhabitants of Maglemose sites were hunters and fishers who were armed with bows and arrows. These sites occur in northern Europe in Poland, Germany, Scandinavia, England and also in the southern North Sea area which was then still dry land. This culture may be dated to between 8000 and 5000 BC. The settlements often occur near lakes so that much of their material culture survives. Bone harpoons and spears for hunting and fishing, microlithic flint arrow-heads as well as primitive stone axes and adzes all appear. Antler was used for hafting the axes and adzes as well as for awls, needles and spearheads. These people had learned how to make good adhesive from birchbark by applying heat, and this birch-tar is the oldest known artificial substance made by man in Europe. The basis of the food supply was hunting, perhaps with the aid of the dog, and this was supplemented by the gathering of berries and fruit. The main animals exploited were red deer, followed by roe deer, elk, aurochs and pig.

Other animals identified at mesolithic sites where dogs have been found include sheep at one Russian site, seal, horse, badger, otter, beaver, bear, marten, wolf, fox, lynx, cat, hare, rabbit, hamster, hedgehog, squirrel, vole, mouse, turtle, fish and birds (see Table No. 12). In connection with the wild fauna the cattle found at Star Carr must be mentioned. These Maglemose cattle were found to vary considerably in size (see Jewell 1962, Fig. 18) and it has been suggested that two sizes of cattle may be present (Clark 1954). After a careful examination Jewell came to the conclusion that the difference in size was purely a result of sexual dimorphism and was not due to the presence of wild and domestic cattle.

The dog occurs at sites in Russia, Germany, Denmark, Norway, Sweden and Britain (see Tables Nos. 12 and 14a). There are three instances of Azilian dogs in Russia, and five of Tardenoisian dogs (Birula 1930, Dmitrieva 1960, Gromova 1953). The only instance of racial identification occurs in the latter context, where the turbary dog was distinguished at Mourzak-Koba (Gromova 1953). The dog found at Senckenberger Moor in Germany is probably the oldest known European dog (Mertens 1936). It occurred associated with the bones of an aurochs, and Mertens says that both animals were drowned shortly after, or whilst the dog was eating the aurochs. Unmistakable domestication characteristics were visible on the dog's skull (basal length 168 mm.) and Mertens regards this dog as the ancestor of the *intermedius* variety.

Two distinct breeds of dogs have been found at Maglemose sites in Denmark. The larger of the two is attributed to *Canis f. inostranzewi* and occurs at Holmegaard (Degerbøl 1928), Øgaarde (Mathiassen 1943) and Sværdborg (Brinkmann 1924, Degerbøl 1927) and the smaller, which occurs at the last two sites, is thought to be *Canis f. palustris ladogensis*, the large turbary dog. Considerable variation was found in other bones also, indicating the presence of these two breeds, and several bones which lay close to those of a wolf in measurements were also found. After various calculations Brinkmann

(1924) came to the conclusion that the dogs found at the Norwegian site of Viste were probably attributable to the *inostranzewi* race or else to a cross-breed with a wolf, and the smaller dog belonged to the turbary breed. It is interesting to note that out of the sixty skulls examined by Brinkmann from mesolithic sites and Ertebølle sites in Scandinavia, two out of every five sets of teeth had anomalies. He attributed this to the lack of nourishment during the early years of the dog's life. The type of dog found in Sweden is not known (Althin 1954).

The dog was finally proven to be present at Star Carr in Yorkshire by Degerbøl (1961). A skull and some limb bones were shown to originate from a domestic animal and fell within the range of the Maglemose dogs in Denmark. The basal length of the skull was 155 mm., which places it just within the range of the large turbary dog. Only a single bone was found at Thatcham which could be attributed to the dog. It is smaller than similar bones from Star Carr and compares reasonably well with the dog from Øgaarde (Wymer 1960).

From this it is clear that two breeds of dog were known during the late mesolithic in Europe. The larger is probably *Canis f. inostranzewi* and the smaller *Canis f. palustris ladogensis*. The evidence indicates that the local wolves were domesticated and resulted in at least the larger breed observed. The large teeth found in the smaller dog shows that they had evolved comparatively recently, and the similarity with the *inostranzewi* teeth that has been noted in Scandinavia strongly suggests that they evolved from the latter group.

At the time that these dogs were domesticated in northern Europe and probably used to facilitate hunting, an aceramic neolithic culture had been established in south-east Europe. At the base of the tell of Argissa in Thessaly there was discovered an occupation layer with no pottery, but with much flint, obsidian, stone and bone implements and evidence for agriculture. The flints include several microlithic forms, some of which were evidently used as sickle blades since the characteristic sheen was present. There were no large stone implements, and axes were absent. This last fact is reminiscent of Jericho. The date of this aceramic occupation is thought to be before 6000 BC. Since the discovery of this site, others with similar characteristics have been found and provide evidence for the cultivation of plants, but it is not yet known whether domestic animals were present at these sites. Another site at which an aceramic neolithic level is claimed is that of La Adam in Dobrogea near the Black Sea coast (Radulesco & Samson 1962). The flint industry is described as poor and polished stone ware is still absent. Recently Bökönyi identified some of the osteological remains from the 'post-palaeolithic' levels of this site and found bones of a hippopotamus, so it is necessary to treat the evidence from this site with a certain amount of reserve.

In the aceramic levels of Argissa it is seen that ovicaprids were the most important domesticated animal, forming more than two-thirds of the total remains (see Fig. 5a, Table No. 13; Milojčić 1962). Cattle, pigs and dogs were present in small quantities. Amongst the ovicaprid bones only the sheep is known with certainty, and considerable variation in their size was apparent. The majority, however, are of a fairly strong race. Two exceptionally robust horn cores compare well with the description of the sheep found at Tepe Siyalk in Persia, but there was no first hand material available for direct comparison. The Siyalk sheep are assigned to the *vignei* group. There was no apparent relationship between the sheep from Argissa and the moufflon of the western Mediterranean (*Ovis musimon*), the northern form of the *orientalis* group, or with the *ammon* sheep of mid Asia. A little more similarity was found with the southern *orientalis* group. Hence Boessneck concludes that the large Argissa sheep belong to the *vignei* group known from Anau and Tepe Siyalk. The smaller sheep compare in size with those of the later neolithic in Europe, and in this connection the evidence from Anau is recalled. Here Duerst found evidence for the evolution of the turbary sheep from the mountain sheep (*O. vignei*) and this may well be what was in the process of happening at Argissa.

A large sheep's cranium was found at La Adam (cave of Adam V) in Rumania, and was well preserved with definite characteristics of domestication (Radulesco & Samson 1962). It has been compared with two types of wild sheep, the European moufflon and a representative of the *ammon* sheep, and was dissimilar to both as were the Argissa remains, but it has not been compared with any domesticated animals. When the descriptions of the La Adam and Argissa sheep are compared, it is seen that they have some features in common. If in fact they are of the same species this would imply the presence of the domesticated mountain sheep *O. vignei* in Greece and Rumania.

The cattle found at Argissa are the least important of the main domestic animals and compare well in size with the material from central Europe (see Fig. 5a & Table No. 13). Some of the pig bones were still close to the wild boar at this site, and both the pig and cow are absent from La Adam. The only record of a dog also comes from Argissa, and of the two bones found, one falls within the range of the turbary breed and the other is slightly larger (Milojčić 1962).

Evidence for the cultivation of both wheat and barley has been found at aceramic sites in Greece, and from this evidence it is clear that wheat was the dominant crop. Examination of daub from aceramic levels at Argissa revealed the presence of einkorn and emmer, and there were also a few instances of unidentified wheat. Only a handful of carbonised grain was found, most of which can be attributed to einkorn (Milojčić 1962). Evidence from the aceramic levels of Ghediki show that emmer was the basic crop and that einkorn was also present, but only emmer wheat has been identified at Achilleion, Sesklo and Soufli (Renfrew 1966; see Table No. 13c). Barley has been found at all of the sites mentioned, and is known to be present in very small quantities at Argissa and Ghediki (Milojčić 1962, Renfrew 1966). The four-rowed glumed variety was identified by Hopf at the first site and both naked and glumed two-rowed barley were found at Ghediki. Hulled two-rowed barley has also been found at Sesklo (Renfrew 1966). A single seed of millet, probably the broomcorn variety, was found at Argissa, and lentils occur here and at Ghediki. The status of these legumes at the first site is uncertain, but those from Ghediki were almost certainly cultivated. The Pistachio nut should also be mentioned as it occurs frequently at Sesklo, and appears to be an important element in the diet. These nuts were also of significance during this period in the Near East.

The earliest evidence for farming in Europe comes from Greece where an aceramic culture was established and based its economy upon the breeding of sheep and cultivation of emmer. Cattle, pigs and dogs were also present in small quantities as were einkorn and various types of barley. It is also highly probable that lentils were being cultivated.

Another site which must be mentioned at this stage is the cave of Tash Ayir in the Crimea. The fauna of this cave has been examined most recently by Dmitrieva (1960), and the analysis raises the possibility of pig domestication from early Mesolithic times. The first level in which these pigs occur is the late Magdalenian/early Azilian, and they are also present in the Azilian and Tardenoisian horizons (see Table No. 14a). However, Dmitrieva stresses that this cannot be regarded as a definite statement that there were domestic pigs at this stage, but rather that there is the possibility. The pigs in question are smaller than the usual wild pig found at this site, and the distinction between the two pigs is made solely on the difference in size; no characteristics of domestication have been found, and the material is scarce in these early levels. From the description given, it seems as though these small Crimean pigs could have much in common with the small wild pigs that have been found in Greece by Boessneck and other authorities. Another similarity lies in the environment. The Crimea is very like Greece in certain areas, with dry mountainous regions and sub-tropical valleys, so that if the small Greek pigs are the result of local environmental conditions, as seems highly probable, it seems also probable that this is the explanation for the small pigs that have been found at Tash Ayir.

The site of Kammenia Mogila lies to the north of the Crimea on the lower Dniepr, and domestic cattle and ovicaprids together with dog are reported to be present (see Fig. 4 & Table No. 14b; Pidoplicko 1956; Radulesco & Samson 1962). The site is described as having affinities to the Tardenoisian culture, but there appears to be no reason to assume that it is particularly early, although pottery was unknown. It seems probable that this occupation is contemporary with the early neolithic of Starčevo-Körös to the west.

Wild cattle and pigs occur frequently at mesolithic sites in western Europe and have often been found in conjunction with the dog in the cultures mentioned earlier. There are, however, a few reports that do not agree with the general impression obtained of these animals and these will now be considered. The reports in question are those in which the cattle and pig remains are described as originating from small individuals, whose height differs considerably from that of the accepted minimum for aurochs and boars. Such cases occur in Azilian, Tardenoisian, Sauveterrian and Asturian contexts. The first two cultures have been considered earlier in connection with the domestication of the dog. The Sauveterrian culture is slightly earlier than the Tardenoisian culture and occurs in western Europe between 7000 and 4900, according to available carbon 14 dates. Small, narrow flint flakes in the form of elongated triangles are characteristic, and trapeze shapes occur occasionally. The bone industry is poor in comparison with other late Mesolithic cultures. Red and roe deer, elk and aurochs were the basis of the hunting economy and fishing was also practised. The Asturian culture supersedes the Azilian culture along the coasts of northern Spain and Portugal. The basic tool is a chipped pebble and shell fish occur in profusion. This culture continued until well into the neolithic period and dates as late as 3000 have been obtained.

Small cattle are reported from sites of the Sauveterrian, Tardenoisian and Azilian cultures, as well as from a few other apparently mesolithic sites (see Table No. 15). The small Sauveterrian cattle found at Unang were separated from remains of the neolithic period by 40 cm. of sterile soil. There is no record of large individuals, and there appears to be no chance of contamination (Paccard 1956). Both Sauveterrian and Tardenoisian cultures have been found at Moita do Sebastião in Portugal (Roche 1960). A small-sized bovine was found in the context of these cultures together with bones of the much larger aurochs. The dentition of the two animals was entirely different, and after a careful examination of the bones Zbyszewski reached the conclusion that the smaller animal was domesticated.

Two French sites provide evidence for small cattle in a Tardenoisian context, namely Belloy-sur-Somme and Cuzoul de Gramat. The osteological remains from the first site are certainly of domestic animals (Salomonsson 1960b), whereas those from Cuzoul de Gramat are said to be small-sized and comparable to remains found at Er Yoh (Lacam 1944) These bones were found in the second and third Tardenoisian layers together with other remains of possibly domesticated animals. These cattle bones are too small to have originated from a bison.

The Azilian instances of small cattle occur at two French and one Swiss site. A bovine of very small size is reported from Colomb à Meaudre and Balme de Glos, together with a large animal (Bouchud 1956); the size is so diminished that it cannot be accounted for by sexual dimorphism and the bones are also too small to have originated from a bison. The remains from the Swiss site of Salève are assigned to the turbary breed of cattle by Studer, and agree well with finds of the neolithic period (Schenk 1912, 122). Studer had no doubt as to their domestic status. The exact context of the remaining cattle is not known, other than that they are thought to be of mesolithic date, and the cattle bones found at Ringneill in Ireland are said to be almost indistinguishable from those of a modern domestic ox (Jope 1955).

Small pigs are reported from both Tardenoisian and Azilian sites (see Table No. 15). The bones found at Belloy-sur-Somme are thought to be of domesticated animals (Salomonsson 1960b) and there is also a possibility of a centre of pig domestication in the Crimea (Stoliar 1959). This last theory has arisen as a result of investigations of the fauna of both Azilian and Tardenoisian sites in this region by Stoliar, who found that the fauna of the Tardenoisian levels appeared to be more specialised than that of the Azilian levels. In the former context bones of the large pig *Sus scrofa attila ferus* were common. Stoliar doubts whether this was the natural habitat of the species, and suggests that it was possible that the inhabitants kept this animal within a confined area. Gromova says, according to Stoliar, that there was an abundance of pig remains at mesolithic sites in the Crimea, and that the majority were remains of suckling pigs. These could form as much as three-quarters of the pig bones.

The only claim for a domestic pig in an Azilian context comes from Salève in Switzerland where Studer identified the turbary breed (Schenk 1912). Bones of small pigs have also been found at other sites, and in two instances these are thought to belong to the turbary breed (see Table No. 15; Cayeux 1960, 1962, Jope 1955, Péquart 1926).

From the above evidence it appears that small cattle and pigs were known in a late mesolithic context. The remains found at the French site of Belloy-sur-Somme may be definitely considered as being contemporary with neolithic communities, since sherds of pottery were found in level 3 which bore two impressions of barley. In the remaining cases there is, however, no such evidence for a definite overlap of these two epochs. In one or two instances, such as at Salève in Switzerland, the bones almost certainly stem from domesticated animals, but in the remaining cases all that is known is that these small individuals were present.

Another interesting occurrence in the context of the mesolithic cultures mentioned is the presence of bones of sheep. Sheep are generally thought to have been extinct on the European mainland since the end of the Pleistocene, or Palaeolithic, but the following evidence questions that fact. As is seen from Table 15, ovicaprids have been reported from sites of the Sauveterrian, Tardenoisian, Azilian and Asturian cultures.

The only known instance of sheep in a Sauveterrian context comes from Three Holes Cave in Devon, where Zeuner reported a few bones of sheep (1964, 193). The evidence from Tardenoisian sites is more abundant and the most interesting instance arises in the south of France at a site known as Châteauneuf-Les-Martigues. Ducos (1958) found over sixty bones of a small sheep which exhibited close agreement with the turbary sheep of the neolithic period in both size and character (see Fig. 5b & Table No. 16). The site was carefully excavated and recorded, and there is no reason to suspect contamination from the later neolithic levels. The size of the sheep reported from the third Tardenoisian horizon at Sauveterre is unknown (Coulonges 1935), but both these remains and those from the other sites are known to be in the same state of preservation as the other osteological remains from this context (Lacam 1944, Péquart 1937, Salomonsson 1960b).

Bones of sheep identified at the two French Azilian sites are described as originating from animals of very small size (Bouchud 1956a & b). Bouchud reports that the majority of bones of European palaeolithic sheep are similar in length to those of the Asiatic moufflon, but that these Azilian sheep are much smaller and similar to the neolithic sheep. This suggests that they show similarity to the other mesolithic sheep which may be described as 'turbary'. The other instance of sheep occurs at Salève in Switzerland, and the goat is recorded at Baie Herculane in Rumania by Bökönyi (Nicolaescu-Plopsor 1957).

Sheep also appear in an Asturian context in Spain and sheep or goat are present at Mugem in Portugal (Obermaier 1924). These finds all occur in the coastal shell mounds, and carbon 14 dates suggest that this culture is in fact fairly late and contemporary with the early neolithic in this region. There are several other instances of sheep or goat in a mesolithic context, the majority of which occur in France. It is interesting to note that in his list of animals known in the Basse Province during the Azilian period, Fournier (1901) includes an ovicaprid, thought to be the goat. The possibility that this goat could in fact be a small goat-like sheep, as found at other mesolithic sites, should be considered.

From this evidence it is clear that sheep were present during the late mesolithic in Europe, and that the majority of cases occur in France. There are three possible explanations for their presence. These sheep are wild animals which survived from the Final Pleistocene (late palaeolithic) until well into the Post Glacial (late mesolithic) times, or animals domesticated by the local mesolithic populations, or finally they could represent contact with external neolithic communities. As far as the last possibility is concerned, it can be seen from Fig. 140 that many of the sites involved lie outside the area occupied by the Initial Colonisation cultures. This implies that the people occupying these mesolithic sites in France, for instance, could either have obtained their sheep by distant trade with the coastal Impressed Ware communities, or else from contact with the Chassey culture. The earliest date for the Impressed Ware in France is around 4200 and that for Chassey is around 3400, thus implying that both Tardenoisian and Azilian cultures would have survived until at least 4000, and probably for another 600 years in certain regions. There are, unfortunately, no carbon 14 dates for the Azilian culture, although in some cases it can be shown to be contemporary with the Tardenoisian culture. Most of the evidence favours a date of between 6000 and 4000 for the Tardenoisian culture, but at one German site a date of as late as 3300 has been obtained (Birsmatten). From this it is seen that contact between the mesolithic and neolithic societies would be feasible.

As far as domestication by the local mesolithic communities is concerned, this necessarily implies the presence of wild sheep in the vicinity. It is generally thought that sheep became extinct on the European mainland at the end of the Palaeolithic. They are reported, however, to have survived on certain Mediterranean islands such as Corsica and Sardinia (Zeuner 1964). The northern tip of Corsica lies on the same degree of latitude as the southernmost point of France where sheep have been found in a Tardenoisian context. This southern region of France is noted for its Mediterranean climate of hot dry summers and mild winters, which does not differ notably from the climate of Corsica. Since the environmental conditions are similar in the two areas, it is probable that if the sheep did in fact manage to survive in one region, that they also did so in the other. It is therefore proposed here that sheep could have survived in southern France until the late mesolithic period.

Another factor which is of importance to this enquiry is that during the Palaeolithic, sheep were always extremely rare in Europe. They have been identified at a few sites only, which are listed by Zeuner (1964), so that they could not be expected to be present at many sites of the later mesolithic. This has proved to be the case. Most of the European palaeolithic sheep were of large size and similar to the Asiatic and European moufflon, but there are, however, one or two instances of small wild sheep. These occur at Pech de l'Aze in a Mousterian context (Bouchud 1955) and at the Grotte de l'Observatoire in Monaco. The bones found at the first site showed close agreement in size with those of small sheep found in Spain today. From this it appears that several sheep of both the Palaeolithic and the Mesolithic periods were a good deal smaller than the European moufflon. Lundholm (1949) has pointed out that the actual mechanics for a small species emerging from a larger one are the same for both wild and domesticated animals. He applies this to horses, but it is equally applicable to sheep, and he reckons that dwarfs in wild communities can occur fairly rapidly, perhaps in as little as a hundred years. Sewell Wright (1931) investigated the changes in size of wild animals on a purely mathematical basis. He found that in a small isolated group there is a greater probability of reduction in size than there is of an increase in size or of the size remaining the same (Lundholm 1949, 218-219).

Indeed, dwarfing in unfavourable circumstances is a relatively common botanical phenomenon, and several examples of dwarf plants surviving in extreme conditions when the original species appears to die out are known. One example is the dwarf polyploid juniper of the Himalayas, and another small version of this plant occurs in the mountainous areas of Britain. One of the best examples of this size reduction is scurvy grass (*Cochlearia officinalis* L.). There are in all four forms, of which the smallest is that found in the mountains where the conditions are less favourable. These were originally classed as four different species as the variation in size was so great, and it was Linnaeus who demonstrated that they were in fact all members of the same species that were affected by, and had adapted themselves to, different environments.

The exact status of the mesolithic sheep in France and other regions of Europe cannot be decided with confidence on the evidence available at present. It is, however, clear that small sheep, some closely

26

resembling the turbary sheep of the neolithic, were present at several sites. They were by no means common, nor would this be expected, since they were also rare during the palaeolithic. However, the writer thinks it most probable that these sheep represent a diminutive form of the wild sheep of the later Palaeolithic, which managed to survive the climatic changes. Although they are said to resemble the later domestic animals, no evidence for their domestication has yet been given. They were either wild or herded, and if left without external influence, may have resulted in a situation similar to that observed at Zawi Chemi Shanidar. As to the exact nature of the small cattle and pigs that have been observed in a similar context, no conclusions can be made. Their presence does not fit in with the general impression obtained of the wild animals of this period.

The other cultural group to be considered is that of Ertebølle-Ellerbek, which is found along the coasts of Denmark, southern Sweden and Germany. Isotopic dating places these cultures between 3800 and 2900 BC. Initially they were contemporary with the north European mesolithic communities, but latterly the TRB culture is found in the same area. The pottery is coarse and consists of pointed-based pots. The stone industry includes flake and greenstone axes which occasionally are ground to shape, and arrowheads represent the microlithic element. The bone and antler forms of the true meso-lithic were to a large extent replaced by flint, but perforated axes, antler sleeves for stone axes and bone combs are found. Fish were caught with bone hooks and a line rather than harpooned.

The coastal settlements are characterised by shell heaps, or 'Kjøk-kenmøddinger'. The sources of food are basically fishing, shellfish collecting and hunting. The dog is present at several of these sites, and at a few late settlements cattle, sheep, goat and pig occur. Amongst the hunted animals were red and roe deer, elk, aurochs, pigs, seals (Greenland, gray and ringed), horse, otter, badger, beaver, bear, marten, fox, wolf, lynx, wild cat, polecat, squirrel, hare, hedgehog, dolphin and killer whale. There were also many types of fish caught, including bottom feeders, and many species of birds (see Table No. 17a).

Domestic cattle and pig are recorded at more sites than are sheep or goat (see Table No. 17b). Next to the large bones of the aurochs, bones of a medium-sized animal were found and in some instances they are said to be unmistakably bones of domesticated animals (Troels-Smith 1958, Mathiassen 1940, Nobis 1962). The presence of these smaller animals was recorded as early as 1906, when Thomsen and Jessen, who had excavated the Danish site of Brabrand, reported that half of the bovine bones they found could well be regarded as originating from domesticated animals. Relatively small animals were also reported from other sites, such as Dyrholmen, but were thought to be best regarded as being of wild origin in the light of knowledge at that time (Degerbøl 1942). The definite presence of cattle in Germany was established by Nobis (1962) after a detailed analysis of the shoulder blades, and at an earlier date was proposed by Mestorf (1904). Bones of aurochs and cattle were the second most common, next to those of red deer, in the last case (see Fig. 91, Table No. 18), and the bones of the wild aurochs were a third as large again as those of the domestic. The presence of domestic pigs was first established by Pira (1909) for the site of Ringsjön in Sweden. Most of the pig remains were of wild animals, but amongst the bones of the domestic stock was one jaw fragment which included the crista that was so much reduced in size that the possibility of the animal being castrated must be considered. Domestic pigs, close to their wild ancestors, were later found in Germany and Denmark (see Table No. 17b). Sheep or goat have been found in all three countries, with only a few remains being recorded at each site. In most instances it is the sheep that has been identified, with no known cases of goat.

Apart from these domestic animals, there are many occurrences of dogs and at the majority of these sites the dog is the only known domestic animal (see Table No. 17b). In most cases the breed could not be established, but when this information was possible to obtain, two breeds were observed. The smaller of the two is the more frequent and represents the turbary breed whereas the larger is thought to represent *Canis f. intermedius, Canis f. inostranzewi* or *Canis f. matris optimae* (Brinkmann 1924, Degerbøl 1927, Hauck 1950, Thomsen & Jessen 1906, Winge 1904). The situation is similar to that observed at the other mesolithic sites in Scandinavia which were discussed earlier. There are several instances of the large turbary dog, *Canis f. palustris ladogensis*, and also a single case of the miniature dog *Canis f. spaletti* (Brinkmann 1924, Degerbøl 1928).

In addition to breeding animals, claims that the Ertebølle people cultivated plants have also been made. Impressions of both wheat and barley have been found at Ertebølle-Ellerbek sites, and einkorn, emmer, club wheat and naked barley have all been identified (Helbaek 1954, Rydbeck 1938, Troels-Smith 1953). No trace of carbonised grains has been found. However, all these impressions occur on sherds of TRB pottery, and although Helbaek conducted a careful examination of Ertebølle sherds, there were no indications of any cereal impressions. The presence of wheat and barley in this context merely illustrates the already known fact that these cereals were cultivated by the TRB communities.

28

There is evidence for the presence of domestic cattle, ovicaprids and pigs in an Ertebølle context, but they only occur at a very small proportion of the sites, whereas the dog is a much more common feature. The cattle include medium-sized and large animals, most of the pigs were still fairly large, and two types of dog were bred. There is little doubt that the dogs were actually reared by the Ertebølle inhabitants, but it is obvious that the sheep could not have been domesticated by them. The main problem to arise is whether the cattle and pigs were domesticated by the Ertebølle people, or whether they are actually animals of the TRB communities. There is ample evidence for contact between these two cultures, and this is particularly well illustrated at Muldbjerg where four-fifths of the sherds can be attributed to TRB pottery, and only a fifth to Ertebølle pottery. The claim that the Ertebølle folk cultivated wheat and barley is seen above to be incorrect. The sheep must originate from the same source as do the plant imprints, namely the nearby TRB settlements. It is clear that the Ertebølle people would come into contact with domestic animals other than the dog, and if in fact they did domesticate their own cattle and pigs, the TRB culture must have been the impetus behind this action. It seems probable that at least the medium-sized animals did in fact originate from TRB stocks, but the large individuals could represent local domestication by either the TRB or Ertebølle culture.

It has been shown that two breeds of dog were known in mesolithic Europe, and that the inhabitants of Scandinavia had domesticated the local wolves to obtain these animals somewhere between 8000 and 5000 BC. As well as dogs, small cattle and pigs are reported from Sauveterrian, Tardenoisian, Azilian and Asturian sites, but it cannot be ascertained whether they were small wild or domesticated animals. Sheep were present in these four contexts, and in several instances are seen to be small and closely resemble the later turbary sheep of the neolithic. It is suggested that they represent a diminutive form of the late Palaeolithic sheep of Europe which managed to adapt themselves to the climatic changes of the period. It is also seen that the agricultural activities of the Ertebølle-Ellerbek culture are largely attributable to the TRB communities, although it is possible that they did domesticate a few aurochs and boars. Their dogs on the other hand were an internal acquisition, and two breeds were present as in the other mesolithic societies of this area.

3. The Initial Agricultural Colonisation of Europe

The earliest evidence for agriculture in Europe occurs in the aceramic tell settlements in Greece, which can be placed in the late seventh and early sixth millennium BC. It was not, however, until the fifth millennium that expansion took place and the knowledge of agriculture was transmitted over the greater part of Europe. Following the Aceramic sites in Greece came a group of settlements which can be best described as Early Agricultural Neolithic. They all have certain elements in common, such as painted pottery, figurines, bone spatulae and a macrolithic flint industry. Three cultures are responsible for the transmission of this new economy over the rest of Europe, namely those of Starčevo-Körös, Impressed Ware and Linear Pottery. These cultural groups represent the impetus behind the transmission of agriculture over Europe and they may be called the Initial Colonisation cultures.

The Early Agricultural Neolithic of Greece has various different components. The earliest is known as the Proto-Sesklo culture and it may be placed before 5000 BC. It is characterised by fine, monochrome, burnished pottery, which is usually red in colour and its connections lie in Anatolia. Slightly later than this, a group of sites with pottery with fingertip or Cardium shell impressions occurs, and these have an essentially coastal distribution. They are related to the cardial Impressed Ware of the Adriatic and Black Sea coasts and to those in France and Spain. This culture, together with that of Proto-Sesklo, led to the emergence of the rich Sesklo culture which developed in Thessaly between 5000 and 4400 BC. The pottery is fine, usually consisting of red-slipped burnished ware, which often bears black and white painted rectilinear patterns. The flame design is also typical. The stone ware includes vases; otherwise it is a macrolithic blade industry. The settlements are relatively small and consist of the usual rectangular mud-walled houses. The evidence for hunting of red deer, possibly aurochs, and boar shows that this was not of importance to the economy.

Evidence for the animal husbandry of the Proto-Sesklo period comes from two sites known as Argissa (Boessneck 1962) and Otzaki (Boessneck 1955). Cattle, sheep, goat, pig and dog were all bred, and it is seen that ovicaprids were the most important element in the economy (see Fig. 6a, Table No. 21). The sheep are medium to large in size, and there is evidence for hornless animals indicating a fairly advanced form of domestication. The goats were fairly powerful as were some of the cattle. Pigs were less important, and dogs appear in very small quantities at Otzaki and have been assigned to the turbary breed.

The fingertip and Cardium impressed ware sites, called the Vor- or Pre-Sesklo phase by Milojčić (1962), also has an economy based upon ovicaprid breeding (see Fig. 6b, Table No. 21). As is the case in the preceding Proto-Sesklo phase, hornless animals were bred together with individuals closely resembling the wild sheep and goat from which they were domesticated (Boessneck 1962). Cattle were more important than pigs. The cattle show affinity to the aurochs, although there is some variation in their size, and the pigs are mostly of the turbary type (Milojčić 1962). The dog found at Otzaki is also attributed to this breed.

Another Early Agricultural site is that of Nea Nikomedeia. It contains no cardial or fingertip impressed pottery, and shows more affinity with the Sesklo sites than with the others. However, carbon 14 dates place it earlier than the majority of Sesklo sites, namely at around 5600 BC (5607±91; P-1202). Here again sheep and goat breeding was the mainstay of the economy, with a smaller proportion of cattle and pig (Rodden 1962; see Fig. 7). Cattle are slightly less frequent than pig.

Evidence for the Sesklo culture indicates a change in the economy from the preceding Proto-Sesklo and Pre-Sesklo cultures, and comes from the site of Otzaki where the preceding cultures have also been found (Boessneck 1962). The pig is now more important than both sheep and goat, and cattle are the least important of the three main domestic animals (see Figs. 6c, 6d, Table No. 21). The majority of these animals were medium to small in size and fall within the range of the turbary pig, but there is also a larger and more primitive-looking animal present. These are probably the results of local domestication. The pig of this period can be compared with the modern pigs in this area. Papadopoulo (1934) gives a good description of them. The body is tall and slender with long legs, the head of medium size with a long and slender snout and medium length horizontal ears. Greece lies within the distribution of both the large *Sus scrofa ferus* and of the smaller *Sus mediterraneus* and it would seem probable that the smaller pig was domesticated to produce the turbary animals (Boessneck 1955). Both the cattle and the ovicaprid stock resemble that of the preceding early agricultural stages.

Evidence for plant cultivation during the early neolithic in Greece comes from three sites which may be placed before the Sesklo culture, and two of the true Sesklo culture (see Table No. 19). The earliest and most abundant evidence for plant cultivation during the pottery neolithic comes from Soufli, where the basic crop is seen to have been emmer, followed by hulled two-rowed barley (Renfrew 1966). The only other cereal known to have been cultivated is einkorn. Wheat and barley, together with a large quantity of lentils, were cultivated at Nea Nikomedeia (Rodden 1962). At the type-site of the Sesklo culture a single grain of emmer was detected in a similar context to that of the remains from Soufli. The only instances of plants in a Sesklo context come from Servia where hard wheat and lentils are thought to have been cultivated (Heurtley 1939) and from Tsani where barley was found (Wace & Thompson 1912).

From this it is apparent that ovicaprids were the basic domestic animal of the Proto-Sesklo and Pre-Sesklo cultures, as was the case in the earlier Aceramic period. They are also the dominant animal at the other Early Agricultural site of Nea Nikomedeia which has Sesklo affiliations, but at one later site of the Sesklo culture the economy is orientated towards pig-breeding. The other basic domestic animals are also bred at this stage, and emmer appears to have been the main crop, with hulled two-rowed barley and einkorn also being cultivated.

The Starčevo-Körös Karanovo I culture is found in Bulgaria, Yugoslavia, Rumania and Hungary where the sites have been dated to between 5100 and 4200 BC. It is slightly later than the Sesklo culture to the south, which on present evidence appears to have provided the impulse behind the emergence of this new cultural group especially in the West Balkans. The three classes of pottery found include rough, rusticated ware with fingertip impressions, which occurs mostly in south-east Hungary and Rumania, a plain buff or yellow burnished ware, and a fine hard painted pottery. The latter is usually fairly thick, with a red or more rarely white slip. The painted decoration is rectilinear and curvilinear, and is black or white, or black and white on a red ground, and occasionally black and red on a white ground. The flints have retouched edges and are generally thin and of medium length. Unperforated axe/adzes also occur, and the bone industry is not particularly rich. The houses are square, rectangular or trapeze shaped, and they are grouped into settlements found near the base of tells in eastern Europe.

Hunting was insignificant as a means of procuring food, its products generally forming less than a fifth of the osteological remains. The most interesting fact to arise from the examination of the wild animals is the presence of the donkey, which was thought to have been extinct on the European mainland since the end of the Pleistocene. Recently, however, there have been various reports of this equoid in a neolithic context, so that its presence until at least the early neolithic must now be accepted. Other animals to be hunted include red and roe deer, pig, aurochs, horse, otter, beaver, polecat, cat, fox, wolf, badger, hare, turtle, fish and birds (see Table No. 20a).

The osteological remains from fourteen sites are now considered (see Table No. 20b). The only statistical evidence comes from Hungary, where ovicaprids are seen to be the dominant feature, as the evidence from Maroslele-Pana shows (Bökönyi 1964; see Fig. 8, Table No. 22). The importance of these animals at Hódmezövásárhely-Bodzaspart and Lebo cannot be determined since the statistics apply to the neolithic as a whole, and so include remains from the Linear Pottery and subsequent cultures. Statistics from the remaining sites are not available, but sheep are said to be the dominant animal at Szarvas-Szappanos although this does not apply to Tiszapart (Kutzian 1947, p. 10). The number of bones involved in both cases is unknown. Cattle were also bred, as were pigs and dogs, but at Maroslele-Pana pigs were of very little importance and are comparable to the dog in numbers.

The ovicaprid stock varied considerably, with strong, medium and weak horned animals all being bred. The hornless sheep that are recorded at Maroslele-Pana compare well with those found in the Early Agricultural Neolithic at Otzaki in Greece, the main difference being that the examples from the Hungarian site are slightly smaller (Bökönyi 1964). In connection with sheep domestication the alleged presence of the moufflon at Opoljenik must be mentioned (Kutzian 1947, p. 10). The presence of large moufflon-like sheep is known from the early neolithic of Europe, so that it seems most probable that this is a large domesticated animal resembling its wild prototype. However, it must be remembered that the moufflon occurs on the islands of Corsica and Sardinia and that this animal may have survived in southern France.

The variation amongst the cattle stock is also considerable, with some animals lying very close to the aurochs and on occasions indistinguishable from them, and others being reduced in size (Bökönyi 1959, 1964). The majority were of medium size, and local aurochs domestication was probably practised in Hungary. Pigs are the least important of the domestic animals and are absent from several sites; where an indication of their size has been obtained they appear to have been small as were the dogs (Bökönyi 1964).

Little evidence for plant cultivation survives. Einkorn and emmer were cultivated together with an unidentified form of barley and millet (see Table No. 25). The authenticity of the millet has, however, been questioned by various authors (Garašanin 1958). The legumes identified include vetch at Karanovo I (Georgiev 1961) and a bean at Banyata (Garašanin 1958).

The Impressed Ware culture has an essentially coastal distribution and is found to the west of the Starčevo-Körös culture along the coast of the Adriatic and Mediterranean Sea. Isotopic dating places it between 4700 and 3800 BC. The most characteristic feature of the pottery is the occurrence of impressions of the Cardium shell. This gives the culture its other name of Cardial Impressed Ware. In appearance this pottery is similar to some of the rougher Starčevo pots, and in Greece and Yugoslavia fingertip impressions occur in both cultures. Although the pottery is not so well executed, both the bone and flint industries are richer than those of Starčevo-Körös.

Red and roe deer, aurochs, wild pig, chamois, wolf, badger, lynx, cat, rabbit, fox, hare and fish were all hunted, and in some areas in France the rabbit was one of the main sources of food (Châteauneuf; see Table No. 16), and in others the boar was more important (Roucadour; see Table No. 28).

Osteological evidence is only available from six sites (see Table No. 27), and the statistics from Châteauneuf-Les-Martigues show that sheep breeding was the basis of the economy (Ducos 1958, see Fig. 10, Table No. 16). It is the turbary breed that is present throughout, with no indication of a larger animal. Sheep are also present at another two French sites, but there has been no definite occurrence of the goat in this area. Both ovicaprids were, however, found at Stentinello in Sicily, and the goat is known from Yugoslavia (Strobel 1890, Benac 1961). In addition sheep are known from the cave of Arene Candide (Brea 1946).

Both large and small breeds of cattle were being kept in this context. The two breeds are present together in Sicily, with the larger the more frequent of the two, but at Châteauneuf-Les-Martigues only the smaller variety of cattle could be established as being definitely domesticated (Strobel 1890, Ducos 1958). It seems probable that the large cattle found at Roucadour were also wild in origin (Ducos 1957).

Pigs are only known to have been domesticated in two instances, namely at Stentinello where the turbary breed was present (Strobel 1890), and at Unang where the breed could not be established (Paccard 1952). It seems likely that the large proportion of pigs found at Roucadour is of wild stock, although the possibility of a few domesticated or semi-domesticated animals being present cannot be completely excluded (Ducos 1957, 1966). Those from Châteauneuf are known definitely to be of wild origin (Ducos 1958). The single

34

instance of dog in this context occurs at Stentinello in Sicily where the turbary breed, together with its miniature form, have been identified (Strobel 1890).

The only site to provide evidence of the crops grown by the Impressed Ware culture is that of Coveta de l'Or in Spain which has carbon 14 dates of 4560 ± 160 (KN–51) and 4315 ± 75 (H–1754/1208). Several thousand carbonised grains were identified, which show that the basic crop was bread wheat (*Triticum aestivum*). Emmer was also present, as were einkorn and club wheat in smaller quantities. Amongst the numerous grains of barley both naked and glumed could be distinguished, with the former much more common than the latter (Hopf & Schubart 1965).

The Linear Pottery culture has the widest distribution of the three Initial Colonisation cultures, and is found in Hungary, Rumania, western Russia, Poland, Czechoslovakia, Austria, Germany, Holland and eastern France. The earliest phase may be dated at around 4600–4400 BC and the latest to 3700 BC. The characteristic pottery is incised and may be divided into three phases. The earliest is found in the Alföldi area of Hungary, from where it spreads to the north-east and west of Hungary, and to south-west and east Slovakia, Moravia, Bohemia, south-east Germany, west Germany and hence to the Rhine valley and Holland. The pottery contains much organic material, is orange in colour and bears thick incised lines which form curvilinear and linear patterns. The shapes of the pots at this stage are more sophisticated than during the later stages.

The mid phase of this culture has the widest distribution. It has spread up to Holland, and is also found in Poland and north-east Rumania. In the eastern area of its distribution the Tisza and Bükk cultures have emerged. In the central area the Notenkopf style of ornamentation has evolved, and in the west the 'Filled-in band' style developed. The former is similar to incised musical notes, and the latter consists of parallel lines which are filled in with dots.

The late phase is characterised by the development of these two types of patterns, and has a similar distribution to that of the mid phase. The 'Notenkopf' design degenerates into 'Stichbandkeramik', and the 'Filled-in Band' leads to the emergence of the Rössen and Altheim cultures.

The flint industry varies in the geographical sense rather than with the differing phases. In the central area the blades are long and have only a little retouching, and in the north-west large wide blades with more retouching are found. Arrowheads occur in this last area but never in the central area. They are also absent in Poland and the Ukraine where large end scrapers appear. In the central area high-backed shoe-last axes are found. The bone industry is usually poor and very little survives.

The Linear Pottery settlements are composed of large rectangular houses, averaging 20 by 100 feet, constructed out of solid timber posts covered with daub. Occasionally these houses are grouped together in an ordered pattern. The settlements were occupied for a period of time, perhaps ten years, and then abandoned and re-inhabited at a later date. At Bylany in Czechoslovakia several such occupations have been found and the site probably had a life span of between 600 and 900 years. In other areas such as Holland the occupation seems to have been more permanent. It has been suggested that this semi-migratory system may have been carried out owing to local soil exhaustion, so that by the time of re-occupation the environment would once again be fertile, and suitable for raising crops and animals. These settlements are usually found on the loess soil of central Europe, and pollen analysis shows that these were forested, or at least lightly wooded. The trees would have to be cleared and the most probable method employed would be that of slash and burn, with the resultant ash enriching the fertile loess.

The wild fauna usually accounts for between a tenth and a fifth of the total, but at one or two late sites proportions as high as a half have been noted. Red and roe deer, elk, aurochs, pig, horse, bear, beaver, badger, wolf, fox, hare, hamster, turtle, birds and fish were all used to supplement the diet provided by the domestic animals (see Table No. 29).

This rich culture is, from the osteological and botanical point of view, the best documented of all European neolithic cultures. Evidence of animal breeding is obtained from well over a hundred sites from all parts of Europe, and many of these provide detailed statistics showing which of the animals were the most important to the economy (see Tables Nos. 30-63). As is seen from these tables, cattle are present at most of the sites and in nearly every instance are the dominant feature (see Figs. 9-47). Sheep, goat and pig were also being bred to a lesser extent, but the remains of dog are remarkably few in number. Since there are numerous instances of sites where several hundreds, or even thousands, of bones have been identified, the impression obtained from the percentages may be regarded as giving an accurate picture of the economy.

The majority of the cattle were of medium size, as is shown particularly in Germany (Müller 1964), but both large and small animals are also present in this country and in Rumania. Bones of large individuals, some still close to the aurochs, are more common than those of small animals, and it is apparent that local aurochs domestication must have been practised in many different areas. The average height of these animals has been calculated by Müller as being around 1400 mm., with some as small as 1240 mm., and others up to 1520 mm. One of the most interesting facts to arise from investigations of the Linear Pottery cattle found in Germany was the presence of oxen. There are two main ways of distinguishing bones of oxen from those of bulls or cows. The first is on the basis of the long bones, when examples occur which are too large to belong to young animals, yet still have the epiphyses detached. Since castration slows up the fusion of the epiphyses and diaphyses it is probable that these bones belong to oxen. The second method depends on the remains of horn cores. When parts of a large core are found which are too thin walled to have come from a bull, it is again probable that the example originated from a castrated animal. The first site at which their presence was demonstrated was Hohlstedt (Müller 1961), and later they were also shown to be present at many sites in the Magdeburg-Halle-Erfurt district of Germany (Müller 1964). The most striking fact of all is that in this last mentioned area of Germany where over three thousand bones of domestic cattle alone were found, oxen account for nearly half of the male animals. This method of controlling the size of the stock as well as making certain animals more manageable has been attested from settlements of the earliest phases. In connection with this fact the question of the use of the oxen as a source of draught power and the possible use of a wheeled vehicle must be mentioned. Once the castration of cattle was satisfactorily accomplished and the animals became docile, they could be harnessed to a plough or to a simple cart in order to provide draught power. Since wood only survives under special conditions which are not found in the loess soil upon which the Linear Pottery sites are based, there are no surviving ploughs or carts, but it is nonetheless conceivable that some did in fact exist. If a slide-car were present in a simple form and dragged on two poles protruding behind the box of the vehicle, it is possible that during the later stages of the culture simple wheels, or a solid log forming one very thick wheel, had been invented. At present the earliest certain evidence for a wheeled vehicle in Europe comes from the pottery model of a wagon found at Budakalász in Hungary in a burial of the Baden culture, dated to between 2900 and 2400 BC.

On average, cattle account for between a half and three-fifths of the domestic stock. The evidence also indicates that as the culture progressed they rose in importance from a half to nearly three quarters of the herded animals.

Sheep, goat and pig are found at rather less sites than cattle, but they are nonetheless a fairly constant feature in the domestic stock.

At some sites ovicaprids are more important than pigs, and at others this situation is reversed (see Figs. 9-47, Tables Nos. 30-63). In order to investigate this apparent random choice for preference of ovicaprids or pigs, the various phases of the Linear Pottery culture must be examined a little more closely. In order to do this, the ten statistically optimum sites from the osteological point of view, whose phases are known, are considered. In the table below, the sites together with their phase and the position of importance of ovicaprids and pigs are noted, together with the total number of bones found.

Site	Phase	Ovicaprids	Pig	Bones
Györ-Pápai vám	Early/Mid	2nd	3rd	842
Hohlstedt	Early	2nd	3rd	341
Halle-Trotha	Early	2nd	3rd	366
Barleben-Schweinemästerei	Early/Mid	2nd	3rd	231
Gatersleben	Mid	2nd	3rd	307
Tröbsdorf	Early/Mid	1st/2nd	3rd	377
Traian	Late	3rd	2nd	337
Barleben-Schweinemästerei (B–graves)	Late	3rd	2nd	294
Floreşti	Late	Absent	2nd	298
Magdeburg-Prester	Late	3rd	2nd	769

From this table it becomes apparent that ovicaprids are more important than pigs during the first two phases of the Linear Pottery culture, but that during the late stage pigs become more numerous. Indeed, when the statistics obtained by Müller (1964) for the various phases in central Germany are examined, this same fall in the importance of sheep and goat is apparent. The reason for this change in the economy is most probably attributable to an adaption to the local environment by these farmers. New stock of both sheep and goat could only be obtained by trade from the Near East, so that improvement would be difficult. The forested loess soil upon which these Linear Pottery settlements were based, however, would provide ample opportunity to domesticate the local wild pigs and so keep up a healthy and strong pig population.

Both sheep and goat have been distinguished at numerous sites, and it is found that sheep occur more frequently than do goats. When Müller examined the material from central Germany he found that bones of sheep were twice as common as those of goats (201 bones of sheep as against 92 of goats). The horn cores of the two animals were, however, present in approximately equal numbers, and for this reason Müller raises the possibility that the female sheep may have been hornless. Unfortunately, no well preserved skulls were found in order to find direct evidence for the presence of hornless sheep. As they were known in the earlier Starčevo-Körös culture, it is reasonable to assume that at least some of these sheep were in fact hornless. Many finds illustrate the divergent character amongst this ovicaprid stock. Cores of both moufflon-like sheep as well as those resembling turbary animals have been found, and a similar variation was found amongst the goats with a few animals that must have still been fairly close to their ancestor, the bezoar. Amongst the vast material assembled by Müller were a few complete metatarsals and metacarpals from which the height of the animals could be calculated. The results show that most sheep were between 500 and 600 mm. in height and the goats between 550 and 650 mm., with a few powerful animals of both species exceeding this.

The majority of pigs appear to have been of medium size, and those found by Müller which are placed in this category fall within the range of the turbary pigs of Switzerland. There were, however, next to these pigs, many examples of animals which could be related osteologically to the local wild swine, and these represent the indigenous domestication of these animals.

Remarkably few bones of dog have been found in a Linear Pottery context. They are present at less than a fifth of the sites considered (see Table No. 30) and at sites where a statistical analysis was possible, it is seen that they account for only a small proportion of the domestic animals (see Figs. 11-47). In many instances dogs are completely absent. A more or less complete skeleton of a dog survives at Hurbanovo in Czechoslovakia, where it was carefully buried and accompanied by a pot of the late Linear Pottery style (Ambros 1953). It has been assigned to the turbary breed. Where an idea of the size of the dogs has been attainable, they appear to be medium and large turbary dogs. There are one or two instances of more powerful animals, as at Grossgrabe (Müller 1964) and Regensburg-Purkelgut (Boessneck 1958), and in the last case it could not be decided whether a very large dog or wolf was present. Despite the absence of bones, Müller observed some indirect evidence for the presence of dogs at several sites. On many of the animal bones that he identified, he found teeth marks that were not of human origin. Since these could not belong to cattle, sheep, goat or pig, they could only come from a wild carnivore or dog. The former, however, would most likely have taken the bone and flesh away and not have gnawed it within the area of the settlement. These bones, therefore, must bear the marks of dogs' teeth.

39

Before considering the cultivation of plants in this context, it is necessary to make a few remarks about the position of the horse. There have been various claims for its domestic status, usually resting upon the finds of red deer antler cheek pieces for bits. The best known of these comes from Goldbach near Halberstadt in Austria (Barthold 1912), and a similar claim is made at Zauschwitz (Hančar 1956). The cheek pieces from Goldbach were found in a pit together with sherds of the Linear Pottery style and of the Bronze Age. No satisfactory explanation of the association of these antler objects with the Linear Pottery rather than Bronze Age period is given, so it seems most reasonable to assume that they do in fact originate from the later period. Their shape and general appearance is similar to known examples from the Bronze Age. Bones of horses are rare at Linear Pottery sites, and no osteoligical evidence for their domestication has been found.

Both wheat and barley were cultivated, and wheat occurs at more sites than does barley (see Table No. 65). Five different species of wheat have been identified, namely einkorn, emmer, bread wheat, club wheat and hard wheat. Of these emmer is the most common, with only a single instance of each of the last three species. Although bread wheat is only known at Nezwicka, it is reported, together with emmer, as being present in large quantities (Chernush 1963, 31). A large quantity of grain was recovered from Bylany in Czechoslovakia, and nearly all is attributable to emmer (Soudsky 1963). It is also the main crop at Zilgendorf (Hopf, personal communication). At the remaining sites too few grains could be identified for any conclusions regarding their relative importance to be made. Barley appears to have been much less common than wheat. It occurs at fewer sites and there is no record of its being present in large amounts. There is no definite identification of the kind of barley grown, but at one site a multi-rowed form was present (Klichowska 1959), and it seems possible that a naked variety was present at a further site (Buttler 1936). This suggests the presence of six-rowed naked barley, which agrees with what one would expect from the consideration of other cultures.

Impressions of the northern variety of millet (*Panicum miliaceum*), of rye and oats have also been found in this context. All of these occur in small quantities only, usually with only a single instance at any particular site. It is unlikely that rye and oats represent anything other than a weed amongst the crops of wheat and barley.

In addition to cereals, there is one instance of flax occurring at Köln-Lindenthal where a large heap of carbonised seeds was found (Buttler 1936) and three instances of peas. One of these is in Russia

(Nezwicka; Chernush 1963) and the other two in Germany (Eisenberg and Tröbsdorf; Butschkow 1935, Schmidt 1956).

An interesting and important aspect of cereal cultivation is the method in which the crop was stored for future use. The grain may be divided into two categories, that used for sowing for the following years crop and that which was kept for human consumption. The former is found in granaries or pits, and the latter in large storage vessels. The evidence from several sites indicates that large amounts of grain were kept, and the methods of storage are well illustrated at Bylany (Soudsky 1963). Several large pots were found in the houses, which were evidently used for grain storage, and groups of four storage pits have been found outside the houses. These pits were presumably daubed every year and then burnt to provide disinfection, and this is seen to occur ten or eleven times in each pit. Hence the minimum period for which the pits were used is ten or eleven years.

Ovens were also found outside the houses, and these appear to have been used for parching the grain that was stored for food. When grain is kept for consumption it is necessary that it should not germinate, and in order to prevent this the grain has to be heated or parched. These ovens are usually grouped in threes or fours, and carbonised grain has been found in their vicinity.

The chief forms of evidence for the practice of agriculture are those which are the most direct, that is the actual objects of domestication and cultivation. There are, however, several indirect forms of evidence of which the best known is pollen analysis. Research in this field in Holland has shown the arrival of the Linear Pottery colonists into the area by the change in vegetation (see p. 80).

The sickles used to harvest the grain can be reconstructed from surviving antler hafts and flint blades. Microscopic examination and chemical analysis have shown that these small flint blades were used for cutting some form of silica-containing plants, either wild or cultivated. There have been many discussions as to whether shaft-hole axes were used as primitive ploughshares or not. Many of these axes have various chips and scratches on them, as though they had been knocked and dragged against some sharp objects, such as stones, in a field. They occur in various shapes and sizes and usually have the pointed end blunted as though from extensive use.

From this discussion it is clear that the Initial Colonisation cultures had economies based upon the exploitation of different animals, although the components of their fields do not differ very greatly. Sheep and goat were the animals most commonly found at sites of the Early Agricultural Neolithic in Greece and of the Starčevo-Körös culture, with large and small individuals as well as hornless sheep

41

known. Large cattle together with turbary pigs and dogs were also present. Wheat appears to have been the main crop, with both einkorn and emmer represented. Sheep are also the basic animal in the Impressed Ware economy, with goats, cattle, pigs and dogs present to a lesser extent. The main crop was bread wheat followed by emmer, barley, club wheat and einkorn. The Linear Pottery farmers were essentially cattle breeders, who also kept sheep, goats and pigs together with a few dogs. Emmer was more important than einkorn in this context, and bread and club wheat, hard wheat, barley, millet, flax and perhaps peas were also cultivated.

4. Subsequent Development in South-east and Central Europe

Following the Initial Colonisation cultures, a series of cultures developed throughout Europe, all of which either bred animals or cultivated plants to some extent. The subsistence-economics of these societies in south-east and central Europe are considered in this chapter.

The Boian culture developed to the north of the Sesklo culture in south-east Rumania and northern Bulgaria and according to current dating is placed between 4100 and 3800 BC. It is divided into five stratigraphical phases. The pottery bears spiral and meander patterns outlined with channelled or incised lines, and from phase III onwards sporadic painted ware occurs. In the northern area of its distribution white on red painted pots occur. The stone industry contains perforated axes for the first time, but otherwise it follows the Starčevo-Körös tradition. Copper appears occasionally in phases IV and V. The parallels to this culture lie to the north-west in Vinča B$_2$ and C.

Red and roe deer, aurochs, pig, horse, otter, badger, fox, lynx, hare and polecat were all hunted, and many fish bones have been found at the settlements. This means of procuring food remained unimportant throughout the culture, varying between a fiftieth and a fifth of the osteological remains (see Tables Nos. 68 & 69). On average hunting accounts for a tenth of the bones found.

Evidence from ten sites is considered (see Table No. 67). The two instances in which a statistical analysis of the bones was possible, namely Bogata and Tangîru, both demonstrate the fact that cattle were the most frequent of the domestic animals (see Figs. 48-53, Tables Nos. 68, 69; Necrasov & Haimovici 1959b & d). They are also reported to be the main animal at another site (Paul 1962). Both ovicaprids and pigs were also bred, although pigs appear to have been of diverse importance, as their striking absence at Bogata shows.

Two different breeds of cattle have been distinguished in this context. They both occur together, and the more frequent of the two is of the turbary breed, whereas the larger is closely allied to the aurochs. Amongst the goats kept there is evidence for individuals closely resembling the wild bezoar, as well as the more common smaller animals. The pigs were small and slender, and the evidence from Tangîru shows that they were seldom allowed to attain maturity (Necrasov & Haimovici 1959d). Nearly all the remains of dog can be assigned to the turbary breed, with a single exception which may

43

originate from a somewhat larger individual (Necrasov & Haimovici 1959d).

The evidence for plant cultivation is once again limited. There is no evidence for the relative importance of the different components of the fields, but it is known that einkorn and emmer and an unspecified form of millet were cultivated at Tangîru (Childe 1957) and Vidra (Gaul 1948).

The economy of the Boian culture was similar to that of the Linear Pottery colonists, with cattle breeding the basis of the economy. Ovicaprids and dogs were also present, and pigs were of diverse importance. There is only a little evidence for plant cultivation, and the presence of einkorn, emmer and millet has been attested.

The Hamangia culture has been divided into four typological phases, and it is confined to the low-lying area of Dobrogea in southeast Rumania. It occupies the same period in time as the Boian culture, namely 4100–3800 BC. The pottery has comb or shell impressions, or incised lines, and may be compared with the pottery of the southern Bug area. It is generally self-coloured, although in the later stages white on red and graphite painting occurs. The stone industry is somewhat richer than that of Starčeco-Körös. Hunting was of little importance to this culture. It accounts for less than a tenth of the food supply and the animals represented include red deer, roe deer, aurochs, pig, donkey, fox, otter, beaver, cat, hare and dolphin (see Table No. 70).

As was the case in the Boian culture, cattle are more frequent than ovicaprids or pigs, and both large and small animals were being bred. A careful study of the domestic bovine remains at Techirghiol showed that there was a clear transition between these two types, with no animals of intermediate size present (Necrasov & Haimovici 1962b; see Fig. 54 & Table No. 70). There were also abundant bones of cattle at Cernavoda together with the other domestic animals (Necrasov & Haimovici 1959a), and they are again represented at La Adam (Radulesco & Samson 1962). Goats seem to have been more common than sheep (Necrasov & Haimovici 1962b), and the remains indicates that the breeds were similar to those of the Boian culture. The extremely small proportion of pig remains from Techirghiol indicates the presence of the turbary breed, which is about twice as common as the dog at this site (Necrasov & Haimovici 1962b; see Fig. 54 & Table No. 70).

The only instance of plant cultivation in a Hamangia context comes from Techirghiol (Necrasov & Haimovici 1962b). Various types of carbonised wheat grains were present in considerable quantities, but these have not as yet been identified. It is not known whether barley

44

or millet were represented amongst this find, but it is clear that they could only have been of secondary importance to the economy.

Hence it may be concluded that the Hamangia culture had an economy based upon cattle breeding and wheat cultivation. Sheep, goats, pigs and dogs were also bred, but the other crops raised are not yet known.

There is only a little evidence from the Veselinovo culture of the Maritsa valley in Bulgaria. At present this cultural group is dated to between 4400 and 4200 and the pottery shows a complete break with the preceding Starčevo-Körös tradition. It is self-coloured, generally buff or grey, occasionally burnished and has characteristic handles. Axes and adzes occur but are never perforated. Generally the stone industry follows that of Starčevo-Körös. Some connections of this culture appear to be with the Late Chalcolithic of Anatolia.

The only evidence for agricultural activity comes from Banyata where it is known that both einkorn and emmer were cultivated. There is no indication of their relative importance (Garašanin 1958).

The Russian evidence to be considered in this chapter may be divided into three groups, namely evidence from the Pontic sub-neolithic, Pontic neolithic and North Russian neolithic. The definition of the sub-neolithic given by Gimbutas (1956) is the period in which people continued their semi-nomadic way of life but had learned to make pottery. This may be compared with the Ertebølle culture of Scandinavia. The pottery of both groups is similar, and the stone industry is mesolithic in character. Most settlements reveal the collection of mussels and other shells, as well as the hunting of red deer, roe deer, aurochs, pig, horse, wolf, beaver, hare, fox, badger, cat, polecat, hamster, small rodents, marsh turtle, tortoise, birds and fish (see Table No. 71a).

The only domestic animal known from the earliest sub-neolithic levels is the dog. It is present at Igren 8 (Dobrovolskii 1949), Shulaev (Bodianskii 1949) and Surskii (Danylenko 1950), and also at the later sub-neolithic levels of the first two sites. During this later stage other domestic animals begin to make an appearance. Cattle occur at both these sites, and the sheep is known at the second.

Gradually this sub-neolithic phase changes its character and more domestic animals, pottery and neolithic stone working techniques appear. The domestic pig appears for the first time, and the goat can be definitely identified. There is very little evidence for the dating of this period, but it can probably be placed somewhere in the late fourth or early third millennium.

The North Russian evidence comes from sites where a mixture of Pitted Ware and Corded Ware occurs, and so can be placed around

2500 to 2000 BC. Reindeer, red and roe deer, elk, aurochs, bison, pig, horse, lynx, otter, badger, marten, wolverine, bear, beaver, wild cat, polecat, mink, wolf, fox, squirrel, hare, hedgehog, guinea-pig and vole, as well as seal and turtle are known from these sites. Hunting was of much greater importance than domestication to the economy of these northern sites (see Table No. 71). Ovicaprids are not definitely known from this context, and it is not clear whether the cattle and pigs, said to be of the turbary breed, which were found at Bologoe, originate from this horizon (Gandert 1930). One fact that is clear, however, is that the dog was of importance and valued at this time (Paaver 1965). Careful burials of more or less complete skeletons were recovered at Visokoe with a human burial, and at Volosovo (Gandert 1930). The former has been assigned to the *Canis f. poutiatini* breed by Studer and the latter *Canis f. palustris ladogensis* by Anuncin. The Volosovo dog probably died from a blow on the head, after which it was carefully deposited in a pit. This species of dog is also present at Bologoe and Ladogasee (Gandert 1930), and in addition a second larger dog was present at Bologoe and has been attributed to *Canis f. inostranzewi*.

There is no evidence for plant cultivation, although the usual cereals might be expected during the Pontic neolithic, and perhaps also from the northern area.

Seven cultures from central Europe are considered together, forming the Central European neolithic. These are Vinča, Butmir, Bükk, Szilmeg, Tisza, Herpály and Lengyel, and they are either contemporary with or follow the Linear Pottery culture in this area between 4300 and 3500.

The Vinča culture is the Serbian equivalent of the Veselinovo culture, and so has connections with Anatolia. Generally the pottery has more decoration, and finer channeling occurs. It is divided into phases A, B_1, B_2, C and D. Phase A is equivalent to Starčevo-Körös, the B_1 and B_2 phases are known as Vinča-Tordos and the C and D phases as Vinča-Pločnik. The culture is thought to cover a period from 4200 to 3500 BC.

The Butmir culture is basically a Bosnian mixture of Vinča and late Linear Pottery with Adriatic influences. According to current dating it is placed around 3500. The Bükk culture is a Linear Pottery development in east Slovakia and north-east Hungary, and is found in both caves and settlements on the upper Tisza river around 4100. A local variant of the Linear Pottery culture in the region of the middle Tisza is known as the Szilmeg culture, and it contains some painted ware.

The Tisza culture is divided into two phases and again it originates as a local development of Linear Pottery in the middle Tisza valley. It

46

extends partly into the Bükk area to the north. Tisza 11 is contemporary with the late Linear Pottery sites and also with the late Boian culture to the south. At present it is dated to 3900–3700.

The Herpály pottery is usually brown on buff painted ware with rectilinear designs and is very thin. It occurs in the Alföldi area and is slightly later than Tisza 11. It developed from late Linear Pottery and from the painted pottery of Transylvania. The main phase of the Lengyel culture is contemporary with Gumelniţa in Rumania and Tisza-Polgár in Hungary, and the beginning of its development is placed around 3600 and is contemporary with Herpály. The early pottery was painted after firing in white, red, yellow and black on a grey ground. Later the painting disappears and the pots resemble those of the Tisza-Polgár culture. Copper is occasionally found in this context.

The wild animals that were hunted do not differ notably from those of the Linear Pottery culture, with red deer, roe deer, aurochs and pigs the chief representatives. In certain cultures, however, there is a much higher proportion of wild animals than is usual. This is true of the Herpály culture, where aurochs were hunted in large numbers, and in all hunting accounts for three-quarters of the osteological remains. About half of the animal bones of the Lengyel culture may also be attributed to wild animals (see Tables Nos. 77-80).

As may be seen from Table No. 72, cattle are known from all of these contexts, and in every case they are the dominant feature in the economy (see Figs. 55-62). Ovicaprids and pigs were also bred, with pigs the more frequent of the two, and the dog occurs in small quantities in all cultures. The breed of cattle present often could not be determined, but they are shown to be the dominant animal at two sites of the Vinča culture (Gornja Tuzla, Dudeşti; Ćović 1961, Benac 1961, Comsa 1959a), three sites of the Butmir culture (Butmir, Danilo, Smilčić; Korosec 1958, Benac 1961), one instance in the Bükk culture (Borod-Derekegyházi dülö; Bökönyi 1959, see Fig. 55), three instances in the Szilmeg culture (Lebo, Polgár-Basatanya, Szilmeg; Bökönyi 1959) and five in the Tisza culture (Hódmezövásárhely, Hódmezövásárhely-Gorzsa-Cukortanya, Polgár-Csoszhalom, Szegvár-Tüzköves and Lebo; Bökönyi 1959, Gaal 1931). The same is true of the Herpály sites (Berettyószentmárton, Herpály; Bökönyi 1959, see Figs. 59 & 60) and the two Lengyel sites (Pécsvárad-Arangyhegy, Zengovárköny; Bökönyi 1959, see Figs. 61 & 62). In both of these last cultures, the economy was orientated towards hunting rather than domestication and at the Herpály sites the aurochs alone accounts for between two-fifths and half of the bones identified (see Tables Nos. 77, 78). This animal is two to four times as common as its domestic counterpart. The aurochs was clearly the object of intensified hunting, and it is probable that its prevalence is due to the fact that it was in the process of being domesticated in large numbers. In these various cultures, animals similar to the aurochs, others resembling turbary cattle, as well as intermediate types have all been identified. On average cattle account for between half and three-quarters of the domestic stock.

Both sheep and goat were being bred and were less frequent than pigs in Vinča, Szilmeg, Tisza, Herpály and Lengyel contexts. The only instance of their exceeding pigs occurs at sites of the Butmir culture, where the statistics are unknown (Benac 1961). Horn cores resembling those of the bezoar goat are recorded from Hungary, and indicate contact with the Near East (Gaal 1931), but otherwise both sheep and goat are thought to be medium-sized.

With the exception of the Butmir culture, pigs are more common than ovicaprids; the extent to which pigs exceed them can be seen from Figs. 9, 55-62. Both the small turbary pig and the larger *scrofa* breed are represented, but it is the larger animal that is the more frequent of the two. Although wild animals are important to the economy of both the Herpály and Lengyel cultures, boar hunting was of no great importance unlike that of aurochs, so it appears that local domestication was not practised to the same extent.

Dogs occur in small quantities in all cultures, but it is only at the Tisza site of Hódmezővásárhely that the breed could be determined. In this case the turbary dog was present (Gaal 1931). This breed is also thought to be present at the Lengyel site of Eggendorf (Hauck 1944). There are various other instances of dogs from unspecified neolithic contexts, mostly in Austria, where larger individuals are present (see Table No. 72).

The cultivation of wheat is attested for the Vinča, Butmir and Lengyel cultures, and that of barley for the Butmir, Lengyel and possibly Bükk cultures (see Table No. 81). In addition to these cereals, broomcorn has been identified in a Bükk context and Italian millet in a Lengyel context. Further instances of these cereals occur at other neolithic sites where the cultural connections are not known (see Table No. 81).

Einkorn and emmer form the basis of the wheat crop. They are the only form of wheat identified at Lisicici and Lug in Yugoslavia (see Table No. 82). Impressions of wheat are more frequent than those of barley, but no remains of carbonised wheat were found whereas a large quantity of carbonised four and six-rowed barley occurs (Hopf 1958; see Table No. 82). Werneck (1949, 1961) has demonstrated the presence of both einkorn and emmer at Lengyel sites in Austria. They are the only species present and emmer accounts for around three-quarters of the crop. Bread and club wheat have only been found at two sites, and there is no record of their being of much importance relative to einkorn or emmer.

The occurrence of a four-rowed naked barley in Yugoslavia is of interest since it is regarded as a hybrid between the two and six-rowed forms. It is a rare occurrence in a neolithic context, although in this case it accounts for the majority of the grains of barley, with only a small proportion of the six-rowed variety present. The only instance of two-rowed barley occurs in a Lengyel context (Dombai 1960).

The two instances of rye, one at a Butmir site and the other in either a Lengyel or a Linear Pottery context, must both represent the wild rye which is found in the Carpathians and southwards into the Balkans. The same applies to the possible occurrence of oats (Neuweiler 1905). The cultural connections of the single instance of flax at the type site of the Lengyel culture are unknown, but flax was probably known to most if not all of the cultures mentioned (Neuweiler 1905). The pea and the bean are also present at various sites, and are assumed to have been cultivated, although no definite evidence for this is given (see Table No. 81).

The archaeological cultures which followed the Initial Colonisation cultures in south-east and central Europe had various common elements in their subsistence economics. The Boian culture which developed in an area previously occupied by sheep and goat breeders, became a basically cattle breeding culture, as did the Hamangia culture. The Vinča, Butmir, Bükk, Szilmeg, Tisza, Herpály and Lengyel cultures of central Europe followed the example of the Linear Pottery colonists and maintained cattle as their basic domestic animal. In European Russia the dog is the only domestic animal during the early sub-neolithic, but during the latter stages of this period and during the ensuing neolithic the full range of domestic animals begins to appear. In the northern area the dog is the main domestic animal.

The evidence for plant cultivation is less abundant, but it is clear that both wheat and barley were known and cultivated by most societies. There are more instances of wheat than of barley in the southern area, and einkorn, emmer, hard wheat together with possibly four-rowed barley, millet and peas were cultivated. It is only in the central area that an analysis of the relative importance of the different types of wheat has been possible. Emmer was the main crop of the Lengyel culture with einkorn of secondary importance. Other cereals account for only a very small proportion of the remains. The beginning of the rise in popularity of barley is attested to the south, in the region of the Butmir culture. It is also seen that this is the only context in central Europe where sheep and goat are seen to be more common than pigs, and so connects this culture with Anatolia as well as with central Europe. Further connections with the south have been seen in the pottery ornamentations which are reminiscent of those on Early Cycladic vases (Childe 1957, p. 93).

The agricultural habits of the Starčevo-Körös and allied cultures were superseded by the tradition of the Linear Pottery culture in northern Bulgaria and Rumania, and in both this region and in central Europe the breeding of cattle together with the cultivation of emmer, and to a lesser extent einkorn, remain the basis of the subsistence-economics until the advent of the copper trading cultures.

5. Western and Northern Europe

Many different neolithic cultures developed in western and northern Europe after the arrival of the Linear Pottery and Impressed Ware farmers. Some of these contain much evidence for their agricultural activities, but for other communities, particularly those in the south-west, direct evidence is lacking. It must be made clear that this lack of evidence is not due to the absence of domesticated animals and plants, but rather to the opinion of some excavators that finds of animal bones or carbonised plants were irrelevant and unimportant.

The Cortaillod culture of Switzerland represents one of the best documented cultures in Europe. This is due to the exceptional circumstances of preservation. The culture developed between 3200 and 2600 and consisted of lakeside villages of rectangular houses, which were eventually submerged beneath the rising lakes. Owing to the waterlogged conditions many objects of bone and wood, as well as plant remains, survived and were first discovered by archaeologists at the end of the last century. Specialists were called in and a detailed analysis of the bone and plant material was made.

The pottery is fairly simple in design, and usually has a round base, resembling leather prototypes. Flat-based pots can also occur. This culture may be divided into two phases, and in the late phase the pottery designs are rather more sophisticated, and Rössen and Michelsberg affinities may be detected. The pots of both phases are often perforated with small holes near the rim. Axes and occasional adzes occur, but otherwise the stone industry could be developed from the mesolithic tradition.

At most sites hunting is still a valuable part of the economy. Generally wild animals account for about half the total fauna, although at the richest site only a quarter of the bones could be attributed to wild species (see Tables Nos. 85-95). Of these, red deer is by far the most frequent animal, with roe deer, elk, chamois, aurochs, bison, pig, horse, wolf, fox, badger, otter, pine and beech marten, polecat, beaver, bear, lynx, cat, weasel, hare, hedgehog, mouse and squirrel also represented. Bones of birds and fish are also found (see Table No. 83). The Pfyn group of sites is also considered here. There are several marked differences between these and the Cortaillod culture, but the flint, bone and wood industries link these sites with those of the Cortaillod culture rather than the Michelsberg culture. They are thought to be contemporary with the late Cortaillod phase.

The osteological remains from 22 sites have been analysed (see Table No. 84), and from this it is clear that cattle are the predominant feature in the economy. Sheep and goat were also domesticated but at the majority of sites are slightly less common than pigs, and dogs are recorded at nearly every site in relatively high proportions (see Figs. 63-72).

Amongst the cattle it is the turbary breed that predominates. Some sites, such as Burgäschisee Sud-ouest, reveal that the stock was almost exclusively turbary, and at others a substantial proportion of domestic animals resembling the aurochs was found (Josien 1956, Hescheler & Rüeger 1939, 1942, Studer 1883). The size of these animals has been calculated as being 1150 mm. and 1360 mm. respectively, which compares with the aurochs variation of between 1450 mm. to 1600 mm. (Hescheler & Rüeger 1942). Some idea of the appearance of the turbary breed is obtained by comparison with the Simmentaler cattle of today, which they resemble very closely. Hunting of the aurochs was of no great importance to the economy, and neither was its domestication. This is well illustrated at Burgäschisee Süd, where there was only a very small proportion of domesticated animals, and the red deer is seen to be the most common animal (Table No. 85).

Sheep and goat have been found at all the sites considered, as have cattle, and where the two species could be distinguished, sheep are usually more common than goats (Josien 1956, Studer 1883, Josien 1956, Hescheler & Rüeger 1942). The remains can be assigned almost exclusively to the turbary breeds, and there is a single case in which a hornless animal was found. This occurs at Seematte-Gelfingen where a hornless sheep's skull was found, and also at this site there was a loose horn core which bore evidence of pressure being applied to the inner and outer surfaces (Hescheler & Rüeger 1942, p. 437). From this it seems probable that the inhabitants were trying intentionally to produce hornless sheep in preference to horned animals. Indirect evidence for the presence of ovicaprids was obtained from Egozwil III. As yet there is no detailed report from this site, but Guyan (1955) conducted a biological examination of the faeces found in Field II, and it was found that they contained pollen of *Caltha palustris* (marsh marigold), which is a plant that cattle and pigs never touch.

Domestic pigs have been found at most of the sites mentioned, and the majority of the remains fall within the range of variation of the turbary pig. At many sites this was the only breed that could be found, but at Burgäschisee Sud, where the economy was orientated towards hunting, there were also many bones that could not be assigned with certainty to either domestic or wild animals (Stampfli 1962; see Table No. 85). This may indicate the practice of local domestication.

However, at all the other rich sites, such as St. Aubin, Burgäschisee Sud-ouest and Egozwil II, there was no indication of local domestication or large domestic pigs.

Dogs attain their greatest importance at the hunting site of Burgäschisee Sud where they account for a fifth of the domestic animals Stampfli 1962; see Fig.63 & Table No.85). The dogs bred by the Cortaillod people were of more or less constant size, and represent small and medium-sized turbary animals. Slightly larger dogs have been found in small numbers at two sites, and these lie between the *palustris* and *intermedius* breeds (Reverdin 1927, Kuhn 1935). Amongst the dog bones at St. Aubin there were a few jaws which showed traces of disarticulation. It appears that these animals were forcibly killed and that the high proportion of young dogs at this site was intentional.

At the Pfyn site of Niederwil, pigs are much more common than ovicaprids, and also exceed cattle when the number of individuals is considered (Clason 1964; see Fig.72 & Table No.94).

There is much evidence for both the cultivation and gathering of plants, owing to the special conditions of preservation of the remains. Many berries and fruits were collected to supplement the diet. These include apples, pears, plums, sloes, cherries, raspberries, blackberries, bilberries, strawberries and elderberries. Hazel nuts also appear to have been eaten in large quantities. Both wheat and barley were cultivated and wheat occurs in more instances than does barley (see Table No. 96). Einkorn, emmer, club wheat and bread wheat were all known, and by far the most frequent of these was club wheat (*Triticum aestivo-compactum*). Its importance is best illustrated at Thun where a large quantity of grain was recovered (Rytz 1930), and also at Niederwil (Waterbolk & Zeist 1964). In addition there were several sites at which it was the only form of wheat known. The other naked wheat, bread wheat, was far less common, as were the two glumed wheats. Where the relative quantities of wheat and barley have been distinguished, barley is seen to be of little significance (Rytz 1930; Waterbolk & Zeist 1964). There are only two cases in which the spike type could be determined, and both show the presence of the six-rowed variety.

Apart from these cereals, there were one or two instances of both Italian and broomcorn millet, and several occurrences of peas and lentils (see Table No.96). The first legume is the more common and has been found mixed with wheat and barley (Rytz 1930), and is the only legume that was definitely cultivated.

Another important cultivated plant to the Cortaillod people was flax. There has been some confusion over the type of flax involved, but Helbaek (1959a) has shown that this Swiss Neolithic flax was derived from the Near Eastern *Linum bienne*. Neuweiler thought that the flax he identified was descended from the wild species found in Austria and Switzerland, and he called it *Linum austriaceum*, and the other early specialist in this field, Heer, thought that the Swiss flax was descended from *Linum angustifolium*, which is now better known as *Linum bienne*. Helbaek was able to demonstrate conclusively that Heer was correct by examination of the ring cells of the seed coat of flax, which showed agreement between the Swiss and Near Eastern examples. Also the chromosome number of Austrian flax was different from that found at the Swiss sites, which in turn agreed with that of *Linum bienne*. Hence it can be concluded that the Swiss flax was derived from the Near Eastern *Linum bienne*, and it is called *Linum usitatissimum*. This oil-bearing plant is known to have been present in large quantities at Niederwil, where only wheat and poppy seeds are known in similar proportions. Its presence has also been demonstrated in the pollen diagrams (Troels-Smith 1955), and a linen fabric was also found (Rytz 1946).

Poppy was also a popular plant, but its exact status does not appear to have been thoroughly investigated. These seeds must have been of great significance to the Cortaillod people, judging by their frequency at some sites, as might be expected from parallels of certain modern primitive tribes.

It is seen that cattle breeding was the basis of the Cortaillod economy together with the cultivation of club wheat. Sheep, goat and pigs were also kept, as was the dog, and the turbary breed of these animals are dominant in all cases. Pigs are of greater importance at the Pfyn sites than at the true Cortaillod sites. Einkorn, emmer, bread wheat, barley, millet, flax and peas were also cultivated.

The Cortaillod culture is superseded by the Horgen and Michelsberg cultures in Switzerland. According to current dating the former is placed at 2700–2300 and the latter at 2800–2500 BC. The Horgen pottery is coarse and badly baked, some vases have splayed bases and others have rounded bases. The stone material is generally local in origin and perforated axes occur. During this period there is a general deterioration in architecture, with houses often becoming smaller than in the Cortaillod settlements. The pottery, antler sleeves and arc pendants are reminiscent of the SOM culture of northern France.

The Michelsberg culture is concentrated to the north of the Cortaillod area, in moor villages in Switzerland and Württemberg, and in hilltop camps in south-west Germany. The most distinctive pot form is the tulip-shaped beaker, but pots with round and flat bases, jugs with handles, and flat plates also occur. Some similarities with the TRB culture are seen. The Michelsberg settlers are known to have worked flint mines in Belgium. Their houses were rectangular and usually sub-divided into two rooms with a hearth in the inner and oven in the outer. Copper occurs at a few late settlements. This culture is partially contemporary with that of Cortaillod and Rössen in the west, and to the east it supersedes Rössen.

Hunting accounts for two-fifths to half of the osteological remains in both cultures, and there is a noticeable drop in the proportions of wild animals in the late Horgen period. Red and roe deer, elk, aurochs, bison, pig, horse, bear, wolf, fox, marten, lynx, cat, otter, beaver, badger, hare, squirrel, birds, fish and turtle are all represented (see Table No. 97). Together with sites of these two cultures, settlements which are known to be of neolithic date but whose exact cultural connections are not known, are considered.

The economy of the Horgen and Michelsberg cultures was different. The former concentrated upon the breeding of pigs and the latter exploited cattle to a greater extent. The rich sites of Auvernier III (Reverdin 1932b) and St. Aubin III (Reverdin 1930) both illustrate the composition of the Horgen economy (see Figs. 73, 74 & Tables Nos. 99, 100). Following the pigs, which are attributable to the turbary breed, came cattle, and these belonged to the same small species. Sheep were more common than goats, and they once again belonged to the turbary variety. Both this form of dog as well as its miniature form *Canis f. spaletti* were also bred (Kuhn 1932).

Both large and small cattle are present at Michelsberg sites and the small breed is the more common of the two, as has for instance been demonstrated at Ossingen (Kuhn 1932; see Fig. 75, Table No. 101). One of the striking features about this site is the complete absence of both sheep and goat, although these animals are known to have been present at other Michelsberg sites (Kuhn 1932, 1935). Pigs were more popular than ovicaprids, and belong exclusively to the turbary race (Kuhn 1932, 1935). The two breeds of dog noted for the Horgen culture are present in this context.

The same range of domestic animals is apparent from the neolithic sites, and turbary animals are prevalent amongst all the species. There is a possibility of a larger breed of dog at Wangen where *Canis f. leineri* has been identified, but it could not be stated with certainty whether these bones came from the neolithic or Bronze Age levels (Vogel 1933).

Very little is known about the cultivated plants of the Horgen culture. Wheat has been found in this context, but its variety could not be ascertained (Neuweiler 1930, 1935). Einkorn, emmer, club wheat and six-rowed barley were all cultivated in the Michelsberg settlements. Of these it is naked wheat that occurs in larger quantities than any other grain, although in the pollen diagrams barley occurs more frequently than wheat at Thayngen-Weiher (Guyan 1955). Flax was cultivated by both cultures, and both Italian millet and broomcorn occur as well as poppy seeds and peas (see Table No. 102).

The origin of naked wheats is interesting. There is no ancestral wild form, and it is thought to have developed as a result of chromosome aberration of emmer. It has been shown that club wheat was the main crop of both the Cortaillod and Michelsberg communities in Switzerland, and this therefore implies the dominance of emmer and its allied wheats amongst these societies. This agrees with the results of other neolithic cultures. The Cortaillod culture is one of the earliest known European cultures to centre its cultivation upon naked wheats, and it is suggested here that this chromosome aberration may have taken place in the central alpine zone of Europe as a result of the environmental conditions. It is possible that this took place in the highest cultivation zones, which would be exposed to more ultraviolet and cosmic radiation, and when the advantages of a glumeless wheat were realised, the grain was generally traded for sowing at lower altitudes.

The majority of sites to be considered as Italian Neolithic cannot be attributed to any particular cultural group (see Table No. 104). Those that can however belong to the Molfetta, Bocca Quadrata and Lagozza cultures. This lack of identification is chiefly due to reports of the late nineteenth and early twentieth centuries which describe the sites as 'neolithic'. The Molfetta culture is characterised by red burnished pottery with lightly incised rectilinear patterns. Occasionally, it is lighter in colour with red or red and black designs. Black vessels reminiscent of the late neolithic in Greece also occur. The settlements consist of several houses and pasture land within ditched enclosures. This culture is found in Apulia around 3200–2900 BC.

The Bocca Quadrata culture, as its name suggests, is characterised by square-mouthed pots and is found in northern Italy in the late fourth and early third millennium. The Lagozza pottery is similar to that of Late Cortaillod but is better made and has a more sharply carinated shoulder. This culture occurs in northern Italy around 2900–2700. Microlithic elements are present in the stone industry indicating mesolithic survival.

The proportions of wild animals relative to the domestic stock is unknown in all cases. Bones of red and roe deer, elk, aurochs, bison, pig, horse, donkey, fox, wolf, cat, lynx, badger, beaver, otter, marmot, hyena, hare, porcupine, bear and birds have all been identified (see Table No. 103).

Cattle are only known from a Molfetta context, and in one instance are more common than pigs, although their relationship to ovicaprids is not given (Rellini 1942). Sheep and possibly goats are known to have been bred by all three cultures, and pigs occur in the Molfetta and Bocca Quadrata cultures (see Table No. 104). Some idea of the nature of these domestic animals is obtained from the remaining 26 neolithic sites. Both the *brachyceros* and *primigenius* breeds of cattle occur at several sites, and the smaller variety are slightly more common. At one site cattle are known to be more important than the other domestic animals (Strobel 1886). The ovicaprid stock showed considerable variation in its composition. As well as the turbary breeds, a very small breed of sheep is recorded (Almagro 1955), together with a larger breed (Strobel 1877), and a 'wild goat' is also said to be present (Peet 1909). The occurrence of animals resembling the bezoar goat of the Near East are known from several sites of the neolithic period in Eastern Europe, and this is presumably another instance indicating the connection that was maintained with the Near East in order to obtain new stock. The turbary breed of pig is recorded more often than the *scrofa* breed, but they only occur rarely together (Strobel 1877, 1886).

Dogs are known at sites of the Molfetta and Bocca Quadrata cultures as well as at other neolithic sites (see Table No. 104). Where the species has been determined the turbary breed is the most frequent, and a larger breed is also thought to be present in one instance (Strobel 1890, Hauck 1950).

The only evidence for plant cultivation indicates that bread wheat and spelt were known together with millet and seeds of lentils (Goiran 1889, Neuweiler 1905). It is probable that other species of wheat as well as barley were also present.

The Chassey-Chalain culture is found in most fertile regions of France between 3400 and 2300 BC. The pottery is reminiscent of the Cortaillod ware, with simple round-based pots, but these sometimes bear hatched rectilinear patterns unlike their Swiss counterparts. Vase supports are also characteristic and other pot forms include the flat plate as found in the Michelsberg culture, and pots with perforated lugs. Mesolithic connections are visible in the stone industry, and amber and arc-shaped pendants are found at some late sites. The settlements take the form of fortified camps, often on hill tops, and the inhabitants lived in irregular oval huts. The dead were usually buried within the enclosures.

Red and roe deer, aurochs, bison, pig, horse, donkey, wolf, marten, fox, bear, badger, cat, lynx, hedgehog, rabbit, hare, weasel, vole, toad, mouse, birds and fish have all been identified in this context, but hunting does not appear to have been of much importance to the economy (see Table No. 105).

In order to discuss the economy of this culture, it is necessary to consider two separate areas, the first covers the greater part of this culture's distribution over central France, and the second consists of the small area to the south which borders the Mediterranean and was formerly occupied by the Impressed Ware colonists.

Within the large central area it is seen that cattle form the basis of the economy, with sheep, goat, pigs and dogs also being bred and of secondary importance (see Figs. 76, 79, 80; Ducos 1957, Ficatier 1885, Burnez & Case 1966, Perrault 1870, Prevost 1958, Sauter 1860). Two sizes of cattle have been noted, with the smaller of the two slightly more frequent, as at Fort Harrouard and Roucadour. At Genissait and Les Matignons however, all cattle have been assigned to the turbary breed (Burnez & Case 1966; Sauter 1860). Ducos (1957) demonstrates the presence of intermediate-sized animals as well. He made scatter diagrams for astragali and for the first and second phalanx, plotting the length of the bone against its transverse diameter, and on the resultant graphs there were three areas of maximum density. The one nearest the origin represents turbary cattle, the one furthest away the large domestic cattle, and an intermediate form is therefore also present. Both sheep and goat have been identified in this context. Some sheep have been assigned to the turbary breed, and there is one definite instance of horn cores of relatively large animals (Burnez & Case 1966). Ovicaprids are present in approximately the same numbers as domestic pigs. There are, however, a few instances in the south in which this last animal is completely absent from the domestic range, despite the fact that many bones were recovered during excavations (Ducos 1958).

There are two main sites which represent the economy of the Chassey-Chalain culture in the south of France. These are Château-neuf-Les-Martigues (Ducos 1958) and St. Benoît (Audras 1955). In this district it is the breeding of ovicaprids and not cattle that forms the basis of the economy (see Figs. 78, 81 & Tables Nos. 15, 109). Sheep account for three-quarters of the domestic stock and are mostly within the range of the turbary animals. There were also a few goats present. Cattle were bred, and are composed mainly of turbary individuals with a few larger animals as well. As mentioned above, the pigs at one site are of wild origin, and at the other it could not be decided whether they were wild or domesticated.

Dogs occur at several sites, and in both areas under consideration the turbary breed is known (Ducos 1957, 1958, Sauter 1860). The most detailed investigation of canine remains was made at the beginning of the century by Hue (1906) who examined the numerous skeletal remains from Chalain and Clairvaux. His general conclusions were that the turbary dog was the basic breed, but there were one or two instances in which a slight deviation from this breed was visible. These animals, which were a little larger, he called *Canis f. Le Mirei* and *Canis f. Girardoti*, and he regarded them as having evolved from specialised breeding of the turbary dogs.

Wheat was widely cultivated and was more common than barley. Einkorn emmer, bread wheat and spelt have all been recorded (see Table No. 110), and in one instance emmer is the most frequent wheat and in another it is bread wheat (Coquillat 1956). Six-rowed barley was cultivated, but in most cases the variety was indeterminate. It is notable that this cereal was entirely absent at Trou Arnaud where a large quantity of bread wheat was found (Coquillat 1956). Broom-corn, flax, poppy seeds and legumes are also recorded at one or two sites, but there is no indication that they were represented in large amounts.

The majority of the sites of the Chassey culture practised an economy based upon cattle breeding, but in southern France there was an area where the communities continued to be sheep farmers as they were in the preceding neolithic period. The implication is that there was a long tradition of sheep farming in this neighbourhood, which did not change with the introduction of a new pottery style. Wheat was the main crop with emmer and bread wheat its chief constituents.

Following the Chassey-Chalain culture in France were the Lagozza, Michelsberg and Horgen/som cultures. The first two are known also in Italy, Switzerland and Germany, but the som culture originated in the district around the Seine-Oise-Marne rivers in northern and central France. It may be approximately placed between 2500 and 2100 BC and so is the latest of the three cultural groups. It is essentially an adaption of the Megalithic 'religion' to the chalk downs of this area. The grave goods include Horgen pottery, a neolithic stone industry with arc pendants, bone, shell, beads of amber and a few copper finds. Trepanned skulls also occur. Red deer, roe deer, pig, horse, fox, wolf, rabbit, hare and birds have been identified at various sites (see Table No. 111).

As is seen from Table No. 112, cattle are known from all three cultures, and where the relative frequency of the domestic animals was ascertainable, they are the dominant species in two out of three cases (Ducos 1958, 1957, Paccard 1952). Both the *primigenius* and *brachyceros* animals were being bred. There is one instance of the turbary breed being dominant at a Lagozza site (Paccard 1952), and both breeds were present in equal numbers at a Horgen/SOM site (Ducos 1957, see Table No. 28). To the south, in the Mediterranean Lagozza context at Châteauneuf, it is the turbary sheep that accounts for over three-quarters of the domestic stock as during the earlier neolithic (Ducos 1958, see Table No. 16). In general pigs are less common than either cattle or ovicaprids, and as at Chassey sites, they were often of wild or indeterminate status. There are no definite instances of dogs in this context. There is, however, a possibility of the domestication of the horse at Roucadour (Ducos 1957; see Table No. 28). This occurs in a Horgen/SOM context and so belongs to the late neolithic period. At this stage there is a marked increase in the frequency of the horse bones, which rise from a twenty-fifth to a quarter of the osteological remains. Ducos thinks that these animals, a large proportion of which were young, are probably wild, but their increased numbers and the abundance of young animals supports Lundholm's theory that horses were being domesticated at the end of the neolithic period (see p. 68, 101).

There is little evidence for cultivated plants. Emmer, club wheat and naked barley were cultivated in a Horgen context, and broomcorn and legumes occur in this culture as well as at another site of an unknown culture (Galan & Arnal 1956; Neuweiler 1905).

To the east of France on the vast north European plain in Poland, Germany and Scandinavia there developed an effective farming culture that had much influence on both the early neolithic of Scandinavia and on the late neolithic in Germany. This was the TRB or Trichterr and becher culture. At present isotopic dating places it between 3000 and 2500 and it is divided into three phases A, B and C. The main type of pot is the funnel beaker, but amphorae and flat clay discs or baking plates are also common. During phases B and C the necks of the funnel beakers become longer and collared flasks appear. Pots of phase B may have cord impressions beneath the rim and are round bottomed, and during phase C the pots are more fully decorated, with pits, ribs and cord impressions employed to form vertical patterns. The stone industry includes thin-butted polished axes and polygonal battle axes together with mesolithic flake axes. The blade industry is inferior to that of the Ertebølle culture. Amber occurs and copper imports are found rarely in phase C. Many burials of this last phase have been found. These occur in megalithic 'dolmens', usually composed of four upright stones and a single large capstone, and are large enough for one extended burial (about 6' 6" by 3'). Phase C is sometimes referred to as the 'dolmen' period.

It is convenient also to consider at this point the late offshoots of this culture. These are the Walternienburg-Bernburg and Salzmunder groups. The second developed out of the TRB culture in the Lower Saale and Havelland area and led to the evolution of the first. The pottery is more angular than that of TRB itself, and burials occur in pit graves with megalithic cists. Late Dutch sites with TRB affinities are also considered here.

Hunting was of marked importance at some sites, ranging from less than a twentieth to a third of the osteological remains (see Tables Nos. 113, 115-120). The animals identified include red and roe deer, aurochs, pig, bear, horse, badger, fox, beaver, otter, cat, marten, seal, polecat, birds and fish.

The full complement of domestic animals was bred in this context, and it is seen that of these cattle occur more frequently than any of the other animals (see Table No. 114). Not only are they present at more sites than the other animals, but they are also more numerous at the individual sites. At the Polish sites they represent over half of the domestic stock (see Figs. 82-85, Tables Nos. 115-118; Krysiak 1950, 1956, 1957, Kubaswiecz 1958). In most cases these cattle can be attributed to exclusively *primigenius* animals, but at one site a few smaller turbary-like animals were also present. At the German sites an even higher proportion of cattle is revealed. They account for four-fifths or more of the stock (see Figs. 86, 87 & Tables Nos. 119, 120) and the majority of the animals is clearly related to the aurochs with only a small proportion of turbary animals (Behrens 1958, Nobis 1962). There are also many instances of individuals which could be either wild or domesticated, indicating that local domestication of the aurochs was probably practised. The osteological remains from Weissenfels are particularly rich and well preserved and illustrate these points well (Behrens 1958). At this site, as at the Polish sites, definite evidence for castration has been found. Although the proportions have not been calculated, the number of oxen do not appear to have been as great as in the Linear Pottery culture, where they account for about half of the male animals. One notable burial occurs at Gehofen where six cattle, three goats, three pigs, seven dogs and a horse all accompanied the burial of six human skeletons (Behrens 1953). Polled or hornless cattle are also known in the Salzmunder variant of this culture (Müller 1963). This is probably the earliest find of its kind, with other instances known from the Copper Age in Poland and Russia. However, the majority of animals at this site still have average length horns. Cattle burials occur in a Walternienburg-Bernburg context associated with human remains (Behrens 1966, Schwarz 1950, Sprockhoff 1938). Cattle are once again the dominant feature at Dutch sites, where there is a possibility of local aurochs domestication as well as breeding of turbary animals (Modderman 1959, Clason 1967). There have also been various finds of cattle bones in the Danish bogs, where they have been found together with TRB pots, and proved to be of this period by means of pollen analysis (Becker 1947, 1952). Settlement sites in Denmark also show the same importance of cattle as in Poland and Germany.

Turbary sheep, hornless sheep and medium and large goats all occur at various sites, and are generally less important than both cattle and pigs (see Figs. 82-87, Tables Nos. 115-120). Amongst the goats were animals that resembled the wild bezoar *Capra aegagrus*, and others with drill-like horns called *Capra prisca*. At first this last type of goat was thought to be a separate species, but later it was shown that it, like all other domestic European goats, originated from the bezoar. Ovicaprids also occur in the various offshoots of the TRB culture, but there is no record of their being represented in large numbers. Both turbary sheep and goats occur in Scandinavia, both in individual bog finds and at settlement sites (Becker 1947, 1952, Clason 1967, Forssander 1941, Mathiassen 1940).

Pigs are the second most frequent of the three basic domestic animals. At the four main Polish sites all the bones belonged to a large animal closely resembling the local boar (see Figs. 82-85, Tables Nos. 115-118; Krysiak 1950, 1956, 1957, Kubaswiecz 1958). A large variation in the size of pigs is seen amongst the German sites. Many are large and similar to the local wild animals, and others are smaller and resemble the turbary breed (see Figs. 86, 87, Tables Nos. 119, 120; Behrens 1953, Nobis 1962). The majority of finds is attributed to the large *scrofa* form of pig. The same results are apparent from Scandinavia (Mathiassen 1940).

Dogs occur in small proportions in all areas, and the majority can be related to the turbary and allied breeds. Evidence from the Polish sites suggests that the turbary dogs there may have had their brains extracted after death (Krysiak 1950, 1956). Many bones of dogs were found at Weissenfels in Germany, and in all over twenty animals, nine of which are represented by more or less complete skeletons, were found. These have all been attributed to the same breed, namely the large turbary dog *Canis f. palustris ladogensis* (Behrens 1953). There is also one instance of the miniature dog *Canis f. spaletti* (Nobis 1962) and one of a larger dog thought to be *Canis f. inostranzewi* (Schoetensack 1908).

The horse is generally thought to have been hunted in this context, but there is one definite claim for its domestication. This occurs at Ustowie in Poland (Kubaswiecz 1958). Fragments of the cranium and teeth show that this horse was of a relatively large domestic form, and no bones of wild horses were found. The horses from the other Polish sites are assigned to small wild tarpan-like animals (*Equus caballus gmelini*). Behrens (1953) could not decide whether the small amount of horse bones found at Weissenfels were of wild or domestic origin, and it is probable that the horse skeletons reported in the context of the Walternienburg-Bernburg culture at Tangermünde (Sprockhoff 1938) and Calbe (Niklasson 1925) are in fact burials of cattle (Behrens 1962, 1964).

Several varieties of wheat, as well as barley and flax were cultivated by the TRB people. The wheats include einkorn, emmer, club wheat, bread wheat and spelt, and of these emmer occurs at more sites than the other wheats, followed closely by einkorn (see Table No. 121). As is seen, impressions and a few carbonised remains have been found at various sites in Poland, Germany, Denmark and Sweden, but there are only three instances in which considerable amounts of grain were found and could be identified. The richest site was that of Lietfeld in Germany, where several thousand carbonised grains were recovered. Wheat was clearly the basic crop, with only a very small proportion of barley. Investigation of the wheat revealed that einkorn was twice as frequent as emmer, and no other species was identified (see Table No. 122; Hopf 1957). In comparison with modern grain, that from Lietfeld seems to have been a little shorter, but just as wide, and in some cases wider, than modern grain. At the Danish site of Store Valby einkorn and emmer occur more frequently than club wheat or barley, but since these two wheats are morphologically so similar, their relative quantities could not be determined (Helbaek 1954). In Sweden however, the situation is reversed, and at one site, Mogetorp, barley was twice as common as wheat (Schiemann 1958). There was no indication of varieties other than the six-rowed naked barley (Schiemann 1958, Hjelmqvist 1955, 1958). Over the remaining area occupied by the TRB culture there is no evidence to suggest that barley was an important crop, and club wheat, bread wheat and spelt are only present in small amounts at a few sites (see Table No. 121). As well as the cultivation of six-rowed barley, the evidence from Lietfeld proved that four-rowed glumed barley was grown (Hopf 1958).

There is only a single instance of millet in this context, and it belongs to the broomcorn variety (Netolitsky 1930), and two cases of flax (Hopf 1958, Klichowska 1959, Gimbutas 1956). Flax seeds form only a very small proportion of the remains at Lietfeld, with barley two to three times as common (see Table No. 122). The absence of flax at other sites may be due to the small amount of plant remains that survive rather than to its total absence. However, it should be remembered that this is not the only oil-producing plant to be found in this area.

The economy of the TRB culture was centred upon cattle breeding with pigs slightly more frequent than ovicaprids, and both of secondary importance. The cattle account for half to three-quarters of the livestock and were basically *primigenius* in character, with a few turbary animals only. The sheep and dogs are chiefly of the turbary breed, but large pigs are more common than small. Einkorn and emmer were the main crop in Germany, Poland and Denmark, with club wheat, bread wheat, spelt, barley, millet and flax also cultivated. In Sweden, however, barley becomes the chief crop and is basically of the six-rowed type. This dominance of barley in the northern area of the TRB culture is probably due to the climatic conditions, since barley being a more hardy plant is better suited to a cold climate than wheat.

In Poland there are various sites which cannot be attributed to the Linear Pottery, TRB, or Single Grave cultures and may only be described as being neolithic. Evidence for the breeding of cattle, ovicaprids, pigs and dogs has been found at these sites (see Table No. 123). The cattle were of mixed character, with both large and small animals present (Bökönyi & Kubaswiecz 1961, Hilzheimer 1920), and amongst the ovicaprid remains was the skull of a goat attributed to *Capra prisca* (Adametz 1928). Nothing is known of the pigs that were bred, but a wide range in the sizes of dogs is recorded by Hauck (1950). Amongst the cultivated plants at this group of sites there was einkorn, club wheat, bread wheat and spelt (Klichowska 1959, Netolitsky 1930), and some form of multi-rowed barley (Burchardówna 1952).

Two main cultures represent the Later German Neolithic period. These are the Rössen and Michelsberg cultures. According to current dating the former is placed between 3500 and 2900 BC and it originated in western Bohemia and Saxo-Thuringia from whence it spread to Switzerland and eastern France. It evolved from the late phase of the Linear Pottery culture. The pots are usually round-based, and bear rectilinear patterns reminiscent of basketry. Rings which serve as vase stands also occur. Stone arrow heads and mace heads are often found, together with antler axes. The Michelsberg culture in Germany may be considered to be slightly earlier than its Swiss counterpart, namely around 3100 to 2600.

The wild animals which have been identified at these German sites include red and roe deer, elk, aurochs, pig, bear, horse, donkey, badger, otter, marten, wild cat, lynx, wolf, fox, beaver, hedgehog, hare, turtle, fish and birds (see Table No. 124). Although no exact statistics are available hunting seems to have been an important source of food. The red deer was the most common of these wild animals.

Cattle, sheep, goat, pig and dog are all known from sites of the Rössen culture, but in no instance was an analysis of their relative importance possible (see Table No. 125). All the cattle bones from at least one site are known to be of large individuals, and it was often impossible to distinguish the wild from the domestic animals (Boessneck 1958). The dog has been attributed to the turbary breed (Paret 1930). The same range of domestic animals occurs in a Michelsberg context (see Table No. 125). Although no statistics were available, it is known that at Ehrenstein the turbary pig was the basic domestic animal (Paret 1955). Large cattle were also being bred at this site, and both these and the turbary breed occur at other sites (Schoetensack 1908, Reinerth 1929). Amongst the ovicaprids at Ehrenstein were goats that resembled the bezoar, as well as turbary sheep. Small and medium-sized dogs were also bred, and the majority are attributable to the turbary breed (Paret 1955).

As well as sites of the Rössen and Michelsberg cultures, there are many German sites of the neolithic which contain bones of domestic animals, but have not been attributed to any particular cultural group (see Table No. 125). Both large and small domestic cattle, sheep, goat and pigs have been found. At one of these sites, pigs outnumber cattle (see Fig. 88 & Table No. 120; Nobis 1955) and at another ovicaprids were more common (see Fig. 89 & Table No. 126; Schoetensack 1908). At both this and other sites sheep were more common than goats. As well as the turbary dogs, larger dogs attributed to *Canis f. matris optimae* (Schoetensack 1908, Lindner 1961) and *Canis f. inostranzewi* (Hauck 1950) have been identified. The dominance of pigs at one site suggests a link with the Michelsberg culture, and the dominance of ovicaprids at another may mean that the site belongs to the late neolithic or copper age (see Chapter VI).

There are two claims for horse domestication. One occurs at Riedschachen, but nothing is known about the remains and no reason for domesticity is given. They were found in the upper levels of the site (Reinerth 1929). Nobis (1955) also thought that the domestic horse was present at Berlin, but the cultural context is not known and only a single bone was found. The horse burial reported from Engers is most probably that of an ox (Behrens 1964).

The plant cultivation of the Rössen culture does not appear to have followed any particular pattern. A large quantity of grain was recovered at two sites, Ur-Fulerum (Schiemann 1954) and Wahlitz (Hopf 1957), and at the first site barley was the most common cereal forming two-thirds of the remains, and at the second club wheat forms the same proportion of the fifty thousand identified seeds. Although emmer is totally absent from Wahlitz, it accounts for a third of the cereal remains at Ur-Fulerum, and einkorn is represented in small amounts at Wahlitz, but is absent at the second site, as was club wheat. Three varieties of barley were identified at Ur-Fulerum, and these were four-rowed glumed barley, which forms half of the cereal crop, four-rowed naked and six-rowed glumed barley which form only a small proportion of the barley grains. The absence of six-rowed naked barley, the most usual neolithic variety, is striking. The spike-type of the barley at Wahlitz is not known, but as a whole this cereal forms a third of the remains.

Barley is also the most frequent cereal found at Ehrenstein in a Michelsberg context (Bertsch 1955). It accounts for two-thirds of the plant remains and only the six-rowed species is known with certainty. Barley is again the most frequent crop at Reute Waldsee, which is also thought to belong to the Michelsberg culture (Paret 1935). Einkorn and emmer were also cultivated at Ehrenstein, and these two wheats together with club wheat are known from Reute Waldsee. The other wheat identified in this context is spelt (see Table No. 127).

There are also several identifications of einkorn, emmer, club wheat and barley at 'neolithic' sites (see Table No. 127). The only case in which the relative frequency of grain is known occurs at the Passage Grave of Dötlingen, where the three varieties of wheat are less common than barley (Patzöld 1958).

The other plant known to have been cultivated was flax. This oil-bearing plant has been identified at three sites in a Michelsberg context, but its absence at the rich Rössen sites is striking. In connection with the cultivation of flax it is interesting to note that examination of the interior of sherds found at Dötlingen revealed that they originated from vessels that had served as containers for plant oil (Patzöld 1958). The two main plants to yield oil are flax and dog-wood. The last plant was identified in quantity at the Michelsberg site of Ehrenstein, and it is possible that it replaced flax as an oil-producing plant in some cultures.

Large and small cattle, ovicaprids, pigs and dogs were bred during the German Neolithic, and in one instance pigs were the dominant feature of the Michelsberg economy. Six-rowed barley was the main crop in this context, but the Rössen culture does not appear to have followed any particular pattern of plant cultivation, with club wheat dominant at one site and barley at another.

The TRB culture of the north European plain was ancestral to the

Scandinavian Middle Neolithic, which at present is placed between 2600 and 2200. This period is characterised by a series of settlement sites and large passage graves. The graves replace the earlier dolmens to a great extent and are also constructed of large stones. The tomb is entered by a narrow passage and the burials occur in chambers placed at the end of the passage and symmetrically on either side. As many as a hundred skeletons may occur in one tomb.

The pottery includes the earlier funnel beakers, and they may bear vertical arrangements of cord impressions as in the earlier TRB C phase. Deep incisions also occur as a form of decoration. Pedestal bowls, angular vases similar to those of Walternienburg-Bernburg, and later more rounded forms all appear. Stone elements include double axes, daggers, arrowheads and mace heads as well as specialised tools. Metal was imported from central Europe and amber was the main export. Many settlements have been found in Denmark, and they include both apsidal and rectangular buildings.

Hunting was of very little significance and at one important site it accounts for less than a fiftieth of the osteological remains. The animals exploited include red and roe deer, elk, aurochs, pig, seal, horse, otter, badger, marten, bear, wolf, fox, cat, polecat, squirrel, hedgehog, hare, turtle, birds and fish (see Table No. 128).

Cattle, ovicaprids and pigs have all been found at the majority of sites to be considered (see Table No. 129). Cattle were clearly the dominant animal, and this is particularly well illustrated at the rich site of Bundsø where somewhere in the region of ten thousand bones were identified (Degerbøl 1939). Nearly all these animals can be attributed to the turbary breed, and show close agreement with the animals bred at Swiss neolithic sites. The difference in size between these animals and the domesticated aurochs is well illustrated by the basal circumference of the horn cores, with the small domestic animals having a circumference of 130 mm., and the aurochs of 335 mm. There were, however, a few further cranial remains which do not comply with the turbary characteristics and represent more powerful animals. These have been assigned by Degerbøl to domesticated aurochs. The evidence from other sites also suggests this prevalence of turbary cattle (Winther 1943, Degerbøl 1928, Winge 1904).

The second most frequent animal at Bundsø was the pig, all of which show close agreement with the turbary breed. No intermediate individuals lying between this and the wild pig have been found (Degerbøl 1939). The majority of sheep remains at this site can also be attributed to this small breed, and characteristic bones were often encountered. Only a very few goat bones were identified. Another breed of sheep is, however, also present. Comparative measurements show that it is the Copper sheep *Ovis aries studeri*, which is character-ised by large outswept horns with a triangular cross-section. This type of sheep which resembles the moufflon closely is extremely rare during the neolithic period, but has been identified at sites of the Single Grave Complex in Switzerland. Single Graves and Corded Ware appear in Denmark during the second half of the Passage Grave or Middle Neolithic period, so that the occurrence of these large sheep can be connected with the Single Grave Complex. They are another example of contact between the two cultural groups. The nature of the sheep and goats present at the remaining sites is not known.

The other domestic animal, the dog, was found at fewer sites (see Table No. 129). Several distinctive skulls were found at Bundsø, the most powerful of which can be attributed to the large turbary dog *Canis f. palustris ladogensis*, and the remainder all belong to *Canis f. palustris*. This uniformity of breed is born out by the other bones found at this site (Degerbøl 1939). At another site both a large and a small dog are reported (Winge 1904).

Bones of horses have been identified at various sites, but it is only at the late sites of Lindø and Lindskov that there is thought to be a possibility of domestication (Brønsted 1957, p. 268). The number of horse bones increases greatly towards the end of the Neolithic period and it is thought that this coincides with their domestication (Lund-holm 1949). It is generally felt that the Single Grave people brought the idea of horse domestication to Denmark, but if this is so they domesticated the local wild stock and did not bring their own stock with them. Since the Single Grave complex appears in Scandinavia towards the end of the Middle Neolithic, the occurrence of domestic horses at late Passage Grave sites is perfectly feasible.

A great deal of work has been done in Scandinavia on the botanical evidence obtained from sites. Both wheat and barley have been iden-tified at numerous sites of the Middle Neolithic period in Denmark and Sweden, and einkorn, emmer, club wheat, possibly bread wheat, and six-rowed barley were all cultivated (see Table No. 130). The evidence from Denmark is considered first. In the majority of cases the presence of the cereal is attested by either a small number of pottery impressions, or a few carbonised grains, so that the relative frequency of the types of wheat and barley cannot be ascertained. There were, however, two sites at which a large quantity of grain was preserved. These sites, Bundsø (Jessen 1939) and Blandebjerg (Win-ther 1943), show that the main crop was einkorn, and at the second site it was the only wheat identified and accounts for all but a twentieth of the cereal remains. At Bundsø wheat forms nine-tenths of the

68

cereals, and emmer is about half as frequent as einkorn. There was also a very small proportion of naked wheat, amongst which club wheat was present. Barley was relatively unimportant, with six-rowed naked barley as well as glumed barley being cultivated (Jessen 1939, Winther 1943). It is also seen to be less important than wheat at other sites where the species are not known (Helbaek 1952).

Einkorn and emmer are the basic wheats found in Sweden (see Table No. 130). They are more important than barley, and at the richest site, Vastra Hoby, einkorn is the more frequent of the two (Hjelmqvist 1955). For the Swedish material as a whole this same result applies (Hjelmqvist 1952, 1955). Both naked and glumed barley have been identified by Hjelmqvist, but they account for only a small proportion of the cereals.

The agriculture of the Scandinavian Middle Neolithic was based upon cattle breeding and the cultivation of einkorn. The cattle stock was almost exclusively turbary, and this breed of pig was more common than sheep or goat. Amongst the ovicaprid remains were bones of the Copper sheep, illustrating the contact between the Single Grave and Middle Neolithic communities. The main breed of dog was the turbary animal, and at a few late sites the domestic horse may have been known, and was probably introduced by the Single Grave complex. Apart from the cultivation of einkorn, emmer, club wheat and barley are also known. This and T R B are the only cultures known to have had einkorn as a main constituent of the crop in their fields.

Along the coast-line of Scandinavia and the Baltic, partially contemporary with the Middle Neolithic, there developed a culture known as Pitted Ware. It is placed between 2400 and 2200. The pots have rounded bases and are ornamented with rows of pits and comb impressions. In the western part of its distribution the pots may have a concave neck profile. Adzes, chisels, celts, mace heads, slate knives and darts are all present and in nearly all areas Maglemose type harpoons and bone points illustrate the strong mesolithic background.

Evidence for animal breeding has so far only been found in Sweden, and at the majority of sites hunting was of much importance. Wild pig and seal are the most common animals, and some sites clearly have their economy based upon the exploitation of one or other of these animals. Other animals identified include red deer, roe deer, elk, aurochs, horse, bear, otter, beaver, badger, marten, wolf, fox, wild cat, lynx, hare, fish and birds as well as porpoise (see Table No. 132). The foxes found on the island of Stora Karslö are of interest since they are all small in comparison with modern animals and only rarely attain medium size. Zeuner said that several of the foxes he identified at sites in Switzerland were also of similar size, and many show traces of arthritis, which only occurs as a result of domestication (Piggott, personal communication). This raises the possibility that some of the Swedish foxes may have been domesticated.

The agricultural economy of Pitted Ware settlements was centred upon pig breeding rather than on cattle or ovicaprid breeding. This is shown clearly at several sites. In some instances it was impossible to decide whether the pig bones originated from wild or domesticated animals, as is the case at Västerbjers where pigs account for over four-fifths of the fauna (see Fig. 90 & Table No. 134; Stenberger, Dahr & Munthe 1943). Pira (1909) analysed the bones of pig found at several sites in detail and divided them into four groups. The first represents wild animals, the second the initial stages of domestication, and the following groups the various stages of domestication, placing the turbary animals in group 5. One site at which pigs were particularly prevalent was found to have animals that could nearly all be considered as being in the initial stages of domestication (Hemmor, group 2). Hence it appears that this area was a centre of domestication, and from other reports of similar sites it seems that there were several centres of pig domestication associated with the Pitted Ware culture (Pira 1909, 1927, Forssander 1941, Frodin 1910, Bagge & Kjellmark 1939, Lidén 1940). Although the large *scrofa* pig is the one most frequently encountered there are also instances of the small turbary animals, as on the island site of Stora Karslö, where it is the more numerous of the two. Several transitional animals were also present.

Amongst the cattle remains there are many bones of large animals, some of which could belong to either domestic or wild species, and also bones of animals which fall within the turbary range. This small breed was the dominant type at Stora Karslö, where turbary pigs are also more common than the usual larger species (Pira 1927). The evidence, therefore, suggests that aurochs domestication was practised, although not on the same scale as was boar domestication. Sheep and goat are also well represented in this context (see Table No. 133), and the most detailed information comes from Stora Karslö. Sheep were more frequent than goats, and all identifiable goat bones belong to the small turbary breed (Pira 1927). This, however, is not the case with the sheep. All the sheep bones show close agreement with each other, and they resemble those of the moufflon closely. Some measurements agree completely with those for the Sardinian moufflon, and others show slight divergences, which Pira says would arise as the result of primitive domestication. These differences include slightly weaker horn cores. From the description that Pira gives, and from what Degerbøl says about the large sheep found at the Middle Neolithic site of Bunsdø in Denmark, the two types of sheep appear to be closely related. Hence it is probable that both can be attributed to the Copper sheep *Ovis aries studeri*. The Single Grave folk reached Sweden during the period of the Middle Neolithic and Pitted Ware cultures, so that both Scandinavian instances of this large sheep may be connected with the expansion of the Single Grave Complex.

The other domestic animal present at Pitted Ware sites is the dog. At sites where hunting was of great significance the dog was one of the most common domestic animals (Stenberger, Dahr & Munthe 1943). In most cases the turbary breed is present, but large dogs closely resembling the wolf also occur (Frodin 1910, Pira 1927). There is a possibility of first generation domesticated wolves being present at Stora Karslö, where the teeth suggest these animals were reared in captivity (Pira 1927).

Amongst the cultivated plants of this culture are einkorn, emmer, naked wheat and barley (see Table No. 135). Many carbonised grains were found at Alvastra, and all have been assigned to barley (Frodin 1910). The six-rowed naked version is known to have been cultivated. When the sherds were examined for impressions of cereals there were again no cases of wheat, but both naked and glumed barley were present (Hjelmqvist 1955). All the other instances of plants at Pitted Ware sites occur in small numbers only (Hjelmqvist 1955, Lidén 1940).

The Middle Neolithic and Single Grave communities were the basis of the Late Neolithic in Scandinavia. This period is characterised by extremely fine flint daggers, and axes, sickles and arrowheads also occur. The basic pot is of a flower-pot shape and decorated with zig-zag bands. Long stone cists, and upper, ground and bottom graves form the methods of burial. Imported bronzes from Italy, central Europe and Britain are contemporary, and amber was still exported. Pins and other ornaments of Unetiče type link this period in part at least with the Bronze age of central Europe.

Most of the evidence for farming concerns the plants cultivated. Pigs are known to have been domesticated, but the absence of cattle and ovicaprids can be attributed to the fact that as yet no site with a large quantity of bones has been found (Jarbe 1950; see Table No. 133). There is, however, a possible occurrence of the domestic horse. This occurs at Ulltorpsbach where the skull of a horse was found with a flint dagger embedded in the suture of the forehead (Lundholm 1949). The dagger dates the find to the Late Neolithic period or later, and pollen analysis confirms the former date. Osteologically Lundholm found that it was impossible to tell whether the horse was in the initial stages of domestication or whether it was still wild. Since horses become increasingly common at this time, he favours the theory that this animal was kept in a confined area by man and then sacrificed.

Einkorn, emmer, club or bread wheat and barley were cultivated during the late neolithic (see Table No. 135). Although evidence was obtained from nearly a dozen sites, the material only consists of a few plant impressions or carbonised grains, so that there is insufficient evidence to draw conclusion as to the relative importance of these different cereals (Brønsted 1957, 390-393, Hjelmqvist 1955, Schnittger 1910).

There are also several instances of domestic animals and cultivated plants at sites whose cultural connections are not known (see Tables Nos. 133, 135). The evidence shows that cattle, ovicaprids, pigs and dogs were bred and that some form of wheat and barley were cultivated.

The earliest agricultural settlements in the British Isles belong to the Windmill Hill culture, and were found in the south on the chalk downs of Wessex. At present, carbon 14 dates place them between 3200 and 2600 BC. The pottery used was well made, dark and often burnished, and usually had rounded bases. Plain bowls are common, but shoulders also occur as do lugs. Various flint mines have been found, and both chipped, and chipped and polished axes are frequently encountered. Leaf-shaped arrowheads, scrapers and flake knives also occur. There are various characteristic sites at which this culture is found, amongst which are the causewayed camps. These earthworks are constructed from broken concentric rings of a bank and ditch, and range in diameter from 250 feet to 1000 feet. It is clear that these were not settlement sites, and recently it has been suggested that they may have been a rallying point for the various tribes in the vicinity. Another distinctive monument is the earthen long barrow. These trapezoid or sub-rectangular earth mounds cover, in many instances, wooden chambers for collective burial at the proximal end, and they vary in length from 100 to 400 feet. The material for this mound is usually derived from the flanking ditches.

The wild animals that were hunted include red deer, roe deer, aurochs, horse, pig, badger, fox, cat and hare. The few statistics that are available suggest that hunting was unimportant to the economy (see Table No. 136).

Cattle occur at more sites than the other domestic animals, and they are also more numerous than ovicaprids or pigs (see Table No. 137). The type site of Windmill Hill illustrates the relative importance of these animals (see Fig. 92 & Table No. 138; Smith 1965). They are the dominant feature for both the pre-enclosure occupation and for the occupation following the construction of the ditch. All the cattle were of large size and there is no indication of the turbary breed. Histograms and graphs to illustrate the size of these cattle relative to those found at Star Carr and the Danish Maglemose sites can be seen in Fig. 94. Cattle appear to be the dominant animal also at other causewayed camps (Curwen 1931, Jackson 1943, Lidell 1931–35, Piggott 1952, Trow-Smith 1957), and they are a common occurrence in the earthen long barrows. In many cases it was difficult to distinguish the wild and domesticated animals. These bones occur in all parts of the sites including ditches, forecourts, mortuary enclosures and the mound material itself. At one site five skulls were found placed under a central cairn (Piggott 1954b), and at another there was a possible domestic ox hide burial (Grigson 1966).

Ovicaprids are less important than pigs in the pre-enclosure 'settlement' at Windmill Hill, but are more important than pigs in the later phase (see Fig. 92 & Table No. 138). Their increase could be due to increased land clearance activity between the two phases, so that pasturage conditions became more favourable to sheep and goat. Both the sheep and the goats at this site can be attributed to the turbary breed, and complete skeletons of these have been found and may be seen in Avebury Museum. It is also probable that this small sheep was being bred at Maiden Castle (Jackson 1943). Bones of ovicaprids have not been found at as many long barrows as have cattle, but they do occur in most parts of the sites; only sheep are known with certainty (Drew & Piggott 1936, Morgan 1959, Pitt-Rivers 1898).

The pigs bred at Windmill Hill are said to be fairly large, whereas the remains found at Whitehawk were of smaller animals (Smith 1965, Trow-Smith 1957). At one long barrow the pigs were small in stature (Piggott & Drew 1936), and at another it could not be decided whether the bones found belonged to wild or domesticated animals (Morgan 1959). An indication of a local pig cult was found at one site where there was a deposit of twenty jaws, and in one ritual hole behind the façade of the tomb there was a pig's scapula carefully placed on its end (Piggott 1954b).

Dogs have only been found at three sites, but in all cases it is known that the turbary breed was present. At both Maiden Castle and Windmill Hill complete skeletons were recovered (Jackson 1943, Smith 1965).

The cultivation of einkorn, emmer, bread wheat, possibly club wheat as well as barley is attested for this culture (see Table No. 139). Of these cereals, emmer dominated the early fields (see Table No.

73

140b). The proportion of einkorn was very small, and on a statistical basis it is probable that nearly all of the ambiguous einkorn-emmer impressions belong to emmer. Naked wheats were rare, and none were found at the type-site, where over a hundred impressions were identified (Helbaek 1952, Smith 1965). Both naked and hulled barley were present in small amounts with the former the more frequent of the two. In Helbaek's opinion all finds are probably of the six-rowed variety (Helbaek 1952). The other plant to have been grown was flax, which occurs only at Windmill Hill itself, and is thought to belong to *Linum usitatissimum* (Helbaek 1952; Smith 1965).

The agriculture of the Windmill Hill culture was based upon cattle breeding and emmer cultivation. From the size of the emmer grains Helbaek was able to conclude that this plant was well suited to its environment and that farming techniques were highly skilled. Turbary sheep and goats, as well as larger pigs and small dogs, were also bred, and einkorn, naked wheat, barley and flax were cultivated in small quantities.

Cultures of the third millennium in the British Isles which have evidence for agricultural practice include those of Abingdon, Ronaldsway, Rinyo-Clacton and Knockadoon. Abingdon pottery is found in the Upper Thames valley. A bowl with a flattened horizontal rim is the most common form and a fair amount of white grit is usually present in the clay. The Ronaldsway culture is found on the Isle of Man, and is characterised by deep pots, perhaps up to three feet deep, of Windmill Hill type. There are two areas in which the Rinyo-Clacton culture occurs, namely Orkney and Shetland, and southern England from Wessex to the East Anglian coast. The pottery is decorated with channels or grooves which form geometric patterns. The vessels may have either flat or round bases. An Irish version of the Windmill Hill culture is known as Knockadoon, and its distinctive features are similar to those for Windmill Hill.

Red and roe deer, aurochs, pig, horse, bear, otter, fox, pine marten, cat, weasel, hare, vole, birds and fish were all hunted (see Table No. 141). Apart from these animals, bones of whale were found at Skara Brae in Orkney, where the vertebrae were used as vessels and the jaws were probably used to support the roofs of houses. The porpoise has been found in Ireland.

Cattle were the most common animal at the causewayed camp of Abingdon, with sheep, goat and pig also being bred (Case 1956), and at the type-site of the Ronaldsway culture cattle, which resembled the turbary rather than the *primigenius* breed of Windmill Hill, were found together with ovicaprids (Piggott 1954b). The full complement of domestic animals has been found at sites of the Rinyo-Clacton culture (see Table No. 142). Cattle and pigs were the basic domestic animals, and at the only site where statistics were available, Durrington Walls, the economy was based upon pig breeding (see Fig. 93 & Table No. 143; Stone, Piggott & Booth 1954). These pigs were relatively small in size. The cattle on the other hand were large, and at one site are said to be slightly more abundant than pigs (Stone 1958; Stone & Young 1948).

The economy of the Knockadoon culture was similar to that of Windmill Hill, as might be expected. The evidence from Lough Gur shows clearly that cattle breeding was of great importance, with ovicaprids, pigs and dogs of much less significance (O'Riordain 1954). O'Riordain reports that the canine remains from this site are of either a large dog or small wolf, but Hauck (1950) thinks that the dog was definitely present. Studer also identified bones from this site, and attributed some to *Canis f. intermedius*.

Amongst the osteological remains from Irish kitchen middens were some which have been attributed to a dog resembling a sheep dog in size, and others to pigs which may have been domesticated (Mitchell 1947, 1956). Otherwise the fauna was composed entirely of wild animals, fish and shells.

Another important site to be considered is that of Skara Brae in the Orkneys (Childe 1931). The cattle found at this site are said to differ from any other neolithic cattle found in Britain, and bulls, cows and possibly oxen are said to be present. The evidence from complete skulls suggests that these animals had been pole-axed, and in some instances the fragments of bone that would have been driven inwards by the blow have been found inside the skulls. Polled or hornless cattle were also present, which is a rare occurrence during the neolithic. These animals are on the whole large in size, but are said to differ from the usual domestic aurochs. The ovicaprid horns are described as being heavy, widely divergent and strongly curved, and they are all ascribed to sheep. Sheep were present in large numbers, but were less common than cattle. These animals have not been compared with the large sheep found at Bundsø in Denmark or Stora Karslö in Sweden, but their descriptions have several features in common. Those from Bundsø are known to belong to the Copper sheep and represent recently domesticated moufflons. No remains of dogs have been found at this site, and it could not be decided whether the small proportion of pig bones originated from wild or domesticated animals.

There is a small amount of evidence for the cultivation of wheat and barley (see Table No. 144). Emmer is the only wheat to be identified and it occurs at the type-site of the Abingdon culture, and naked barley is also known to have been cultivated (Helbaek 1952, Jessen & Helbaek 1944).

Cattle breeding was of much importance to the British economy, but during the Rinyo-Clacton culture the popularity of pig breeding rose to exceed that of cattle in at least one instance. Sheep and goats were bred, and large animals are known from Orkney. The dog was present and both wheat and barley were cultivated.

There are many instances of osteological remains being found in the Chambered Tombs of the British Isles. The ones considered here may be divided into five groups, namely Severn-Cotswold, Derbyshire, Clyde-Carlingford, Boyne, Caithness-Zetland and allied tombs. There are two distinct groups from which these tombs may be derived, namely gallery graves and passage graves. There is no clear structural distinction between the corridor and chambers in gallery graves, but there is a definite distinction between these in passage graves. Gallery graves are usually covered by long cairns and passage graves by round mounds. The former probably resulted in the Severn-Cotswold, Derbyshire and Clyde-Carlingford tombs and the latter in the Boyne and Caithness-Zetland groups. These tombs are often constructed of large stone slabs, and in a few instances in Ireland and Scotland they are built of smaller horizontal slabs.

Once the tombs were built, and the appropriate skeletons placed inside, often in a state of disarticulation, the chambers and passage were on occasion filled with earth in which there was a mixture of sherds, flints and bone. Apart from remains of domestic animals, bones of wild animals were often found in these tombs. Those identified include red and roe deer, aurochs, pig, horse, fox, cat and possibly wolf (see Table No. 145). In the north of Scotland a very large selection of bird bones has been found as well as several types of fish, and squirrel, otter and vole.

There are numerous identifications of bones of cattle, ovicaprids, pigs and dogs in these Chambered Tombs (see Table No. 146). Cattle occur more frequently than do the other animals, and in general very little information is available other than the actual presence of the animal at an individual site. There has been no racial identification of the cattle from the Severn-Cotswold group, although the animals from Notgrove are thought to be relatively small in size (Clifford 1937). Bones of cattle occur more frequently than those of other domestic animals at West Kennet (Piggott 1962). The osteological remains from the Boyne tomb of Bryn Celli Ddu are of interest, since the skeleton of an ox was discovered in the forecourt of this tomb, placed centrally to the entrance of the cairn. It is thought that this animal belongs to the turbary breed (Piggott 1954b). In his investiga-

76

tion of the Scottish material, Ritchie (1920) found that the cattle were fairly small and bore similarity to the turbary breed. The probable dominance of small cattle in these tombs resembles the situation found in Poland. The cattle of the Windmill Hill culture were predominantly large and the same applies to cattle found at settlement sites in Poland (Bökönyi & Kubaswiecz 1961), but those animals found in the tombs of both countries were distinctly smaller.

Only the goat is known with certainty amongst the ovicaprid bones from the Severn-Cotswold tombs (Crawford 1925), and at the tomb of West Kennet these animals were less numerous than cattle and pigs (Piggott 1962). There are many instances of sheep in the Caithness-Zetland tombs, but none of goat. When Ritchie examined some of this material he came to the conclusion that the turbary sheep was the only breed present. The only detailed investigation since then comes from Quoyness. Zeuner (1951) did an analysis of ovicaprid cranial remains, and found a close agreement with semi-wild and undeveloped breeds. He came to the conclusion that they belonged to a primitive race with some moufflon characteristics. Many similarities to the Soay sheep were noted, but the two were not identical. No comparisons have been made between these remains and those found at Skara Brae in Orkney, Stora Karslö in Sweden and Bundsø in Denmark, but all are said to have moufflon characteristics. Sheep were the most frequent of the animals found at Blackhammer, where the breed is unkown (Henshall 1963).

The pig is less common than both cattle and ovicaprids in this context, and there are several instances of large animals which could be either wild or domesticated. Nothing is known of the size of the remaining animals. Pigs occur frequently at West Kennet (Piggott 1962), but only rarely at Scottish tombs (Henshall 1963).

Dogs are well represented in all groups of the Chambered Tombs but no racial identifications have been made (see Table No. 146). There is one instance of a large dog or wolf at Notgrove, where the former possibility is thought to be the more likely one (Clifford 1937), and amongst the Scottish material the remains from Burray and Cuween Hill are of especial interest (Henshall 1963). In the former tomb a dog's skull was carefully deposited in each of the seven chambers and also in the passage; only one of the skulls has been preserved. On the floor of the tomb at Cuween Hill there were twenty-four dog skulls, and further bones were found in the rammed filling. The dog was the only domestic animal present on the floor of the tomb.

A few impressions of cereals have been found on pots that were recovered from Chambered Tombs (see Table No. 147). Barley is the only cereal known from the Severn-Cotswold group, where Helbaek identified the six-rowed naked variety on a sherd of Peter-borough ware (Helbaek 1952). Einkorn and emmer are known from a Clyde-Carlingford tomb (Jessen & Helbaek 1944), and the only other instance of this cereal occurs at a Boyne tomb (Piggott 1954b). The remaining impressions are at Scottish sites where naked and hulled barley have been found (Jessen & Helbaek 1944).

Cattle occur more frequently than any other domestic animal in the Chambered Tombs of the British Isles, and are of smaller size than the animals usually found at settlement sites. Goats and turbary sheep were bred, and in Scotland a moufflon-like sheep was also present. Dogs were fairly common in these tombs, but pigs occur rarely. Einkorn, emmer and barley were cultivated but are only present at a few sites as impressions on pottery.

In the area of north-west Europe under discussion here, another method has been employed to detect the presence of farming communities. This is pollen analysis, and it was first discussed by Iversen (1941), who showed how the technique could be used to illustrate the proximity of farming communities in certain areas. These communities first appear at the zone viia/b transition. Half-way through zone vii some important changes were noted in the mixed oak forests of Denmark. These took the form of a rapid fall in *Ulmus* (elm) and *Hedera* (ivy) and an increase in *Fraxinus* (ash). These changes appear to have taken place over the whole of Denmark on both fertile and infertile land. Iversen showed that this vegetational change could not be the result of a sudden decrease in temperature since there is a sudden increase in the pollen of herbaceous plants, nor could it be the result of the lowering of the ground water level after a dry period. It was entirely due to man's influence. The evidence also indicates that fire was the method by which the dense forests were cleared. Charcoal deposits were found just beneath the level of the fall in elm pollen. The zone before this decline, viia, is known as the At-lantic period, and the zone afterwards, viib, as the sub-Boreal period.

Troels-Smith also considers the various possibilities for the cause of the elm decline. The presence of an elm disease, as in recent years in America, would be possible, but difficult to prove and rather unlikely. The decline cannot be due to soil deterioration since this would produce a gradual fall and not the rapid one that is observed. Troels-Smith also dismisses the idea of a climatic change, supporting his view by the finds of grape vine pollen in Denmark. He comes to the conclusion that the change in the pollen diagram must be due to human interference. He found two elm declines, and attributed the first to the feeding of cattle and the second to cattle feeding and cultivation. This interpretation has been questioned, and a different explanation is given for this phenomenon in Britain.

After the decline in the forest, regeneration took place fairly rapidly. The first trees to appear were *Betula* (birch) and *Alnus* (alder). These have a greater power of dispersal than *Quercus* (oak) and are also attracted by light open areas in the forest. Their prevalence is probably slightly exaggerated since they take only 10-12 years to flower and produce pollen whereas oak takes between 30 and 40 years. After this, *Betula* falls in frequency as more trees come into the cleared area. At the minimum in the mixed oak forest there is a corresponding maximum in the *Plantago* (plantain) curve and herbaceous plants are more frequent than before. At this stage there was also an increase in certain weeds, which are known as the weeds of cultivation. These include *Artemisia*, *Rumex* and the *Chenopodiaceae*. The presence of these weeds is often the best guide to the presence of cereals, since wheat and barley are self-pollinating and so do not produce very much pollen.

Sometimes, however, cereal pollen has been detected. Firbas (1937) pointed out that it could be distinguished from wild grasses, both on the pollen structure and on the size (Iversen 1941). Cereal pollen is thick-walled, has a large pore and well marked ring and on the whole is larger than that of grasses. The value taken for the minimum size of cereal pollen varies, but Iversen regards pollen with a diameter greater than 35μ as being that of cereals.

Pollen diagrams have been constructed for many Scandinavian sites. The distinctive features mentioned above have been found at sites of the Ertebølle, TRB, and Middle Neolithic periods, and also at some late neolithic sites in Sweden (Iversen 1949, Troels-Smith 1960, Hjelmqvist 1958, Florin 1958). Hafsten (1960) gives evidence for the introduction of agriculture into the Oslo area of Norway at the zone VIIa/b transition. The characteristic minimum in the mixed oak forest at the point of the maximum of the weeds of cultivation is clearly represented, as was the expected charcoal layer. Hafsten attributes these changes to an immigration in the Dolmen period (TRB C). The increase in weed pollen at a slightly later stage is attributed to expansion during the flint dagger period of the late neolithic. The earliest evidence for agriculture in western Norway does not occur until the end of the Passage Grave period and it is conceivable that it did not happen before the Stone Cist period of the late neolithic (Faegri 1944). Agriculture was never very extensive in this region, as might be expected, since there is very little evidence for the neolithic as a whole. Faegri concludes that the mesolithic Nostvet hunter-fisher culture came to a sudden end all along the coast of western

Norway, and that it was quickly followed by a neolithic farming culture (the Vespestad culture) in Jæren, which did not reach Bømlo until a few centuries later. These two cultures are not contemporary, unlike the Danish Ertebølle and TRB cultures.

The same zone-transition features that have been observed in Denmark have also been found in Holland. A detailed analysis of Linear Pottery sites showed these characteristics (Bodemonderzoek Berichten 1955, *Palaeo-historia* VI-VII, 1958-9). There is also evidence for cultivation from the burial mounds of the TRB, Single Grave and Bell Beaker cultures (Groenman van Waateringe 1961).

Investigations in Germany have been carried out in the area around the Federsee and Bodensee settlements (Müller 1947). On the basis of profiles obtained showing the change in *Ulmus*, the appearance of *Plantago* and cereal pollen, Müller came to three conclusions. These are that agriculture was well known in the area of Federsee before the late neolithic settlements, that there was very little activity after this until the early Bronze Age when the region may have been inhabited. At a later date it was re-inhabited until the Middle Ages. Investigations carried out at two Linear Pottery sites revealed traces of exceptionally early cereal pollen (Milojčić 1960). At Gatersleben this pollen, together with *Plantago*, appears in zone VI (early Atlantic) and at Brux cereal pollen is found in zone vb (Boreal). On the basis of these two finds it has been claimed that cereal cultivation was already practised during the Mesolithic. *Plantago* was, of course, present in open areas during the mesolithic period so that its presence does not imply the practice of agriculture, and in order to be sure that the pollen of cereals is present it is necessary to examine the structure of the pollen grain as well as its size.

Pollen analysis in Switzerland has been carried out around the sites of Thayngen-Weiher and Burgäschisee (Troels-Smith 1955). Both areas show the presence of agriculture, with the former the clearer of the two. Both the elm aud ivy decline, together with the presence of cereal and plantain pollen have been observed. Much cereal pollen was found and a microscopic analysis showed that it was nearly all of barley (Analysis 10).

Pollen diagrams have also been constructed for the region in southwest France near Biarritz, and also at two places in Brittany. The transition zone in the south has been dated to 3150 ± 130 BC (Q-314) by carbon 14. Originally Mouligna was identified as an Asturian site, but later western neolithic pottery was found associated with this industry, showing that the two were contemporary. The presence of charcoal together with a high percentage of *Pteridium* (bracken) pollen and low values of *Pinus* and *Corylus* indicates deforestation, and it seems probable that land clearance was being carried out (Laplace-Jauretsche 1953). Two bogs in Brittany show the *Ulmus* decline and *Plantago* increase (Radiocarbon 1963). At the first site two horizons were observed and dated to 3460±60 (GrN–1983) and 1830±55 (GrN–2175) and at the second the only horizon was dated to 1990± 75 (GrN–2161). The early date corresponds with the first appearance of neolithic farmers, and the later date to the arrival of herdsmen in the area (Radiocarbon 1963).

Pollen analysis has been carried out in various localities in the British Isles. These include Cambridgeshire, Norfolk, Yorkshire, the Lake District, Lanarkshire, Perthshire, Co. Derry, Co. Limerick, Co. Antrim, Co. Derby and Co. Galway. The zone VIIa/b transition in Cambridgeshire has been dated to 3400 BC (Clark & Godwin 1962), and in the Lake District the same transition is placed around 3000 BC (Godwin, Walker & Willis 1957). The *Ulmus* decline found in Cambridge also occurs in Norfolk accompanied by the pollen of herbaceous plants, grasses and plantain (Godwin & Tallantire 1951). There is no evidence for a neolithic occupation on the Yorkshire moors described by Dimbleby (1952, 1954, 1961), but there are various mesolithic and bronze age sites. Evidence shows that the forest became more open after the mesolithic and an abundance of charcoal suggests that it was cleared by fire. In several areas towards the centre of the then forested moors there were no traces of weeds of cultivation, implying that cultivation never extended over the main area of the present day moor. Two elm declines were found in several areas of the Lake District. The primary decline is accompanied by a small amount of *Plantago* pollen, but the secondary decline is much more marked, with greater amounts of *Plantago*, the appearance of *Artemisia* and *Rumex* in significant quantities, and an increase in the pollen of *Gramineae*. This is taken to represent the true 'Landnam' phase. It is also significant that the elm decline was more intense in the diagrams obtained in areas that lie close to the Langdale axe factories (Pennington 1964, 1965). Similar features have been observed in Scotland (Durno 1965).

The major part of the Irish work on this subject has been done by Mitchell (1954, 1965), Morrison (1959) and Smith (1958, 1961, 1962). Various indications of land clearance have been found in all the counties mentioned, and the sharp elm decline, increase in herbaceous plants and grasses and the presence of *Plantago* and weeds of cultivation have been found in most cases. At one site this transition has been dated to around 3300 BC (Smith 1958; Smith & Willis 1965). Two separate elm declines were found in Co. Antrim and Co. Meath by Morrison, and he regards the earlier and less distinct decrease as representing the sub-zone transition, and the later as representing the arrival of agricultural communities into the area. This is similar to the situation encountered by Oldfield and others in the Lake District, and the same situation in Denmark is given a different interpretation by Troels-Smith.

The utilisation of elm leaves and branches as fodder has been described by Troels-Smith (1954, 1955, 1960). The lower branches of the elm trees would be collected, stored and fed to the stalled cattle, or alternatively eaten directly by the cattle themselves. The elm would take seven or eight years to produce pollen again, by which time the new pollen bearing twigs would have been reaped. The result is that the trees continue to thrive but produce no pollen. Both Iversen (1949, 1960) and Troels-Smith (1954, 1955, 1960) report this method of husbandry still being practised in several areas of Europe. These include Norway, Switzerland, Italy, Rumania and Bosnia. Troels-Smith believes that these early neolithic cattle were kept in stalls rather than allowed to wander free, since plants such as *Allium* would be eliminated immediately by untethered cattle. He also concludes that the pasture area was small since the *Gramineae* curve does not rise appreciably and there is still a relatively small quantity of *Plantago*. Troels-Smith also shows that ivy was probably used as fodder in both Denmark and Switzerland. The fact that cattle eat ivy has been recorded in classical literature (Theophrastus in 286 BC); in Egypt ivy was consecrated to Osiris, and as recently as 1953 Iversen saw a farmer gathering a basket of ivy for his cattle in Italy. There is also a possibility that mistletoe was used as fodder, perhaps in winter when food was scarce. This method of nutrition is recorded by Theophrastus (286 BC) and Pliny (AD 23–79), and today some Greek peasants feed it to both cattle and goats in the belief that it will make them fertile and keep away illness. It was used as fodder in France, Belgium, Austria and Germany earlier this century, and is said to have increased milk yield and to turn the butter 'a nice yellow colour'.

6. Late Neolithic and Copper Age Agriculture

During the latter part of the neolithic in western and central Europe there is evidence for trading with the early metal producing societies of the Near East and eastern Europe. These late neolithic and copper age cultures in Europe include sites at which evidence for animal breeding and plant cultivation has been obtained. These are now considered.

The Greek late Neolithic and Copper Age period is composed of two cultures known as Dimini and Larissa. The first is confined to eastern Thessaly and the second lies to the west in Thessaly, Macedonia and central Greece. The Larissa culture is considered by Milojčić to be slightly later than Dimini, but Holmberg has brought forward evidence to suggest it may be a little earlier and contemporary with Vinča. These cultures may be placed somewhere between 4200 and 3200. Characteristics of the Dimini culture include painted pottery with spiral and meander patterns which are sometimes tricoloured, but the pots are generally inferior to those of Sesklo. They bear some similarity to the Gumelni a pottery further north. The patterns are usually white, black or incised on a buff, brown or red ground. Perforated axes rather than adzes are used for the first time and a small amount of copper and gold imports occur. The Larissa pottery on the other hand is either white and black painted ware or black burnished ware, and when decoration occurs it is usually in the form of rectilinear patterns rather than spirals. Red deer, roe deer, aurochs, pig and either water or marsh turtle have been identified in this context, but their proportion relative to the domestic animals remains small (see Tables Nos. 13, 21).

The osteological remains from Dimini sites show that sheep and goat breeding formed the basis of the economy. Cattle, pigs and dogs were also bred. The evidence comes from stratified sites which have been considered earlier, namely Argissa, Arapi, and Otzaki, and in all cases the ovicaprids predominate (Boessneck 1955, 1962; see Figs. 95-97, Tables Nos. 13 & 21). Both sheep and goat have been identified and the stock was basically of medium size, although considerable variation on either side of this has been noted. Pigs were slightly less important and all appear to have been of small and medium size and are comparable with the turbary pig of central Europe. Cattle are the least important of the three main domestic animals, and there is no indication of animals over 115 cm. in height. Some bones compare

83

well with those of the earlier Proto-Sesklo period. Very few remains of dog have been found; they are only known from Otzaki where evidence for small and medium-sized turbary animals is present (Boessneck 1955; see Fig. 97, Table No. 21).

Evidence of farming during the Larissa culture comes once again from Otzaki, and here a change is visible from the economy of the other cultures. Cattle become the dominant feature for the first time in Greece, followed closely by sheep and goat. This situation is indicative of the change that was to follow later, when cattle become the dominant feature of the Bronze Age economy (Boessneck 1955; see Fig. 98, Table No. 21). Other instances of domestic animals at late neolithic sites have been noted, but no further information was available (Heurtley 1939, Mylonas 1929).

There is evidence for the cultivation of three cereals as well as legumes during the Dimini culture. Wheat is represented by both einkorn and emmer. In the early phase of this culture at Sesklo a thousand grains were identified and all have been attributed to emmer and in the later Rachmani variant of this culture it is again the only cereal represented (Renfrew 1966). The wheat found at Rachmani itself has not been identified (Wace & Thompson 1912, Renfrew 1966). The beginning of the rise in popularity of barley is attested at the late Dimini site of Pyrasos, where six-rowed hulled barley forms nearly three-quarters of the cereal remains, the other components being emmer and einkorn (Renfrew 1966). The other instances of barley have not had the spike-type determined (Wace & Thompson 1912). The main legume to be identified is the pea, and lentils are also recorded at the later Rachmani site (Renfrew 1966, Wace & Thompson 1912). Figs, almonds, pears, acorns and pistachio nuts were collected and have been found at various settlements (Renfrew 1966).

Ovicaprid breeding was the dominant feature in the Dimini economy, but during the Larissa phase a change to cattle breeding is seen at at least one site. This anticipates the Bronze Age economy, as does the popularity of barley at one late site. Elsewhere emmer was the main crop, and today this region of Greece is noted for its excellent wheat.

To the north, the Gumelniţa culture developed in Bulgaria and Wallachia and the Salcuţa culture in Oltenia. Both cultures are divided into four phases which are contemporary and are placed approximately between 3700 and 3200. The Gumelniţa pottery continues in the late Boian tradition, namely painted ware with spiral meander patterns, but it is of better quality. The flint and stone industry is also derived from that of Boian, with many long blades occurring, and the bone industry is much richer although similar. Substantial quantities of copper are found for the first time. The Salcuţa culture is not as rich as that of Gumelniţa. It has basically the same characteristics, but the pottery is different in that there is very little painted decoration, and instead graphite painting, fine rustication and wave impressions occur. Both cultures are contemporary with Vinča-Pločnik in east-central Europe, and with late Tripolye A, Triploye B and Ci in European Russia.

The evidence indicates that hunting and fishing played only a small role in the economy, probably yielding less than a twentieth of the meat supply. The animals hunted include red deer, roe deer, aurochs, pig, bear, horse, half-ass, chamois, marten, badger, wild cat, lynx, beaver, wolf, fox, hare, tortoise, polecat, stoat, weasel, turtle, birds and fish (see Table No. 148a). Of these animals, red deer is the species most frequently encountered.

Domestic animals are known from twenty-six sites and where a statistical analysis of their relative importance has been obtained cattle are seen to have been the dominant species (Necrasov & Haim-ovici 1959; see Figs. 99-101, Tables Nos. 69, 149). Sheep, goats, pigs and dogs were also being bred. At the site of Tangîru two types of cattle have been distinguished, one large and the other small, and the smaller is the more frequent of the two. Information regarding the animal breeding activities for the first three phases of this culture have been obtained here, and the dominance of cattle becomes estab-lished as the culture progresses, with a distinct decline in the impor-tance of ovicaprid breeding and a corresponding increase in the number of pigs (see Figs. 99a-d). Where a distinction has been pos-sible goats appear to outnumber sheep, and two types of the former species have been identified. These are *Capra hircus* and *Capra aegagrus*, and the smaller is the more common breed. The latter identification suggests contact with the Near East. The breed of sheep could not be determined. All the pigs on the other hand were small and slender and there was a large proportion of young animals. At another site, how-ever, there is evidence showing that the indigenous *scrofa* pig had been recently domesticated (Paunescu 1962). Although no exact figures are given, it is known that cattle were the predominant animal, excluding dog, at the Bulgarian cave site of Devetaki (Mikov & Dzambzov 1960) and also at the Rumanian site of Luncavita (Comsa 1962). Many bones of dogs have been found at the Bulgarian site, and it is notable that the economy of this site was based upon hunting rather than breeding. Dogs account for only a small proportion of the remains at Tangîru, and two types have been distinguished. One is small in size and belongs to the turbary breed of Rütimeyer, and the

85

other is larger and its exact identification has not been determined. This larger dog was identified as *Canis f. intermedius* in the Boian levels of the site (Necrasov & Haimovici 1959).

The evidence from the Salcuţa culture is less abundant, and it is based upon two sites. Many bones have been found at the type-site of Salcuţa, but the final statistics have not yet been published. Berciu (1961) reports that pigs are the dominant feature in the Salcuţa 1-11b phases, ovicaprids then predominate in phase 11c, and finally during the last phase cattle are more numerous than either of these species. Two breeds of cattle have been found at the other site, and there is also evidence for castration and probable use as tractive power (Berciu 1961, Mateescu 1959, 1962). There were also two breeds of goats present, probably similar to those found at Tangîru.

As well as the domestication of these animals, there are three possible instances of the domestic horse. Claims are made from the Bulgarian sites of Madara and Pod-Grada, but the nature of this evidence is not known (Bibikova 1953). As well as these, the domestic horse was almost certainly present during the Cernavoda culture, which developed partly out of the late phase of the Gumelniţa culture. Horses' hooves were found at the type site, which Berciu reports as belonging to domesticated animals. At this late stage the inhabitants were basically sheep farmers, with only a small proportion of cattle and pigs (Berciu 1961).

The evidence obtained from the cultivated plants shows that wheat was the main crop and it has been found at all of the sites considered (see Table No. 150). Barley and millet were also cultivated. Einkorn, emmer and bread wheat have been identified, but nothing is known of their relative importance (Bibikova 1953, Gaul 1948, Georgiev 1961, Piggott, personal communication). There has been no closer identification of the few cases of barley and millet. However, a detailed report on the plant remains of this period is shortly to be published by Jane Renfrew. Evidence for grain storage was found at Salcuţa. Many large pottery vessels were discovered, and grain was often found in their immediate vicinity. There were also several mattocks, which could serve as hoes, usually manufactured out of red deer antler. In all cases they were perforated, and were probably strapped on to a wooden shaft with leather bands. A single stone hoe was also found (Berciu 1961).

The agricultural economy of the Gumelniţa and Salcuţa cultures was different. The former concentrated on cattle breeding, and ovicaprids and pigs appear to complement each other. During the Salcuţa culture the evidence available suggests that pigs, ovicaprids and cattle become the dominant species in turn. Wheat and barley were cultivated in both cultures, and millet is also present in the Salcuţa culture.

The basic cultural group of this period in north-east Rumania was that of Cucuteni. This is essentially the Rumanian version of the Tripolye culture. It is generally thought to be slightly earlier than its Russian counterpart, and is very difficult to distinguish from it. It is divided into three basic phases, Pre-Cucuteni, Cucuteni A and B which equate with Tripolye A, B and C respectively. Hunting was of greater importance in the later stages, and accounts for between a half and two-thirds of the osteological remains during the Cucuteni A-B period. In the earlier stage it forms between a fifth and a third of the remains.

Cattle, sheep, goat, pigs and dogs are all known to have been bred, and of these cattle are the dominant species (see Figs. 102a-c, Table No. 152, 34). The nature of the herd is best seen from the evidence of Hăbăseşti and Traian. Both large and small breeds have been distinguished, but at the first site the latter is more numerous, and at the second the former occurs more frequently. The animals found at Traian were slaughtered at between two and three years of age whereas those found at Hăbăseşti varied between four and seven years. Both ovicaprids and pigs were considerably less important to the economy, and two breeds of sheep and two of goats have been distinguished at these sites. There was one instance of a goat's horn that closely resembled that of the wild bezoar (Dumitrescu 1954). Both large and small pigs were found at Hăbăseşti, but at Traian only a relatively large breed was identified (Necrasov & Haimovici 1959, 1962). The turbary dog as well as one with some wolf-like characteristics are also known in this context (Dumitrescu 1954, Necrasov & Haimovici 1959, 1962). The only definite claim for a domestic horse comes from a Cucuteni B site, Ruptura-Folteşti, but nothing is known of the finds (Berciu 1961). The equoid bones recovered during the 1957 excavations at Traian are placed in an 'Uncertain' category by Necrasov and Haimovici, and the single bone found in 1959 is attributed to a wild animal.

Wheat is the only cereal to have been found at Cucuteni sites (see Table No. 153). Bread and club wheat are the sole species to have been identified (Dumitrescu 1954), but the large amount of carbonised wheat found at Izvore has not yet been closely examined (Vulpe 1957). The vetch found at Hăbăseşti is also thought to have been cultivated.

Cattle breeding and wheat cultivation were the basis of the Cucuteni agriculture. Both large and small breeds of all the domestic animals have been identified, and there is also a possibility of horse domestication during the final stages of this culture. Naked wheats are

87

the only cereal known to have been cultivated, although it is probable that further work will reveal the presence of other wheats as well as barley.

The Tripolye culture developed on the fertile black earth of the Ukraine during the period 3800–2900. It equates with the Rumanian Pre-Cucuteni and Cucuteni period. The pottery shows sophisticated geometric designs which are painted on red or white bases and outlined by either channelled grooves, red, black or white paint; occasionally three colours occur on the pottery. This culture is sub-divided into phases A, Bi, Bii, Ci, Cii and G on the basis of stylistic variations in the geometric designs. Stone implements from sites are characteristically neolithic and are generally local in origin. Metal is found in association with the middle phases and implements of metal become common in the later stages. Gold trinkets have been found, and in phase C amber finds suggest contact with the east Baltic neolithic cultures. The average Tripolye village consists of between thirty and forty long rectangular houses arranged on arcs of concentric circles of between 200 m. and 500 m. in diameter. Occasionally much larger villages comprising 150 houses are encountered.

As is seen from Figs. 104-118 and Tables Nos. 156-174, there is no consistent factor for the importance of hunting relative to domestication as a means of food supply. During phase A hunting accounts for a fifth to three-fifths of the meat supply, during phase B for a twentieth to two-fifths, during phase Ci the range of variation is from an eighth to two-thirds, during phase Cii from a fiftieth to a half and finally in phase G between a tenth and nine-tenths. The animals exploited include red deer, roe deer, elk, antelope, aurochs, boar, horse, ass, bear, badger, beaver, otter, wolverine, marten, polecat, wild cat, wolf, fox, lynx, hare, squirrel, hamster, mole, hedgehog, rodents, European marsh turtle, river tortoise, frog, birds and fish (see Table No. 154).

The settlements of phase A may be divided into two groups, namely those which had their economy centred upon pig breeding and those which concentrated rather on cattle breeding. The first group of villages is best represented by one known as Luka-Vrublevetskaia, where over eight thousand bones have been identified (Bibikova 1956; see Fig. 104a, Table No. 156). Pigs are more than twice as common as any other domestic animal, and all fall within the range of the turbary breed. It is interesting to note that at this site there were also numerous clay models of pigs which have finely modelled snouts, eye sockets and also holes for the insertion of tusks. Both large and small cattle were also being raised as well as many of intermediate size, and the slightly less numerous ovicaprid remains include skulls of hornless sheep. The dogs fall into the turbary category, with one example of the larger *ladogensis* variety. At Soloncheny I pigs are more frequent than cattle when the number of individuals are considered, although this is not true of the number of bones (see Fig. 104b & Table No. 166; Bibikova 1963). The cattle-breeding sites are best represented by Bernova-Luka and Sabatinovka II (Bibikova 1963, Hausler 1956, Mdanylenko & Makarevych 1956). The stock does not differ from that of the pig-breeding communities, but they are clearly more important than all of the other domesticated animals (see Figs. 105a, 106a & Tables Nos. 157b, 165a). There is very little difference between the numbers of ovicaprids and pigs at these sites.

During stage B this latter emphasis on cattle breeding becomes dominant, although in one instance pig breeding continues to be of significance (Polivanov-Jar, see Fig. 180a & Table No. 168; Bibikova 1963). The importance of cattle is demonstrated at the rich sites of Khalepye, Kolomiischina, Novi Ruseşti and Sabatinovka I (see Figs. 106a-110a, Tables Nos. 36, 157-158, 167; Bibikova 1963, Hančar 1956, Makarevych 1952, 1956). There are also several other instances in which cattle bones occur more frequently than those of other domestic animals. Both large and small animals were bred, some villages preferring one variety, and others another. During the 1949 excavations at Sabatinovka I a bull's skull was found with the horn cores purposely cut off. It lay inside a house and close to it was a female figurine. Ovicaprids and pigs were bred in varying quantities, and both large and small pigs have been identified. The large breed is closely related to the local wild boar which indicates local domestication. At some sites sheep were entirely absent and only goats identified and at others the situation is reversed (Bibikova 1963). Some of the sheep are known to have had well developed horns (Hančar 1956). Dogs account for a small proportion of the osteological remains, and as in phase A only the turbary breed has been identified.

The subsistence-economics of Tripoly e Ci represent a continuation of the pattern of phase B. Cattle remain the dominant feature as is illustrated at Troyanov, Pavoloc and Sandraki (see Figs. 112a-113b, Tables Nos. 169b, 170, 171b; Bibikova 1953, 1963, Lahodovska 1956). Two breeds have been encountered at most sites, and the relative importance of sheep, goat and pigs varied.

With the onset of stage Cii there was, however, a distinct change in the economy. Cattle breeding gave way to a resurgence in sheep farming, and horses also become an important element for the first time. The sudden dominance in sheep farming is well illustrated at Usatovo, where they clearly outnumber cattle (see Fig. 115, Table No. 163; Bibikova 1963, Hančar 1956, Lahodovska 1952). Nearly all these bones can be attributed to the small turbary sheep and the significance of pig breeding is minimal at this stage. There is no indication of the type of dog that was bred. The rise in the importance of the horse is shown at this site, where it exceeds both pigs and dogs (see Fig. 115), and it is also well demonstrated at Gorodsk where horse remains are more frequently encountered than those of any other domestic animal (Bibikova 1963, Hančar 1956; see Fig. 116, Table No. 164). At this stage it was almost certainly domesticated, but there has been some controversy over the status of the horse in the earlier stages of the Tripolye culture. It is reported to have been definitely domesticated at Luka-Vrublevetskaia during stage A, after a detailed examination of the bones. The early domestic horse reported from this site was small, sturdy and had a relatively large head; it was half as common as the dog. Bones from some other sites are said to agree morphologically with these, although their status cannot be determined with confidence (Hančar 1956, Bibikova 1953). Hančar takes the point of view that all the horses of the Tripolye culture were domesticated.

The other domestic animal known in this context is the camel. It has been found at the Cii sites of Gorodsk (Hančar 1956) and Veremje (Bibikova 1953), and it is thought to be the Bactrian camel that is represented.

The evidence from stage G is less abundant, but cattle, sheep, goat, pig, dog and horse were all kept. No exceptionally rich sites in the osteological sense have been reported, and the statistics that are available show no clear tendency to breed one animal rather than another (see Figs. 114b, 117a, 118; Tables Nos. 172-174).

Plant cultivation was widely practised in the Tripolye culture, and the crops show considerable variety with wheat, barley, and millet all present. Wheat occurs more frequently than the other cereals, being present at all the sites considered, and in all four varieties have so far been distinguished (see Table No. 176). These are emmer, hard wheat, bread wheat and club wheat. The most frequently encountered of these is bread wheat, with only a single instance of the other naked wheat and of emmer. The proportion of these various kinds of wheats relative to each other is not known, and there are also several instances in which the type of wheat has not been specified. Barley is also a frequent occurrence and only the six-rowed species has been identified. There are two instances of it, at Kolomiischina and Vladimirovka, and both are attributed to the dense-eared erect variety (Passek 1949). Glumed barley, spike type indeterminate, is known, but there are no known occurrences of a naked barley. Millet also played an important role in the agriculture of this culture. It has been found at more sites than has barley, but it is not stated whether it is

Panicum miliaceum or *Seteria italica* that is present (Passek 1949). This is the first European culture in which the importance of millet can be established, and it must be considered as an essential element in the Tripolyan economy.

Apart from finds of carbonised grain or impressions in pottery, some interesting information and insight into the ritual practices of this culture have been obtained by a detailed examination of the female figurines. These were found to be full of grain of all three kinds, and the best known come from Bernova-Luka and Luka-Vrublevetskaia. There were nearly 250 figurines at the last site, six of which were broken and showed traces of grain throughout their bodies. A further 60 bore evidence of grain impressions on their surface. These were then X-rayed in order to ascertain the density of the grain, and it was discovered that the specimens that showed only a few grain impressions on the surface, were in fact stuffed with grain. As a result of these investigations, the question arose as to whether the statues that had no superficial grain impressions were made of a clay that had been tempered with flour. The figurines that were examined were found to be made of a very porous clay. In addition they had small hollows in their surface and in one of these the impression of a broken grain was identified. Bibikov thought that these figurines had been made with a clay that had been tempered with roughly ground flour (Bibikov 1951). Another characteristic of these models is their roughly made appearance. It has been suggested that this was because they were made hurriedly and perhaps used for a short time only. Bibikov suggests that the figurines were thrown into the fire almost immediately after their manufacture whilst the clay was still wet, and that these activities took place during specific seasons of the year, probably just before the arrival of spring. The figurines from the other site, Bernova-Luka, indicated similar results which were demonstrated by Hausler (1956). He calculated that these figurines had to be fired within three minutes of the grain being mixed with the damp clay since, if the grains had been lying longer in damp surroundings, they would have swollen and their transverse furrows would not have been preserved.

During the initial stage A of this culture there were two differing strains in the economy. The first was based upon pig farming and the second upon cattle farming. It is the second form of economy that becomes dominant in phase B and remains so during phase ci. At sites of Tripolye cii, however, there is a complete change, and sheep farming becomes the predominant factor. Horses were definitely domesticated at this stage, and they may have been sporadically domesticated as early as stage A. The camel also makes an appearance during

91

cii. No concrete conclusions can be made concerning the animal breeding of phase G, but at present there seems to have been no uniformity at the sites considered. Wheat, barley and millet were all of importance to the economy of the Tripolye culture, and bread wheat has been found at more sites than any other cereal. There is, however, no statistical analysis of the relative importance of these cereals, and no inferences concerning the various phases can be made.

The Hungarian Copper Age is composed of three cultures known as Tisza-Polgár, Bodrogkeresztur and Baden. The first is contemporary with that of Gumelniţa and so can be placed at 3600–3200, Bodrogkeresztur is partly contemporary with Cucuteni B and so is around 3200–3000, and the Baden culture developed between 2900 and 2400. The first two cultures are confined to Hungary, but the Baden culture also occurs with variations in eastern Austria, and through east and central Czechoslovakia northwards to the Elbe.

The Bodrogkeresztur culture developed from that of Tisza-Polgár and both are known from a large number of cemeteries and a few settlement sites. The pottery continues in the late Lengyel tradition, with the characteristic 'milk jug' emerging by the late Bodrogkeresztur period. Decoration only occurs rarely, and consists of cross-hatched meander patterns. The stone industry can also be assigned to Lengyel ancestry. Large copper axe/adzes with their blades perpendicular to each other at either end of the implement head are most distinctive of these two periods. Hammer-ended axes, knives, spiral armbands, copper and gold decorative discs have also been found.

Baden pottery is usually self-coloured, fairly dark, and has distinctive large ribbon handles rising above the level of the rim of the pot. Channelled decoration is common and gives the culture its other name of Channelled Ware. Amongst various clay models that have been found, one of a wagon with four solid disc wheels is of especial interest, and represents the earliest direct evidence for wheeled vehicles in central Europe. The stone industry does not differ much from that of the preceding two cultures, but metal is not so common. The axe/adze is no longer present but neck rings occur for the first time.

The wild fauna of this copper age period which is found at settlements and cemeteries is composed of red and roe deer, aurochs, pig, horse, hare, cat, turtle, fish and birds (see Table No. 177). At all sites the domestic animals are much more frequently represented than are the wild.

Only a small quantity of bones has been found at the majority of Tisza-Polgár sites, but at the burial ground at Polgár-Basatanya pigs are more common than the other animals (see Fig. 103, Table No. 75; Bökönyi 1959). Ovicaprids and cattle were also bred, as was the dog (see Table No. 168). The economic value of the animals at settlements of the Bodrogkeresztur culture shows cattle as the main feature with ovicaprids and pigs considerably less important. The burial grounds, however, indicate that the economic and ritual values were not the same, and here sheep and goat predominate (see Figs. 119-122, Tables Nos. 180-182, 75; Bökönyi 1959). The two Baden settlements of Budapest-Andorutca and Székely-Zöldteltk contained more bones of sheep and goat than of other animals, and cattle were more common than pigs (see Figs. 124-125, Tables Nos. 182-183; Bökönyi 1959). However, in the graves cattle were more frequent and there are a few instances of careful burials of these animals. The best known comes from Alsonmédi, where the burials of two cows and two calves were found (Bökönyi 1951). All four animals can be related to the aurochs, as the more or less complete skeletons show, and the height of the cows was around 130-133 cm., and that of one calf (15-18 months), 120 cm. These animals had been carefully placed in the graves and must represent some form of sacrifice. Another complete cow's skeleton was found beneath a Baden pot at Üllö (Bökönyi & Kubaswiecz 1961), and these animals were also of importance in the graves of Polgár-Basatanya (Bökönyi 1959). Many pig bones were also found at the last site (see Fig. 123). The only occurrence of a probably domesticated horse is in the graves at Deszk, where the worked distal end of a metacarpal was found; the animal was small and slender and may represent the first instance of the domestic horse in Hungary (Bökönyi 1959). A tooth was found in a Bodrogkersztur grave, but since the grave had been opened its authenticity is doubtful (Bökönyi 1959). There is no evidence for the hunting of wild horses during this period.

The Hungarian Copper Age sites may be divided into two groups, the settlements and the graves, of which the first reflect the economic value of the different animals and the second reflect their ritual significance. Nothing can be said about the economy of the Tisza-Polgár culture, but pigs were of ritual importance at one site. Cattle dominate at settlements of the Bodrogkeresztur culture and sheep and goat in the graves; during the Baden culture this situation is reversed, with ovicaprids being bred in large quantities, and cattle of great ritual significance.

Further evidence for the Baden culture is obtained from Austria, Czechoslovakia and Poland. Sheep and goat dominate the economy at Ossarn (Bayer 1928), and the headless burial of a calf was discovered at the Czechoslovakian site of Šarovce (Ambros 1958,

Novotny 1958). The only other animal known to be of ritual significance in Czechoslovakia was the dog. Complete skeletons have been found at three sites, some of which occur in association with human burials (Behrens 1964, Vlček 1953, Zikmundova 1962).

The only evidence for the cultivation of cereals in a Baden context comes from Ossarn, where a pot containing between 25 and 30 gm. of wheat was discovered. This was almost entirely einkorn, with a small proportion of emmer (Bayer 1928). No other cereals were present.

There is a little evidence for agriculture during the Mondsee-Altheim culture-period in Austria. This culture is slightly later than that of Baden, and lies to the west in Austria and Bavaria. The pottery is coarse and decorated with incised concentric rings, and the incisions are filled in with white paste in the Mondsee region; cordons appear elsewhere. Stone axes, adzes, mace heads, daggers, arrowheads as well as flat copper axes, rhomboid daggers and ornaments also occur. The wild fauna consists of red and roe deer, wild pig, chamois, wild cat, bear, lynx, fox, beaver and wolf. Various fishes have also been identified (see Table No. 184).

Cattle, pigs and dogs are known in the context of this culture, but since only a few bones have been found, the absence of sheep and goat is not significant (Amschler 1949). The cattle and dogs both belong to the turbary breed, and the pigs have been attributed to the larger *scrofa* variety. Emmer and club wheat, four and six-rowed barley as well as millet and flax have been found at the type site of Mondsee (Much 1876, 1879, Buschan 1895, Hofmann 1924, Neuweiler 1905). At another site the millet has been identified as the Italian variety (Netolitsky 1914, Werneck 1949).

Further evidence for the domestication of animals and cultivation of plants has been found at sites which are known to be of the Copper Age period, but whose cultural group is not known, in Austria (Teutsch 1903, Hauck 1950), Czechoslovakia (Ehrlich 1956, Zikmundova 1962, Kuhn 1960) and Italy (see Table No. 185, Trump 1960, Tongiorgi 1956, Malavotti 1953). At one Italian site sheep and goats are known to be the most frequent domestic animal encountered (see Fig. 127, Table No. 186). The sheep are attributed to the turbary breed.

The Swiss Copper Age site of Uerikon on the other hand contained more bones of cattle than of sheep and goat (see Fig. 126, Table No. 188; Rüeger 1944). They appear to be almost exclusively of turbary stock. At other sites the sheep, goats and pigs can also be attributed to this breed (see Table No. 187; Rütimeyer 1860, Schenk 1912). There is no instance of the relative importance of crops being known

94

at Copper Age sites, excluding those of the Single Grave Complex, in Switzerland. It is, however, known that emmer and club wheat, six-rowed barley, two varieties of millet, flax and possibly poppy were cultivated (see Table No. 189).

The cultural connections of many of the French Copper Age sites is also unknown. A few, however, are known to belong to the Peu Richard culture which is characterised by channelled and incised ware, and occasionally contains small amounts of copper. It is placed around 2600 to 2200. Bones of red deer, roe deer, aurochs, pig, horse, fox, badger, hare, rabbit, squirrel, vole and hedgehog have been identified as well as a possible bone of wolf. These usually account for a tenth to a quarter of the fauna, although in one instance the wild animals form well over half of the osteological remains (see Tables Nos. 190-196).

The full range of domestic animals is known from sites of the Peu Richard culture, and the evidence from Les Matignons shows that turbary cattle are the basis of the economy (see Fig. 77 & Table No. 108; Burnez & Case 1966).

The most information regarding the remaining Copper Age sites comes from a group of four sites examined by Josien (1957). The relative importance of the animals has been ascertained in all cases, and it is seen that sheep and goat were dominant (see Figs. 128-131, Tables Nos. 192-195). Sheep were more common than goats, and they have been attributed to the turbary breed as have the cattle. The pigs are also small in size but it is not certain that they are of turbary stock. Josien thinks that their small stature could be attributable to the local vegetation which does not favour pig breeding, and they are the least important of the basic domestic animals. The complete absence of cattle at another site, known as Trache Deux, is striking since many bones have been identified. In this case sheep were bred in large quantities, followed closely by pigs (see Fig. 132, Table No. 196; Josien 1962). Goats appear to have been completely absent, and both the sheep and pigs were large with no indication of the turbary variety. Dogs were bred during this period, but nothing is known of their race other than that at two sites they were too large to belong to the *palustris* group (Josien 1957, 1962).

The osteological evidence indicates that cattle were the most important animal bred at Peu Richard settlements, but that sheep and goat were numerous at a group of sites in southern and western France. There is no evidence concerning the crops raised at this stage.

The information from the Iberian Peninsular comes from the Los Millares culture and from a few other sites known to be of the Copper Age period. The Los Millares pottery can be derived from the preceding Almerían neolithic ware. The shapes include vessels with rounded or pointed bases which were undecorated during the neolithic, but now some have incised patterns which include occuli motives. Occasionally these are painted in black on a light background. Extremely fine flint work was being done, and small objects of bone and ivory such as V-perforated buttons and toggles appear. Metallurgy was also of importance with copper, silver and gold all being worked. The basic form was a fairly simple copper dagger with a rib down the centre of one face. Nothing is known of the importance of hunting as opposed to domestication, but it may be assumed that the usual wild animals were being killed to supplement the food and to provide skins.

Cattle, goats and pigs are known from the Portuguese Copper Age site of Vila Nova de São Pedro (Behrens 1964), and turbary cattle have been recorded at Spanish sites (Staffe 1943). There is no further osteological evidence, since it was discarded during numerous excavations. The remains of plants, however, had a more favourable fate, and at several sites carbonised grain was kept and identified by botanists. Wheat and barley are both known to have been cultivated, and amongst the wheat remains there is a single instance of emmer and several of club wheat and bread wheat (see Table No. 197). The richest site was that of Almizaraque, where the last two species occur in abundance, with the former slightly more frequent than the latter (Neuweiler 1935, Santa-Olalla 1946, Tellez 1954). The only instance in which the spike-type of the barley cultivated has been identified also occurs at this site, and it was six-rowed, and again the only known case of flax comes from Almizaraque. Some small carbonised seeds were found in one of the chambers of the tombs and identified as *Linum usitatissimum*. The only legume that was of significance was the bean, *Vicia faba v. celtica nana*, and it has been found at several sites and was definitely cultivated (de Paco 1957, Tellez 1954, Sangmeister & Schubart 1964).

The farming practice of the inhabitants of northern Europe must now be considered. The groups to be discussed may be divided into the German Late Neolithic and Copper Age, and the Single Grave Complex.

This period in southern Germany is represented to a large extent by the Altheim and Horgen cultures, and the Altheim culture is regarded as being an eastern extension of the Horgen culture. They may be placed around 2700–2300. The pottery is fairly rough, decorated with cordons and includes handled jugs; there is none of the decoration that is found in the Mondsee region of Austria. However, other elements such as the stone and metal industries are similar to those found in Austria. The settlements take the form of fortified hilltop camps or lakeside villages. Hunting was practised and the animals exploited include red and roe deer, elk, aurochs, bison, pig, bear, horse, beaver, otter, badger, wolf, fox, cat, turtle, birds and fishes. On the whole hunting accounts for less than a quarter of the osteological remains (see Table No. 198).

Cattle, ovicaprids, pigs and dogs are all known from Altheim sites, and of these cattle are the main feature (see Figs. 133-135, Tables Nos. 199-202). The majority of the cattle were of small or medium size, with a few instances of animals that lay near the aurochs variation. In addition certain evidence for castration was found at the type-site of Altheim (Boessneck 1956). No definite racial identification of the sheep and goat bred at the four sites considered by Boessneck was possible, but it appears that no very large or very small animals were known. Amongst the pigs were both the turbary and *scrofa* varieties, and they varied in importance at the different sites (Boessneck 1956). There were also two breeds of dog, the turbary dog and the larger *intermedius* dog (Boessneck 1956). It is highly probable that the horse was known as a domestic animal at the sites of Pesternacker and Alternerdingen, where they are about as numerous as ovicaprids or pigs (Boessneck 1956). These animals are described as being of medium size, 140-145 cm. to the withers, robust, but not of cold-blooded stock. Boessneck thinks that the forerunner was the Prze-walskii horse and that they were probably domesticated, although this cannot be stated with complete certainty.

The evidence from the Horgen culture indicates that pigs were the chief domestic animal, as was the case at sites of this culture in Swit-zerland. Two breeds were known, but the majority of animals lay within the maximum for turbary pigs as is shown at Sipplingen (see Fig. 136 & Table No. 203; Vogel 1933). The cattle at this site are described as lying between the turbary and recent Simmentaler cattle in appearance, and the sheep were more common than the goats, and both can be ascribed to the turbary breeds. Most of the dogs belong to this breed, but the *intermedius* as well as the miniature *spaletti* animals were also present. The horse is reported as having been domesticated at another site, but nothing further is known about these remains (Reinerth 1929). The only known instance of plant cultivation during this period occurs in a Horgen context, and emmer, barley and broomcorn millet have been identified (Bertsch 1954). Domestic animals have also been found at other Copper Age sites whose cultural connections are uncertain (see Table No. 199).

Cattle were the most frequent animal found at Altheim settlements, ovicaprids and pigs were of about equal importance, and the domestic horse was also probably known. This animal was of warm-blooded or eastern stock. The economy of the Horgen culture was different, despite the fact that the Altheim culture is regarded as being an eastern extension of the Horgen culture. It had its economy based upon pig farming as do Swiss sites of this culture, with cattle, ovicaprids, dogs and possibly the horse bred to a lesser extent. Wheat, barley and millet were being cultivated.

There is much evidence for the animals and plants raised in the context of the Single Grave Complex, most of which comes from the ritual offerings made when some member of a particular tribe was buried. This Complex is composed of several cultures which have many features in common. Included here are the Corded Ware sites of Germany, Poland and Switzerland, the Swedish Boat Axe culture and the Single Graves of Jutland, Germany and Holland. The time-span of these groups is considerable, with Corded Ware overlapping the late Baden culture and extending into the early Bronze Age. The complex as a whole may be placed around 2800–2000.

The elements in common to these cultural groups include single, contracted skeletons in all early graves, a beaker-shaped pot decorated with cord impressions, stone battle-axes and necklaces of bored teeth. The earliest Single Graves are those below ground level, called Bottom or Flat Graves, they are followed by Ground Graves which are constructed on the land surface, and Upper Graves which occur in mounds above ground level. These last graves are contemporary with the Danish Stone Cist period and may be placed at about 2000.

Some people hold the view that Corded Ware originated in central Germany and Bohemia, but others believe that it originated somewhere in southern Russia shortly after the end of the Tripolye culture, and from there spread as far west as Switzerland. The pot forms include long-necked beakers and amphorae, both of which are richly ornamented with cord impressions around the upper portion of the pot. The cemeteries of this group include flat graves and barrows. Small copper rings and spirals, amber objects and trepanned skulls are all known.

The other cultural group considered here is that of Globular Amphorae. This culture is concentrated in Germany with extensions to the south, east and west and it is largely contemporary with the Corded Ware sites in this area. The pots have a rounded base and vertical-sided neck with two small handles. It resembles a squat beaker, and has incised cross-hatching around the upper half of the vessel. Flint, stone and bone implements, amber beads, bone ring pendants, a few copper and occasionally bronze objects have been associated with Globular Amphorae.

The animals that were hunted include red deer, roe deer, elk, aurochs, bison, pig, horse, beaver, badger, otter, bear, wolf, fox, marten, wolverine, cat, hare, seal, porpoise, tortoise, various fishes and birds. A large quantity of wild animals is represented at one of the northern Polish sites, but in Switzerland where the greatest number of bones has been found, the wild fauna accounts for about a quarter of the osteological remains (see Tables Nos. 205, 207-209). In connection with the evidence for agriculture in this context it must be mentioned that there is no evidence for this period in Denmark. This is because no settlement sites have yet been found, and also that in the graves themselves no bones have survived. This is a result of local soil conditions, and the only indication of human burials is a dark stain outline of the skeleton.

The evidence from the graves is considered first, followed by that found at settlement sites. Cattle, sheep, goats, pigs and dogs are all well represented in burials of the Single Grave Complex (see Table No. 206). Excluding the evidence from Sweden, which is extremely fragmentary, cattle are most common and the osteological remains often include complete skeletons of sacrificed animals. Most of these cattle belong to the turbary breed and at two Polish sites, Adolfin and Brzesc Kujawski, dwarf animals have been found. They lie between 1089 mm. and 1165 mm. in height. Another interesting fact to emerge from the last site is that all cattle appear to have had their horn cores deliberately cut off near the base before they were buried (Bökönyi & Kubaswiecz 1961, Swiezynski 1958). This fact may account for the absence of horn cores at other sites in central Europe, if it were practised as part of the ritual burial of these animals. This dominance of cattle in the graves is particularly noticeable at the Globular Amphorae sites of Poland and Germany. Sheep and goat have been found at more Single Grave sites than have pigs, and a few ritual burials of these animals are known, including those of a small goat and large pig. One of the most remarkable sites is that found at Föllik in Austria. Inside this grave there were discovered the burials of a cow and calf, ewe and lamb, goat and kid, and mare and foal together with the skull of a third horse. The bovine remains again indicate the turbary breed, and resemblances to the modern alpine cattle of the Zillertal and to the short-horned Pinzgauer cattle are apparent (Amschler 1949). The goat is known to be of the *prisca* group, but the breed of sheep is unknown. Amschler came to the conclusion that the horses belonged to the representative of the Arabian horse, *Equus caballus L. orientalis*. This animal was of medium size and lies within the range of the modern Arabian horses, and was domesticated. There are also other reported instances of domestic

99

horses in burials of the Single Grave Complex. One claim is made at Złota in Poland, but after a careful examination Behrens could not accept their association with Corded Ware since there were no associated finds (Behrens 1962). The skeleton of a horse was discovered at the Swedish site of Hvellinge in 1860, but the excavator and all subsequent authorities have been unable to decide whether or not it was contemporary with the grave (Behrens 1962, Lundholm 1949). Another claim for domestication occurs in Poland (Weick-Luisenthal; Kilian 1955, Gimbutas 1956), and a skeleton of a horse (or a cow?) was found in Germany (Langendorf; Behrens 1964).

Apart from the skeleton of the horse mentioned above, the osteological remains found in Sweden are extremely scarce and in a bad state of preservation. Most of these belong to either sheep or goat, and consist of one or two worked bones found in the graves (Møhl 1962). There was, however, one complete dog's skeleton which has been attributed to the turbary breed.

Many skeletons of dogs were recovered from the Polish site of Złota during the 1926–27 excavations. Most of the dogs are very similar in size and can be attributed to the large turbary breed, *Canis f. palustris ladogensis* (Wodzicki 1935). At another site there is evidence for a larger animal, thought to be *Canis f. matris optimae* (Niezabitowski 1928). There are also several instances of perforated dogs' teeth and these probably served as necklaces and dress ornamentation. At one Czechoslovakian site known as Marefy there were 421 dogs' teeth and a further 56 imitations of these teeth, ornamenting the dress of an old woman. It would have taken the teeth of a minimum of 22 dogs to provide this trimming (Neustupny 1961). The high instance of dog bones at Single Grave sites is striking, since they are normally the least frequent of the domestic animals, but in this context they occur at more sites than does any other domestic animal (see Table No. 206).

The evidence from settlement sites is found mainly in Switzerland. No uniform picture emerges from the three richest sites, but there appear to have been two strains in the economy. The first is based upon the breeding of sheep and goat and occurs at Auvernier II and Baldegg, and in the second cattle and pigs were of greater importance as is illustrated at Utoquai (see Figs. 137-139, Tables Nos. 99, 207-208; Hescheler 1940, Kuhn 1932, Reverdin 1932). Since there is much similarity between the sites of Uerikon and Utoquai, it is probable that the former site is also of the Corded Ware culture, but this is not known for certain. Cattle were the dominant feature at Uerikon (see p. 94). The cattle are basically of turbary stock with a few larger animals also present and the pigs can also be assigned to the turbary breed, and in two instances miniature pigs are recorded (Studer 1883). The remains of sheep are of interest. The main breed was the turbary sheep, but there were also bones of a larger animal which lay within the range of variation of the Copper Sheep, *Ovis aries studeri*. The horns were slightly smaller than those of the moufflon, and Studer regards them as originating from a domesticated moufflon. Duerst (1904) also examined these remains and came to the same conclusion. This sheep is known from Scandinavia in a Passage Grave and Pitted Ware context, and possibly also from Britain in Chambered Tombs. Dogs form a small proportion of osteological remains at the Swiss sites, and both the small *Canis f. palustris* and the larger *Canis f. matris optimae* have been identified (Hescheler 1920, 1940, Studer 1883).

The last domestic animal to be considered is the horse. Its domesticity at Baldegg has been established by comparison with remains of Helveto-Gallic horses (Hescheler & Rüeger 1940), and amongst the remains at Amberg and Meyer two different types of horses are said to be present (Rütimeyer 1860, 1861, Hescheler 1920). Both are assumed to have been of wild origin, but if the difference in size is greater than that indicated by Lundholm (1949), it seems probable that one of these animals must have been brought there by man and so be at least semi-domesticated. There is also a strong possibility of the domestic horse being present at the neolithic village of Dummersee in Germany. Reinerth originally reported them to be of definite domestic status, and if this is true Lundholm says they represent the earliest instance of domestic horses in this region of Europe. According to Lundholm the basis of the argument for their domesticity rests on the size variation that was apparent amongst the remains. However, he has shown that there was a variation in size amongst wild post-glacial horses, so that this factor alone can be no proof of domestication. Some of these bones survive and have been examined by Nobis (1955) and Vogel (1933), and both came to the conclusion that whereas some of the bones are certainly those of wild animals, there were also a few that can be attributed to domestic horses.

The main crops to have been cultivated in the Single Grave Complex are wheat, barley, millet and flax, and of these wheat and barley are most frequently encountered. There is only a single instance of einkorn, but emmer and naked wheat are known from several sites (see Table No. 210). Emmer is the only wheat known from Poland, and it is the most frequent grain to be encountered at Utoquai in Switzerland, and the second most common at Meyer (Neuweiler 1924, 1930). At this last site the basic cereal was club wheat, and between three and four litres of it were recovered; this is also the main cereal at Robenhausen (Heer 1865, Neuweiler 1905). The absence of wheat at Swedish sites is notable, and only barley occurs here, although elsewhere in the Single Grave Complex it has been shown to be of much less significance than wheat. The six-rowed variety is known from Switzerland (Heer 1865, Neuweiler 1924) and both naked and glumed barley have been identified as pottery impressions in Denmark. Only naked barley is known with certainty from Sweden despite a thorough investigation of the pottery by Hjelmqvist (Brønsted 1957, Hjelmqvist 1955, 1962). Both millet and flax are present in Switzerland. The two varieties of millet, *Panicum miliaceum* and *Seteria italica*, occur in small quantities (Neuweiler 1905, 1924, Heer 1865), but many carbonised seeds of flax are reported (Neuweiler 1905, 1924, 1930, Heer 1865). Neuweiler originally identified the flax as *Linum cf. austriaceum*, but it has recently been shown that they are in fact *Linum usitatissimum* (Helbaek 1959a). The seeds of the pea and the poppy have also been found in Switzerland (see Table No. 210).

It is interesting to note, that whilst no cereal remains were found at Succase in northern Poland, Ehrlich (1934) reports a large quantity of carbonised acorns. These could have been ground into flour for human consumption, or alternatively used as fodder for pigs. Another aspect of plant cultivation was brought to light by the discovery of criss-cross plough furrows under a Single Grave tumulus at Aldrupgaarde in Jutland (Kjaerum 1954). The network of markings were found at the base of the whole excavated area, and are orientated east-west and north-north-east—south-south-west. These plough furrows vary in width from 3 to 10 cm., and are on average 30 cm. apart. This is the only site at which plough furrows of this period are known, and they are the earliest so far discovered in continental Europe.

From the above discussion it is apparent that cattle were the most important ritual animal of the Single Grave Complex, and there are many instances of careful burials of these animals. In several cases they are known to have had their horns removed before burial, perhaps at some sacrificial ceremony. Other domestic animals also occur in graves, and the domestic horse appears occasionally in both burials and at settlement sites. Some communities concentrated on the rearing of sheep and goat and others on cattle. Amongst the bones of sheep, which were mostly of turbary stock, there was evidence for an animal which resembled the moufflon and does not appear to have been domesticated for very long. Wheat, barley, millet and flax were all cultivated, and in the southern area club wheat and emmer are dominant amongst the cereals, whereas to the north in Sweden it is probable that barley was the basic crop. The dominance of cattle in the graves and also the emphasis upon sheep breeding at certain sites suggests contact with the Baden culture to the east. On the other hand the presence of certain communities that were chiefly cattle breeders indicates the survival of the preceding neolithic method of subsistence-economics.

From the examination of these late neolithic and Copper Age sites throughout Europe, it appears that they had various different economies, with some cultures preferring to breed cattle, others ovicaprids, and a few bred more pigs. The basically cattle breeding economies include those of Gumelniţa, Salcuţa IV, Cucuteni, some sites of Tripolye A together with nearly all sites of Tripolye B and ci, Bodrogkeresztur, Peu Richard and Altheim, and those who bred more pigs include Salcuţa 1-11b, Tripolye A, and the late German Horgen sites, which agree with the Swiss Horgen sites considered in Chapter V. The sheep rearing communities include those of Dimini, Salcuţa 11c, Tripolye cii, Cernavoda, Baden, some Swiss Corded Ware settlements, and the French Copper Age.

It has been shown earlier that most of the cultures that developed in central Europe followed the Linear Pottery tradition of cattle farming. Indeed this tradition became so strong that its influence spread to the south, as illustrated by the Boian culture, and also to the north and west, as the evidence from France and Britain has shown. The Gumelniţa pottery as well as its flint and stone industry are all developed from the preceding Boian culture, as are many aspects of the Salcuţa culture. There are also certain indirect elements in common between the Tripolye-Cucuteni culture and the Linear Pottery culture. The connection lies in the Pre-Cucuteni phase, which appears to have developed from a Linear Pottery and Vinča (Dudeşti) ancestry, and it is from this that the Tripolye and Cucuteni cultures evolved.

Both the pottery and stone industry of the Bodrogkeresztur culture can be assigned to Lengyel ancestry, and Peu Richard evolved from the so-called Western Neolithic cultures with the additions of new decoration on the pottery and the presence of metal. The Altheim culture has many similarities with the Horgen culture and so may be related to the middle Neolithic. Hence it is seen that all of the cattle-breeding cultures of this period have strong connections with the preceding neolithic, and they appear to have derived their economy from this same period. All of these communities have developed in established cattle breeding areas and continued the tradition of farming, pottery and stone manufacture that had been practised for several hundreds of years.

There is no apparent connection between the three pig-breeding cultures. During the late stages of the Linear Pottery culture it was seen that pigs became of greater importance to the economy. It is possible that this increase in pig-breeding resulted in the emergence of one or two basically pig farming cultures. This may be regarded partially as an adaption to the local environment, which supported many pigs, and these may have proved to be much easier to domesticate than the alternative aurochs.

More striking than either the emphasis on cattle or on pig, is the presence of many sheep and goat at this stage in Europe, as ovicaprid breeding was on a decline during the late Linear Pottery period, and new stock could only be obtained as a result of trade with the Near Eastern cultures. At first there seems to be very little in common between these communities. The pottery of the Dimini culture may be tri-coloured, and has white, black or incised spiral meander patterns on a buff, brown or red ground. The Salcuṭa pottery on the other hand is very rarely painted in colours, and instead graphite painting and decoration by means of rustication and wave impressions is found. The Cernavoda culture developed from that of Gumelniṭa, together with influence from the south, and its pottery is basically grey burnished ware with little decoration. The Tripolye pottery was of very sophisticated design. Complicated geometric patterns are painted in red, black or white or alternatively outlined with channelled grooves. In addition to these forms, during the late cii stage plain cord-ornamented pots appear but are not so common. The Baden culture is best known for its channelled or grooved decorated ware. The vessels are usually self-coloured, fairly dark and many pots have distinctive ribbon handles. The Swiss Corded Ware vessels are again different. The main form is a long necked beaker or amphora which is richly ornamented with cord impressions over the upper portion of the vessel. Both plain and decorated pots have been found at the French Copper Age sites considered by Josien; the decoration may take the form of grooved channels, diamond-shaped reliefs or incised chevrons. From this it is clear that there is no overall factor in common between the pottery of the Dimini, Salcuṭa iic, Cernavoda, Tripolye cii, Baden, Swiss Corded Ware and French Copper Age cultures. Some of these cultures may be linked by their methods of ornamenting the pottery, but this is the only similarity to emerge and it is not a general one. Channelled decoration is recorded in the contexts of the Baden and French Copper Age sites, and channels are used to outline some Tripolye motifs. Cord impressions are characteristic of the Swiss pottery, and they also occur on some pots of the Tripolye cii phase. Since both channelled decoration and cord impressions occur in several other cultural connections at this time, it cannot be regarded as a significant link between these cultures.

The stone industry in these different contexts does not differ notably from those of the preceding neolithic cultures. Perforated axes occur for the first time in Greece in a Dimini context, and battle axes are known from Swiss Corded Ware sites and possibly from Tripolye cii sites.

One feature in common to all these cultures is the occurrence of copper. Both copper and gold are found in small quantities at Dimini settlements, and small copper axes and gold ring pendants have been discovered. Copper occurs a little more frequently in both the Salcuța and Cernavoda cultures. The axes of the Dimini culture are found together with copper adzes and double spiral pins which are similar to Anatolian models. Copper beads, axes and adzes occur in Tripolye B, and during stage cii daggers with a midrib on one face only and small rings and spirals in copper, gold or silver are all present. During the Baden culture there is relatively little copper and the most characteristic forms are diadems and torques with rolled terminals. Torques from graves can be matched by examples from Chalcolithic graves in Anatolia. Axes, rhomboid and triangular daggers are all found at Swiss Corded Ware sites, and daggers and occasional gold objects are found in southern France.

From this it appears that the Dimini, Salcuța iic, Cernavoda, Tripolye cii, Baden, Swiss Corded Ware and French Copper Age sites have one common factor. There is no substantial similarity in their pottery, some groups have painted ware and others plain ware, but the most obvious link, apart from their subsistence-economics, lies in the presence of copper at the majority of sites.

Although these were by no means the first copper containing cultures in their respective areas, they do contain features which dissociate them from the other earlier cultures. The chief early copper age cultures of eastern Europe are those of Gumelnița, Cucuteni, Tripolye B and ci, Tisza-Polgár and Bodrogkeresztur and all of these contain substantial amounts of copper, which appears to be derived from the local Carpathian ore. With the exception of the Tisza-Polgár culture, for which there is no evidence, all of these cultures have an economy centred upon the breeding of cattle, and also many strong connections with the earlier neolithic of this region. In other words the breeding of cattle in the earlier copper age may be linked with the production of ore from the Carpathians, and this was carried out by societies with strong local neolithic backgrounds.

However, there appears to have been a decline in this Carpathian centre around 3000, and subsequently copper is not so common in eastern Europe, and many of the copper objects found are derived by trade from the Caucasus and Near East. Analysis of some of the copper from a Tripolye cii context has shown that it is derived from the Caucasus, and that found at Baden sites has strong connections with Anatolia and the Near East, as has the Cernavoda copper. These cultures in which the amount of copper found declines and is imported from the south, are basically sheep-farming societies. Links between the Near East and eastern Europe are also apparent in various details of the pottery. For example, the flanged handles found in the Baden culture are encountered in the Chalcolithic at Mersin, as well as at Troy. The clay model of a wagon found in a Baden context can link this area with Mesopotamia where the wheel was probably first invented.

Isotopic dating of these cultures has an interesting result. The Dimini culture may be placed between 3900–3200, Salcuţa iic to between 3500 and 3300, Cernavoda to 2800–2300, Tripolye cii to 3100–2900, the Baden culture to 2900–2400. The approximate dates of the Swiss Corded Ware sites are thought to be between 2500 and 2000, and those of the French Copper Age 2400–2000. When the time span of these cultures is mapped over their known areas of distribution, it is seen that there is a continuous spread of these ovicaprid-breeding and copper-trading societies from Greece through eastern and central Europe to western Europe (see Fig. 142). Their origin must be placed somewhere in the Near East. As yet there is insufficient evidence to locate the exact areas or centres of origin, but they must have evolved during the fifth millennium, and been both breeding and domesticating sheep, and producing vast quantities of copper objects. The regions in the Near East in which copper ore is found and can be mined are the highland zones of Iran and Anatolia, and so it is almost certain that the impetus behind these European cultures is to be found somewhere within these two neighbourhoods. On purely theoretical grounds this places their origin either in the mid and late Chalcolithic of the hilly region of Iran, or in the early and mid Chalcolithic of Anatolia.

One of the chief problems that would arise for the ovicaprid-breeders in Europe would be the problem of obtaining new stock. It would be impossible to domesticate the animals themselves, as the cattle and pig breeders could do, so that either the stock would have to be maintained without external means, or else new stock would have to be acquired by trade from the Near East. If the latter solution was the one adopted, it is probable that some of the ovicaprids at these sites should closely resemble the wild sheep and goats of the Near East. A few such animals have been identified. Boessneck (1962) reports an exceptionally large sheep from Otzaki in a Dimini context, and others have been found at Corded Ware sites in Switzerland. A sheep, described by Duerst as being very close in appearance to the European moufflon, was identified at Utoquai, and another was found at Greng. Duerst called this sheep the Copper Sheep, *Ovis aries studeri*. There is, however, very little difference between the Asiatic and European moufflons, particularly in the early stages of domestication, so that these large sheep may equally well belong to the Asiatic variety. If this is so, as seems probable, it would show better agreement with the archaeological evidence which indicates that there was a considerable amount of trade being conducted between Europe and the Near East. There has been no detailed analysis of the sheep found in either the Cernavoda or Salcuța cultures, and the majority of sheep at Tripolye cii sites are of the turbary breed, but it is unknown whether or not there was any indication of a larger breed.

There is further indirect evidence for the presence of large sheep amongst the stock of the Single Grave people. At the Scandinavian Middle Neolithic site of Bundsø a large sheep that compares well with the Copper sheep found in Switzerland was identified, and it is at this time that the Single Grave folk first appear in Denmark, and trade between the two societies can be established in many instances. There is also the possibility of a similar sheep being present at the Swedish island site of Stora Karslö in a Pitted Ware context, which again overlaps with the Single Grave immigration. So far no actual Single Grave settlements have been found in this region of northern Europe, but if one were found, it is highly probable that amongst the bones of sheep there would be a few remains indicating the presence of a large moufflon-like animal.

From the above evidence it is therefore concluded that the ovicaprid breeding cultures spread over Europe from Greece to France between 3900 and 2000, and that they were ancestral to the chief copper trading cultures of this period. Their origin is placed in the Near East in the fifth millennium, and new stock was obtained sporadically from this region.

The last animal to have been domesticated in the period under consideration is the horse. Since much of the evidence for its evolution as a domestic species rests upon osteological finds of the Bronze Age rather than from the Neolithic or Copper Age, the question of horse domestication cannot be fully investigated in this present context. There is no evidence for the domestication of the true horse during the Chalcolithic of the Near East, although there are two probable instances of half-ass and one of donkey domestication.

Wild horses may be divided into two main groups, the eastern and the western. The eastern includes the Przewalskii horse and the tarpan, and the western consists of the large *germanicus* horse and the smaller *miohippus* horse. The Przewalskii horse has always been confined to Asia, and both this and the tarpan have been found in the Near East during the neolithic period. Of the European horses the larger breed is found in Scandinavia and Germany, and the smaller *miohippus* to the south of this. The distribution of the wild tarpan extends into southern Russia and eastern Europe.

The earliest European culture in which the question of horse domestication arises is the Tripolye culture. Horses are present at all stages although their status is not always known, but it is clear that the horse was an important domestic animal by period cii. There is one definite report of its domesticity in the early stage A, the decision being reached after a careful examination by two experts. Therefore it would appear that the horse was probably bred, or at least herded, sporadically during the early stages, and that by the final phases it had become an important domestic animal. There is no indication that this was a gradual process, indeed it appears rather to have been a rapid change which coincided with the increase in sheep farming and also in copper trade during Tripolye cii.

The other East European claim for domestic horses comes from the Cernavoda culture, where some hooves were found, and it occurs, as do the Russian horses, at a time when sheep farming suddenly dominates the economy. On the basis of tooth diagrams, Lundholm (1949) concluded that the tarpan is the progenitor of the Russian and Rumanian domestic horses. There is a single instance of a domestic horse's tooth in a Copper Age grave in Hungary (Deszk B) reported by Bökönyi (1959), and another claim comes from the Baden site of Ossarn in Austria, where again ovicaprids dominate the economy.

There has been much speculation as to the status of the horse during the Single Grave Complex. Several claims have been shown to be unfounded (Behrens 1962, 1964), but the horse was certainly present as a domestic animal at Baldegg in Switzerland, again in conjunction with a high proportion of sheep. Two different sizes of horses are reported from Amberg and Meyer by Rütimeyer, and both are attributed to wild animals. It is also almost certain that a domesticated horse was buried at Föllik, and that the two animals present were related to the Arabian horse, which indicates a Przewalskii or tarpan-like animal. There is again a strong possibility of domestication at the megalithic village of Dummersee in Germany, which is contemporary with the early Single Grave Complex, and another claim is made for the equoid remains from Weick-Luisenthal.

Boessneck thinks that the horses he found at some sites of the

Altheim culture were domesticated. These horses were definitely of the eastern and not the western group, and he thought that they were probably Przewalskii horses. They also agree well with measurements given by Amschler for the horses found at Föllik. Since the Altheim horses are of the eastern group, they must have been brought to southern Germany by some external community, and this community must have obtained their domesticated, or semi-domesticated, horses from the east. The only archaeological culture known to have had a wide distribution including Germany and eastern Europe, and to have been contemporary with the Altheim culture, is the Single Grave Complex, and the evidence from this complex itself indicates that horses were at any rate sporadically known as domesticated animals. For this reason it appears that the Single Grave Folk brought domestic horses with them to central Europe, and that they obtained these animals in the eastern area of their distribution. This fact strengthens the claim that this Complex had an eastern origin rather than a western one.

There is also a possibility of horse domestication at the Swedish site of Hvellinge in a Boat Axe context, and also at late Passage Grave settlements in Denmark, just after the arrival of the Single Grave herdsmen. This evidence is much in favour of the view that the domestic horse was known in Scandinavia during the late neolithic and Copper Age periods, and that the Single Grave Complex was the impetus behind this innovation. However, the horses that were domesticated at this time in Scandinavia were of the indigenous *germanicus* stock, and not of an imported breed, so that the Single Grave people must have domesticated the local horses. Since no Single Grave settlements are known from Scandinavia this fact cannot be established directly, although the evidence from other regions of Europe indicates that this assumption is correct.

The above information shows that the horse was known as a domestic animal during the Copper Age period over a large area of Europe. The first type to be domesticated belonged to the eastern group and was the tarpan, and its spread can be directly linked with a marked increase in sheep farming and with the mounting trade in copper from the Near East. It occurs at sites of the Tripolye cii, Cernavoda, Baden and Swiss Corded Ware cultures. An eastern horse, either Przewalskii or tarpan, is known in a Single Grave context as well as in an Altheim context and was domesticated, and to the north the appearance of the domestic horse may be connected with the expansion of the Single Grave Complex. Local wild horses were being sporadically domesticated by the indigenous communities.

Résumé

The earliest evidence for agriculture in the Near East takes the form
of domestication of sheep followed by that of goat, and this was
accomplished between 9000 and 7000 BC. Towards the end of this
period plants were first cultivated, including einkorn, emmer and
barley, and then the dog was domesticated. The first certain occurrence of domestic cattle and pigs is in the late neolithic of Anatolia
and the Chalcolithic of Mesopotamia, which are contemporary at
around 5000 BC. Legumes were now being cultivated, as was flax.
The donkey, and in all probability the half-ass, were domesticated
towards the end of the Chalcolithic period, and the camel was also
known. No evidence has been found to suggest that the horse itself
was domesticated at this stage.

Two breeds of dog were present during the later Mesolithic in
Europe, and the inhabitants of Scandinavia domesticated the local
wolves to obtain these animals somewhere between 8000 and 5000.
Reports have been made of small cattle and pigs in Sauveterrian,
Tardenoisian, Azilian and Asturian contexts, but there is insufficient
evidence to prove that they were domesticated. It is also shown here
that sheep have been identified in these same contexts. They are said,
in several instances, to be small and to resemble the later turbary
sheep of the neolithic. The writer suggests that they may represent a
diminutive form of the late Palaeolithic sheep of Europe which managed to adapt themselves to the environmental changes that occurred
between the Final Pleistocene and Holocene periods. The agricultural activities of the Ertebølle/Ellerbek culture are largely attributable to the TRB communities, although they did domesticate their
own dogs, and may have domesticated some aurochs and boars as a
result of contact with the TRB culture.

The Initial Agricultural Colonisation of Europe began before 5000
BC in Greece, and agricultural settlements were found in Holland
before 4000 BC. Sheep and goat were the basic domestic animals of
the Early Agricultural Neolithic of Greece and of the Starčevo-Körös
culture, with cattle, pigs and dogs bred to a lesser extent. Wheat was
the main crop, with einkorn and emmer the chief representatives.
Sheep were also the main domestic animal of the Impressed Ware
economy, and bread wheat was probably the most important cereal
crop, with emmer, einkorn, barley and club wheat also cultivated.
The Linear Pottery culture was responsible for the transmission of

agriculture across Europe from Hungary to Holland, and these colonists were essentially cattle breeders and they castrated a large proportion of these animals. Emmer was an important crop, and einkorn, bread wheat, club wheat, hard wheat, barley, millet, flax and perhaps peas were cultivated.

The agricultural activities of the cultures that developed after the Initial Colonisation followed the tradition of the Linear Pottery culture. The influence of this last cultural group spread to the south, into northern Bulgaria and Rumania, and also to the west and north as is shown by the evidence from France, Scandinavia and Britain. In all these areas as well as in central Europe, cattle breeding and wheat cultivation remain the basis of the subsistence-economics until the end of the neolithic period. There were, however, one or two societies which preferred to breed pigs to cattle, and these may have emerged from the late stage of the Linear Pottery culture, when pigs are shown to have increased in importance at the expense of ovicaprids.

There are two main animal breeding traditions apparent during the Copper Age in Europe. The first is centred upon cattle rearing, and this was the basis of the subsistence-economics of the early copper mining cultures which had strong local neolithic traditions, and derived their ore from the Carpathians. The second tradition was based upon the breeding of ovicaprids. These ovicaprid-breeding cultures spread over Europe within the period 3900 to 2000 from Greece to France, and their origin is placed somewhere in the Near East in the fifth millennium. Their appearance in east-central Europe coincides with the decline of the Carpathian copper centre around 3000, and after this most of the copper in this area is derived by trade from the south, in particular from Anatolia and the Near East. The evidence shows that these ovicaprid-breeding and metal trading societies also obtained fresh stock of sheep from this same source.

It is at this stage that the horse, in the form of the tarpan, appears to have first been domesticated. The earliest evidence comes from the Tripolye culture of southern Russia, and its spread over the rest of Europe is linked with the increase in sheep farming and with the mounting trade in copper from the south. The first appearance of this new acquisition to the domestic stock in northern Europe may be connected with the Single Grave Complex, and the local wild horses may have been sporadically domesticated at this stage.

Bibliography

Admetz, L., 1925. Kraniologische Untersuchung des Wildrindes von Pamiatkowo. *Arb. d. Lehrkanzel f. Terz. a.d. Hochschule f. Bodenkultur in Wien* (1925).

Admetz, L., 1928. Über neolithische Ziegen des östlichen Mitteleuropas. *Zeitschr. f. Tierzucht u. Züchtungsbiol.* Bd. XII (1928).

Almagro, M., 1955. Excavaciones de 1954 en la 'Caverna dei Pipistrelli'. *Rivista de Studi Ligurii* (1955), 5-31.

Althin, C.-A., 1954. *The Chronology of the Stone Age Settlement of Scania, Sweden*, I, Lund.

Althin, C.-A., 1954. Man and environment. A view of the Mesolithic Material in southern Scandinavia. *Medd. Lunds Univ. Hist. Mus.* (1954), 269-294.

Ambros, C., 1953. Nalez Kostrý Psa z Obdobi volutove keramiky v Hurbanove na Slovensku. *Arch. Roz.* V (1954), 447-450.

Ambros, C., 1958. Kultový zvieraci Hrob z Obdobia Kanelovanej keramiky v Šarovciach. *Arch. Roz.* X (1958), 476.

Amende, E. & Frauendorf, E., 1926. Eine schnurkeramische Wohngrube in der Flur Scheldnitz bei Rositz (Kr. Altenburg). *Jahrb. f. Mitteldeutsch. Vorgesch.* XIV (1926), 27-35.

Amschler, J.W., 1949. Ur- und frühgeschichtliche Haustierfunde aus Österreich. *Arch. Aust.* III (1949), 1-70.

Audras, J.Ph. & Heyard, J., 1955. La Faune des grottes de Saint-Benoît. *Bull. Mus. d'Anthrop. Préh. Monaco* II (1955). 229-242.

Arne, T., 1945. *Excavations at Shah Tepe, Iran.*

Baer, A., 1959. Die Michelsberg-Kultur in der Schweiz. *Mon. z. Ur- u. frühgesch. d. Schweiz*, Bd. XII. Basel, 1959.

Bagge, A. & Kjellmark, K., 1939. *Stenåldersboplatserna vid Siretorp i Blekinge.*

Bailloud, G., *et al.*, 1961. Fond de cabane néolithique danubienne sablière du Petit-Vaux. *Bull. Soc. Préhist. Franç.* LVIII, 5-6 (1961), 480-484.

Banner, J., 1954. Funde der Köröskultur von Hódmezövásárhely-Bodzaspart. *Acta Arch. Hung.* III-IV (1953–54), 1-8.

Banner, J., 1960. The Neolithic settlement of the Kremenyak Hill at Csoka (Čoka). *Acta Arch. Hung.* XII (1960), 1-56.

Baro, N. J., 1881. *Aggtelek.*

Barral, L., 1960. Grotte de la Madeleine (Hérault). *Bull. Mus. d'Anthrop. Préh. Monaco* VII (1960), 5-74.

Barta, J., 1956. Neoliticke Osídlenie Jaskýň pri Poráči na Slovensku. *Arch. Ro*ʒ. VIII (1965), 633-639.

Bate, D. M. A., 1937. See Garrod & Bate (1937).

Bate, D. M. A., 1937. Report on Animal Remains, in: Clifford (1937).

Battaglia, R., 1959. Preistoria del Veneto e della Venezia Giulia. *Bull. di paletnol. it.* (1959), 67-83.

La Baume, W., 1949. Die ältesten europäischen Haustiere. *Verh. d. deutsch. Zool.* Kiel, 1948.

Bayer, J., 1928. Die Ossarner Kultur, eine äneolithische Mischkultur im östlichen Mitteleuropa. *Eiszeit u. Urgeschichte* V (1928), 60-120.

Beck, P., *et al.*, 1930-31. Der neolithische Pfahlbau Thun. *Mitt. Naturf. Ges. Bern* (1930-31).

Becker, A., 1927. Ausgrabungen am Haneklint Gemarkung Athensleben. *Jahrb. f. Mitteldeutsch. Vorgesch.* XV (1927), 43.

Becker, C. J., 1947. Mosefunde Lehar frå yngre Stenålder. *Aarbøger* (1947), 1-318.

Becker, C. J., 1952. Ørnekul paa Nekselø. *Aarbøger* (1952), 60-107.

Becker, C. J., 1954. Stenålderbebyggelsen ved Store Valby i Vestsjælland. *Aarbøger* (1954), 127-197.

Behrens, H., 1952. Wichtige Fund meldungen und Neuererwerbung des Jahres 1951. *Jahrb. f. Mitteldeutsch. Vorgesch.* XXXVI (1952), 283-286.

Behrens, H., 1953. Ein Siedlungs-und Begräbnisplatz der Trichterbecherkultur bei Weissenfels an der Saale. *Jahrb. f. Mitteldeutsch. Vorgesch.* (1953), 67-108.

Behrens, H., 1955. Wichtige Fundmeldungen und Neuererwerbung des Jahres 1953. *Jahrb. f. Mitteldeutsch. Vorgesch.* XXXIX (1955), 194-199.

Behrens, H., 1962. Quellenkritische Bemerkungen zu einigen neolithisch-frühmetallzeitlichen Pferd-Skelettfunden in Europa. *Zeitschr. f. Tierzucht u. Züchtungsbiol.* LXXVI (1962), 2.

Behrens, H., 1964. Die neolithisch-frühmetallzeitlichen Tierskelettfunde der Alten Welt. *Veröffentlichungen des Landesmuseums für Vorgeschichte in Halle*, Heft 19.

Benac, A., 1952. *Prehistorijsko naselje Nebo i problem butmirske Kulture.*

Benac, A., 1961. Studien zur Stein- u. Kupferzeit im Nordwestlichen Balkan. *Ber. Rom. Germ. Komm.* XLII (1961), 1-170.

Benac, A. & Brodar, M., 1958. Crvena Stijena—1956. *Glasnilo Zemaljskog Muʒeja u Sarajevu* N.S. 13 (1958), 1 ff., 29-30.

Benesch, F., 1941. Die Festung Hutberg, eine jung-nordische Mischsiedlung bei Wallendorf.

Berciu, D., *et al.*, 1958. Săpăturile de la Cernavoda. *Mat. si Cercet. Arheol.* VI (1958), 95-105.

Berciu, D., 1961. *Contributii la Problemele Neoliticului in Rumania in Lumina noilor Cercetari.*

Bertsch, K., 1931. Paläobotanische Monographie des Federseerieds. *Bibliotheca Botanica* CIII (1931), 1-126. Stuttgart.

Bertsch, K., 1955. *Früchte u. Samen,* in : Paret (1955).

Bibikova, S. N., 1949. Pre-Tripolyan settlement at Luka-Vrublevetskaia on the Middle Dniestr. *Arch. Pam. Ukr. S.S.R.* 11 (1949), Kiev.

Bibikova, S. N., 1951. Female clay figurines of Early Agricultural Tribes in South-east Europe. *Sov. Arkh.* XV (1951).

Bibikova, V. J., 1953. Fauna rannetripolskogo poseleniia Luka-Vrublevetskaia. *M.I.A.* tom. 38 (1953), 411-458.

Bibikova, V. I., 1963. Izistorii golotsenovoi fauni pozvonočnikh v Vostočnoi Europě. (On the history of the Holocene fauna in east Europe). *Pirodnaya Obstanovka i fauni Prošlovo* I. Institut Zoologii Acad. Sci. Ukr. S.S.R. Kiev (1963), 119-147.

Bichir, Gh. & Dogan, E., 1962. Săpături arheologice la Mindrisca. *Mat. si Cercet. Arheol.* VIII (1962), 291-300.

Birula, A., 1930. Communication préliminaire sur les carnivores quaternaires de la Crimée (in Russian). *Compte rendu de l'Académie des Sciences de l'URSS* (1930), 139-144.

Blanc, J. J., 1953. La Grotte de Terrevaine-La Ciotat. *Bull. Soc. Préhist. Franç.* LIII (1953), 133-151.

Blance, B., 1960. The Origin and Development of the Early Bronze Age in the Iberian Peninsula, Ph.D. (Edinburgh University).

Bocquet, A., 1962. Découverte d'une nouvelle nécropole protohistorique dans la région de Grenobloisse, à Saint-Paul-de-Varces. *Bull. Soc. Préhist. Franç.* LIX, 3-4 (1962), 156-164.

Bodianskii, O., 1949. Neolithic site on the Island of Shulaev. *Arch. Pam. Ukr. SSR* 11 (1949), Kiev.

Boessneck, J., 1955. Zu den Tierknochen aus neolithischen Siedlungen Thessaliens. *Ber. Rom. Germ. Komm.* XXXVI (1955), 1-51.

Boessneck, J., 1956. *Studien an Vor- und frühgeschichtlichen Tierreste Bayerns*: I. Tierknochen aus spätneolitischen Siedlungen Bayerns.

Boessneck, J., 1958. *Studien an vor- und frühgeschichtlichen Tierreste Bayerns*: II. Zur Entwicklung vor- und frühgeschichtlichen Haus- und Wildtiere Bayerns.

Boessneck, J., 1960. Zu den Tierknochenfunden aus der präkeramischen Schicht der Argissa Magula. *Germania* XXXVIII (1960), 336-340.

Boessneck, J., 1962. Die Tierreste aus der Argissa Magula vom präkeramischen Neolitkum bis zur MBA, in: Milojčić (1962).

Bökönyi, S., 1951. Untersuchung der Haustierfunde aus dem Gräberfeld von Alsonmédi. *Acta Arch. Hung.* I (1951), 72-78.

Bökönyi, S., 1954. Eine Pleistozän-Eselart in Neolithikum der Ungarischen Tiefebene. *Acta Arch. Hung.* III-IV (1953-54), 9-21.

Bökönyi, S., 1959. Die frühalluviale Wirbeltierfauna Ungarns. *Acta Arch. Hung.* XI (1959), 39-102.

Bökönyi, S., 1964. A Maroslele-Panai Neolitikus telep gerinces faunája. *Arch. Ért.* XCI (1964), 87-93.

Bökönyi, S. & Kubasiewicz, M., 1961. *Neolithische Tiere Polens u. Ungarns in Ausgrabungen.* Teil I: Das Hausrind.

Böttcher, G., 1963. Eine Siedlung der Linienbandkeramik von Tornau, Kr. Hohenmöslen. *Jahrb. f. Mitteldeutsch. Vorgesch.* XLVII (1963), 121-126.

Bouchud, J., 1955. Deux Espèces rares au Moustérien découvertes au Pech de l'Aze. *Bull. Soc. Préhist. Franç.* LXI, 1-2 (1955), 89-93.

Bouchud, J., 1956a. La Faune épimagdalénienne et romanelloazilienne en Dauphine. *Bull. Mus. d'Anthrop. Préh. Monaco* III (1956), 177.

Bouchud, J., 1956b. La Faune de L'Abri Pagès. *L'Anthrop.* LX, 5-6 (1956), 444-446.

Braidwood, R. J., 1952. *The Near East and the Foundations for Civilisation.*

Braidwood, R. J., 1953a. The earliest village communities of southwestern Asia. *Journ. World History* I (1953), 278.

Braidwood, R. J., *et al.*, 1953b. Did Man once live by beer alone? *Amerc. Anthrop.* IV (1953), 315.

Braidwood, R. J., 1954. Food gathering to food production. *Agric. Hist.* XXVIII, 2 (1954).

Braidwood & Reed, 1957. The Achievement and Early Consequences of Food Production: A Consideration of the Archaeological and Natural Historical Evidence. *Cold Spring Harbor Symposia on Quantitive Biology* XXII (1957), 19. USA.

Braidwood, R. J., 1958a. Near Eastern Prehistory. *Science* CXXVII (1958), 1419-1430.

Braidwood, R. J., 1958b. Über die Anwendung der Radiokarbon-Chronologie für das Verständnis der ersten Dorfkultur-Gemeinschaften in Südwestasien. *Anz. d. phil. hist. Klasse der Österreichischen Akad. d. Wissenschaften* XIX (1958), 249. Wien.

116

Braidwood & Braidwood, 1959. Excavations in the Plain of Antioch. *Oriental Inst. Pub.* LXI (1959). Chicago.

Braidwood, R. J., 1960. Preliminary investigations concerning the Origins of Food Production in Iranian Kurdistan. *Advancement of Science* (1960), 214. London.

Braidwood, R. J., 1961. The Iranian Prehistoric Project 1959–60. *Iranica Antiqua* I (1961).

Braidwood, R. J., 1962. *Further investigations of the Paleo-ecological aspects of the appearance of Food production on the Hilly Flanks of the Fertile Crescent in South western Asia.* Report to The National Science Fdn., USA.

Braidwood, R. J., 1962. The earliest village Communities of South-western Asia reconsidered, in: *Atti del VI Congresso Internazionale delle Scienze Preistoriche e Protostoriche*—I relazioni generali.

Braidwood, R. J. & Howe, B., 1960. *Prehistoric Investigations in Iraqi-Kurdistan.*

Braidwood, R. J., Howe, B. & Negahban, E. O., 1960. Near Eastern Prehistory. *Science* CXXXI (May 1960), 1536-1541.

Braidwood, R. J. & Negahban, E. O., 1960. Near Eastern Prehistory. *Science* (1960), 2.

Braidwood, R. J. & Willey, G. R., 1962. *Courses toward Urban Life.*

Brea, L. B., 1946. *Gli scavi nella caverna delle Arene Candide.*

Brinkmann, A., 1924. Canidenstudien V-VI. *Bergens Mus. Aarbok* (1923–24) Naturr. raekke No. 7.

Broholm, H. C., 1928. Langø fundet. En Boplads frå der Ældre Stenålder paa Fyn. *Aarbøger* (1928), 129-190.

Brønsted, J., 1957. *Danmarks Oldtid i Stenalderen.*

Burnez, A., 1957. La Station du Terrier de Biard. *Bull. Soc. Préhist. Franç.* LIV, 9 (1957), 535-549.

Burnez, Cl. & Case H., 1966. Les Camps Néolithiques des Matignons à Juillac-le-Coq. *Gallia* IX (1966), 131-245.

Burchardówna, H., 1952. Rosliny upraune u pradziejach Polski. *Prze. Arch.* IX (1952), 153-176.

Buschan, G., 1895. *Vorgeschichtliche Botanik der Kulturpflanzen der alten Zeit auf Grunde prähistorischer Funde* (Breslau).

Butschkow, H., 1935. Die bandkeramiken Stilarten Mitteldeutschlands. *Jahrb. f. Mitteldeutsch. Vorgesch.* XXIII (1933), 1-218.

Buttler, W. & Haberey, W., 1936. *Die bandkeramische Ansiedlung bei Köln-Lindenthal.*

Calzoni, U., 1939. Un fondo di capanna scoperta presso Norcia (Umbria). *Bull. di paletnol. it.* III (1939), 37-50.

Cannarella, D., 1961. Relazione preliminare sullo scavo della

Grotta Azzurra di Samatorza (Trieste). *Bull. di paletnol. it.* XIII (1961), 213.

Case, H. J., 1956. The Neolithic Causewayed Camp of Abingdon, Berks. *Ant. Journ.* XXXVI (1956), 11-30.

Cayeux, L., 1960. Note sur un ancien habitat néolithique occidental à la limite des anciens marais du Havre. *Bull. Soc. Préhist. Franç.* LVII, 9-10 (1960), 553-556.

Cayeux, L., 1962. Habitat néolithique dans les tourbes du sous-sol du Havre. *Bull. Soc. Préhist. Franç.* LIX, 7-8 (1962), 548-557.

Chernuch, E. K., 1962. Neolit i Eneolit y uga jevropyerjiskoyi chasti SSSR. *M.I.A.* CII (1962).

Childe, V. G., 1931. Final Report on the Operations at Skara Brae. *Proc. Soc. Antiq. Scot.* LXV (1930–31), 27-77.

Childe, V. G., 1957. *The Dawn of European Civilisation* (6th Edition).

Clark, J. G. D., 1936. *The mesolithic settlement of north Europe.*

Clark, J. G. D., 1954. *Excavations at Star Carr.*

Clark, J. G. D., 1958. Blade and Trapeze Industries of the European Stone Age. *Proc. Prehist. Soc.* XXIV (1958), 24-42.

Clark, J. G. D. & Godwin, H., 1962. The Neolithic in the Cambridgeshire Fens. *Antiq.* XXXVI (1962), 10-23.

Clason, A. T., 1964. The animal remains and implements of bone and red deer antler from Niederwil. 2nd Atlantic Collegium Gröningen (April 1964).

Clason, A. T., 1967. Animal and Man in Holland's Past. *Palaeohistoria* XII A & B (1967), 1-246, 1-190.

Clifford, E. M., 1937. *Notgrove Long Barrow, Gloucestershire.*

Clutton-Brock, J., 1962. Near Eastern Canids and the affinities of the Natufian Dogs. *Zeitschr. f. Tierzucht u. Züchtungsbiol.* Band 76, Heft 2-3.

Colle, J. R., 1959. Sondage dans la fosse du camp néolithique de la Garde de Barzan (Charente-Maritime). *Bull. Soc. Préhist. Franç.* LVI, 1-2 (1959), 38-40.

Colle, J. R., 1962. Un Fond de cabane 'peu-richardien' à Barzan. *Bull. Soc. Préhist. Franç.* LIX, 1-2 (1962), 42-44.

Comsa, E., 1959. Săpăturile de la Dudeşti. *Mat. si Cercet. Arheol.* V (1959), 91.

Comsa, E., 1962a. Săpături arheologice le Luncaviţa. *Mat. si Cercet. Arheol.* VIII (1962), 221-226.

Comsa, E., *et. al.*, 1962b. Săpături arheologice la Techirghiol. *Mat. si Cercet. Arheol.* VIII (1962), 165-175.

Comsa, E., 1962c. Săpături arheologice la Boian-Varaste. *Mat. si Cercet. Arheol.* VIII (1962), 205-212.

Constantini, E., 1953. Mobilier funéraire de dolmens de la région des 'Grands Causses'. *Geneva* (1953), 85-99.

Constantini G., 1957. L'Ossuaire du Monna. *Bull. Soc. Préhist. Franç.* LIV, 5-6 (1957), 257-271.

Constantini, G., 1958. Dolmen du Mas Rougous. *Bull. Soc. Préhist. Franç.* LV, 11-12 (1958), 695.

Coon, C.S., 1951. Cave explorations in Iran 1949. Pennsylvania Univ. Mus. Mon.

Coquillat, M., 1956. Baumes-Sourde; Trou Arnaud, Aubenas. *Cahiers rhodaniens III* (1956) *Inst. Intern. d'Études Ligures*.

Coulonges, L., 1935. Les Gisements préhistoriques de Sauveterre-la-Lemance. *Arch. Inst. pal. hum.* XIV (1935), 1-54.

Čović, B., 1960–61. Rezultati Sondiranja na preistoriskom naselju u Gornjoj Tuzli. *Glasnik Zemaljskog Muzeja u Sarajevu*, N.S. XV (1960–61), 79 ff.

Crawford, O.G.S., 1925. *The Long Barrows of the Cotswolds*.

Cunnington, M., 1929. *Woodhenge*.

Cunnington, M., 1931. The 'Sanctuary' on Overton Hill near Avebury. *Wilts. Arch. Mag.* XLV (1931), 300-335.

Curwen, E., 1931. Excavations in the Trundle, 1930. *Sussex Arch. Coll.* LXXII (1931), 100-149.

Dahr, E., 1936. Studien über Hunde aus primitiven Steinzeit-kulturen in Nordeuropa. *Lunds Univ. Årsskrift*, N.F. Aud. 2, Bd. XXXII (1936).

Dahr, E., 1943. Skelettreste von zahmen Hunden auf dem Västerbjers Wohnplatz, in: Stenberger (1943).

Danylenko, V.M., 1950. Do pitannia pro rannii neolit piudennoi Naddniprianshschini. *Arkheologiia* tom. III (1950), 119-151.

David, A.I., & Markevič, V.I., 1967. Fauna Mlekopitayuščikh poceleniya Noviye Ruşeşti I. (The fauna of Herbivores from the settlement of Novi Ruşeşti I). *Isvestia Acedemii Nauk Moldavskoi S.S.R.* IV (1967), 3-25.

Degerbøl, M., 1927. Über prähistorische dänische Hunde. *Vidensk. Medd. frå Dansk. nat. Foren.* LXXXIV (1927).

Degerbøl, M., 1928. Mindre Bidrag til Danmarks forhistoriske Dyreberden II—Sind andere Haustiere als der Hund aus der älteren Steinzeit (Campignien) Danemarks gefunden worden? *Vidensk. Medd. frå Dansk nat. Foren.* LXXXVI (1928).

Degerbøl, M., 1939. Dyreknogler, in: Mathiassen *et al.* (1939). 99 pp.

Degerbøl, M., 1942. Et Knoglemateriale frå Dyrholm-Bopladsen en Ældre Stenalder-Kokkenmødding, in: Mathiassen (1942).

Degerbøl, M., 1943. Om Dyrelivet i Aamosen ved undlöse paa sjælland i stenålderen. *Nord. Fortidsmind* III, H.3 (1943), 165-204.

Degerbøl, M., 1961. On a find of a Preboreal domestic dog (*Canis familiaris L.*) from Star Carr, Yorkshire, with remarks on other Mesolithic dogs. *Proc. Prehist. Soc.* XXVII (1961), 35-55.

Dehn, W. & Sangmeister, E., 1954. Die Steinzeit in Ries. *Mat. z. bayer. Vorgesch.* III (1954).

Dikaios, P., 1953. *Khirokitia.*

Dimbleby, G. W., 1952. The historical status of Moorland in N.E. Yorkshire. *The New Phytologist* LI (1952).

Dimbleby, G.W., 1954. Pollen Analysis as an aid to the dating of prehistoric monuments. *Proc. Prehist. Soc.* XX (1954), 231-236.

Dimbleby, G.W., 1961. The Ancient Forest of Blackamore. *Antiq.* XXXV (1961), 123-128.

Dinu, M., 1959. Santierul arheologice de la Valea Lupului. *Mat. si Cercet. Arheol.* V (1959), 247.

Dmitrieva, E. L., 1960. Fauna Krimskikh stoyanok Zamil Koba II n Tash-Ayir I. (The fauna of the Crimean sites Zamil Koba II and Tash Ayir I). *Materiale* XCI (1960), 166-187.

Dobrovolskii, A., 1949. Vosma Igrenska neolitichna stoianka. *Ark. Pam. URSR*, tom. II (1949), 243-251.

Dombay, J., 1960. Die Siedlung und das Gräberfeld in Zengövarkony. *Arch. Hung.* XXXVII (1960).

Ducos, P., 1957. Étude de la faune du gisement néolithique de Roucadour (Lot). *Bull. Mus. d'Anthrop. Préh. Monaco* IV (1957), 165-188.

Ducos, P., 1958. Le Gisement de Châteauneuf-Les-Martigues—les mammifères et les problèmes de domestication. *Bull. Mus. d'Anthrop. Préh. Monaco* V (1958).

Duerst, J., 1904. Über ein neues prähistorisches Hausschaf (*Ovis aries studeri*) und dessen Herkunft. *Viertelj. Naturf. Ges. Zürich* XLIX, 17 (1904).

Dumitrescu, V., 1954. Hăbășești. *Monographie Arheologica* (Acad. Repub. Pop. Romine, Bucuresti) (1954).

Durand-Tullon, A. & Poulain-Josien, T., 1958. Le Dolmen à couloir du 'Sotch de la Gardie'. *Bull. Soc. Préhist. Franç.* LV (1958), 497-506.

Durno, S.E., 1965. Pollen Analytical Evidence for 'Landnam' from Two Scottish Sites. *Trans. Bot. Soc. Edinb.* XL, 1 (1965), 13-19.

Džambzov, N., 1963. Lovéc Cave. *Izvestia I.A.I.* XXVI (1963), 236-238.

Ehrlich, B., 1934. Ein jungsteinzeitliches Dorf der Schnurkerami-ker in Succase, Kr. Elbing. *Altschlesien* v (1934), 60-66.
Ehrlich, R., 1956. Homolka: a neolithic fortified village in Bohemia. *Archaeology* ix (1956), 233.
Escalon de Fonton, M., 1956. Préhistoire de la Basse-Provence. *Préhist.* xii (1956), 1-148.

Fægri, K., 1944. On the introduction of agriculture in Western Norway. *Geol. Foren. Forh.* Bd. 66 (1944), Stockholm.
Ficatier, A., 1885. Mémoire sur de nouvelles fouilles entreprises dans la grotte de Nermont. *Ass. Franç. Adv. Sciences*, Grenoble (1885), 506-508.
Florin, S., 1958. *Vrå kulturen (K.V.H.A.)*.
Forrer, R., 1908. *Urgeschichte des Europäers*.
Forssander, J. E., 1941. Den sydsvenska bopladskulturen. *Medd. Lunds Univ. Hist. Mus.* iii (1941), 128-152.
Fournier, M., 1901. Recherches sur la préhistoire de la Basse-Provence. *Ann. de la Faculté des Sciences de Marseille* xi (1901), 165.
Fraser, F. C. & King, J. E., 1950. Second Interim Report on the Animal Remains from Star Carr, Seamer. *Proc. Prehist. Soc.* xvi (1950), 124-129.
Frickhinger, E., 1932. Spiralkeramische Siedlung bei Herkheim. *Germania* xvi (1932), 187-190.
Frickhinger, E., 1934. Spiralkeramische Siedlung bei Nähermem-mingen. *Germania* xviii (1934), 252-257.
Frödin, O., 1906. En svensk kjokkenmödding. *Ymer* H.1 (1906), 17-35.
Frödin, O., 1910. Ein schwedischer Pfahlbau aus der Steinzeit. *Mannus* ii (1910).

Gaál, I., 1931. A Hódmezövásárhely i Neolitkori Telep Gerinces Maradvanyai. *Annales Historico-Naturales Musei Nationalis Hungarici* xxvii (1930–31).
Gabalowna, L., 1958. Pochowki bydlece kultury amfor kulistych ze stanowiska 4 w Brzesciu Kujawskum w swietie podobnych znalezisk kultur srodkowoeuropejskich. *Prace i Materialy Muzeum Kodzkiego* iv (1958).
Galan, Abbé A. & Arnal, J., 1956. De l'Argenteuillien à la Perte du Cros, Saillac (Lot). *Bull. Soc. Préhist. Franç.* liii (1956), 255-261.
Gandert, O., 1930. Forschungen zur Geschichte des Haushundes. *Mannus-Bibl.* xlvi (1930).
Garašanin, D. A., 1952. *Stačrevačka Kultura*.

Garašanin, M.V., 1958. Neolithikum und Bronzezeit in Serbien und Makedonien. *Ber. Rom. Germ. Komm.* XXXIX (1958), 1 ff.

Garrod, D.A.E., & Bate, C.M.A., 1937. *The Stone Age of Mount Carmel.*

Garstang, J., 1953. *Prehistoric Mersin.*

Gaul, J.H., 1948. *The Neolithic Period in Bulgaria.*

Georgiev, G.I., 1961. Kulturgruppen der Jungsteinzeit und der Kupferzeit in der Ebene von Thrazien, in: *L'Europe à la fin de l'âge de la pierre*—Acad. Tchécoslovaque des Sciences, Prague (1961).

Gersbach, E., Mahling, 1962. Schwörstadt. *Bad. Fundber* XXII (1962), 242.

Ghirshman, R., 1939. *Fouilles de Siyalk I-II.*

Gillot, X., 1907. Note sur les graines trouvées dans les foyers du camp de Chassey (Somme-et-Loire). *Congrès Préh.* (Autun) (1907), 393.

Gimbutas, M., 1956. The Prehistory of Eastern Europe, I. *American School of Prehistoric Research*, Bulletin No. 20 (1956).

Goiran, A., 1889. Flora delle capanne del M. Loffa. *Bull. di paletnol. it.* XV (1889).

Glasbergen, W., *et al.*, 1961. De neolithische Neerzettingen te Vlaardingen (Z.H.). *I.P.P. Univ. Amsterdam, Instituut voor Prae-en Protohistorie* (1961).

Glob, P.V., 1942. Pflüge vom Walle-Typus aus Dänemark. *Acta Arch.* XIII (1942), 258-272.

Glob, P.V., 1954. Plough carvings in the Val Camonica. *Kuml* IV (1954), 15-26.

Godwin, H., 1956. *History of the British Flora.*

Godwin, H. & Tallantine, P.A., 1951. Studies in the Post-glacial History of British Vegetation. *Journal of Ecology* XXXIX (1951).

Godwin, H., Walker, D., Willis, E.H., 1957. Radiocarbon dating and post glacial vegetational history: Scaleby Moss. *Proc. Royal Soc.*, B, CXLVII (1957), 352-366.

Gotze, W., 1936. Jungsteinzeitliche Bestattung von Mutter und Kind mit zwei Rindern bei Beindorf, Kr. Köthen. *Jahrschr. f. sächs.-thür. Ländern* XXIV (1936), 91.

Grigson, C., 1966. The Animal Remains from Fussell's Lodge Long Barrow, in: Ashbee, P. The Fussell's Lodge Long Barrow, Excavations 1957. *Archaeologia* C (1966), 63-73.

Grimes, W.F., 1960. Excavations on Defence Sites 1939–1945. Part I: Mainly Neolithic-Bronze Age.

Grimm, P., 1938. Die Salzmunder-Kultur in Mitteldeutschland. *Jahrb. f. Mitteldeutsch. Vorgesch.* XXIX (1918–38), 1-104.

Groenmen-van Waateringe, W., 1961. Palynologisch onderzoek

van drie laat-neolithische Tumuli te St. Walrick by Overasselt (Gld.). *I.P.P. Univ. Amsterdam, Instituut voor Prae- en Protohistoire* (1961).

Gromova, V., 1940. Beiträge zur Geschichte der Hausziege und der ältesten Haustiere USSR, in: *Problems of Origin and Evolution and Formation of the Races of Domestic Animals* (1940), Moscow.

Gromova, V., 1953. Fauna pozronochnykh Tardenuazkoi stoianki Murzak-Koba u Krymu. *Paleolit i Neolit SSSR* (1953), 489-563.

Grössler, D., 1909. Die Tongefässe der Glockenbeckerkultur und ihre Verbreitung. *Jahrb. f. Mitteldeutsch. Vorgesch.* VIII (1909), 1-86.

Gubitza, K., 1905. Opoljenik. *Arch. Ért.* XXV (1905), 246-247.

Guyan, W., 1942. Mitteilung über eine jungsteinzeitliche Kulturgruppe von der Gruthalde bei Herblingen. *Zeitschr. f. Schweiz. Arch. u. Kunstgesch.* IV, H.2 (1942), 65.

Guyan, W., 1955. Das jungsteinzeitliche Moordorf von Thayngen-Weiher, in: *Das Pfahlbauproblem.*

Guyan, W., 1957. Weiher bei Thayngen. *Ur-Schweiz* XXI (1957), No. 2.

Hafsten, U., 1960. Pollen analytical investigations on history of agriculture in Oslo and Mjøsa regions. *Viking* XXIV (1960), 1-42.

Hančar, F., 1956. Das Pferd in prähistorischer und früherhistorischer Zeit. *Wiener Beiträge zur Kulturgeschichte und Linguistik* IX (1956).

Hartuchi, N., 1957. Săpăturile de la Brailita. *Mat. si Cercet. Arheol.* III (1957), 129.

Hauck, E., 1944. Die Hunde der ur- und frühgeschichtlichen Bewohner Niederdonaus. *Niederdonau Natur und Kultur* XXVII (1944).

Hauck, E., 1950. Abstammung, Ur- und Frühgeschichte des Haushundes. *Prähistorische Forschungen:* herausgegeben von Anthrop. Ges. Wien. H.1 (1950).

Häusler, A., 1959. Fragen der ältesten Landwirtschaft in Osteuropa. *Wiss. Zeitschr. Martin Luther Univ. Halle-Wittenberg* VIII, 4/5, (1959), 755.

Heer, O., 1865. Die Pflanzen der Pfahlbauten. *Mitt. Antiq. Ges. Zürich* (1865).

Helbaek, H., 1952. Early crops in Southern England. *Proc. Prehist. Soc.* XVIII (1952), 194-233.

Helbaek, H., 1954. *Store Valby—Kornavl i Danmarks Første neolitiske Fase.*

Helbaek, H., 1954. Prehistoric food plants and weeds in Denmark. *Danmarks Geol. Undersøgelse* (1954).

Helbaek, H., 1959a. Notes on the Evolution and History of *Linum*. *Kuml* (1959), 103-141.

Helbaek, H., 1959b. Domestication of Food Plants in the Old World. *Science* cxxx, 3372 (Aug. 1959), 365-373.

Helbaek, H., 1960. Paleoethnobotany of the Near East and Europe, in: Braidwood & Howe, 1960.

Helbaek, H., 1966. Commentary on the Phylogenesis of *Triticum* and *Hordeum*. *Economic Botany* xx, No. 4 Oct.-Dec. (1966), 350-360.

Heller, F., 1955. Fauneninhalt und Schichten der Jungfernhöhle. *Münchner Beiträge* v (1955), 52 ff.

Henrici, P., 1935. Benfyd från boplatsen på Rotekarrslid. *Göteborgs och Bohuslans Forminnes-forenings Tidskrift* (1935), 38-42.

Henrici, P., 1936. Benfyd från boplatsen vid Rörvik. *Göteborgs och Bohuslans Forminnes-forenings Tidskrift* (1936), 82-91.

Henshall, A.S., 1963. *The Chambered Tombs of Scotland* (Vol. I).

Hescheler, K., 1920. Beiträge zur Kenntnis der Pfahlbautenfauna des Neolithikums (die Fauna vom Wauwilersee). *Vierteljahrschr. Naturf. Ges. Zürich* lxv (1920).

Hescheler, K. & Rüeger, J., 1939. Die Wirbeltierreste aus dem neolithischen Pfahlbaudorf Egolzwil 2 nach den Grabungen von 1932-34. *Vierteljahrschr. Naturf. Ges. Zürich* lxxxiv (1939).

Hescheler, K. & Rüeger, J., 1940. Die Wirbeltierreste aus den Pfahlbauten des Baldeggersees nach den Grabungen von 1938 and 1939. *Vierteljahrschr. Naturf. Ges. Zürich* lxxxv (1940).

Hescheler, K. & Rüeger, J., 1942. Die Reste der Haustiere aus den neolithischen Pfahlbaudörfern Egolzwil 2 (Wauwilersee) und Seematte-Gelfingen.

Heurtley, W.A., 1939. *Prehistoric Macedonia*.

Hilzheimer, M., 1926. Unser Wissen von der Entwicklung der Haustierwelt Mitteleuropas. *Ber. Rom. Germ. Komm.* xvii (1925-26), 47-85.

Hjelmqvist, H., 1952. Några sädeskornsavtryck fran Sydsveriges Stenålder. *Bot. Not.* (1952), 330.

Hjelmqvist, H., 1955. Die älteste Geschichte der Kulturpflanzen in Schweden. *Opera Botanica* 1, 3 (1955).

Hjelmqvist, H., 1958. Cereal impressions from the early neolithic habitation at Vätteryd. *Medd. Lunds Univ. Hist. Mus.* (1958), 103-106.

Hjelmqvist, H., 1962. Getreideabdrücke in der Keramik der schwedisch-norwegischen Streitaxtkultur, in: Malmer (1962).

Hoernes, M., 1903. *Der diluviale Mensch in Europa.*

Hofmann, E., 1924. Pflanzenreste der Mondseer Pfahlbauten. *Sitz.-Ber. Acad. Wien* CXXXIII, Abt. I (1924), 379-409.

Hofmann, W., 1951. Vorgeschichtliche Neufunde im Lande Sachsen-Anhalt. *Jahrb. f. Mitteldeutsch. Vorgesch.* XXXV (1951), 215-219.

Hopf, M., 1957. Botanik und Vorgeschichte. *Jahrb. R.G. Zentralmus. Mainz* IV (1957), 1-22.

Hopf, M., 1958. Neolithische Getreidefunde aus Bosnien und Herzegowina. *Glasnik Zemaljskog Muzeja u. Sarajevu,* N.S. 13 (1958), 97-98.

Hopf, M., 1958. Kleinbardorf. *Bay. Vorgesch.* XXIII (1958), 142.

Hopf, M., 1962. Bericht über die Untersuchung von Samen- und Holzkohlenresten von der Argissa Magula aus den präkeramischen bis mittelbronzezeitlichen Schichten, in: Milojčić (1962).

Hopf, M. & Schubart, H., 1965. Getreidefunde aus der Coveta del Or (Prov. Alicant). *Madrider Mitteilungen* VI (1965), 20-38.

Hoyer, H., 1927. Kości Zwierzece wykopane z Ziemianek w Nowy Darominie. *Prze. Arch.* III (1927), 152-155.

Hoyer, H., 1927. Kości zwierzece wykopane z Ziemianek w Nowym Darominie. *Spraw. Arch.* XXXI (1927).

Hue, E., 1906–07. Canis Girardoti des palafittes de Chalain (Jura). *Congrès Préh. de France* (Autun) (1906–07), 399.

Hue, E., 1909. Les Canides des palafittes du Jura français. *V Congrès Préh. de France* (Beauvais) (1909), 463-543.

Iaworsky, C., 1960. La Grotte Pertus II à Méailles (B.-A.). *Bull. Mus. d'Anthrop. Préh. Monaco* VII (1960), 81-152.

Iversen, J., 1941. *Landnam i Danmarks Stenalder—En pollenanalytist Undersøgelse over det første Landbrugs Indvirkning paa Vegetationsudviklingen.*

Iversen, J., 1944. *Viscum, Hedera* and *Ilex* as climatic indicators. *Geol. Foren. Forh.* LX, H.3 (1944).

Iversen, J., 1946. The influence of prehistoric man on Vegetation. *Danmarks Geol. Undersøgelse* IV, Bd. 3, No. 6 (1946).

Jackson, J.W., 1934. Prehistoric domestic animals. *Proc. first int. congr. Preh. Protohist. Sci.* London (1934).

Jackson, J.W., 1943. Animal bones, in: Wheeler, *Maiden Castle.*

Järbe, B., 1950. An inhumation burial from The Stone Cist Period at Kiaby. *Medd. Lunds Univ. Hist. Mus.* (1950), 1-26.

Jaworski, Z., 1938. Czaszki świn z osady Młodszej Epoki Kamiennej we wsi Złota. *Wiadomosci Arch.* xv (1938), 187-201.

Jessen, K., 1939. Kornfund. En yngre Stenålders Boplads paa Als. *Aarbørger* (1939), 65-84.

Jessen, K., 1951. Studies in late quaternary deposits and flora-history of Ireland. *Proc. Roy. Irish Acad.* LII, B.6 (1951), 85.

Jessen, K. & Helbaek, H., 1944. *Cereals in Great Britain and Ireland in prehistoric and early historic times.*

Jewell, P. A., 1962. Changes in size and type of cattle from Pre-historic to Medieval times in Britain. *Zeitschr. f. Tierzucht u. Züchtungsbiol.* LXXVII, H.2 (1962), 159-167.

Jope, M., 1955. Animal remains and mollusca of northern Ireland studied for quaternary ecological research. *Nuffield Quaternary Research Unit* (1954–55).

Josien, T., 1955. Station lacustre d'Auvernier (Lac de Neuchâtel)—étude de la faune. *Bull. Soc. Préhist. Franç.* LII (1955).

Josien, T., 1956. Étude de la faune de gisements néolithiques (niveau Cortaillod) du canton du Berne. *Arch. Suisses d'Anthrop.* (1956).

Josien, T., 1956. Faune chalcolithique du gisement de Bir es-Safadi à Beersheba (Israel). *Bull. Soc. Préhist. Franç.* LIII (1956), 724-726.

Josien, T., 1957a. Le Gisement chalcolithique d'Anis-2-Hortus à Valflaunes (Hérault). *Bull. Soc. Préhist. Franç.* LIV (1957), 98-100.

Josien, T., 1957b. Fonds de cabanes chalcolithiques de la Bergerie Neuve à Lauret (Hérault). *Bull. Soc. Préhist. Franç.* LIV (1957), 94-97.

Josien, T., 1957c. Comparaison des sites chalcolithiques de la Bergerie Neuve et d'Anis-2-Hortus. *Bull. Soc. Préhist. Franç.* LIV (1957), 101-102.

Josien, T., 1957d. Étude de la faune des stations chalcolithiques de Gimel et de la Paillade. *Bull. Soc. Préhist. Franç.* LIV (1957), 757-762.

Josien, T., 1962. See Poulain-Josien (1962).

Kaszab, Z., 1966. New sighting of Przewalski Horses. *Oryx* VIII, No. 6 (Dec. 1966), 345-347.

Kenyon, K., 1960. *Archaeology in the Holy Land.*

Kilian, L., 1935. *Haffküstenkultur und Ursprung der Balten.*

Kirkbride, D., 1966. Five Seasons at the Pre-Pottery neolithic village of Beidha in Jordan. *Palestine Exploration Quarterly* XCVIII, No. 1 (1966), 8-72.

Kisleghi-Nagy, G., 1911. Az obessenyei östelep. *Arch. Ért.* (1911), 161.

Kjærum, P., 1954. Striber på Kryds og tværs. *Kuml* IV (1954), 18-29.

Klichowska, M., 1959. Odciski ziarn zboz i innych gatunkow traw na wamkach naczyn z neolitycznego stanowiska kultury ceramiki wstegowej w Strzelcach w pow. Mogilenskim. *Fontes Arch. Posnan.* X (1959), 101-105.

Klichowska, M., 1962. Krotkie Doniesienia o wynikach Bádàn occiskow Roślinnych na Ceramice i polepie z kilku stanowisk neolitycznych. *Spraw. P.M.A.* XI (1962).

Korosec, J., 1958. *Neolitska naseobina u Danilu Bitinju.*

Kostrzewski, J., 1929. Nouvelles Fouilles et découvertes en Pomeranie polonaise. *Revue Anthrop.* XXXIX, Nos. 10-12 (1929), 388-390.

Kowalczyk, J., 1953. Dwa groby kultury amfor kulistych z Lasu Stockiego i Stoku, pow. Puławy. *Spraw. P.M.A.* tom. V, 1-2 (1953), 38-48.

Krysiak, K., 1950. Szczatki zwierzece z osady neolitycznej w Ćmielowie. *Wiadomosci Arch.* XVII (1950), 165-228.

Krysiak, K., 1951/52. Szczatki zwierzece z osady neolitycznej w Ćmielowie. *Wiadomosci Arch.* XVIII (1951−52), 251-290.

Krysiak, K., 1956. Material zwierzece z osady neolitycznej w Grodku Nadbuzny. *Wiadomosci Arch.* XXIII (1956), 49-60.

Krysiak, K., 1957. Material zwierzece z osady neolityczney w Klementowice pow. Puławy. *Materialy Starozytne* II (1957), 203-206.

Krysiak, K., 1959. Material zwierzecy z wykopalisk w Strzekach w pow. mogilenskim. *Fontes Arch. Posnan.* X (1959), 96-99.

Kubasiewicz, M., 1958. Szczatki zwierzece ze stanowiska neolitycznego w Ustowie, pow. Szczecin. *Mat. Zach. Pom. B.* IV (1958).

Kuhn, E., 1932. Beiträge zur Kenntnis der Säugetierfauna der Schweiz seit dem Neolithikum. *Rev. Suisse de Zool.* (1932).

Kuhn, E., 1935. Die Fauna des Pfahlbaues Obermeilen am Zürichsee. *Vierteljahrschr. Naturf. Ges. Zürich* (1935).

Kuhn, E., 1942. In Guyan (1942).

Kühn, F., 1960. Nálezy obilnin z pravekzch Vzzkumu. *Arch. Roz.* XII (1960), 701-708.

Kulczycka, A., 1961. Materialy Kultury Starzej Ceramiki wstegowej z Zofipola, pow. Preszowice. *Materialy Arch.* III (1961), 19-28.

Kunkel, O., 1955. Die Jungfernhöhle bei Tiefenliern. *Münchner Beiträge* V (1955).

Kutzian, I., 1947. The Körös Culture. *Diss-Pan.* Ser. 11, 23 (1947).

Lacam, R., *et al.*, 1944. Le Gisement mésolithique du Cuzoul de Gramat. *Arch. Inst. de pal. hum. Mém.* XXI (1944), 1-90, Paris.

Lahodovska, O.F., 1952. A preliminary report of the Usatovo expedition in 1948. *Arch. Pam. Ukr. SSR* IV (1952) Kiev, 124-130.

Lahodovska, O.F., 1956. Late Tripolyan Settlement at Sandraki. *Arch. Pam. Ukr. SSR* VI (1956), Kiev.

Lantier, R., 1930. Ausgrabungen und neue Funde in Frankreich aus der Zeit von 1915 bis 1930. *Ber. Rom. Germ. Komm.* XX (1930), 77-147.

Liddell, D.M., 1931–35. Report on the Excavations at Hamburg Fort, Devon. *Proc. Devon Arch. Expl. Soc.* I (1931), 90-120, 162-190; II (1933–36), 135-175.

Lidén, O., 1940. *Sydsvensk Stenålder—Strandboplatserna i Jonstorp.*

Linder, H., 1961. Die altsteinzeitlichen Kulturen der Räuber-Höhle am Schelmengraben bei Sinzing. *Mat. z. bayer. Vorgesch.* XVI (1961).

Lundholm, B., 1949. Abstammung und Domestication des Hauspferdes. *Zoologista Bidrag fran Uppsala* XXVII (1949), 1-289.

Luttschwager, J., 1954. Studien in vorgeschichtlichen Wirbeltieren Schleswig-Holsteins. *Schr. Naturwiss. Verein Schleswig-Holstein* XXVII, H. 1 (1954), 22-33.

Macrea, M., 1958. Santierul arheologic Caşolţ-Boiţa *Mat. si Cercet. Arheol.* IV (1958), 407.

Makarevych, M.L., 1952. Tripolyan settlements near the village of Pavloc. *Arch. Pam. Ukr. SSR.* IV (1952), Kiev.

Makarevych, M.L., 1956. See Mdanylenko & Makarevych (1956).

Malavolti, F., 1952. Ricerche di preistoria emiliana: scavi nella stazione neo-eneolitica del Pescale (Modena). *Bull. di paletnol. It.* N.S. VIII, 4 (1951–52), 13.

Mallowan, M.E.L., & Rose, J.E., 1935. Excavations at Tell Arpachiyah, 1933. *Iraq* II (1935), 1-178.

Malmer, M.P., 1962. Jungneolithische Studien. *Acta Arch. Lund.* VIII, 2 (1962).

Marton, F. & Roska, 1941. *Die Sammlung Zsófia von Torma.*

Masson, V.M., 1961. The First Farmers in Turkmenia. *Antiq.* XXXV (1961), 203-213.

Masson, V.M., 1962. The neolithic farmers of Central Asia. VI Internat. Cong. of preh. & protoh. Sciences, Moscow 1962.

Mateescu, C.N., 1957. Săpături arheologice la Crusovu. *Mat. si Cercet. Arheol.* IV (1957), 103.

Mateescu, C.N., 1958. Săpături arheologice la Vădastra. *Mat. si Cercet. Arheol.* vi (1958), 107.

Mateescu, C.N., 1962. Săpături arheologice la Vădastra. *Mat. si Cercet. Arheol.* viii (1962), 187.

Mathiassen, T., *et al.*, 1939. Bundsø—En ygre stenalders boplads paa Als. *Aarbøger* (1939), 1-198.

Mathiassen, T., 1940. Havnelev—Strandegaard. Et Bidrag til Diskussionen em den yngre stenalders Begyndelse i Danmark. *Aarbøger* (1940), 1-82.

Mathiassen, T., 1942. Dyreholmen. *K.D.V.* 1 (1942).

Mathiassen, T., 1944. The Stone Age Settlement at Trelleborg. *Acta Arch.* xv (1944), 77-98.

Matthias, W., 1953. Zwei schnurkeramische Gräber mit Tierzahnschmuck von Dobris, Kr. Hohenmötsen. *Jahrb. f. Mitteldeutsch. Vorgesch.* xxxvii (1953), 154-160.

Matthias, W., 1956. Ein schnurkeramisches Gräberfeld von Schafstädt. *Jahrb. f. Mitteldeutsch. Vorgesch.* xl (1956), 51-108.

Mdanylenko, V. & Makarevych, M., 1956. Investigations of 1949 of the early Tripolyan settlement at Sabatinovka II. *Arch. Pam. Ukr. SSR* vi (1956), Kiev.

Mellaart, J., 1959. Excavations at Beycesultan—Chalcolithic Sounding. *Anat. Stud.* ix (1959), 38-47.

Mellaart, J., 1962. Excavations at Çatal Hüyük. *Anat. Stud.* xii (1962), 41.

Mertens, R., 1936. Der Hund aus dem Senckenberg-Moor, ein Begleiter des Ur's. *Natur und Volk*, Bd. lxvi (1936), 506. Frankfurt.

Messikommer, H., 1913. *Die Pfahlbauten von Robenhausen.*

Mestorf, J., 1904. Wohnstätten der älteren neolithischen Periode in der Kieler Fohrde. *Ber. d. Schleswig-Holsteinischen Museums vaterländischer Altertümer* xxxi (1904).

Mikov, V. & Dzambov, N., 1960. *Devetaki Cave.*

Millan, G. & Poulain-Josien, T., 1958. Le Dolmen à couloir du Devezas. *Bull. Soc. Préhist. Franç.* lv, 7-8 (1958), 412-421.

Millotte, J.P., 1956. Quelques Précisions sur le camp du Mont Vaudois près d'Héricourt. *Bull. Soc. Préhist. Franç.* liii, 11-12 (1956), 687-691.

Milojčić, V., 1960. Präkeramisches Neolithikum auf der Balkanhalbinsel. *Germania* xxxviii (1960), 320-336.

Milojčić, V., 1962. *Die Deutschen Ausgrabungen auf der Argissa Magula in Thessalien I.*

Mitchell, G.F., 1947. An early kitchen midden in County Louth. *J. County Louth Arch. Soc.* xi, 3 (1947).

Mitchell, G.F., 1954. A pollen diagram from Lough Gur, Co. Limerick. *Proc. Roy. Irish Acad.* LVI C (1954), 481-488.

Mitchell, G.F., 1956. An early kitchen midden at Sutton, Co. Dublin. *Jour. Roy. Soc. Ant. Ireland* LXXXVI (1956), 1-26.

Mitchell, G.F., 1965. Littleton Bog, Tipperary: An Irish Vegetational Record. Geological Soc. of America, Inc. Special Paper 84, (1965).

Modderman, P.J.R., 1953. Een neolithische Woonplaats in de Polder Vriesland onder Hekelingen. *Bodemonderzoek Berichten* IV, 2 (1953), 1-26.

Modderman, P.J.R., 1959. Die bandkeramische Siedlung von Sittard. *Palaeohistoria* VI-VII (1958–59).

Møhl, U., 1962. Übersicht über Knochenfunde aus Gräbern der schwedisch-norwegischen Streitaxtkultur, in: Malmer (1962).

Morgan, F. de M., 1959. Excavation of a Long Barrow at Nutbane, Hants. *Proc. Prehist. Soc.* XXV (1959), 15-51.

Morintz, S. & Preda, C., 1959. Săpăturile de la Spantov. *Mat. si Cercet. Arheol.* V (1959).

Morrison, M.E.S., 1959. Evidence and interpretation of landnam in N.E. Ireland. *Bot. Not.* CXII, 2 (1959).

Much, M., 1876. Dritter Bericht über die Pfahlbau-Forschungen im Mondsee (1875–1876). *Mitt. Anthrop. Ges. Wien* VI (1876), 161-194.

Much, M., 1878–79. Über den Ackerbau der Germanen. *Mitt. Anthrop. Ges. Wien* VIII (1878-79), 203-323.

Müller, H.-H., 1961. Möglichkeiten einer kulturgeschichtlichen Auswertung von ur- und frühgeschichtlichen Tierknochen. *Jahrb. f. Mitteldeutsch. Vorgesch.* XLV (1961), 25-34.

Müller, H.-H., 1963. Hornlose Rinder aus der Salzmunder Höhensiedlung von Halle-Mötzlich. *Jahrb. f. Mitteldeutsch. Vorgesch.* XLVII (1963), 149-156.

Müller, H.-H., 1964. Die Haustiere der Mitteldeutschen Bandkeramiker. *Deutsche Akad. der Wiss. zu Berlin*, Band 17 (1964).

Müller, I., 1947. Der pollenanalytische Nachweis der menschlichen Besiedlung im Federsee- und Bodenseegebiet. *Planta* XXXV (1947), 70-87.

Müller-Karpe, M., 1961. Die spätneolithische Siedlung von Pölling. *Mat. z. bayer. Vorgesch.* XVII (1961).

Mylonas, G.E., 1929. *Excavations at Olynthus: The Neolithic Settlement.*

Necrasov, O., et al., 1959a. Săpăturile de la Cernavoda. *Mat. si Cercet. Arheol.* V (1959), 110-114.

Necrasov, O. & Haimovici, S., 1959b. Fauna din complexele Boian de Linga satul Bogata. *Mat. si Cercet. Arheol.* v (1959), 127.

Necrasov, O. & Haimovici, S., 1959c. Nota asupra resturilor de fauna descoperita in 1956 la Traian-Dealul Fintinilor. *Mat. si Cercet. Arheol.* v (1959).

Necrasov, O. & Haimovici, S., 1959d. Étude de la faune de la station néolithique de Tangîru. *Dacia* III (1959), 561.

Necrasov, O. & Haimovici, S., 1962a. Studiul resturilor de fauna descoperite in 1959 la Traian. *Mat. si Cercet. Arheol.* VIII (1962), 261-266.

Necrasov, O. & Haimovici, S., 1962b. Studiul resturilor de fauna neolitica (Cultura Hamangia) descoperite in cursul săpăturilor de la Techirghiol. *Mat. si Cercet. Arheol.* VIII (1962), 175-185.

Nehring, A., 1884. Referat über das sogenannte Torfschwein. *Verh. Berliner Ges. Anthropol. Ethnol. Urgesch.* (1884), 181-188.

Netolitzky, F., 1914. Die Hirse aus antiken Funden. *Sitz.-Ber. Akad. Wien* CXXIII, Abt. 1 (1914), 725-759.

Netolitzky, F., 1930. Unser Wissen von den alten Kulturpflanzen Mitteleuropas. *Ber. Rom. Germ. Komm.* XX (1930), 14-76.

Neustupny, E. & J., 1961. *Czechoslovakia.*

Neuville, R., 1951. Le Paléolithique and le mésolithique du désert de Judée. *Mém. Inst. Paléont. hum. Paris*, Mém. XXIV (1951), 1-264.

Neuweiler, E., 1905 Die prähistorischen Pflanzenreste Mitteleuropas mit besonderer Berücksichtigung der schweizerischen Funde. *Botan. Exkurs. u. pflanzengeogr. Stud. in der Schweiz.* Zürich (1905).

Neuweiler, E., 1924. Die Pflanzenwelt in der jüngeren Stein- und Bronzezeit der Schweiz. *Mitt. d. Antiq. Ges. Zürich* (1924). Pfahlbauten X Bericht.

Neuweiler, E., 1924. Pflanzenreste aus den Pfahlbauten des ehemaligen Wauwilersees. *Naturf. Ges. Luzern.* IX (1924).

Neuweiler, E., 1925. Pflanzenreste aus den Pfahlbauten vom Hauersee, Greifensee und Zürichsee. *Vierteljahrschr. Naturf. Ges. Zürich* (1925).

Neuweiler, E., 1930. Pflanzenfunde aus dem spätneolithischen Pfahlbau am Utoquai Zürich. *Vierteljahrschr. Naturf. Ges. Zürich* LXXV (1930).

Neuweiler, E., 1935. Nachträge urgeschichtlicher Pflanzen. *Vierteljahrschr. Naturf. Ges. Zürich* LXXX (1935), 98-112.

Neuweiler, E., 1946. Nachträge II urgeschichtlicher Pflanzen. *Vierteljahrschr. Naturf. Ges. Zürich* XCI (1946).

Nicolaescu-Plopsor, *et al.*, 1957. Santierul arheologice Baie Herculane. *Mat. si Cercet. Arheol.* III (1957), 51.

Niederlender, A., Lacam, R., & Arnal, J., 1966. Le Gisement
néolithique de Roucadour III, supplément Gallia. *Préhistoire*
(1966).

Niezabitowski, E., 1928. Szczatki zwierzece z osady Neolitycznej
w Rzucewie na Polskiem wybrzezu Baltyku. *Prze. Arch.* IV
(1928), 64-171.

Niklasson, N., 1925. Studien über die Walternienburg-Bernburger
Kultur. *Jahresschr. Vorgesch. sächs.-thür. Länder* XIII (1925),
1-182.

Niklasson, N., 1927. Gräber mit Bandkeramik aus Provinz Sachsen
und aus Thüringen. *Jahrb. f. Mitteldeutsch. Vorgesch.* XV (1927),
1-28.

Niquet, F., 1937. Die Rössener Kultur in Mitteldeutschland.
Jahrb. f. Mitteldeutsch. Vorgesch. XXVI (1937), 1-111.

Nobis, G., 1955. Die Entwicklung der Haustierwelt Nordwest-
und Mitteldeutschlands in ihrer Beziehung zu landschaftlichen
Gegebenheiten. *Pet. Geo. Mitt.* (1955).

Nobis, G., 1961-62. Die Tierreste prähistorischer Siedlungen aus
dem Satrupholmer Moor. *Zeitschr. f. Tierzucht u. Züchtungsbiol.*
LXXVII (1961-62), 1.

Nosek, S., 1956. Stan i Potrzeby Badán w Zakresie neolitu
Matopolski. *Wiad. Arch.* XXIII (1956), 1-22.

Nougier, L.-R., 1954. Les Grandes Civilisations préhistoriques de la
France. *Bull. Soc. Préhist. Franç.* LI, 8 (1954), 76-81, 89-95.

Novotny, B., 1958. Nové Nálezy Kanelováne Keramiky na
Dolnim Pohroni. *Arch. Roz.* X (1958), 605-617.

Nowothing, W., 1937. Zur Jungsteinzeit Mitteldeutschlands.
Jahrb. f. Mitteldeutsch. Vorgesch. XXV (1937), 1-123.

Obermaier, H., 1924. *Fossil Man in Spain.*

Oldfield, F., 1960. Pollen and Spores—The Coastal Mud-Bed at
Mouligna, Bidart, and the Age of the Asturian Industry in the
Pays Basque. *Mus. National d'Hist. Nat.* (1960), Paris.

Oldfield, F., 1963. Pollen-analysis and man's role in the ecological
history of the south-east Lake District. *Geografiska Annaler* XLV,
1 (1963), 23-40.

O'Riordain, S.P., 1954. *Lough Gur Excavations.*

Paaver, K. L., 1965. Formirovanie teriofauny i izmenčivost
mlekopitayuščikh Pribaltiki v Golotsene, (The Formation of
Herbivores in the Baltic during the Holocene period). Inst.
Zoology and Botany Acad. Sci. of Estonia S.S.R. (1965).

Paccard, M., 1952. Le Gisement sauveterrein et néolithique de la grotte d'Unang, Vaucluse. *Bull. Soc. Préhist. Franç.* XLIX (1952), 226-229.

Paccard, M., 1957. L'Abri de l'église. *Bull. Mus. d'Anthrop. Préh. Monaco* IV (1957), 189-208.

Paco, A. do, 1954. Sementes prehistoricas do Castre de Vila Nova de São Pedro. *Academia Portuguesa da historica*, Ser. 11, V (1954), Lisboa.

Paco, A. do, 1957. *Sementes incarbonizadas do 'Baleal' (Peniche)*.

Papadopoulo, D. O., 1934. Das griechische brachycere Rind. *Zeitschr. f. Tierzucht u. Züchtungsbiol.* XXX (1934), 286 ff.

Paret, O., 1924. Eine Schussenrieder Siedlung bei Cannstatt. *Germania* VIII (1924), 60-65.

Paret, O., 1930. Markgröningen. *Fundberichte a. Schwabens* V (1928–30), 17.

Paret, O., 1935. Der steinzeitliche Pfahlbau von Reute OA Waldsee. *Fundberichte a. Schwabens* VIII (1933–35), 39-45.

Paret, O., 1955. *Das Steinzeitdorf Ehrenstein bei Ulm (Donau)*.

Passek, T. S., 1946. Excavations at Tripolye Settlement of Vladimirovka. *Arch. Pam. Ukr. SSR* 11 (1949), Kiev.

Passek, T. S., 1949. Periodizatsiya Tripolskich Posyelyenii. *M.I.A.* X (1949).

Passek, T. S., 1958. Noveye Otkretiya na territorii SSSR i voprose pozdnyenyeoliticheskich kultur dunayisko-dnyestrouskogo mezhdurechya. *Sov. Arkh.* 1 (1958).

Passek, T. S., 1961. Ramiezemlyedyelcheskiye (Tripolckme) Plyemyena Podnestrovya. *M.I.A.* LXXXIV (1961) 1 ff.

Pätzold, J., 1958. Hinweise auf die jungsteinzeitliche Vegetation bei der Untersuchung eines Steingrabes in Döttlingen. *Germania* XXXVI (1958), 169-185.

Paul, I., 1962. Sondajul arheologic de la Ocna Sibiului. *Mat. si Cercet. Arheol.* VIII (1962), 193-203.

Paunescu, A., *et al.*, 1962. Săpăturile din împrejurimile oraşului Giurgui. *Mat. si Cercet. Arheol.* VIII (1962), 127-139.

Peet, T. E., 1909. *The Stone and Bronze Ages in Italy and Sicily*.

Pennington, W., 1964. Pollen analyses from the deposits of 6 upland tarns in the Lake District. *Philosophical Transactions of the Royal Society of London*, Ser. B, Biological Sciences, No. 746, CCXLVI (1964), 205-244.

Pennington, W., 1965. The interpretation of some post-glacial vegetation diversities at different Lake District sites. *Proc. Roy. Soc.*, B, CLXI (1965), 310-323.

Péquart, St.-J., 1926. Un Kjokkenmodding morbihannais: Er Yoh premier outillage en os découverte dans le Morbihan. *Revue Anthrop. Paris* XXXVI (1926), 206-211.

Péquart, M. & St.-J., 1937. Téviec. *Arch. de l'Inst. de Pal. Hum.* XVIII (1937), 1-223. Paris.

Péquart, M. & St.-J., 1941. Nouvelles Fouilles au mas d'Azil (Ariège). *Préhistoire* VIII (1941), 7-42.

Perkins, D., 1960. The faunal remains of Shanidar Cave and Zawi Chemi Shanidar: 1960 season. *Sumer* XVI (1960), 77-78.

Perrault, E., 1870. *Note sur un foyer au camp de Chassey.*

Perrot, J., 1952. Le Néolithique d'Abou Gosh. *Syria* XXIX (1952).

Petrescu-Dimbovita, M. & Florescu, A., 1959. Săpăturile arheologice de la Trusești. *Mat. si Cercet. Arheol.* VI (1959), 147-155.

Petrescu-Dimbovita, M. & Zaharia, E., 1962. Sondajul arheologic de la Danești. *Mat. si Cercet. Arheol.* VIII (1962), 47-58.

Pidoplicko, I.G., 1938–56. *Materiali do vivčeniia minulih faun U.R.S.R.* I, II.

Piggott, S. & Drew, C.M., 1936. Excavations of Long Barrow 163a on Thickthorn Down, Dorset. *Proc. Prehist. Soc.* II (1936), 77-96.

Piggott, S., 1952. The Neolithic Camp on Whitesheet Hill, Kilmington Parish. *Wilts. Arch. Mag.* LIV (1952), 404-410.

Piggott, S., 1954a. Le Néolithique occidental et le chalcolithique en France. *L'Anthrop.* LVII, 5-6 (1953) & LVIII, 1-2 (1954).

Piggott, S., 1954b. *Neolithic Cultures of the British Isles.*

Piggott, S., 1955. Windmill Hill—East or West? *Proc. Prehist. Soc.* XXI (1955), 96-101.

Piggott, S., 1962. *The West Kennet Long Barrow.*

Pigorini, L., 1893. Stazione neolitica di Alba in provincia di Cuneo. *Bull. di paletnol. it.* XIX (1893), 162-168.

Pigorini, L., 1902. Continuazione della civiltà paleolitica nell'età neolitica. *Bull. di paletnol. it.* XXVIII (1902), 158.

Pira, A., 1909. Studien der Geschichte der Schweinerassen. *Zool. Jahrb. Suppl.* X (1909), 233-426.

Pira, A., 1927. On bone deposits in the cave Stora Forvar on island of Stora Karlsö, Sweden. *Acta Zoologica* (1926), 123-217.

Pitt-Rivers, Lieut.-Gen., 1898. *Excavations at Cranborne Chase.* Vol. IV.

Pleiner, R. & Moucha, V., 1958. Hrob Lidu se Šňórovou Keramikou z Lovosic. *Arch. Roz.* X (1958), 172-177.

Pohlhausen, H., 1954. Jäger, Hirten, Bauern in der aralokaspischen Mittelsteinzeit. *Ber. Rom. Germ. Komm.* XXXV (1954), 1-20.

Poulain-Josien, T., 1962. Faune provenant de la grotte de la Trache 2 (Charente). *Bull. Soc. Préhist. Franç.* LIX, 7-8 (1962), 464-473.

Prévost, R., 1958. L'Habitat néolithique de la montagne de Lumbres (Pas-de-Calais). *Bull. Soc. Préhist. Franç.* LV (1958), 162-165.

Priebe, H., 1938. Die Weltgruppe der Kugelamphorae. *Jahrb. f. Mitteldeutsch. Vorgesch.* XXVIII (1938), 1-129.

Pumpelly, R., 1904. *Anau—Explorations in Turkestan, Expedition of 1904.*

Radulesco, C. & Samson, P., 1962. Sur un centre de domestication du mouton dans le mésolithique de la grotte 'La Adam' en Dobrogea. *Zeitschr. f. Tierzucht u. Züchtungsbiol.* LXXVI (1962), 2.

Rataj, J., 1956. Hurbanovo-Bacherov Majer Neolitické Sídliště. *Arch. Roz.* VIII (1956), 311-325.

Ravoux, G., 1962. Une Nouvelle Station de la garrigue Nimose. *Bull. Soc. Préhist. Franç.* LIX, 11-12 (1962), 792-800.

Reed, C. A., 1960. A Review of the Archaeological Evidence on Animal Domestication in the Near East, in: Braidwood & Howe (1960).

Reed, C. A., 1961–62. Osteological evidences for prehistoric domestication in southwestern Asia. *Zeitschr. f. Tierzucht u. Züchtungsbiol.* Band 76, 1 (1961), 31-38.

Regtereb, V. J. F., 1958. Nieuwe opgravingen van de neolithische nederzetting te Zandwerven, gem. Spanbroek. *West-Frieslands oud en nieuw* XXV (1958), 144-159.

Regtereb, J. F. & Bakker, J. A., 1961. De neolithische Woonplaats te Zandwerven. *I.P.P. Univ. Amsterdam, Instituut voor Prae- en Protohistorie* (1961).

Reinerth, H., 1929. *Das Federseemoor als Siedlungsland des Vorzeitmenschen.*

Reinerth, H., 1939. Ein Dorf der Grossteingräberleute. *Germanen-Erbe* IV:VIII (1939).

Rellini, U., 1938. Grotte preistoriche scoperte presso Parrano (Orvieto). *Bull. di paletnol. it.* II (1938), 115-116.

Rellini, U., 1942. Grotte preistoriche nei monti dell'Uccellina e a Massa Marittima. *Bull. di paletnol. it.* V-VI (1941–42), 236.

Renfrew, J. M., 1966. A report on recent finds of carbonised cereal grains and seeds from prehistoric Thessaly. *Thessalika* V (1966), 21-36.

Reverdin, L., 1921a. La Faune néolithique de St. Aubin (Port-Conty). *Schweizerische Naturf. Ges. Verhandlungen* CII (1921).

Reverdin, L., 1921b. La Faune néolithique de la station de St. Aubin (Port-Conty, Lac de Neuchâtel). *Archives Suisses d'Anthrop.* (1921).

Reverdin, L., 1923. Nouvelles Contributions à l'étude de la faune des stations néolithiques lacustres. *Schweizerische Naturf. Ges. Verhandlungen* (1923).

Reverdin, L., 1927. Étude de la faune néolithique du niveau inférieur de St. Aubin. *Schweizerische Naturf. Ges. Verhandlungen* (1927).

Reverdin, L., 1928. Sur la faune du néolithiques ancien et moyen des stations lacustres. *Archives Suisses Anthrop.* (1928).

Reverdin, L., 1930. La Faune néolithique de la station de Port-Conty (St. Aubin) d'après le matériel recueilli de 1928–1930. *Compte rendu des séances de la société de physique et d'histoire naturelles de Genève*, in: *Archives des Sciences physiques et naturelles* (1930), 83-6.

Reverdin, L., 1932a. Sur la faune du kokkenmodding morbihannais Er Yoh et ses rapports avec celles des stations néolithiques lacustres de la Suisse. *Archives Suisses Anthrop.* (1932).

Reverdin, L., 1932b. Sur la faune du néolithique moyen et récent de la station d'Auvernier, Neuchâtel. *Compte rendu des seances de la société de physiques et d'histoire naturelles de Genève*, in: *Archives des Sciences physiques et naturelles* (1932), 101-5.

Richard, C., 1939. Nuovi scavi nella caverna degli 'Armorari' o 'Parmorari' (Borgio-Verezzi). *Bull. di paletnol. it.* III (1939), 11-24.

Ridola, D., 1925. Le grandi trincee preistoriche di Matera. *Bull. di paletnol. it.* XLV (1925), 85-98.

Ritchie, J., 1920. *The influence of man on animal life in Scotland.*

Roche, Abbé J., 1960. *Gisement mésolithique de Moita de Sebastião (Muge).*

Rodden, R. J., 1962. Excavations at the early Neolithic site at Nea Nikomedeia, Greek Macedonia (1961 Season). *Proc. Prehist. Soc.* XXVIII (1962), 267-288.

Rüeger, J., 1944. Die fauna des Pfahlbaues Uerikon am Zürichsee. *Vierteljahrschr. Naturf. Ges. Zürich* LXXXIX (1944).

Rütimeyer, L., 1860–61. *Die fauna der Pfahlbauten in der Schweiz.*

Rydbeck, O., 1938. Fangkultur und Megalithkultur in der süd-skandinavischen Steinzeit. *Medd. Lunds Univ. Hist. Mus.* (1938), 1-145.

Rytz, W., 1930–31. Die pflänzlichen Funde, in: Beck (1930–31).

Rytz, W., 1946. Über die Früchte und Samen aus dem Pfahlbau Burgäschi-Südwest, in: Tschumi (1946).

Salomonsson, B., 1960a. Eine neuentdeckte steinzeitliche Siedlung auf der Bjare-Halbinsel. *Medd. Lunds Univ. Hist. Mus.* (1960), 5-33.

Salomonsson, B., 1960b. Fouilles à Belloy-sur-Somme en 1952 et 1953. *Medd. Lunds Univ. Hist. Mus.* 1959 (1960), 5-109.

Samoilovskii, I.M., 1952. Relics of the Tripolyan culture in Kiev. *Arkheologiia* VI (1952), Kiev.

Sangmeister, E. & Schubart, H., 1965. Grabungen in der kupferzeitlichen Befestigung von Zambujul/Portugal 1964. *Madrider Mitteilungen* VI (1965), 39-63.

Santa-Olalla, J.M., 1946. Cuadernos de historia primitiva—cereales y plantas de la cultura ibero-sahariana en Almizaraque.

Sarauw, G.F.L., 1903. En stenålders Boplads i Maglemose ved Mullerup. *Aarbøger* (1903), 148-315.

Sauer, C.O., 1952. Agricultural Origins and Dispersals. *American Geog. Soc.* I-III (1952), I-110.

Sauter, M.R., 1959. Saint-Léonard, haut lieu de la préhistoire valaisanne. *Ur-Schweiz* XXII (1958), 1.

Sauter, M.R. & Gallay, A., 1960. Les Matériaux néolithiques et protohistoriques de la station de Génissiat (Ain, France). *Geneva* VIII (1960), 63-111.

Sawicki, L., 1920. Groby megalityczne w Potyrach w Pow. Płońskim z Warszawskiej. *Wiad. Arch.* V (1920), 125-141.

Scheitzel, K., 1965. Müddersheim—eine Ansiedlung der jüngeren Bandkeramik im Rheinland. *Fundamenta* I, Köln.

Schenk, A., 1912. *La Suisse préhistorique—le paléolithique et le néolithique.*

Schiemann, E., 1954. Die Pflanzenreste der Rössener Siedlung Ur-Fulerum bei Essen. *Jahrb. R.G. Zentralmus. Mainz* I (1954), 1-14.

Schiemann, E., 1958. Die Pflanzenfunde in den neolithischen Siedlungen Mogetorp O. Vrå und Brokvarn, in: Florin, S. (1958).

Schlosser, M., 1909. Die Bären- oder Tischhoferhöhle im Kaisertal bei Kufstein. *Abh. Bayer. Akad. Wiss.* XXIV (1909), 385.

Schmidt, B., 1956. Die wichtigsten Neufunde des Jahres 1955 aus dem Lande Sachsen-Anhalt. *Jahrb. f. Mitteldeutsch. Vorgesch.* XL (1955), 285-295.

Schmidt, B., 1959. Wichtige Fundmeldungen und Neuererwerbung des Jahres 1956. *Jahrb. f. Mitteldeutsch. Vorgesch.* XLIII (1959), 304-313.

Schmidt, B., 1960. Wichtige Fundmeldungen und Neuererwerbung des Jahres 1957. *Jahrb. f. Mitteldeutsch. Vorgesch.* XLIV (1960), 328-331.

Schmidt, B., 1961. Wichtige Fundmeldungen und Neuererwerbung des Jahres 1958. *Jahrb. f. Mitteldeutsch. Vorgesch.* XLV (1961), 278-286.

137

Schmidt, B., 1962. Wichtige Fundmeldungen und Neuererwerbung des Jahres 1959. *Jahrb. f. Mitteldeutsch. Vorgesch.* XLVI (1962), 351-364.

Schmidt, B., 1963. Wichtige Fundmeldungen und Neuererwerbung des Jahres 1960. *Jahrb. f. Mitteldeutsch. Vorgesch.* XLVII (1963), 401-408.

Schnittger, B., 1910. Die prähistorischen Feuersteingruben und Kulturlagen bei Kvarnby und Sallerup. *Prähist. Zeitsch.* 11 (1910), 163-186.

Schoetensack, O., 1904-08. Beiträge zur Kenntnis der neolithischen fauna Mitteleuropas. *Verh. naturh. med. Ver. Heidelberg.* N.F. 8 (1904-08).

Schwabedissen, H., 1962. Die Anfänge der Haustierhaltung in Schleswig-Holstein im Lichte der Archäologie. *Zeitschr. f. Tierzucht u. Züchtungsbiol.* LXXVII (1962).

Schwarz, K., 1950. Vorgeschichtliche Neufunde im Lande Sachsen-Anhalt 1948-49. *Jahrb. f. Mitteldeutsch. Vorgesch.* XXXIV (1950), 208-218.

Seitz, H. J., 1952. Aislingen. *Bay. Vorgesch.* XVIII-XIX (1951-52), 225.

Seitz, H. J., 1956. Lauingen. *Bay. Vorgesch.* XXI (1956), 156-157.

Seitz, H. J., 1958. Lauingen und Wittislingen. *Bay. Vorgesch.* XXIII (1958), 142, 147-148.

Seitz, H. J. & R. H., 1960. Hausen. *Bay. Vorgesch.* XXV (1960), 225.

Seitz, H. J. & R. H., 1962. Haunsheim. *Bay. Vorgesch.* XXVII (1962), 264-265.

Smith, A. G., 1958. Pollen analytical investigations of the mire at Fallahogy Td., Co. Derby. *Proc. Roy. Irish Acad.* LIX, B (1958), 329.

Smith, A. G., 1961. Cannons Lough, Kilrea, Co. Derby: Stratigraphy & Pollen Analysis. *Proc. Roy. Irish Acad.* LXI, B (1961).

Smith, A. G. & Willis, E. H., 1962. Radiocarbon dating of the Fallahogy Landnam Phase. *Ulster Journal of Archaeology* XXIV-XXV (1961-62), 16-24.

Smith, I. F., 1964. Windmill Hill and its implications. 2nd Atlantic Colloquium Gröningen (April 1964).

Smith, I. F., 1965. *Windmill Hill and Avebury—excavations by A. Keiller 1925-1939.*

Sneidrova, K., 1955. Jama Keramikou Nalevkovitych Pohárů ve Štolmiri. *Arch. Roz.* VII (1955), 20-22.

Soudský, B., 1955. Vyzkum neolitickeho sídlište u Postoloprtech u R. 1952. *Arch. Roz.* VII (1955), 5-11.

Soudský, B., 1962. The Neolithic Site of Bylany. *Antiq.* XXXVI (1962), 190-200.

Sprockhoff, E., 1938. Die nordische Megalithkultur. Handbuch der Urgeschichte Deutschlands III. Globular Amphora Complex (1938), 120-150.

Staffe, A., 1943. Über zwei Funde vorgeschichtlicher Kurzhornrinder in Spanien. *Zeitschr. f. Tierzucht u. Züchtungsbiol.* LIV (1943).

Stampfli, H., 1962. Die Tierreste der neolitischen Siedlung Seeberg/Burgäschissee-Süd. *Zeitschr. f. Tierzucht u. Züchtungsbiol.* LXXVII (1962), 1.

Stefan, G. & Comsa, E., 1957. Săpăturile arheologice de la Aldeni. *Mat. si Cercet. Arheol.* III (1957), 93.

Stehlin, H.G., 1930–31. Animal bones of Thun, in: Beck (1930–31).

Stenberger, M., Dahr, E. & Munthe, H., 1943. *Das Grabfeld von Västerbjers auf Gotland* (K.V.H.A.).

Stieber, A., 1956. Stations néolithiques d'Alsace. *Bull. Soc. Préhist. Franç.* LIII, 11-12 (1956), 750-758.

Stieber, A., 1960. Nouvelle Station néolithique à Pfettisheim. *Bull. Soc. Préhist. Franç.* LVII, 3-4 (1960), 206-208.

Stone, J.F.S., 1935. Some discoveries at Ratfyn, Amesbury. *Wilts. Arch. Mag.* XLVII (1935), 55-67.

Stone, J.F.S., 1958. *Wessex.*

Stone, J.F.S. & Young, W.E.V., 1948. Two pits of grooved Ware date near Woodhenge. *Wilts. Arch. Mag.* LII (1948), 286.

Stone, J.F.S., Piggott, S., & Booth, A.St.J., 1954. Durrington Walls, Wiltshire. *Ant. Journ.* XXXIV (1954), 155-177.

Strobel, P., 1877. Avanzi animali dei fondi di capanne nel Reggiano. *Bull. di paletnol. it.* III (1877), 45-78.

Strobel, P., 1886. Avanzi di vertebrati prehistorici della valle della Vibrata. *Bull. di paletnol. it.* XII (1886), 162-179.

Strobel, P., 1890. Avanzi animali della stazione neolitica di Stentinello (Siracusa). *Bull. di paletnol. it.* XVI (1890), 201-209.

Strobel, P., 1890. Saggio della fauna mammologica delle stazioni prestoriche dei Monti Lessini, Veronesi. *Bull. di paletnol. it.* XVI (1890), 167-175.

Studer, T., 1883–84. Nachtrag zu dem Aufsatz über die Tierwelt in den Pfahlbauten des Bielersees. *Naturf. Ges. in Bern* (1883–84), 1-99.

Studer, T., 1892. Zwei grosse Hunderassen aus der Steinzeit der Pfahlbauten. *Naturf. Ges. in Bern* (1892).

Sudakov, S.A., 1952. Settlement of the Tripolye culture at Semeniv-Zelenche. *Arch. Pam. Ukr. SSR* IV (1952), Kiev.

Sveshnikov, I.K., 1954. Kultura lineino-lentochnoi keramiki na teritorii verkhnego Podnestrovia i zapadnoi Volyni. *Sov. Arkh*, xx (1954), 101-131.

Swiezynski, K., 1958. Analiza Szcsatkow kootnych neolitycznych Grobow zwierzecych a Brzescia Kujawskiego. *Prace i Materialy Muzeum Kodzkiego* iv (1958).

Sydow, & Kimmig, W., 1962. Jechtingen und Leiselheim. *Bad. Fundber*. xxii (1962), 209-210, 212-214.

Tellez, R. & Ciferri, F., 1954. *Trigos arquelógicos de España*.

Teutsch, J., 1903. Die spätneolithischen Ansiedlungen mit bemalter Keramik am oberen Laufe des Albflusses. *Mitt. präh. Kom. Wien* (1903).

Thomsen, T. & Jessen, A., 1906. Brabrand-Fundet frå den ældre Stenålder. *Aarbøger* (1906), 1-74.

Tongiorgi, E., 1956. Osservazioni paleontologiche nella grotta del Mezzogiorno. *Bull. di paletnol. it.* x (1956), 535-540.

Troels-Smith, J., 1944. Fund af Vitis silvestris Pollen i Danmark. *Dansk. Geol. Forening* x, h.4 (1944).

Troels-Smith, J., 1953. Ertebøllekultur—Bondekultur. *Aarbøger* (1953), 5-62.

Troels-Smith, J., 1955. Pollenanalytische Untersuchungen zu einigen schweizerischen Pfahlbauproblem, in: *Das Pfahlbauproblem*.

Troels-Smith, J., 1960. Ivy, mistletoe and elm Climatic Indicators—Fodder Plants. *Dansk. Geol. Undersøgelse* iv (1960).

Trow-Smith, R., 1957. *A History of British Livestock Husbandry to 1700*.

Trump, D.H., 1961. Scavi a la Starza, Ariano Irpino. *Bull. di paletnol. it.* xiii (1961), 223-231.

Tschumi, O., 1946. Das Pfahlbau von Seeberg Burgäschi-Südwest 1945–46. *Bern-Historisches Museum-Jahrbuch* (1946).

Tschumi, O., 1949. *Urgeschichte der Schweiz*.

Tsundas, C., 1899. *Prehistoric Acropolis of Dimini and Sesklo*.

Turner, W., 1895. On human and animal remains found in cavern at Oban, Argyllshire. *Proc. Soc. Ant. Scot.* v (1895), 410-438.

Veyrier, M., 1949. Clansayes préhistorique. Station néolithique du 'Pas-de-Clavel'. *Bull. Soc. Préhist. Franç.* xlvi, 7-8 (1949), 278-295.

Vizdal, J., 1962. Neolitické Hroby z Oborína na Slovensku. *Arch. Roz.* xiv (1962), 605.

Vlček, E., 1953. Hromadné Kostrové Pohřby s Kanelovanou Keramikou v Nitranském Hrádku na Slovensku. *Arch. Roz.* v (1953), 733-736.

Vogel, R., 1933. Tierreste aus vor- und frühgeschichtlichen Siedlungen Schwabens. *Zoologica* LXXXII, Bd. 31 (1933).

Vogel, R., 1935. Die Tierreste aus Reute OA Waldsee. *Fundber. aus Schwabens* VI-VIII (1931–35).

Vogel, R., 1940. Die alluvialen Säugetiere Württembergs. *Jahrh. Ver. vaterl. Naturkunde Württ.* XCVI (1940), 89-112.

Vogel, R., 1955. Die Tierknochen, in: Paret (1955).

Vogt, E., 1951. Das jungsteinzeitliche Uferdorf Egolzwil III. *Zeitschr. f. schweiz. Arch. u. Kunstgesch.* XIII, H.4 (1951).

Vulpe, R., 1957. *Izvoare, Săpăturile din 1936–1948.*

Wace, A. J. B. & Thompson, M. S., 1912. *Prehistoric Thessaly.*

Wahle, E., 1920. Die Besiedlung Südwestdeutschlands in vorrömischer Zeit nach ihren natürlichen Grundlagen. *Ber. Rom. Germ. Komm.* (1920), 1-73.

Waterbolk, H. G. & Zeist, W. van, 1964. Preliminary report on the neolithic settlement of Niederwil. 2nd Atlantic Colloquium Gröningen (April 1964).

Werneck, H., 1949. *Ur- und frühgeschichtliche Kultur und Nutzpflanzen in der Ostalpen und am Rande des Böhmerwaldes.*

Werneck, H., 1961. Ur- und frühgeschichtliche sowie mittelalterliche Kulturpflanzen und Hölzer aus den Ostalpen und dem südlichen Böhmerwald. *Arch. Aust.* XXX (1961).

Werth, E. & Baas, E., 1934. Wie alt sind Viehzucht und Getreidebau in Deutschland? *Natur und Volk* LXIV (1934), 495.

Westerby, E., 1927. *Stenålderbopladser ved Klampenborg, nogle Bidrag tel studiet af den mesolitiske Periode.*

Wheeler, Sir M., 1943. *Maiden Castle.*

Winge, H., 1904. Om jordfundne Pattedyr frå Danmark. *Vidd. Medd. Naturhist. Foren.* (1904).

Winther, J., 1928. *Lindø, en Boplads frå Danmarks yngre Stenalder.*

Winther, J., 1943. *Blandebjerg.*

Wodzicki, K., 1935. Studja nad prehistorycznemi psami Polski. *Wiad. Arch.* XIII (1935), 1-76.

Wymer, J., 1962. Excavations at the Maglemose site at Thatcham, Berks. *Proc. Prehist. Soc.* XXVIII (1962), 329-361.

Zablocki, J. & Zurowski, J., 1932. *Znalezienie zapasów Lithospermum w dwu Stanowiskach Kultury Malopolskiej.*

Zeuner, F.E., 1951–52. Quoyness: Report on a sheep's skull. *Proc. Soc. Antiq. Scot.* LXXXVI (1951–52).

Zeuner, F.E., 1955. The goats of early Jericho. *Palestine Exploration Quarterly* (1955), 70.

Zeuner, F.E., 1958. Dog and Cat in the Neolithic at Jericho. *Palestine Exploration Quarterly* (1958), 52.

Zeuner, F.E., 1963. *A history of domesticated animals.*

Zikmundova, E., 1960–62. Osteological finds from Aneolithic graves at Brandýsek. *Pam. Arch.* LI (1960), 484-488.

Zukovskiy, P.M. *Cultivated Plants and their wild relatives* (Moscow, 1950). Abridged translation by Hudson. Cambridge, 1962.

Key to Histograms

Scale: 0.8 mm. = 1 %

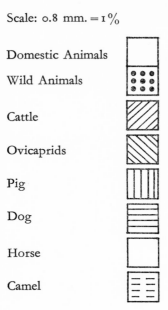

Domestic Animals

Wild Animals

Cattle

Ovicaprids

Pig

Dog

Horse

Camel

The animals are considered in the order listed above throughout, and should any particular species be absent at a site, a gap is left in the appropriate position so that its absence is at once apparent

143

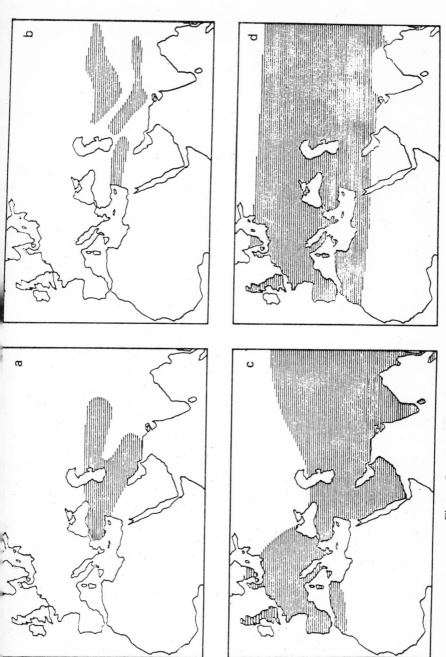

Fig. 1. Generalised distribution of: a, wild goat; b, sheep; c, pig and d, cattle

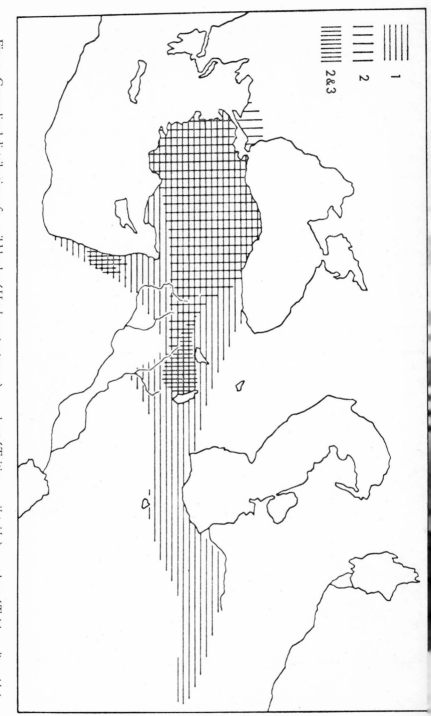

Fig. 2. Generalised distribution of 1, wild barley (*Hordeum spontaneum*); 2, wheat (*Triticum aegilopoides*); 3, wheat (*Triticum dicoccoides*) (after Piggott 1965)

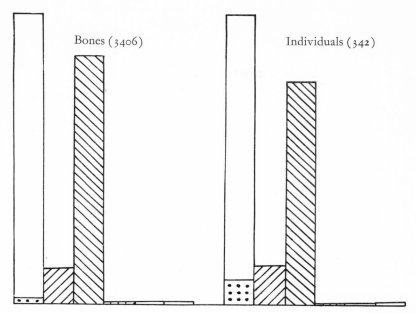

Fig. 3 Bir-es-Safadi (Chalcolithic)

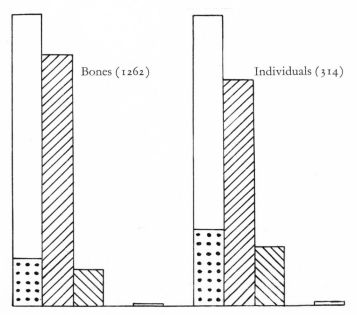

Fig. 4 Kammenaia Mogila (Aceramic)

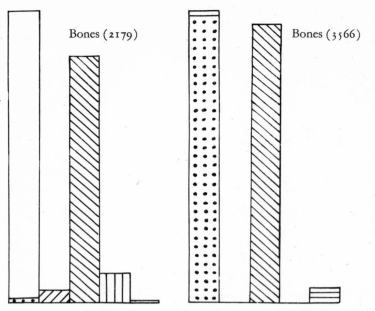

Fig. 5a Argissa (Aceramic) Fig. 5b Châteauneuf-Les-Martigues (Transitional

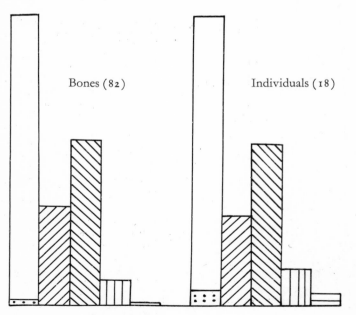

Fig. 6a Otzaki (Proto-Sesklo)

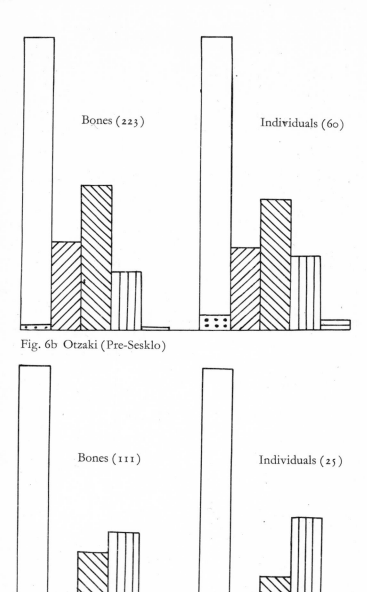

Bones (223)   Individuals (60)

Fig. 6b Otzaki (Pre-Sesklo)

Bones (111)   Individuals (25)

Fig. 6c Otzaki (Early Sesklo)

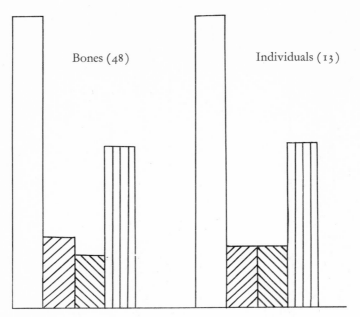

Fig. 6d Otzaki (Late Sesklo)

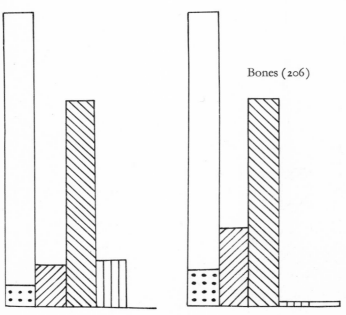

Fig. 7 Nea Nikomedeia

Fig. 8 Maroslele-Pana (Starčevo-Körös)

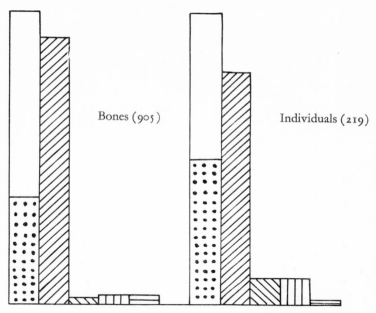

Bones (905)

Individuals (219)

Fig. 9 Lebo (Starčevo-Körös, Linear Pottery, Szilmeg & Tisza)

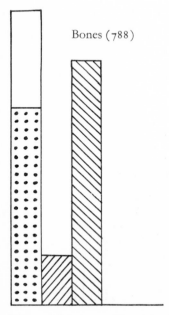

Bones (788)

Fig. 10 Châteauneuf-Les-Martigues (Impressed Ware)

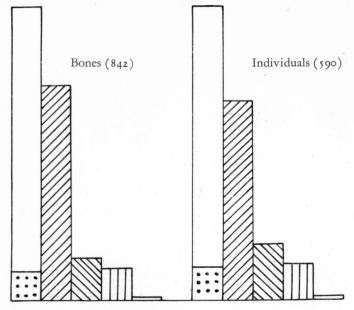

Fig. 11 Györ-Pápai vám (Linear Pottery)

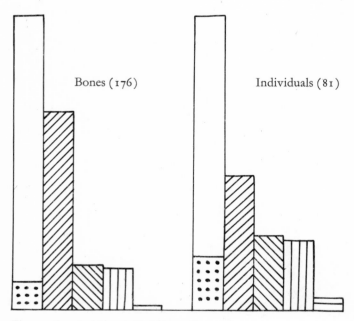

Fig. 12 Pomáz-Zdravlyák (Linear Pottery)

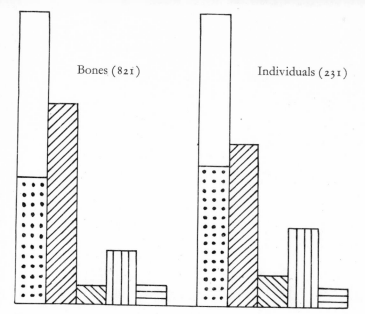

Fig. 13 Szegvár-Tüzköves (Linear Pottery)

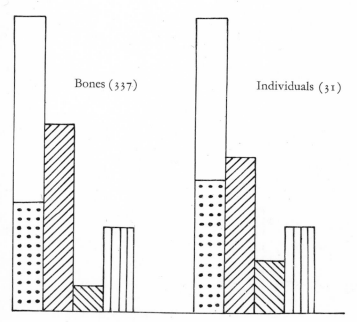

Fig. 14 Traian (Linear Pottery)

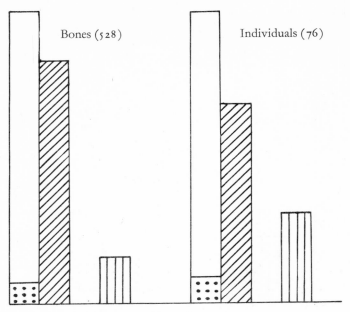

Fig. 15 Florești (1955–58; Linear Pottery)

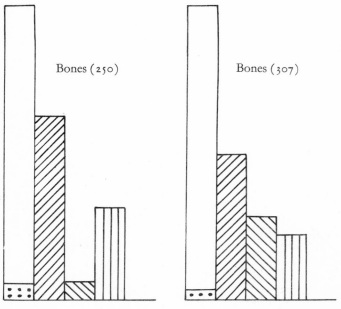

Fig. 16 Florești (houses 1 & 3; Linear Pottery)

Fig. 17 Gatersleben (Linear Pottery)

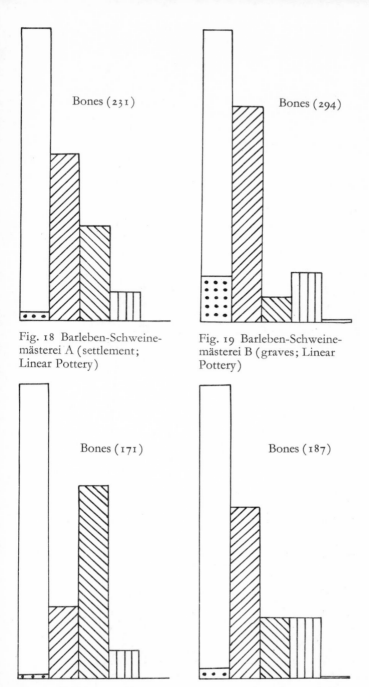

Bones (231)

Fig. 18 Barleben-Schweinemästerei A (settlement;
Linear Pottery)

Bones (294)

Fig. 19 Barleben-Schweinemästerei B (graves; Linear
Pottery)

Bones (171)

Fig. 20 Barleben-Hühner-
farm (Linear Pottery)

Bones (187)

Fig. 21 Bruchstedt (Linear
Pottery)

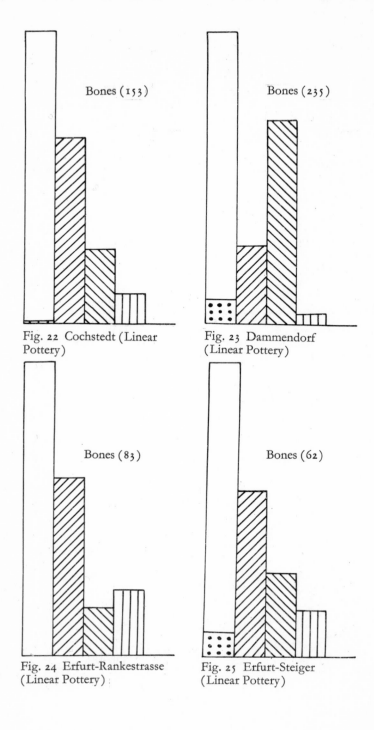

Bones (153)

Fig. 22 Cochstedt (Linear
Pottery)

Bones (235)

Fig. 23 Dammendorf
(Linear Pottery)

Bones (83)

Fig. 24 Erfurt-Rankestrasse
(Linear Pottery)

Bones (62)

Fig. 25 Erfurt-Steiger
(Linear Pottery)

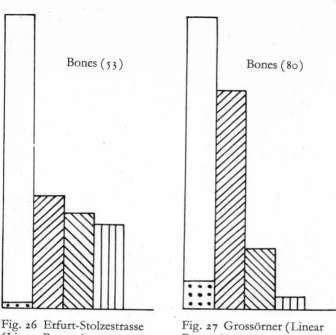

Fig. 26 Erfurt-Stolzestrasse (Linear Pottery)

Fig. 27 Grossörner (Linear Pottery)

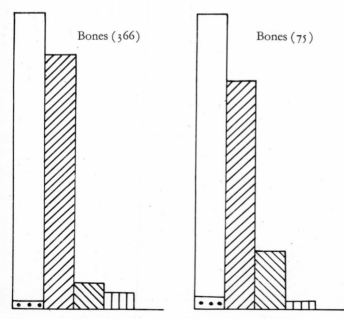

Fig. 28 Halle-Trotha (Linear Pottery)

Fig. 29 Hausneindorf (Linear Pottery)

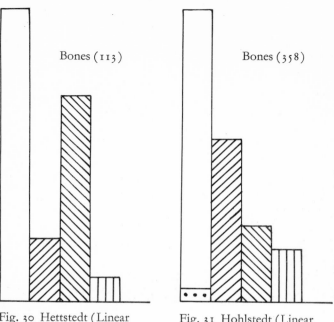

Bones (113)

Fig. 30 Hettstedt (Linear
Pottery)

Bones (358)

Fig. 31 Hohlstedt (Linear
Pottery)

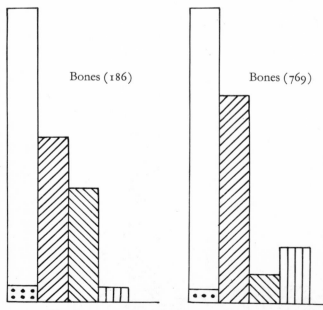

Bones (186)

Fig. 32 Köthen-Geuz
(Linear Pottery)

Bones (769)

Fig. 33 Magdeburg-Prester
(Linear Pottery)

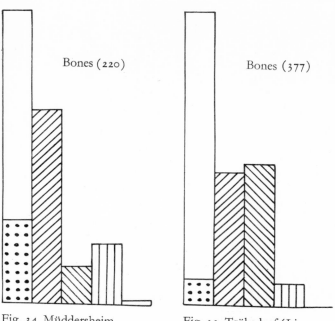

Bones (220)

Fig. 34 Müddersheim
(Linear Pottery)

Bones (377)

Fig. 35 Tröbsdorf (Linear
Pottery)

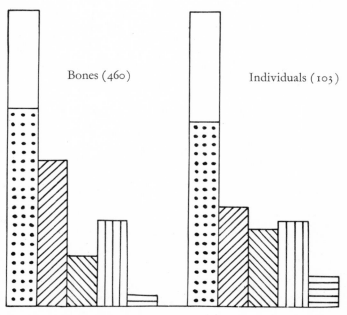

Bones (460)

Individuals (103)

Fig. 36 Regensburg-Purkelgut (Linear Pottery & Rössen)

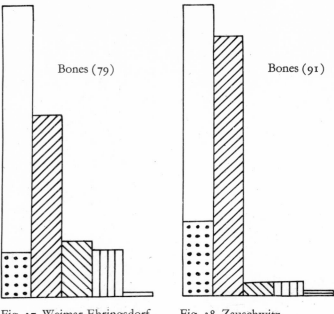

Bones (79)

Bones (91)

Fig. 37 Weimar-Ehringsdorf
(Linear Pottery)

Fig. 38 Zauschwitz
(Linear Pottery)

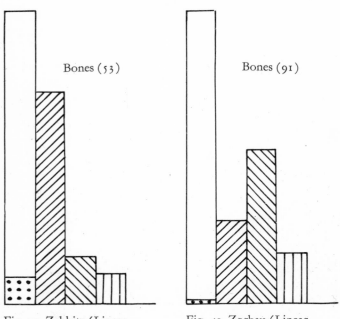

Bones (53)

Bones (91)

Fig. 39 Zehbitz (Linear
Pottery)

Fig. 40 Zorbau (Linear
Pottery)

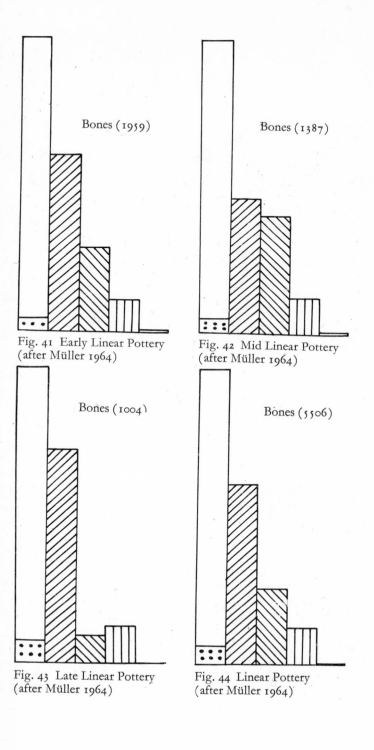

Bones (1959)

Fig. 41 Early Linear Pottery
(after Müller 1964)

Bones (1387)

Fig. 42 Mid Linear Pottery
(after Müller 1964)

Bones (1004)

Fig. 43 Late Linear Pottery
(after Müller 1964)

Bones (5506)

Fig. 44 Linear Pottery
(after Müller 1964)

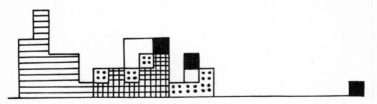

Fig. 45 Comparison of the circumference of horn cores of cattle at
Linear Pottery sites (after Müller 1964)

Domestic cattle   ⊞ Bull   Aurochs   ■ Bull

⊟ Cow   □ Cow

⊡ Ox

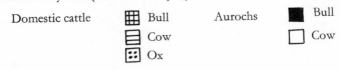

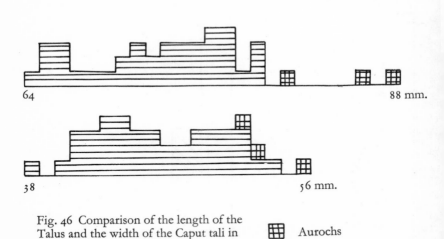

Fig. 46 Comparison of the length of the
Talus and the width of the Caput tali in   ⊞ Aurochs
aurochs and cows (after Müller 1964)   ⊟ Cattle

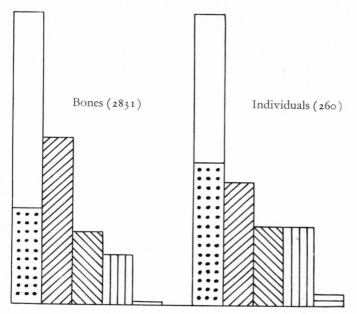

Fig. 47 Novi Rusești (Linear Pottery)

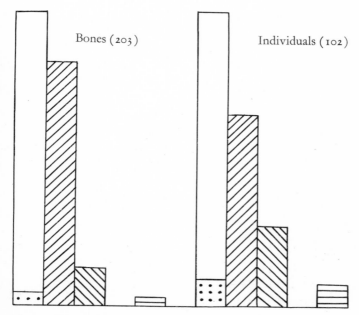

Fig. 48 Bogata (Boian)

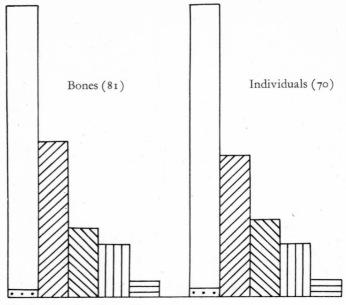

Fig. 49 Tangîru (Boian I)

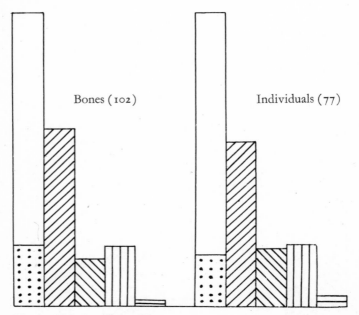

Fig. 50 Tangîru (Boian II)

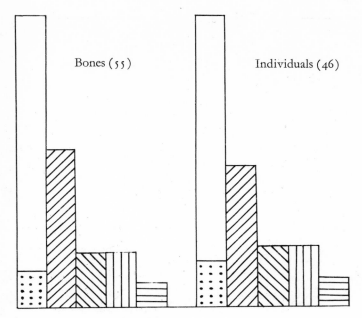

Fig. 51 Tangîru (Boian III)

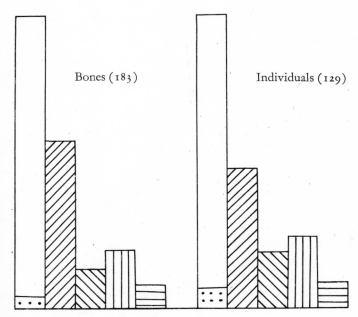

Fig. 52 Tangîru (Boian IV)

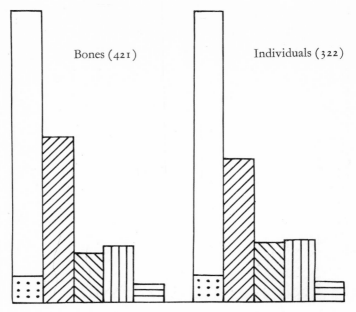

Fig. 53. Tangîru (Boian)

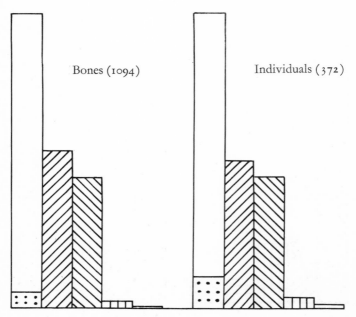

Fig. 54 Techirghiol (Hamangia)

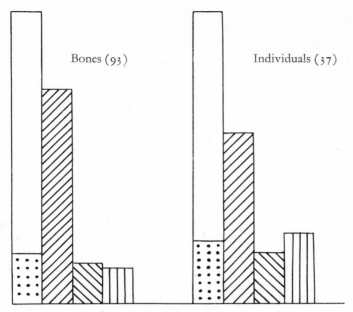

Fig. 55 Borod-Derekegyházi dülö (Bükk)

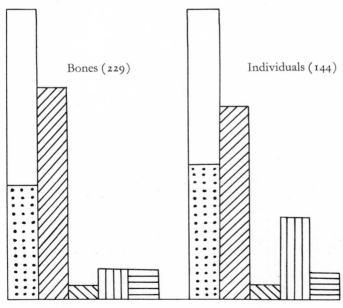

Fig. 56 Hódmezövásárhely-Gorzsa-Cukortanya (Tisza)

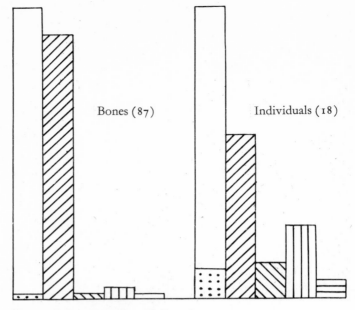

Fig. 57 Polgár-Basatanya (Szilmeg)

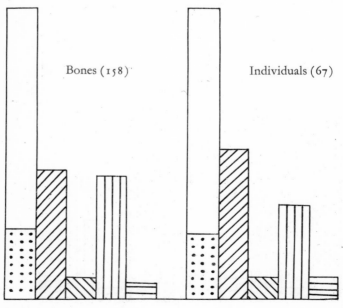

Fig. 58 Szilmeg (Szilmeg)

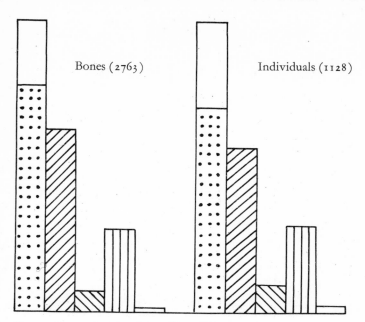

Fig. 59 Berettyószentmárton (Herpálÿ)

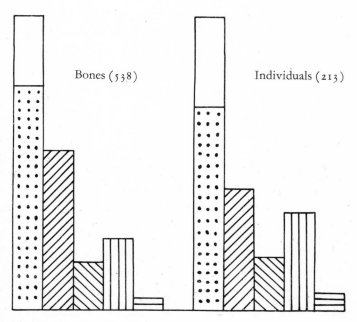

Fig. 60 Herpály (Herpály)

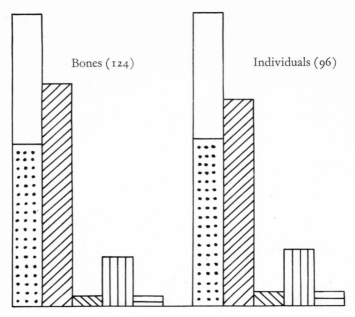

Fig. 61 Pécsvárad-Aranghegy (Lengyel)

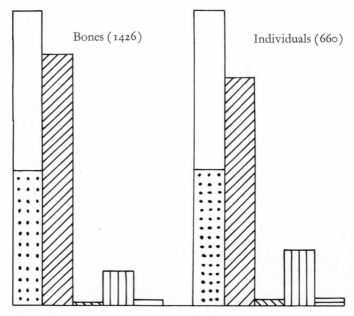

Fig. 62 Zengovárköny (Lengyel)

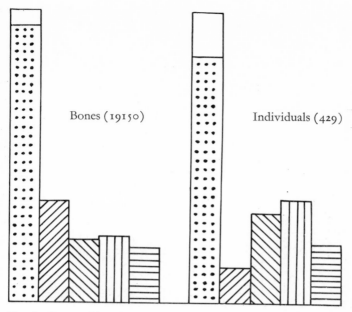

Fig. 63 Burgäschisee Sud (Cortaillod)

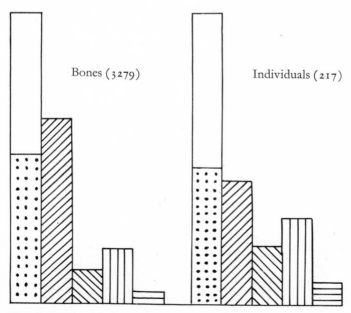

Fig. 64 Burgäschisee Sud-ouest (Cortaillod)

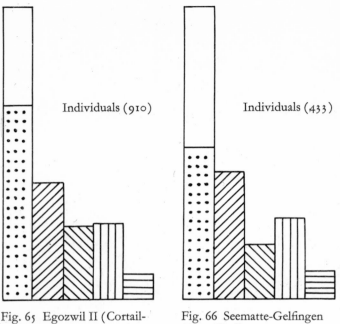

Individuals (910)

Fig. 65 Egozwil II (Cortaillod)

Individuals (433)

Fig. 66 Seematte-Gelfingen
(Cortaillod)

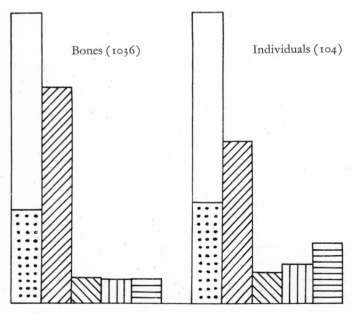

Bones (1036)

Individuals (104)

Fig. 67 Luscherz (Cortaillod)

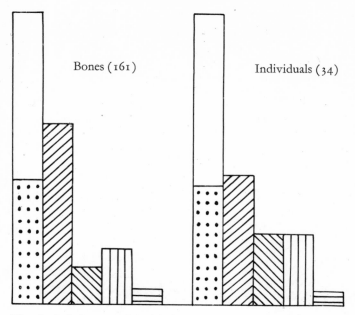

Fig. 68 Lobsigersee (Cortaillod)

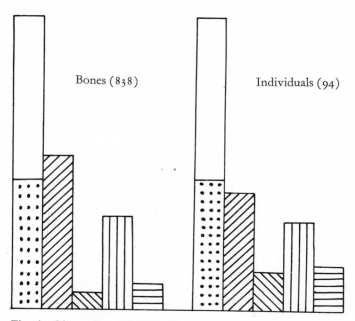

Fig. 69 Obermeilen (Cortaillod)

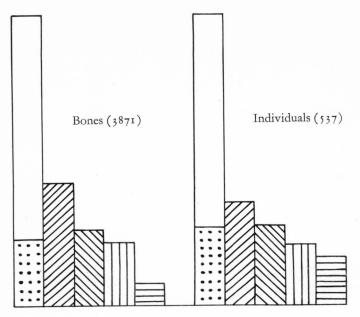

Fig. 70 St. Aubin (Cortaillod)

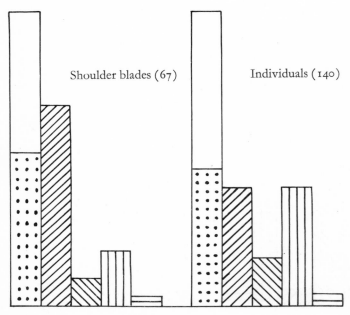

Fig. 71 Wauwil (Cortaillod)

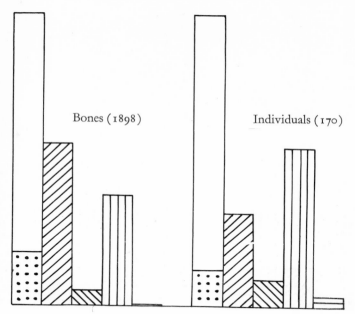

Fig. 72 Niederwil (Cortaillod/Pfyn)

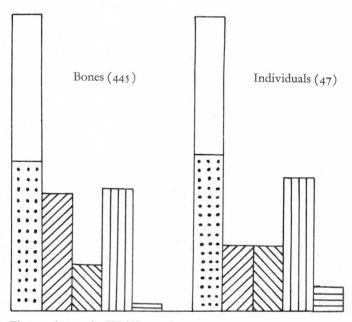

Fig. 73 Auvernier III (Horgen)

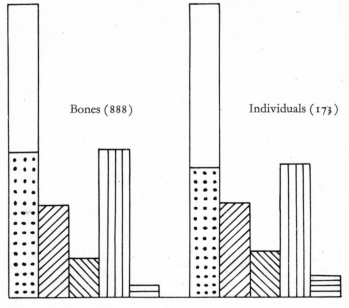

Fig. 74 St. Aubin III (Horgen)

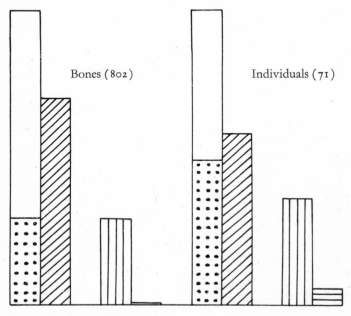

Fig. 75 Ossingen (Michelsberg)

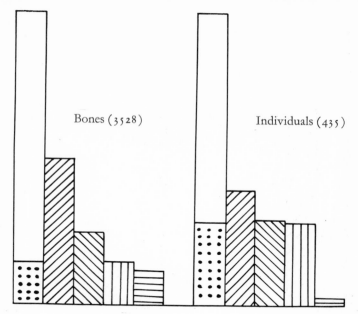

Bones (3528)   Individuals (435)

Fig. 76 Les Matignons (Chassey)

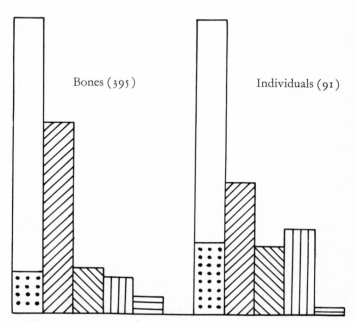

Bones (395)   Individuals (91)

Fig. 77 Les Matignons (Peu Richard)

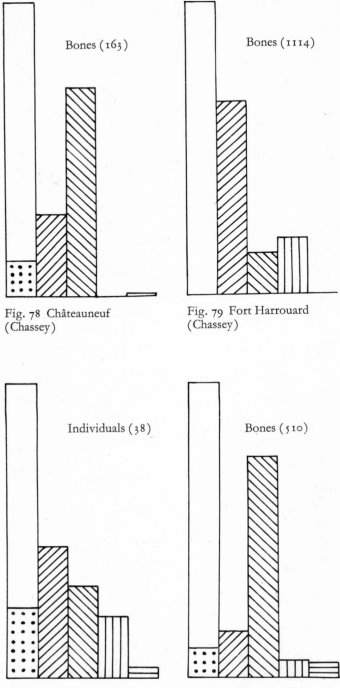

Bones (163)

Fig. 78 Châteauneuf
(Chassey)

Bones (1114)

Fig. 79 Fort Harrouard
(Chassey)

Individuals (38)

Fig. 80 Genissait (Chassey)

Bones (510)

Fig. 81 St. Benoit (Chassey)

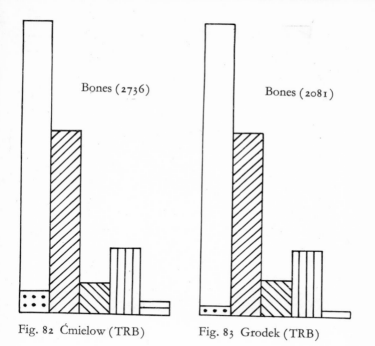

Bones (2736)

Fig. 82 Ćmielow (TRB)

Bones (2081)

Fig. 83 Grodek (TRB)

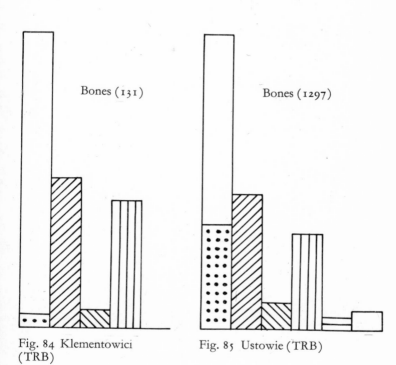

Bones (131)

Fig. 84 Klementowici
(TRB)

Bones (1297)

Fig. 85 Ustowie (TRB)

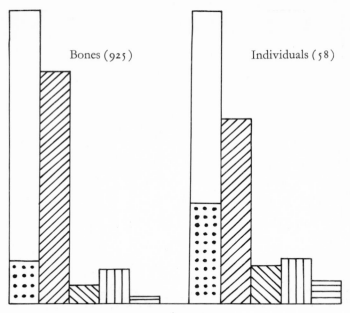

Fig. 86 Fuchsberg-Südensee (TRB)

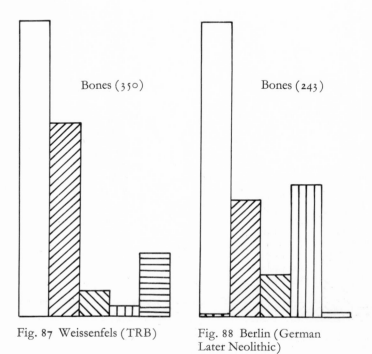

Fig. 87 Weissenfels (TRB)

Fig. 88 Berlin (German Later Neolithic)

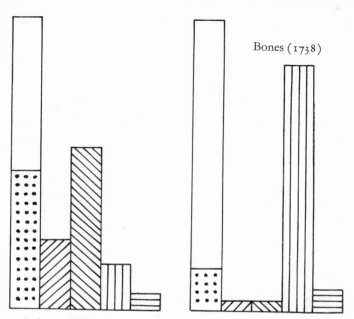

Fig. 89 Einhornhöhle
(German Later Neolithic)

Bones (1738)

Fig. 90 Västerbjers (Pitted
Ware)

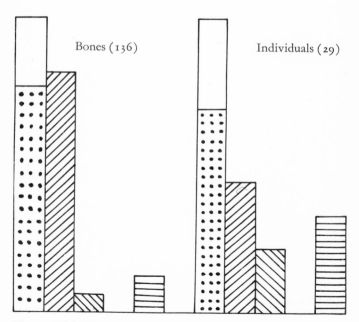

Bones (136)

Individuals (29)

Fig. 91 Kiel-Ellerbek (Ertebølle-Ellerbek)

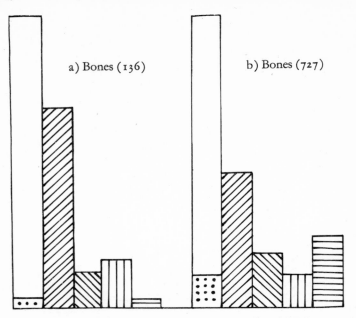

a) Bones (136)   b) Bones (727)

Fig. 92 Windmill Hill a) Pre-enclosure occupation; b) Primary levels of enclosure ditch (Windmill Hill)

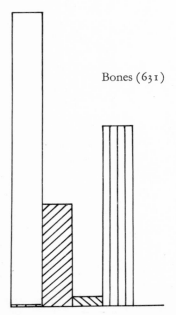

Bones (631)

Fig. 93 Durrington Walls (Rinyo-Clacton)

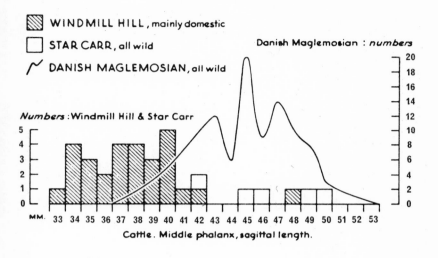

WINDMILL HILL, mainly domestic

STAR CARR, all wild

DANISH MAGLEMOSIAN, all wild

Danish Maglemosian : *numbers*

Numbers : Windmill Hill & Star Carr

Cattle. Middle phalanx, sagittal length.

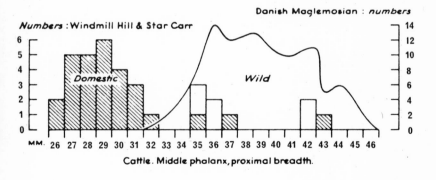

Danish Maglemosian : *numbers*

Numbers : Windmill Hill & Star Carr

Domestic

Wild

Cattle. Middle phalanx, proximal breadth.

Fig. 94 Diagram illustrating the relative sizes of the Windmill Hill cattle with those of the Mesolithic period

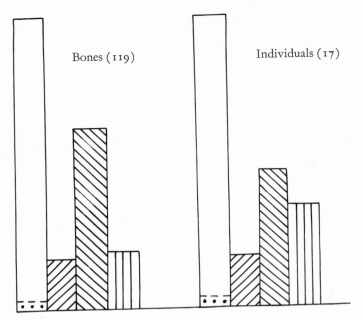

Fig. 95 Argissa (Dimini)

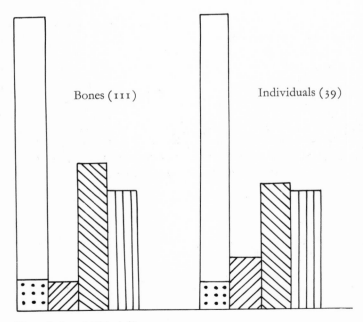

Fig. 96 Arapi (Dimini)

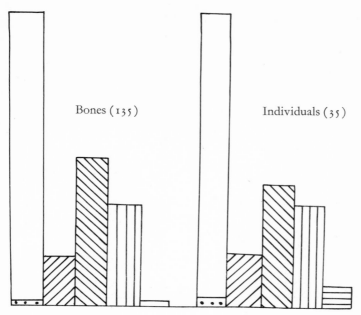

Fig. 97 Otzaki (Dimini)

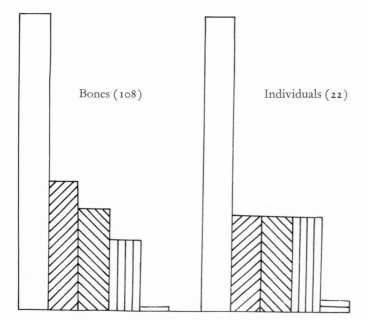

Fig. 98 Otzaki (Larissa-Eutresis)

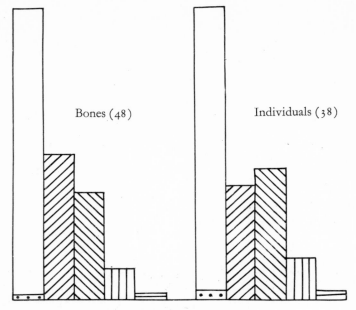

Fig. 99a Tangîru (Gumelniţa I)

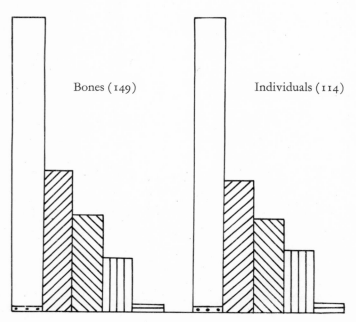

Fig. 99b Tangîru (Gumelniţa II)

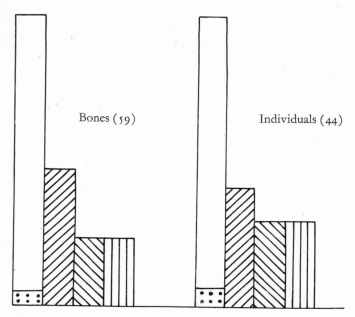

Fig. 99c Tangîru (Gumelniţa III)

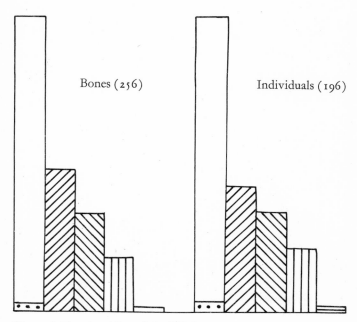

Fig. 99d Tangîru (Gumelniţa I-III)

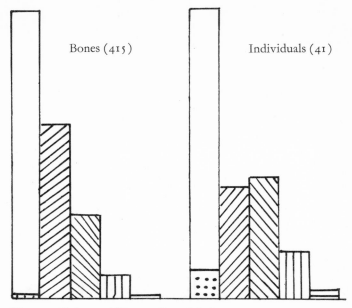

Fig. 100 Vulcănești (Proto- Gumelnița)

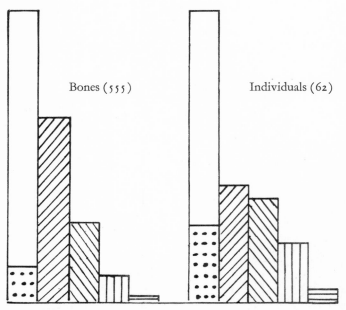

Fig. 101 Bolgrad (Gumelnița)

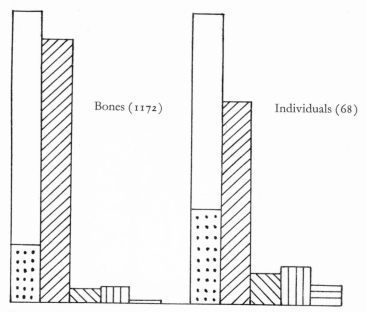

Bones (1172)   Individuals (68)

Fig. 102a Traian (Pre-Cucuteni)

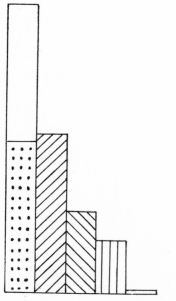

Fig. 102b Traian (Cucuteni, 1957)

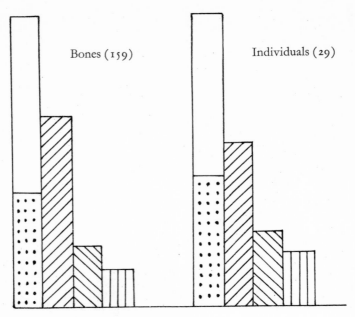

Fig. 102c Traian (Cucuteni A-B, 1959)

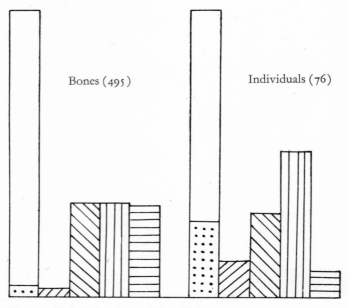

Fig. 103 Polgár-Basatanya (Tisza-Polgár)

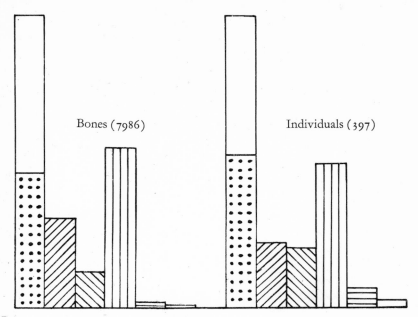

Bones (7986) Individuals (397)

Fig. 104a Luka-Vrublevetskaia (Tripolye A)

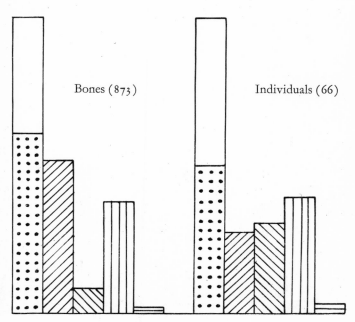

Bones (873) Individuals (66)

Fig. 104b Soloncheny I (Tripolye A)

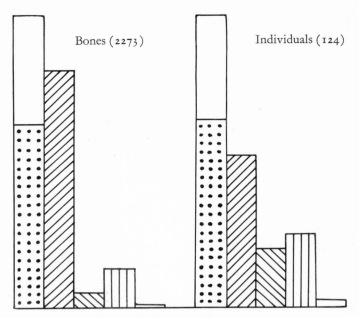

Fig. 105a Bernova-Luka (Tripolye A)

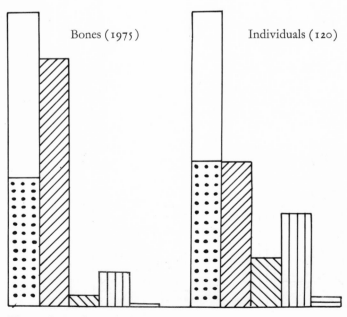

Fig. 105b Lenkovtse (Tripolye A)

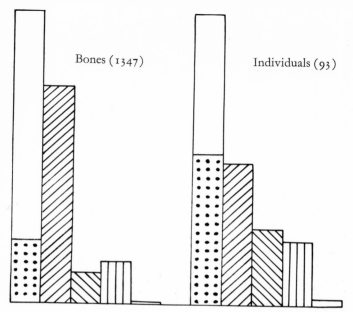

Fig. 106a Sabatinovka II (Tripolye A)

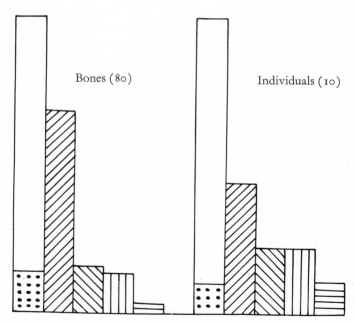

Fig. 106b Sabatinovka I (Tripolye B)

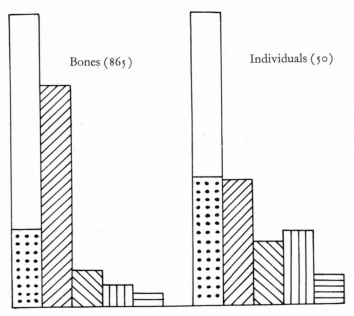

Fig. 107a Sabatinovka (Tripolye B; Hančar 1956)

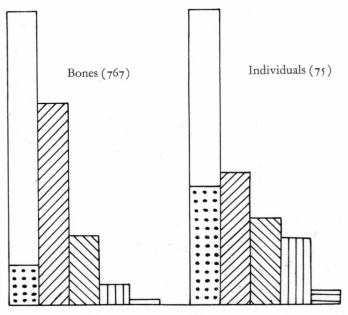

Fig. 107b Kolomiischina (Tripolye B)

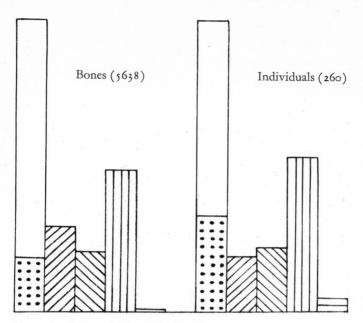

Fig. 108a Polivanov-Jar (Tripolye B)

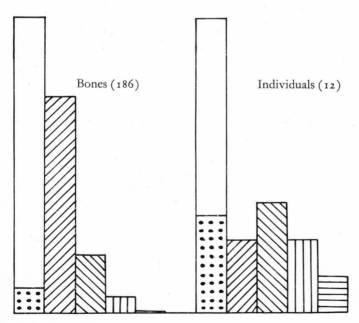

Fig. 108b Vladimirovka (Tripolye B)

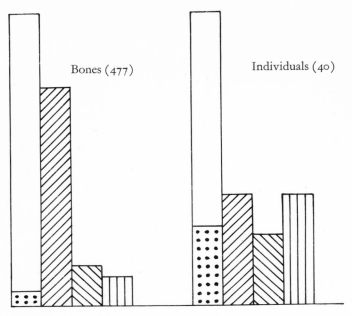

Fig. 109a Khalepye (Tripolye B; Hančar 1956)

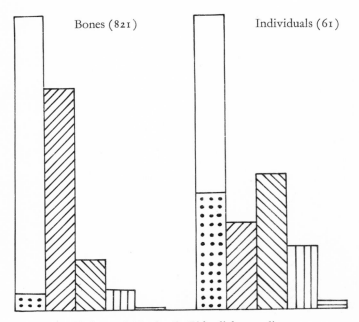

Fig. 109b Khalepye (Tripolye B; Pidoplicko 1956)

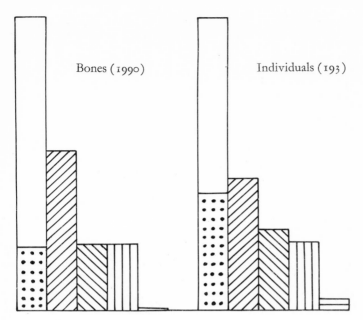

Fig. 110a Novi Rusești (Tripolye B)

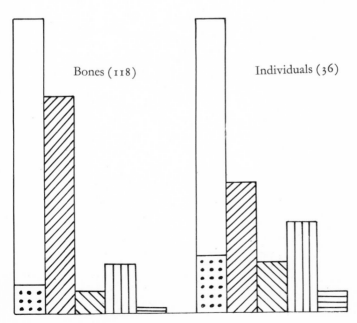

Fig. 110b Krinicki (Tripolye B)

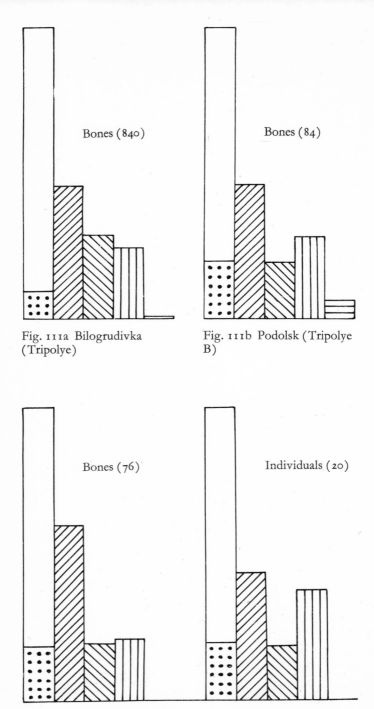

Bones (840)

Fig. 111a Bilogrudivka (Tripolye)

Bones (84)

Fig. 111b Podolsk (Tripolye B)

Bones (76)

Fig. 111c Suskovka (Tripolye C)

Individuals (20)

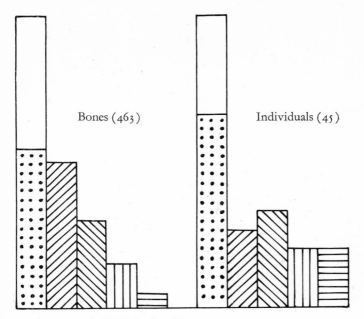

Fig. 112a Sandraki (Tripolye C)

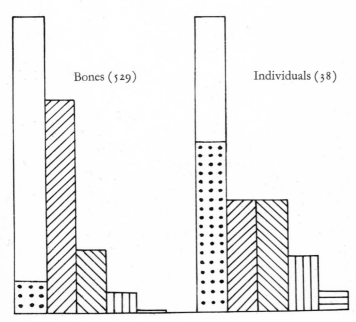

Fig. 112b Pavoloc (Tripolye C)

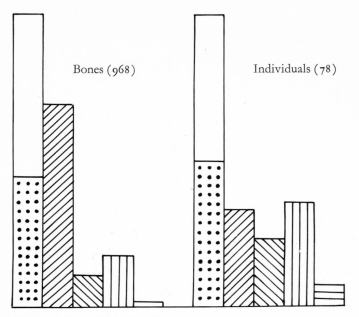

Fig. 113a Stena (Tripolye C)

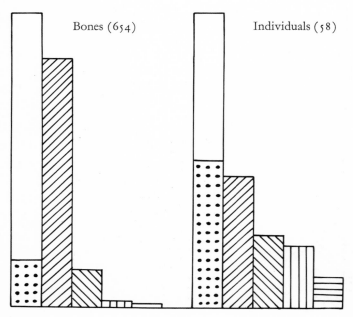

Fig. 113b Troyanov (Tripolye C)

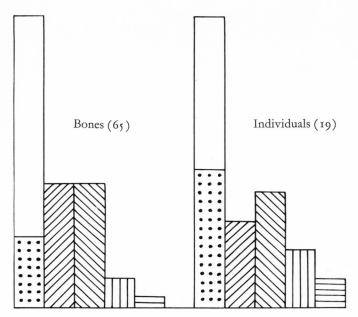

Fig. 114a Andrejevka (Tripolye C)

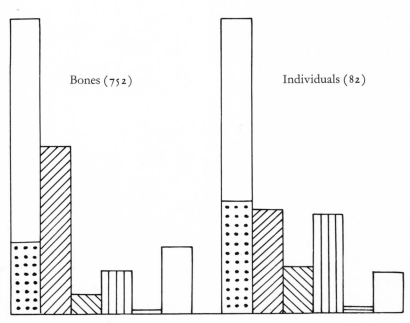

Fig. 114b Podgortse (Tripolye G)

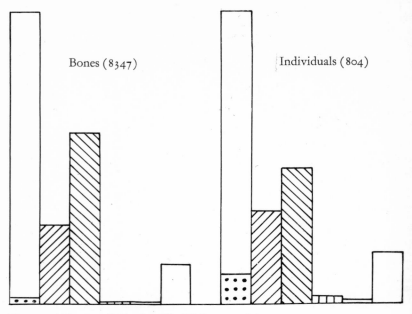

Fig. 115a Usatova (Tripolye Cii; Bibikova 1963)

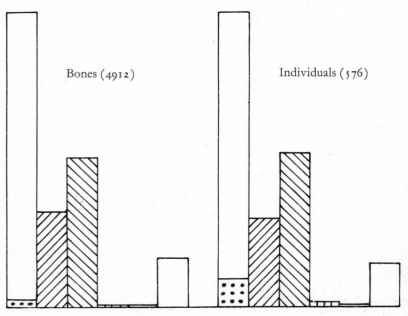

Fig. 115b Usatovo (Tripolye Cii; Hančar 1956)

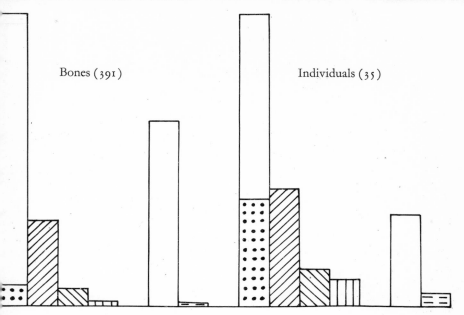

Fig. 116a Gorodsk (Tripolye Cii; Hančar 1956)

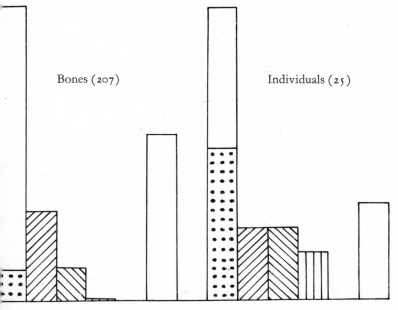

Fig. 116b Gorodsk (Tripolye Cii; Pidoplicko 1956)

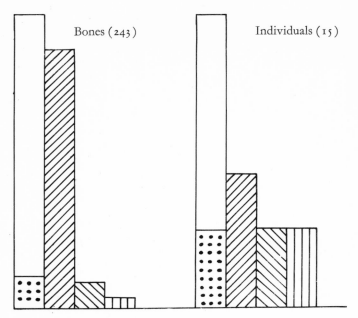

Fig. 117a Kunisivtse (Tripolye G)

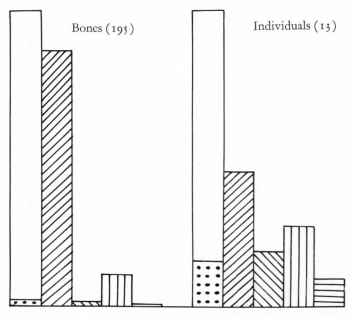

Fig. 117b Kosilovtse (Tripolye C)

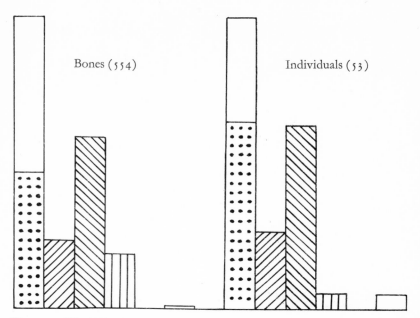

Fig. 118a Kiev (Sirtsi) (Tripolye G)

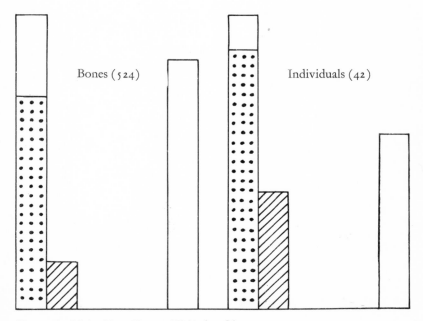

Fig. 118b Molyukhov Bugor (Tripolye G)

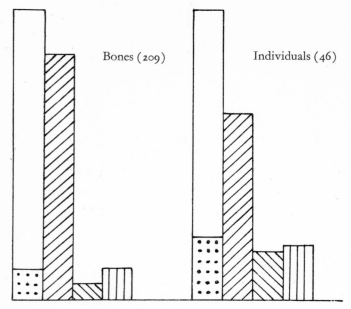

Bones (209)   Individuals (46)

Fig. 119 Derecske-Téglagyár (Bodrogkeresztur)

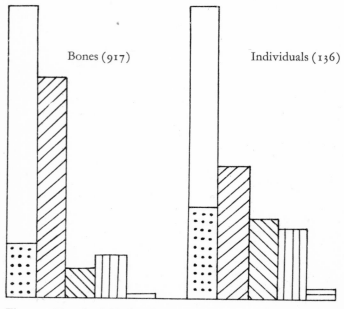

Bones (917)   Individuals (136)

Fig. 120 Tarnabod (Bodrogkeresztur)

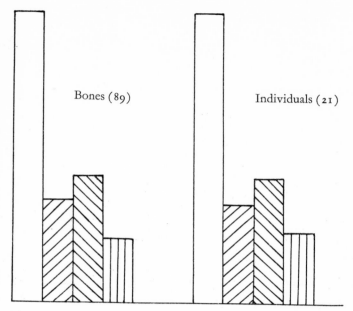

Bones (89)   Individuals (21)

Fig. 121 Szekély-Zöldteltk (Bodrogkeresztur)

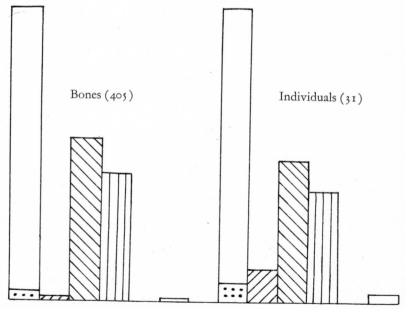

Bones (405)   Individuals (31)

Fig. 122 Polgár-Basatanya (Bodrogkeresztur)

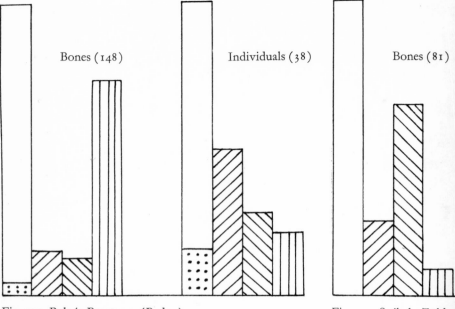

Bones (148) Individuals (38) Bones (81)

Fig. 123 Polgár-Basatanya (Baden) Fig. 124 Székely-Zöldte
(Baden)

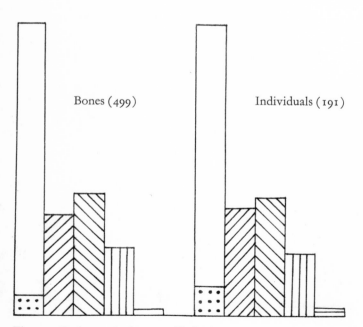

Bones (499) Individuals (191)

Fig. 125 Budapest Andor utca (Baden)

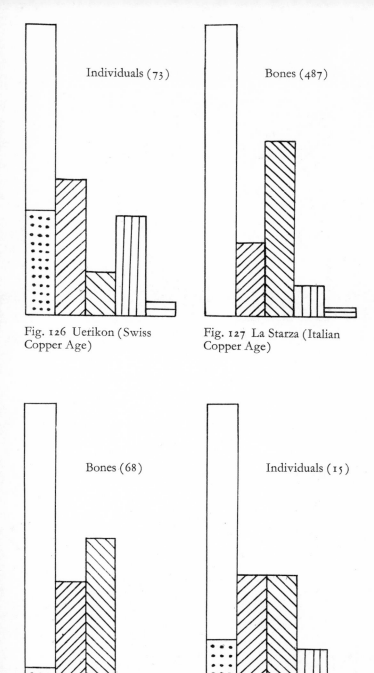

Fig. 126 Uerikon (Swiss
Copper Age)

Fig. 127 La Starza (Italian
Copper Age)

Fig. 128 Anis-Deux-Hortus (French Copper Age)

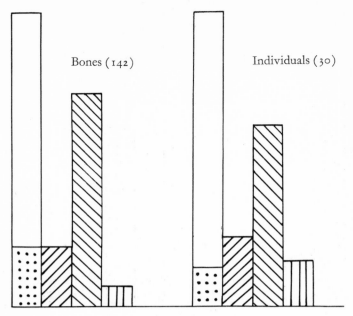

Fig. 129 Bergerie Neuf (French Copper Age)

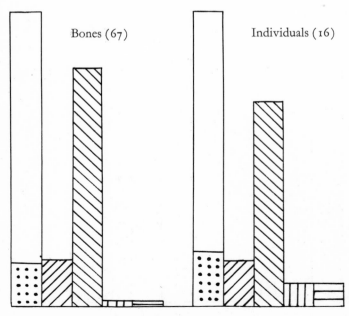

Fig. 130 Gimel (French Copper Age)

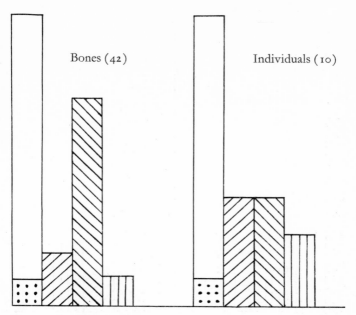

Fig. 131 La Paillade (French Copper Age)

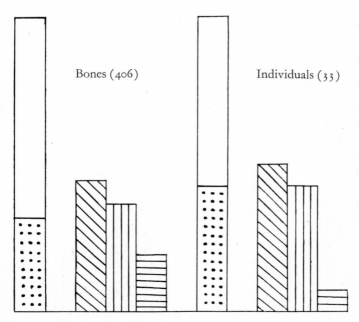

Fig. 132 Trache Deux (French Copper Age)

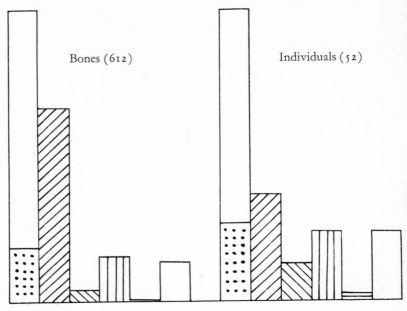

Fig. 133 Altenerdingen (Altheim)

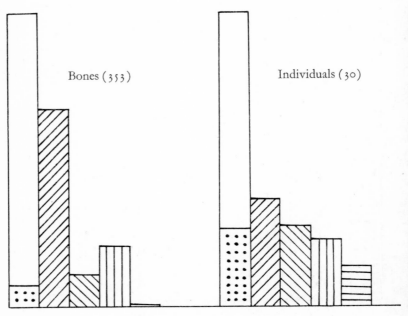

Fig. 134 Altheim (Altheim)

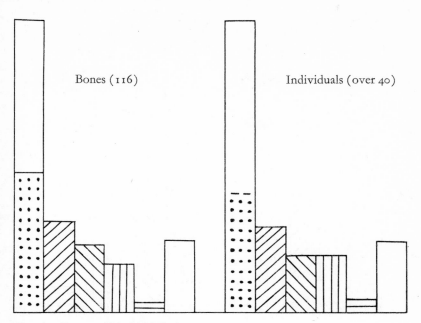

Fig. 135 Pesternacker (Altheim)

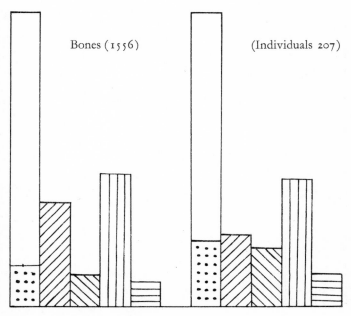

Fig. 136 Sipplingen (Horgen)

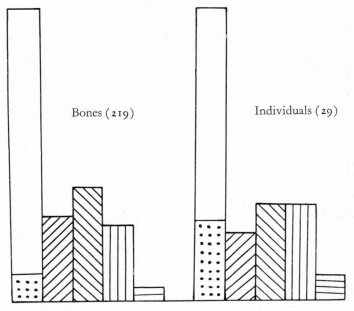

Bones (219)   Individuals (29)

Fig. 137 Auvernier II (Single Grave Complex)

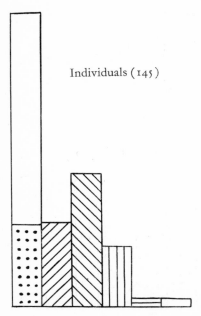

Individuals (145)

Fig. 138 Baldegg (Single Grave Complex)

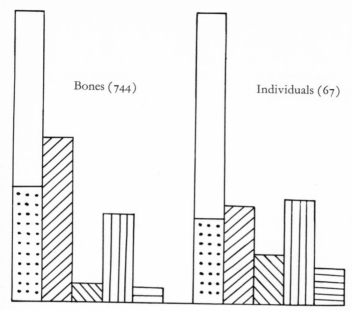

Bones (744)   Individuals (67)

Fig. 139 Utoquai (Single Grave Complex)

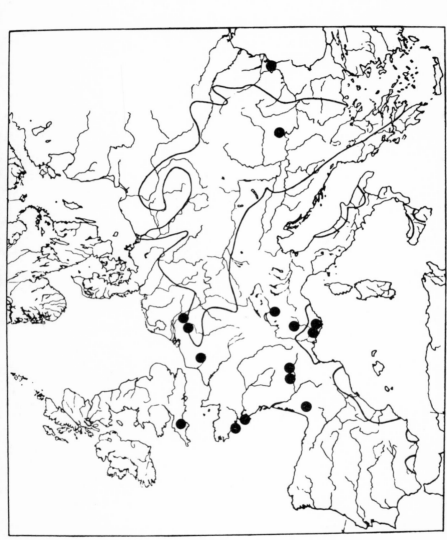

Fig. 140 Map showing the distribution of Mesolithic sheep in Europe relative to the Initial Colonisation cultures

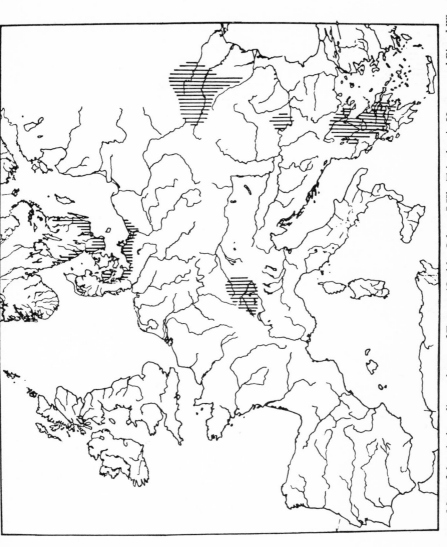

Fig. 141 Map of the pig-breeding cultures of Europe (Sesklo, Salcuta I-IIb, Tripolye A, Horgen and Pitted Ware)

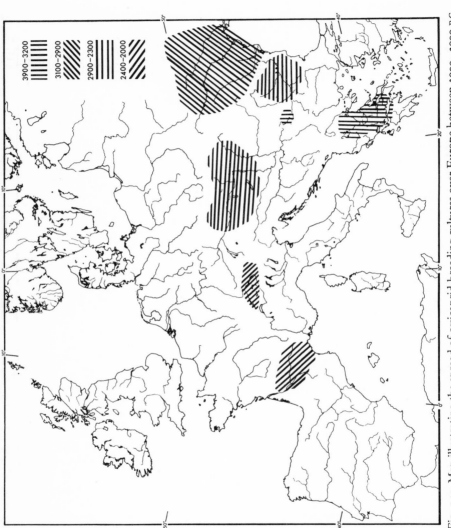

Fig. 142 Map illustrating the spread of ovicaprid-breeding cultures over Europe between 3900–2000 BC

|||	3900–3200
///	3100–2900
⫼	2900–2300
⫽	2400–2000

Tables

Table No. 1

Karim Shahir (Transitional)

Animals	Individuals
Sheep or Goat	17
Deer	3
Pig	4
Cattle	1
Fox	5
Gazelle	1
Hare	1
Tortoise	3
Bird	2
Crab	1
Total	38

Table No. 2

Cultivated Plants of the Aceramic
Neolithic in the Near East

	A	B	C	D
Ali Kosh	x	x	x	
Beidha		x	x	x
Jarmo		x	x	
Hacilar		x	x	x

A—Einkorn; B—Emmer; C—Hulled two-rowed barley;
D—Naked 6-rowed barley.

Table No. 3a

Wild Animals of Neolithic sites in the Near East

	A	B	C	D	E	F	G
Red deer		?			x		
Fallow deer		?			x		
Aurochs	?		x	x	x		?
Pig	?				x	x	?
Gazelle	x	x		x		x	x
Donkey					x		
Equoid			x				
Antelope			x				
Sheep			x		x	x	
Goat						x	
Wolf					x	x	
Fox	x	x				x	
Canid			x				
Leopard					x		
Cat	x						
Tortoise	x						
Birds					x		

A—Abou Gosh; B—'Amuq A & B; C—Anau; D—Belt Cave;
E—Çatal Hüyük; F—Djeitun; G—Tepe Siyalk.

Table No. 3b

Domestic Animals of Neolithic sites in the Near East

	Cattle	Ovicaprids	Pig	Dog
Abou Gosh	?	x	?	
'Amuq A & B	x	x	x	
Anau	x	x		
Belt Cave	?	?		
Çatal Hüyük	x	x		?
Djeitun		x		x
Jarmo		x	x	
Jericho				x
Tepe Siyalk	?	x	?	
Sarab		x		

Table No. 4

Djeitun (Neolithic)

Animals	Individuals
Bezoar goat	58
Wild sheep	18
Sheep and goat	23
Gazelle	27
Various ungulates	51
Pigs	2
Total	179

Table No. 5

Anau	Ia %	Ib %	II %
Cattle	27	25	20
Sheep	22	25	25
Goat	–	–	10
Pig	–	12	15
Dog	–	–	2
Horse	20	28	20
Gazelle	20	7	2
Wolf	11	–	–
Fox	–	2	–
Deer	–	1	–
Camel	–	–	5
Others		–	1

Table No. 6

Cultivated Plants of Neolithic sites in the Near East

	A	B	C	D	E	F	G	H	I
Hacilar	x	x	x		x	x	x		x
Çatal Hüyük	x	x	x			x	x		x
'Amuq A		x						x	
Tell es Sawwan			x			x	x		
Ali Kosh					x	x	x		
Sarab				?				?	
Anau				x	?			x	
Djeitun				x				x	

A—Einkorn; B—Emmer; C—Bread wheat; D—Wheat (unspecified);
E—Hulled two-rowed barley; F—Naked six-rowed barley; G—Hulled
six-rowed barley; H—Barley (unspecified); I—Legumes.

Table No. 7

Wild Animals of the Chalcolithic period in the Near East

	A	B	C	D	E	F	G
Red deer	?	?	?	x			?
Roe deer	?	?	?	x			?
Wild Pig				x			
Gazelle					x	x	
Antelope		x					
Horse							
Half-ass						x	
Sheep						x	
Fox		x					x
Marten					x		x
Weasel					x		
Cat							x
Hare					x		
Tortoise					x		
Frog					x		
Birds					x		

A—'Amuq phase D; B—'Amuq phase E; C—Anau; D—Beycesultan; E—Bir-es-Safadi; F—Dashlydji Depe; G—Gird Banahilk

Table No. 8

Domestic Animals of the Chalcolithic period in the Near East

	Cattle	Ovicaprids	Pig	Dog	Equoid	Camel
Hassuna:						
Hassuna	?	?	?			
Halaf:						
Gird Banahilk	x	x	?	?		
Tell Aswad	?	?				
'Amuq C	x	x	x	x		
Halaf/Ubaid:						
Siabid	x	x	x			
'Amuq D	x	x	x			
'Ubaid:						
Tell Mefesh		x				
Shah Tepe III	x		?			
'Amuq E	x	x	x	x		
Chalcolithic:						
Ain Gedi		x				
Anau Ib	x	x	x			
Anau II	x	x	x	x	x	x
Beycesultan	x	x	x	x		
Bir-es-Safadi	x	x	x	x	x	
Dashlydji Depe	x		x			
Khirbat Bitar		x				
Tepe Siyalk		x		x	x	

Table No. 9

Dashlydji Depe (Chalcolithic)

Animals	Individuals
Domestic;	
Large cattle	4
Small cattle	15
Pig	4
Wild;	
Gazelle	1
Half-ass	1
Wild sheep	1
Total	26

Table No. 10

Bir-es-Safadi (Chalcolithic)

Animals	B.	%	Ind.	%	Domestic % B.	Ind.
Domestic;						
Cattle	409	12.1	46	13.4	12.3	14.6
Sheep & Goat	2918	85.6	263	76.8	87.4	83.8
Pig	1	0.05	1	0.3	0.05	0.3
Dog	2	0.1	1	0.3	0.1	0.3
Donkey	5	0.15	3	1.0	0.15	1.0
Wild;						
Gazelle	8	0.2	2	0.6		
"	8	0.2	1	0.3		
Marten	7	0.2	1	0.3		
Hare	3	0.1	1	0.3		
"	23	0.7	11	3.2		
Birds	16	0.5	9	2.6		
"	5	0.15	2	0.6		
Tortoise	1	0.05	1	0.3		
Wild	71	2.1	314	8.3		
Domestic	3335	97.9	28	91.7		
Total	3406		342			

Table No. 11

Cultivated Plants of the Chalcolithic period in the Near East

	A	B	C	D	E	F
Hassuna;						
Tell Matarrah				x		
Halaf;						
Tell Arpachiyah	x			x	x	
Tell Brak					x	
Mersin	x		x	x		
Chalcolithic;						
Anau		?	x	x		
Beycesultan	?		x			?

A—Emmer; B—Bread wheat; C—Wheat (unspecified);
D—Barley; E—Flax; F—Lentils.

Table No. 12

Wild Animals associated with Mesolithic dogs in Europe

	A	B	C	D	E	F	G	H	I	J	K	L	M	N	O	P	Q	R	S
Dog	x	x	x	x	x	x	x	x	x	x	x	x	x	x	x	x	x	x	x
Red deer			x				x	x	x		x	x	x	x				x	x
Roe deer			x				x	x	x		x	x	x	x				x	x
Elk								x	x		x	x	x	x				x	x
Aurochs						x		x	x		x	x	x	x				x	x
Pig			x				x	x	x		x	x	x	x				x	x
Seal												x							
Sheep			x																
Horse							x												x
Badger	x		x					x			x	x	x					x	x
Otter							x	x				x	x						
Beaver							x	x	x		x	x	x	x				x	x
Bear	x		x								x	x	x						
Marten	x							x			x	x	x					x	x
Wolf	x											x	x	x				x	x
Fox	x		x				x		x		x	x	x					x	x
Lynx	x											x							
Cat	x		x				x		x		x	x	x						x
Hare			x									x					x		

[continued

Table No. 12 [continued]

	A	B	C	D	E	F	G	H	I	J	K	L	M	N	O	P	Q	R	S
Rabbit																			x
Hamster		x																	
Hedgehog								x						x					
Squirrel												x	x						
Vole		x																	x
Mouse		x																	
Turtle								x			x		x						
Birds		x					x		x		x	x	x					x	x
Fish		x				x			x		x	x	x						x

A—Fatna-Koba; B—Kiik-Koba;C—Kukrek-Koba D—Mourzak-Koba;
E—Shan-Koba; F—Sureny II; G—Senckenberg Moor; H—Hallebygaard;
I—Hesselbjerggaard; J—Holmegaard; K—Lundby; L—Maglemose;
M—Øgaarde; N—Svaerdborg; O—Tingbjerggaard; P—Agerod; Q—Viste
R—Star Carr; S—Thatcham.

Table No. 13a

Argissa Magula

Animals	Aceramic		Neolithic	
	Bones	%	Bones	%
Domestic;				
Cattle	103	4.7	32	19.4
Sheep & goat	1820	83.5	86	52.2
Pig	216	9.9	40	24.2
Dog	4	0.2	—	—
Wild;				
Red deer	2	0.1	4	2.4
Deer	4	0.2	—	—
Aurochs	11	0.5	?2	1.2
Pig	?5	0.2	?1	0.6
Horse	—	—	—	—
Fox	1	0.1	—	—
Badger	—	—	—	—
Hare	8	0.4	—	—
Beaver	—	—	—	—
Birds	5	0.2	—	—
Total	2179		165	

Table No. 13b
Argissa Magula

Period	Bones				%			Ind.		
	C	O/C	P	T	C	O/C	P	C	O/C	P
Aceramic	103	1820	216	2139	5	85	10	8	54	19
Early Neolithic	8	7	11	26	—	—	—	2	2	3
Proto-Sesklo	3	5	5	13	—	—	—	2	2	1
Dimini	21	74	24	119	18	62	20	3	8	6

Table No. 13c
Aceramic Neolithic Plants in Greece (from Renfrew 1966)

	Ghediki	%	Achilleion	Sesklo	Argissa	Soufli
Einkorn	2	2.9	—	—	x	—
Emmer	44	61.9	6	6	x	x
Barley—hulled 2rowed	9	12.6	—	1	—	—
naked 2rowed	1	1.5	—	—	—	—
hulled 6rowed	—		—	—	x	—
Millet	—		—	—	x	—
Oats	—		1	—	—	—
Peas	5	7.0	—	5	—	—
Bean/Vetch	4	5.6	—	—	—	—
Lentils	4	5.6	—	—	x	x
Acorns	—		—	1	—	—
Wild Olive	—		—	—	—	x
Pistachio nut	2	2.9	—	74	—	—
Total	71		7	86		

The figures refer to the number of carbonised grains identified

%	
O/C	P
67	23
—	—
—	—
47	35

Table No. 14a

Tash-Ayir (Crimean cave)

	A		B		C		D		E	
	B.	I.	B.	I.	B.	I.	B.	I.	B.	I.
Domestic:										
Cattle	—	—	—	—	—	—	22	2	23	1
Ovicaprids	—	—	—	—	—	—	—	—	1	1
Pig	15	1	22	3	35	2	24	4	193	5
Wild:										
Red deer	—	—	20	2	25	2	29	2	68	3
Roe deer	2	1	5	1	5	1	13	2	47	2
Aurochs	—	—	—	—	—	—	10	1	14	1
Bos	—	—	—	—	—	—	—	—	12	1
Wild pig	8	1	4	1	17	1	26	4	140	5
Pig (?wild)	6	3	20	2	59	4	48	6	259	7
Horse	—	—	—	—	—	—	—	—	2	1
Ass	—	—	—	—	1	1	—	—	1	1
Fox	—	—	—	—	1	1	—	—	—	—
Badger	—	—	—	—	—	—	—	—	1	1
Cat	—	—	—	—	2	1	—	—	1	1
Hare	—	—	6	1	2	1	1	1	23	2
Birds	—	—	3	1	—	—	—	—	62	1
Total	31	6	80	+10	147	14	173	22	847	+31

A—Late Magdalenian/early Azilian; B—Azilian; C—Tardenoisian;
D—Early Neolithic; E—Mid Neolithic.

[continued

Table No. 14a

Zamil-Koba (Crimean cave)

	A		B		C		D	
	B.	I.	B.	I.	B.	I.	B.	I.
Domestic:								
Cattle	—	—	—	—	1	1	—	—
Ovicaprids	—	—	—	—	2	?	11	3
Pig	—	—	—	—	7	2	12	3
Dog	1	1	—	—	3	1	2	2
Wild:								
Red deer	—	—	8	1	27	2	27	3
Roe deer	1	1	4	1	80	6	150	15
Pig	2	1	9	3	60	4	120	7
Horse	—	—	—	—	—	—	1	1
Wolf	—	—	1	1	—	—	—	—
Cat	—	—	—	—	—	—	1	1
Hedgehog	—	—	—	—	1	1	1	1
Hare	—	—	—	—	4	3	21	4
Cetacea	—	—	—	—	4	3	7	5
Buzzard	—	—	1	1	8	?	7	?
Turtle	—	—	—	—	17	4	40	6
Pig (?wild)	5	1	51	2	287	9	508	11
Total	9	4	74	9	501	+36	908	62

(after Dmitrieva 1960).
A—Azilian; B—Tardenoisian; C—Early Neolithic; D—Mid Neolithic.

Table No. 14b

Kammenia Mogila (Russian Aceramic)

	B.	%	I.	%	Domestic % B.	I.
Domestic:						
Cattle	915	72.5	180	57.4	86.8	77.9
Ovicaprids	136	10.8	48	15.4	12.9	20.8
Dog	3	0.2	3	1.0	0.3	1.3
Wild:						
Red deer	10	0.8	1	0.3		
Bison	9	0.7	6	1.9		
Pig	19	1.5	10	3.2		
Horse	140	11.1	50	16.0		
Ass	1	0.1	1	0.3		
Badger	3	0.2	2	0.6		
Fox	1	0.1	1	0.3		

Table No. 14b [continued]

	B.	%	I.	%	Domestic % B.	I.
Wolf	1	0.1	1	0.3		
Hare	2	0.2	2	0.6		
Marmot	1	0.1	1	0.3		
Mole	7	0.5	2	0.6		
Hamster	3	0.2	1	0.3		
Turtle	5	0.4	2	0.6		
Fish	5	0.4	2	0.6		
Birds	1	0.1	1	0.3		
Total	1262		314			
Domestic	1054	83.5	231	73.8		
Wild	208	16.5	83	26.2		

Table No. 15

Controversial domesticated animals of Mesolithic sites

	Small Cattle	Sheep	Small Pig	Dog
Sauveterrian:				
Unang	x			
Three Holes Cave		x		
Sauveterrian and Tardenoisian:				
Moita do Sebastãio	x			
Tardenoisian:				
Belloy-sur-Somme	x	x	x	
Châteauneuf-Les-Martigues		x		
Cuzoul-de-Gramat	x	x		
Sauveterre		x		x
Téviec		x		x
Azilian:				
L'Abri Pages		x		
Balme de Glos	x	x		
Colomb a Meaudre	x			
Saleve	x	x	x	
Baie Herculane		x		
Asturian:				
Mugem		x		x
Others:				
Er Yoh	x	x	x	
Le Perrey	x	x	x	x
Maastricht	x	x		x
Remouchamps		x		
Ringneill	x			
La Adam		x		

Table No. 16

Châteauneuf-Les-Martigues

	Tardenoisian		Early Cardial		Late Cardial and Chassey		Lagozza and Late Chassey	
	No.	%	No.	%	No.	%	No.	%
a) Animals								
Cattle (2)	16	0.4	45	5.7	40	24.5	29	10.3
Sheep	66	1.8	216	27.4	102	62.6	195	69.4
Dog	2	0.1	–	–	1	0.6	–	–
Red deer	15	0.4	21	2.7	–	–	11	3.9
Pig	11	0.3	34	4.3	12	7.4	23	8.2
Fox	9	0.3	2	0.3	1	0.6	–	–
Badger	17	0.5	4	0.5	–	–	–	–
Lynx	17	0.5	1	0.1	–	–	–	–
Cat	1	0.05	1	0.1	–	–	–	–
Rabbit	3382	94.7	461	58.5	7	4.3	21	7.5
Hare	1	0.05	2	0.3	–	–	2	0.7
Microtus (2)	9	0.3	–	–	–	–	–	–
Others	20	0.6	1	0.1	–	–	–	–
Total	3566		788		163		281	
b) Domestic Animals (No. bones)								
Cattle	–	–	45	17.3	40	28.0	29	12.9
Ovicaprids	–	–	216	82.7	102	71.3	195	87.1
Dog	–	–	–	–	1	0.7	–	–
c) Relative frequency of the four main species based on number of individuals								
Cattle	3	11.1	10	20.8	7	33.3	7	21.2
Red deer	7	25.9	5	10.4	–	–	3	9.1
Pig (Wild)	6	22.2	8	16.7	3	14.3	3	9.1
Sheep	11	40.8	25	52.1	11	52.4	20	60.6

Table No. 1/a
Wild Animals of the Ertebølle/Ellerbek culture

	A	B	C	D	E	F	G	H	I	J	K	L	M	N	O	P	Q	R	S	T	U	V	W
Red deer	x	x	x	x	x	x	x	x	x	x	x	x	x	x	x	x	x	x	x	x	x	x	x
Roe deer	x	x	x	x	x	x	x	x	x	x	x		x	x		x	x	x	x	x	x	x	x
Elk			x	x	x	x												x			x	x	
Aurochs	x		x		x	x		x			x	x		x	x	x		x		x	x	x	x
Pig	x	x		x	x	x	x	x	x	x	x	x		x	x	x	x	x			x	x	x
Seal	x		x		x	x	x	x	x	x	x	x	x	x	x	x		x	x	x	x	x	x
Horse											x											x	
Otter	x				x		x			x		x	x						x	x			
Badger	x				x	x															x		
Beaver					x		x		x			x		x									
Bear			x		x																		
Marten			x		x	x	x		x		x		x	x		x		x					
Fox	x	x	x		x	x	x	x	x		x			x									
Wolf	x				x	x	x																
Lynx					x			x															
Wild cat	x	x	x	x	x	x	x	x	x	x	x		x			x	x						
Polecat					x																		
Squirrel					x		x		x			x	x					x					
Hare													x										
Hedgehog													x										
Dolphin			x							x	x							x	x				
Killer whale																	x	x					
Fish			x	x	x	x					x	x					x	x	x	x	x	x	x
Birds			x	x	x	x					x	x					x	x	x	x	x	x	x

A–Aamølle; B–Aasted; C–Brabrand Sø; D–Drøsselholm; E–Dyrholmen; F–Ertebølle; G–Faarevejle; H–Gudumlund; I–Jægerspris; J–Klintesø; K–Langø; L–Muldbjerg; M–Sejrø; N–Sølager; O–Strandegaard; P–Virksund; Q–Visborg; R–Ånnerod; S–Rörvik; T–Rotekärrslid; U–Bregenwedt-Forstermoor; V–Kiel-Ellerbek; W–Mövenberg

Table No. 17b

Domestic Animals of the Ertebølle and Ellerbek Cultures

	Cattle	Ovicaprids	Pig	Dog
Denmark:				
Brabrand Sø	x			x
Drøsselholm			x	x
Dyrholmen	x			x
Langø	?	x	x	x
Muldbjerg	x	x		
Strandegaard	x			
Aamølle				x
Aasted				x
Blocksberg				x
Boling Sø				x
Christainsholm				x
Ertebølle				x
Faarevejle				x
Fannerup				x
Gudumlund				x
Hadsund				x
Havelse				x
Havno				x
Havstrup Sø				x
Jaegerspris				x
Kassemose				x
Klintesø				x
Krabbesholm				x
Mejlgaard				x
Nivaagaard				x
Revelmøse				x
Sejro				x
Sølager				x
Virksund				x
Visborg Bjergbakke				x
Vissinggaard				x
Sweden:				
Ånnerod			?	
Limhamn	?	x	x	x
Ringsjön			x	
Rörvik		x	x	x
Rôtekarrslid				x
Germany:				
Kiel-Ellerbek	x	x	?	x
Mövenberg	x	x	x	x
Bregentwedt-Förstermoor	x			
Husum				x
Klausdorf				x

Table No. 18

Ellerbek (Ertebølle/Ellerbek; after Mestorf 1904)					Domestic %	
Animals	Bones	%	Ind.	%	Bones	Ind.
Domestic:						
Cattle	26	19.1	4	13.8	81.3	44.5
Sheep	2	1.5	2	6.9	6.2	22.2
Dog	4	2.9	3	10.3	12.5	33.3
Wild:						
Red deer	41	30.2	3	10.3		
Roe deer	4	2.9	2	6.9		
Aurochs	27	19.9	4	13.8		
Horse	3	2.2	2	6.9		
Pig	23	16.9	5	17.3		
Seal	3	2.2	2	6.9		
Birds	3	2.2	2	6.9		
Total	136		29			
Wild	104	76.5	20	69.0		
Domestic	32	23.5	9	31.0		

Table No. 19a

Domestic Animals of the Early Agricultural Neolithic in Greece

	Cattle	Ovicaprids	Pig	Dog
Argissa (Proto-Sesklo)	x	x	x	
Otzaki (Proto-Sesklo)	x	x	x	x
Otzaki (Pre-Sesklo)	x	x	x	x
Nea Nikomedeia	x	x	x	
Otzaki (Sesklo)	x	x	x	x
Argissa (Pre Sesklo/Sesklo)	x	x	x	

Table No. 19b

Cultivated Plants of the Early Agricultural Neolithic in Greece

	A	B	C	D	E	F	G
Soufli	x	x			x		x
Sesklo		x					
Nea Nikomedeia				x		x	x
Servia (Sesklo)			x				x
Tsani (Sesklo)						x	

A—Einkorn; B—Emmer; C—Hard wheat; D—Wheat
E—Hulled 2-rowed barley; F—Barley; G—Legumes

Table No. 20a

Wild Animals of the Starcevo-Körös and allied cultures

	A	B	C	D	E	F	G	H	I	J	K	L
Red deer	x	x	x	x	?	x		x	x	x	x	x
Roe deer	x	x	x	?			x	x	x	x		x
Aurochs	x			x		x	x	x				
Pig	x	?	?	x			x	x	?			x
Donkey							x	x				
Horse										x		
Otter								x				
Beaver								x				
Polecat							?					
Cat								x				
Fox	x						x	x				
Wolf										x		
Badger							x	x				
Hare	x						x	x				
Turtle								x	x				
Fish	x	x			x			x	x			
Birds	x	x			x			x				

A—Devetaki; B—Golemata; C—Karanovo; D—Gornja Tuzla; E—Starčevo;
F—Bukovapuszta; G—Hódmezövásárhely-Bodzaspart; H—Lebo;
I—Maroslele-Pana; J—Obessenyo; K—Opoljenik; L—Tiszaug-Topart

Table No. 20b

Domestic Animals of the Starcevo-Körös and allied cultures

	Cattle	Ovicaprids	Pig	Dog
Bulgaria:				
Devetaki	x	x	x	x
Golemata	x	x	x	x
Karanovo I	x	x		
Gornja Tuzla	x			
Yugoslavia:				
Starčevo	x	x		
Rumania:				
Verbiţa	x	x	x	x
Hungary:				
Bukovapuszta	x			
Hódmezövásárhely-Bodzaspart	x	x		
Lebo	x	x	x	x
Maroslele-Pana	x	x	x	x
Obessenyö	x	x		x
Opoljenik	x	x		
Szarvas-Szappanos	x	x		
Tiszaug-Topart	x	x	x	x

Table No. 21a

Otzaki and Arapi Magula

	Bones							Individuals						
Animals	PS	VS	ES	LS	DO	DA	LE	PS	VS	ES	LS	DO	DA	LE
Domestic:														
Cattle	27	65	21	12	20	12	46	5	15	5	3	6	6	7
Ovicaprids	46	108	41	9	65	59	36	9	26	7	3	14	15	7
Pig	7	44	48	27	44	28	25	2	14	12	7	11	14	7
Dog	1	2	1	—	5	—	1	1	2	1	—	3	—	1
Wild:														
Deer	—	3	—	—	1	1	—	—	2	—	—	1	1	—
Pig	1	—	—	—	—	10	—	1	—	—	—	—	2	—
Hare	—	1	—	—	—	—	—	—	1	—	—	—	—	—
Turtle	—	—	—	—	—	1	—	—	—	—	—	—	1	—
Total	82	223	111	48	135	111	108	18	60	25	13	35	39	22

PS—Proto-Sesklo; VS—Vor Sesklo; ES—Early and Mid Sesklo; LS—Late Sesklo;
DO—Dimini (Otzaki); DA—Dimini (Arapi); LE—Larissa-Eutresis.

Table No. 21b

Otzaki and Arapi Magula

	Bones			%			Individuals			%		
Period	C	O/C	P	C	O/C	P	C	O/C	P	C	O/C	P
PS	27	46	7	34	57	9	5	9	2	31	56	13
VS	65	108	44	30	50	20	15	25	14	28	46	26
ES	21	41	48	19	37	44	5	7	12	21	29	50
LS	12	9	27	25	19	56	3	3	8	21.5	21.5	57
DO	20	65	44	16	50	34	6	14	11	19	45	36
DA	12	59	48	10	50	40	6	15	14	17	43	40
LE	46	36	25	43	34	23	7	7	7	33.3	33.3	33.3

PS—Proto-Sesklo; VS—Vor Sesklo; ES—Early and Mid Sesklo; LS—Late Sesklo;
DO—Dimini (Otzaki); DA—Dimini (Arapi); LE—Larissa-Eutresis.

Table No. 22

Maroslele-Pana (Starčevo-Körös)

Animals	Bones	%	Domestic %
Domestic:			
Cattle	48	23.3	26.5
Ovicaprids	127	61.8	70.1
Pig	3	1.4	1.7
Dog	3	1.4	1.7
Wild:			
Red deer	1	0.5	
Roe Deer	5	2.5	
Aurochs	8	3.9	
Pig	1	0.5	
Cat	3	1.4	
Badger	1	0.5	
Fox	3	1.4	
Hare	3	1.4	
Total	206		
Domestic	181	87.9	
Wild	25	12.1	

Table No. 23

Hódmezövásárhely-Bodzaspart (Starčevo-Körös)

Animals	Bones	Individuals
Domestic:		
Cattle	15	5
Ovicaprids	4	3
Wild:		
Roe deer	2	1
Donkey	2	2
Aurochs	2	1
Polecat (?)	1	1
Badger	4	1
Hare	1	1
Small ruminant	4	
Total	35	15

Table No. 24

Lebo (Starčevo-Körös, Szilmeg, Tisza, Linear Pottery)

Animals	1950 Bones	%	1956 Bones	%	Ind.	%	1956 Domestic% Bones	%
Domestic:								
Cattle	64	31.1	521	57.6	88	40.2	91.3	80.0
Ovicaprids	–	–	13	1.4	10	4.6	2.3	9.1
Pig	9	4.4	18	2.0	10	4.6	3.2	9.1
Dog	2	1.0	19	2.1	2	0.9	3.2	1.8
Wild:								
Red deer	34	16.5	49	5.4	18	8.2		
Roe deer	12	5.8	18	2.0	14	6.4		
Aurochs	22	10.7	137	15.2	32	14.6		
Pig	32	15.4	67	7.5	23	10.5		
Donkey	–		2	0.2	2	0.9		
Otter	–		1	0.1	1	0.4		
Beaver	–		1	0.1	1	0.4		
Fox	2	1.0	–		–			
Turtle	8	3.9	8	0.8	2	1.0		
Fish	21	10.2	51	5.6	16	7.3		
Total	206		905		219			
Domestic			571	63.1	110	50.3		
Wild			334	36.9	109	49.7		

Table No. 25

Cultivated Plants of the Starćevo-Körös and allied cultures

	A	B	C	D	E	F
Bulgaria:						
Banyata	x	x				x
Karanovo I	x	x		x		x
Yugoslavia:						
Biserna Obala					x	
Rumania:'						
Salcuţa			?	?		

A–Einkorn; B–Emmer; C–Wheat (unspecified);
D–Barley; E–Millet; F–Legumes.

Table No. 26

Wild Animals of Impressed Ware culture

	A	B	C	D
Red deer	x	?	x	x
Roe deer	x	?		
Aurochs	x			
Pig		?	x	
Chamois	x			
Wolf				x
Badger			x	
Lynx			x	
Cat			x	
Rabbit	x		x	x
Fox			x	
Hare		x	x	
Fish		x		

A—Crvena Stijena; B—Arene Candide;
C—Châteauneuf-Les-Martigues; D—Grotte d'Unang.

Table No. 27

Domestic Animals of the Impressed Ware culture

	Cattle	Ovicaprids	Pig	Dog
Yugoslavia:				
Crvena Stijena		x		
Italy:				
Arene Candide		x		
Stentinello	x	x	x	x
France:				
Châteauneuf	x	x		
Roucadour	?	x		
Unang	?	x	x	

Table No. 28

Roucadour (Neolithic)

a) Animals	Bones	%
Domestic:		
Cattle	1259	29.5
Ovicaprids	123	2.9
Pig (inc. wild)	935	21.9
Dog	23	0.5
Wild:		
Red deer	1066	25.0
Roe deer	192	4.5
Horse (wild and ? dom.)	588	13.8
Wolf	23	0.5
Fox	6	0.1
Bear	17	0.4
Badger	15	0.4
? Cat	8	0.2
Lynx	1	0.05
Beech Marten	2	0.05
Marten	3	0.1
Wolf	2	0.05
Mouse	2	0.05
Total	4265	
Domestic approx.	2340	54.8
Wild approx.	1925	45.2

b) Level	C		B1		B2		A1	
Animals	Ind.	%	Ind.	%	Ind.	%	Ind.	%
Horse	1	3.85	2	2.4	2	2.5	27	24.6
Large cattle	3	11.5	15	18.3	21	26.6	17	15.4
Small cattle	–	–	17	20.7	23	29.1	16	14.6
Sheep	1	3.85	4	4.9	3	3.8	4	3.6
Pig	12	46.2	24	29.3	12	15.2	22	20.0
Red deer	6	23.1	12	14.6	12	15.2	20	18.2
Roe deer	3	11.5	8	9.8	6	7.6	4	3.6
Total	26		82		79		110	

Table No. 29

Wild Animals of the Linear Pottery culture

	A	B	C	D	E	F	G	H	I	J	K	L	M	N	O	P	Q	R	S	T	U	V	W	X	Y	Z
Red deer	x	x	x	x	x	x	x	x	x	x	x	x	x	?	x	x	x	x	x	x	x	?	x			x
Roe deer	x	x	x	x	x	x	x	x			x		x	?	x	x						?	x	x		
Elk																										
Aurochs	x	x	x	x	x		x		x	x	x	x	x			x			x	x		?			x	x
Pig	x	x	x	x	x			x		x	x			x		x	x	x	x						x	
Horse			x	x			x	x	x	x				x			x	x	x				x			
Equoid			x							x																
Bear																							x			
Beaver		x	x	x	x	x					x															
Badger																										
Wolf						x					x															
Fox			x								x		x										x			
Hare	x	x													x											
Hamster																										
Turtle		x	x				x				x															
Birds		x	x																x							
Fish		x	x			x					x															

	A'	B'	C'	D'	E'	F'	G'	H'	I'	J'	K'	L'	M'	N'	O'	P'	Q'	R'	S'	T'	U'	V'	W'	X'	Y'	Z'
Red deer		x	x	x	x	x	x	?		x	x	x	?	x	x	x	x		x		x			x	?	x
Roe deer	x	x	x	x	x	x	?	?		x	x	?	?	x	x	x	x	x	x		x		x	x	?	?
Elk							x																			
Aurochs	x		x	x	x		x			x	x						x	?	x		x	x				
Pig		x	x	x	x	x				x	x				x		x		x		x	x	x			
Horse			x	x	x				x						x		x				x	x	x			
Equoid																										
Bear				x														x								
Beaver																			x							
Badger																x	x			x						
Wolf																										
Fox		x										x					x									
Hare		x			x																					
Hamster		x	x		x																					
Turtle				x																						
Birds																	x									
Fish																	x									

A—Győr-Pápai vám; B—Pomáz-Zdravlyák; C—Szegvár-Tuzköves; D—Traian; E—Florești; F—Luka Vrublevetskaia; G—Strzelce; H—Aislingen; I—Bad Durrenberg; J—Ballenstedt; K—Barleben; L—Bruchstedt; M—Dammendorf; N—Dresden-Cotta; O—Erfurt; P—Gatersleben; Q—Grossörner; R—Hainichen; S—Halle-Trotha; T—Hausneindorf; U—Haneklint; V—Heutingsheim; W—Hohlstedt; X—Holdenstedt; Y—Jersleben; Z—Köln-Lindenthal;

A'—Königsaue; B'—Korner; C'—Köthen-Geuz; D'—Magdeburg-Prester; E'—Muddersheim; F'—Mücheln; G'—Nerkewitz; H'—Offingen I'—Polleben; J'—Quedlinburg; K'—Regensburg-Purkelgut; L'—Rehmsdorf; M'—Reiser; N'—Rossleben; O'—Schlotheim; P'—Sonderhausen; Q'—Tröbsdorf; R'—Waiblingen; S'—Weimar-Ehringsdorf; T'—Wengelsdorf; U'—Wulfen; V'—Zauschwitz; W'—Zehlbitz; X'—Zorbau; Y'—Niedernai; Z'—Sabliere du Petit Vaux.

Table No. 30

Domestic Animals of the Linear Pottery culture

	Cattle	Ovicaprids	Pig	Dog
Hungary:				
Györ-Pápai vám	x	x	x	x
Györ Pandzsa dulo	x			
Lebo	x	x	x	x
Pomáz-Zdravlyák	x	x	x	x
Szegvár-Tuzköves	x	x	x	x
Rumania:				
Danești	x		x	
Glvaneștii Vechi	x	x	x	
Traian	x	x	x	
Russia:				
Florești	x	x	x	
Kötöwania	x	x	x	
Luka-Vrublevetskaia	x	x	x	x
Novi Rusești	x	x	x	x
Torskie	x	x	x	
Poland:				
Debiec	x			
Strzelce	x	x		
Wierzchow Cave	x			
Zofipole	x			
Czechoslovakia:				
Bylany	x	x	x	
Hurbanovo		?		x
Postoloprty			x	
Zelechovice				x
Germany:				
Ahlsdorf	x	x		
Aislingen	?	x	?	
Alterode	x			
Aschara	x	x		
Bad Dürrenberg		x	x	x
Bad Frankenhausen	x	x		
Ballenstedt	x	x	x	
Barleben-Hühnerfarm	x	x	x	
Barleben-Schweinemästerei	x	x	x	x
Bösenburg		x	x	
Braunsbedra	x	x	x	
Bruchstedt	x	x	x	x
Cochstedt	x	x	x	
Dammendorf	x	x	x	

[continued

Table No. 30 [continued]

	Cattle	Ovicaprids	Pig	Dog
Donndorf	x	x	x	
Dorna	x			
Dresden-Cotta			x	
Dresden-Nickern	x			
Dürrenberg		x	x	x
Eisleben	x			
Eitzum	x	x		
Erfurt	x	x		
Esperstedt	x	x	x	
Flomborn	x	x	x	
Frauenpriessnitz	x	x		
Friedensdorf	x		x	
Gatersleben	x	x	x	
Goddula	x			
Grossgrabe	x	x	x	x
Grossörner	x	x	x	
Halberstadt	x			
Hainichen	x	x	x	
Halle-Ammendorf	x			
Halle-Trotha	x	x	x	
Hausneindorf	x	x		
Haneklint	x	x	x	x
Heilgenthal	x	x	x	
Herkheim	x		x	
Hettstedt	x	x	x	
Heutingsheim	x	x	x	
Hohlstedt	x	x	x	
Holdenstedt	x	x	x	
Ingersleben	x		x	
Jersleben	x	x	x	
Keutschen	x	x	x	
Köln-Lindenthal	x	x	x	x
Königsaue	x			
Körner	x	x	x	x
Köthen-Gütersee	x			
Köthen-Geuz	x	x	x	
Lachstedt	x			
Leiselheim	?		?	
Lösau	x	x	x	
Magdeburg-Prester	x	x	x	
Merzien	x			245

[continued

Table No. 30 [continued]

	Cattle	Ovicaprids	Pig	Dog
Müddersheim	x	x	x	x
Mücheln	x	x	x	
Nerkewitz	x	x		x
Nöbeditz	x	x		
Offenau		x		
Öffingen	x	x	x	
Polleben	x	x	x	
Quedlinburg	x	x	x	
Regensburg-Purkelgut	x	x	x	x
Rehmsdorf			x	
Reiser	x	x	x	
Röblingen am See	x			
Rossleben	x	x	x	
Tornau	x			
Schkopau	x			
Schlotheim	x	x	x	x
Schraplau	x	x	x	
Sömmerda	x	x	x	
Sondershausen	x	x	x	
Stedten			x	
Stössen		x	x	
Tröbsdorf	x	x	x	
Tüngeda	x			
Voigtstedt	x			
Waiblingen	?		?	
Weimar-Ehringsdorf	x	x	x	x
Wengelsdorf		x		
Westerhüsen	x	x		
Wittislingen		x		
Wulfen	x	x		
Zauschwitz	x	x	x	x
Zeundorf	x			
Zehbitz	x	x	x	
Zorbau	x	x	x	
Zuffenhausen	?	x	?	
Holland:				
Sittard	x			
France:				
Armeau	?			
Eckbolsheim	x	x	x	
Niedernai	x			
Sabliere du Petit Vaux	x			
Pfettisheim		?		

Table No. 31

Györ-Pápai vám (Linear Pottery)

Animals	Bones	%	Ind.	%	(1952 and 1954)	
Domestic:						
Cattle	555	65.9	354	60.1	73.2	67.7
Ovicaprids	112	13.3	100	17.0	14.8	19.1
Pig	86	10.2	64	10.8	11.4	12.2
Dog	5	0.6	5	0.8	0.6	1.0
Wild:						
Red deer	2	0.2	2	0.3		
Roe deer	5	0.6	5	0.8		
Aurochs	65	7.7	51	8.6		
Pig	9	1.1	8	1.4		
Hare	3	0.4	1	0.2		
Total	842		590			
Domestic	758	90.0	523	88.7		
Wild	84	10.0	67	11.3		

Table No. 32

Pomáz-Zdravlyák (Linear Pottery)

Animals	Bones	%	Ind.	%	Domestic % Bones	Domestic % Ind.
Domestic:						
Cattle	107	60.8	30	37.0	67.8	45.4
Ovicaprids	25	14.2	17	21.0	15.8	25.8
Pig	23	13.1	16	19.8	14.5	24.3
Dog	3	1.7	3	3.7	1.9	4.5
Wild:						
Red deer	3	1.7	2	2.5		
Roe deer	1	0.6	1	1.2		
Aurochs	4	2.2	4	5.0		
Pig	5	2.8	4	5.0		
Beaver	1	0.6	1	1.2		
Hare	1	0.6	1	1.2		
Turtle	2	1.1	1	1.2		
Birds	1	0.6	1	1.2		
Total	176		81			
Domestic	158	89.8	66	81.5		
Wild	18	10.2	15	18.5		

Table No. 33

Szegvár-Tuzköves (Linear Pottery and Tisza)

Animals	Bones	%	Ind.	%	Domestic % Bones	Ind.
Domestic:						
Cattle	317	38.6	67	29.0	68.4	55.8
Ovicaprids	30	3.7	13	5.6	6.5	10.8
Pig	84	10.2	33	14.3	18.2	27.5
Dog	32	3.9	7	3.0	6.9	5.9
Wild:						
Red deer	54	6.6	21	9.1		
Roe deer	18	2.2	14	6.1		
Aurochs	137	16.7	33	14.3		
Pig	60	7.3	23	10.0		
Equoid	1	0.1	1	0.4		
Fox	4	0.5	1	0.4		
Beaver	2	0.3	2	0.9		
Turtle	66	8.0	6	2.6		
Fish	14	1.7	8	3.4		
Birds	2	0.2	2	0.9		
Total	821		231			
Domestic	463	56.4	120	51.9		
Wild	358	43.6	111	48.1		

Table No. 34

Traian

Animals	Linear Pottery				Pre-Cucuteni				Cucuteni A–B			
	Bones	%	Ind.	%	Bones	%	Ind.	%	Bones	%	Ind.	%
Domestic:												
Cattle	134	39.8	9	29.0	849	72.5	32	47.1	63	39.6	9	31.0
Ovicaprids	18	5.3	3	9.7	39	3.3	5	7.4	21	13.2	4	13.8
Pig	60	17.8	5	16.1	48	4.1	6	8.8	12	7.6	3	10.3
Dog	–	–	–	–	4	0.3	3	4.4	–	–	–	–
Wild:												
Red deer	97	28.8	6	19.4	173	14.8	12	17.7	49	30.8	7	24.1
Roe deer	6	1.8	3	9.7	4	0.3	2	2.9	5	3.2	2	6.9
Wild pig	13	3.8	2	6.5	36	3.1	4	5.9	7	4.4	2	6.9
? wild pig	6	1.8	1	3.2	11	0.9	2	2.9	–	–	–	–
Horse	2	0.6	1	3.2	–	–	–	–	1	0.6	1	3.5
Bear	–	–	–	–	–	–	–	–	1	0.6	1	3.5
Beaver	1	0.3	1	3.2	8	0.7	2	2.9	–	–	–	–
Total	337		31		1172		68		159		29	
Domestic	212	62.9	17	54.8	940	80.2	46	67.7	96	60.4	16	55.1
Wild	125	37.1	14	45.2	232	19.8	22	32.3	63	39.6	13	44.9
Domestic:												
Cattle	134	63.2	9	52.9	849	90.3	32	69.5	63	65.6	9	56.3
Ovicaprids	18	8.5	3	17.7	39	4.2	5	10.9	21	21.9	4	25.0
Pig	60	28.3	5	29.4	48	5.1	6	13.1	12	12.5	3	18.7
Dog	–	–	–	–	4	0.4	3	6.5	–	–	–	–

Table No. 35

Florești (Linear Pottery)

a) Houses 1 and 3		b) 1955-58 excavations		
Animals	%B.	Animals	%B.	%Ind.
Cattle	59.0	Cattle	77.5	61.9
Ovicaprids	5.9	Pig	14.8	28.6
Pig	29.5	Wild	7.7	9.5
Wild	5.6			
Total No. Bones	250	Total No. Bones	298	
Total No. individuals	34	Total No. individuals	42	

Table No. 36

Novi Rusești (Linear Pottery & Tripolye B)

	Linear				Pottery		Tripolye		
	B.	%	I.	%	B.	I.	B.	%	I.
Domestic:									
Cattle	1080	38.2	56	21.6	57.0	42.1	854	42.9	52
Goat	473	16.7	36	13.8	24.9	27.1	349	17.6	32
Pig	325	11.5	36	13.8	17.2	27.1	350	17.6	27
Dog	18	0.6	5	1.9	0.9	3.7	8	0.4	4
Wild:									
Red deer	167	5.9	12	4.6			81	4.1	9
Roe deer	90	3.2	14	5.4			49	2.5	5
Elk	10	0.3	3	1.2			3	0.1	2
Aurochs	235	8.3	18	6.9			72	3.6	7
Bison	13	0.5	4	1.5			7	0.2	1
Pig	79	2.8	10	3.8			55	2.8	8
Ass	6	0.2	3	1.2			2	0.1	2
Wolf	27	1.0	6	2.3			8	0.4	3
Fox	25	0.9	8	3.1			4	0.2	3
Bear	27	1.0	5	1.9			9	0.4	3
Badger	32	1.1	6	2.3			4	0.2	2
Marten	9	0.3	3	1.2			1	0.1	1
Wild cat	3	0.1	1	0.4			2	0.1	2
Lynx	10	0.3	3	1.2			3	0.1	2
Hare	66	2.3	11	4.2			16	0.8	5
Beaver	6	0.2	2	0.8			4	0.2	1
Hamster	2	0.1	1	0.4			1	0.1	1
Horse	128	4.5	17	6.5			108	5.4	19
Total	2831		260				1990		193
Domestic	1896	67.0	133	51.1			1561	78.5	115
Wild	935	33.0	127	48.9			429	21.5	78

%	B.	I.
.9	54.8	45.2
.8	22.3	27.8
.0	22.4	23.5
.1	0.5	3.5

.6
.6
.0
.6
.6
.1
.0
.6
.6
.6
.0
.5
.0
.0
.6
.5
.5
.8

.8
.2

Table No. 37a

Eitzum (Linear Pottery)

Animals	Bones
Domestic:	
Cattle	44
Ovicaprids	2
Total	46

Table No. 37b

Jersleben (Linear Pottery)

	Bones	%
Domestic:		
Cattle	47	88.7
Ovicaprids	1	1.9
Pig	1	1.9
Wild:		
Aurochs	3	5.6
Pig	1	1.9
Total	53	

Table No. 38

Barleben-Schweinemästerei (Linear Pottery)

Animals	A Bones	%	B Bones	%	Domestic % A	B
Domestic:						
Cattle	127	55.0	184	62.5	57.0	73.9
Ovicaprids	73	31.6	22	7.5	32.7	8.8
Pig	23	9.9	42	14.3	10.3	16.9
Dog	—	—	1	0.35	—	0.4
Wild:						
Red deer	3	1.3	5	1.7		
Roe deer	—	—	1	0.35		
Pig	3	1.3	28	9.5		
Beaver	—	—	1	0.35		
Wolf	—	—	1	0.35		
Fox	1	0.45	—	—		
Turtle	1	0.45	—	—		
Birds	—	—	3	1.05		
Fish	—	—	1	0.35		
Sturgeon	—	—	5	1.7		
Total	231		294			
Domestic	223		249	84.65		
Wild	8		45	15.35		

A—Settlement; B—Graves

Table No. 39

Barleben-Huhnerfarm (Linear Pottery)

Animals	Bones	%
Domestic:		
Cattle	42	24.5
Ovicaprids	110	64.4
Pig	16	9.3
Wild:		
Aurochs	2	1.2
Pig	1	0.6
Total	171	
Domestic	168	98.2
Wild	3	1.8

Table No. 40

Bruchstedt (Linear Pottery)

Animals	Bones	%	Domestic %
Domestic:			
Cattle	105	56.2	58.3
Ovicaprids	37	19.8	20.6
Pig	37	19.8	20.6
Dog	1	0.5	0.5
Wild:			
Aurochs	7	3.7	
Total	187		

Table No. 41

Cochstedt (Linear Pottery)

Animals	Bones	%
Cattle	97	63.4
Ovicaprids	39	25.5
Pig	16	10.4
Bird	1	0.7
Total	153	

Table No. 42

Dammendorf (Linear Pottery)

Animals	Bones	%	Domestic %
Domestic:			
Cattle	58	24.7	26.9
Ovicaprids	151	64.2	69.9
Pig	7	3.0	3.2
Wild:			
Red deer	3	1.3	
Roe deer	5	2.1	
Aurochs	1	0.4	
Fox	10	4.3	
Total	235		
Domestic	216	91.9	
Wild	19	8.1	

Table No. 43

Erfurt (Linear Pottery)

	A		B		C		B	C
Animals	Bones	%	Bones	%	Bones	%	Domestic %	
Domestic:								
Cattle	50	60.2	32	51.6	20	37.7	56.1	38.
Ovicaprids	14	16.9	16	25.8	17	32.1	28.1	32.
Pig	19	22.9	9	14.5	15	28.3	15.8	28.
Wild:								
Red deer	—	—	1	1.6	—	—		
Roe deer	—	—	3	4.9	1	1.9		
Hare	—	—	1	1.6	—	—		
Total	83		62		53			
Domestic	83		57		52			
Wild	—		5		1			

A—Erfurt Rankestrasse; B—Erfurt Steiger; C—Erfurt Stolzestrasse.

Table No. 44

Gatersleben (Linear Pottery)

Animals	Bones	%	Domestic % Bones
Domestic:			
Cattle	149	48.5	49.8
Ovicaprids	84	27.4	28.1
Pig	66	21.5	22.1
Wild:			
Red deer	2	0.65	
Roe deer	2	0.65	
Pig	4	1.3	
Total	307		
Domestic	299	97.4	
Wild	8	3.6	

Table No. 45

Grossörner (Linear Pottery)

Animals	Bones	%	Domestic %
Domestic:			
Cattle	54	67.5	75.0
Ovicaprids	15	18.8	20.8
Pig	3	3.8	4.2
Wild:			
Red deer	1	1.2	
Pig	2	2.5	
Horse	5	6.2	
Total	80		
Domestic	72	90.1	
Wild	8	9.9	

Table No. 46

Halle-Trotha (Linear Pottery)

Animals	Bones	%	Domestic %
Domestic:			
Cattle	307	83.8	85.9
Ovicaprids	32	8.8	8.7
Pig	18	4.9	5.4
Wild:			
Roe deer	2	0.5	
Aurochs	3	0.9	
Pig	1	0.3	
Horse	1	0.3	
Goose	2	0.5	
Total	366		
Domestic	357	97.5	
Wild	9	2.5	

Table No. 47

Hausneindorf (Linear Pottery)

Animals	Bones	%	Domestic %
Domestic:			
Cattle	56	74.6	77.7
Ovicaprids	14	18.7	19.5
Pig	2	2.7	2.8
Wild:			
Roe deer	1	1.3	
Aurochs	2	2.7	
Total	75		
Domestic	72	96.0	
Wild	3	4.0	

Table No. 48

Hettstedt (Linear Pottery)

Animals	Bones	%
Cattle	24	21.2
Ovicaprids	80	70.8
Pig	9	8.0
Total	113	

Table No. 49

Hohlstedt (Linear Pottery)

Animals	Bones	%	Domestic %
Domestic:			
Cattle	188	52.5	55.1
Ovicaprids	89	24.9	26.1
Pig	64	17.9	18.8
Wild:			
Red deer	3	0.8	
Roe deer	3	0.8	
Horse	2	0.6	
Fox	1	0.3	
Beaver	8	2.2	
Total	358		
Domestic	341	95.3	
Wild	17	4.7	

Table No. 50

Köthen-Geuz (Linear Pottery)

Animals	Bones	%	Domestic %
Domestic:			
Cattle	98	52.7	56.0
Ovicaprids	68	36.6	38.9
Pig	9	4.8	5.1
Wild:			
Roe deer	4	2.2	
Pig	2	1.1	
Fox	1	0.5	
Hare	1	0.5	
Hamster	3	1.6	
Total	186		
Domestic	175	94.1	
Wild	11	5.9	

Table No. 51

Magdeburg-Prester (Linear Pottery)

Animals	Bones	%
Domestic:		
Cattle	538	70.0
Ovicaprids	68	8.9
Pig	130	16.9
Wild:		
Red deer	7	0.9
Roe deer	4	0.5
Pig	11	1.4
Horse	3	0.4
Aurochs	3	0.4
Beaver	1	0.1
Hare	1	0.1
Turtle	1	0.1
Fish	2	0.3
Total	769	
Domestic	736	95.8
Wild	33	4.2

Table No. 52

Müddersheim (Linear Pottery)

Animals	Bones	%	Domestic %
Domestic:			
Cattle	104	47.3	66.7
Ovicaprids	19	8.6	12.2
Pig	32	14.5	20.5
Dog	1	0.5	0.6
Wild:			
Red deer	2	0.9	
Roe deer	2	0.9	
Aurochs	33	15.0	
? Aurochs	16	7.3	
Pig	3	1.3	
Horse	4	1.8	
Hamster	1	0.5	
Birds	1	0.5	
Mussels	2	0.9	
Total	220		
Domestic	156	70.9	
Wild	64	29.1	

Table No. 53

Tröbsdorf (Linear Pottery)

Animals	Bones	%	Domestic %
Domestic:			
Cattle	156	41.3	45.3
Ovicaprids	164	43.5	47.5
Pig	25	6.6	7.2
Wild:			
Red deer	4	1.1	
Roe deer	11	2.9	
Aurochs	1	0.3	
Pig	7	1.8	
Horse	1	0.3	
Fox	3	0.8	
Badger	1	0.3	
Duck	1	0.3	
Fish	3	0.8	
Total	377		
Domestic	345	91.4	
Wild	32	8.6	

Table No. 54

Regensburg-Pürkelgut (Linear Pottery & Rössen)

Animals	Bones	%	Ind.	%	Domestic % Bones	Ind.
Domestic:						
Cattle	74	16.1	13	12.6	49.3	34.2
Ovicaprids	26	5.6	10	9.7	17.4	26.3
Pig	44	9.6	11	10.7	29.3	29.0
Dog	6	1.3	4	3.9	4.0	10.5
Wild:						
Red deer	97	21.1	17	16.5		
Roe deer	10	2.2	6	5.8		
Aurochs	158	34.3	25	24.3		
Pig	34	7.4	13	12.6		
Bear	1	0.2	1	1.0		
Beaver	10	2.2	3	2.9		
Total	460		103			
Domestic	150	32.6	38	36.9		
Wild	310	67.4	65	63.1		

Tables No. 55

Weimar-Ehringsdorf (Linear Pottery)

Animals	Bones	%	Domestic %
Domestic:			
Cattle	42	53.2	62.7
Ovicaprids	13	16.4	19.4
Pig	11	13.9	16.4
Dog	1	1.3	1.5
Wild:			
Red deer	5	6.3	
Roe deer	6	7.6	
Pig	1	1.3	
Total	79		
Domestic	67	84.8	
Wild	12	15.2	

Table No. 56

Zauschwitz (Linear Pottery)

Animals	Bones	%	Domestic %
Domestic:			
Cattle	60	65.9	89.5
Ovicaprids	3	3.3	4.5
Pig	3	3.3	4.5
Dog	1	1.1	1.5
Wild:			
Red deer	6	6.6	
Aurochs	10	11.0	
Pig	7	7.7	
Horse	1	1.1	
Total	91		
Domestic	67	73.6	
Wild	24	26.4	

Table No. 57

Zehbitz (Linear Pottery)

Animals	Bones	%	Domestic %
Domestic:			
Cattle	35	66.0	72.9
Ovicaprids	8	15.1	16.7
Pig	5	9.4	10.4
Wild:			
Roe deer	1	1.9	
Pig	3	5.7	
Horse	1	1.9	
Total	53		
Domestic	48	90.5	
Wild	5	9.5	

Table No. 58

Zorbau (Linear Pottery)

Animals	Bones	%
Domestic:		
Cattle	26	28.6
Ovicaprids	48	52.7
Pig	16	17.6
Wild:		
Red deer	1	1.1
Total	91	

Table No. 59

Keutschen and Tornau (Linear Pottery)

Animals	Keutschen	Tornau
Cattle	9	12
Ovicaprids	17	4
Pig	3	1
Total	29	17

Table No. 60

Esperstedt, Wulfen & Mücheln (Linear Pottery)

Animals	Esperstedt Bones	Wulfen Bones	Mücheln Bones
Domestic:			
Cattle	23	23	19
Ovicaprids	3	2	7
Pig	1	—	10
Wild:			
Red deer	—	3	2
Total	27	28	38

Table No. 61

Holdenstedt, Lösau & Rehmsdorf (Linear Pottery)

Animals	Holdenstedt Bones	Lösau Bones	Rehmsdorf Bones
Domestic:			
Cattle	9	27	—
Ovicaprids	8	3	—
Pig	1	2	2
Wild:			
Roe deer	1	—	—
Fox	—	—	16
Total	19	32	18

Table No. 62

Grossgrabe (Linear Pottery)

Animals	Bones
Cattle	22
Ovicaprids	16
Total	38

Table No. 63

Hainichen (Linear Pottery)

Animals	Bones
Domestic:	
Cattle	15
Ovicaprids	6
Pig	3
Wild:	
Red deer	1
Pig	2
Total	27
Domestic	24
Wild	3

Table No. 64a

Linear Pottery Culture

Animals	E	M	E or M	E & M	L	LP	ΣLP
Domestic:							
Cattle	1122	615	212	1949	677	522	3148
Sheep	63	97	20	180	9	12	201
Goat	31	45	1	77	8	7	92
Sheep or goat	446	400	47	893	75	82	1050
Pig	205	166	60	431	163	60	654
Dog	1	2	4	7	—	2	9
Wild:							
Red deer	20	12	1	33	13	17	63
Roe deer	25	16	—	41	20	15	76
Elk	—	--	—	—	—	1	1
Aurochs	7	1	7	15	10	10	35
Pig	13	10	9	32	18	32	82
Horse	4	2	—	6	5	6	17
Wolf	—	—	—	—	—	1	1
Fox	5	11	—	16	—	16	32
Beaver	8	—	—	8	2	1	11
Badger	1	—	—	1	—	—	1
Hamster	—	3	—	3	—	—	3
Hare	1	1	—	2	1	—	3
Wild duck	1	—	—	1	—	2	3
Wild goose	2	5	—	7	—	1	8
Birds	—	1	1	2	—	—	2
Carp	1	—	—	1	—	—	1
Sturgeon	—	—	—	—	—	5	5
Fish	2	—	—	2	2	1	5
Turtle	1	—	—	1	1	1	3
Total	1959	1387	362	3708	1004	794	5506
Domestic	1868	1325	344	3537	932	685	5154
Wild	91	62	18	171	72	109	352

Table No. 64b

Domestic Animals (Cattle, Ovicaprids and Pigs) in the Linear Pottery Culture

	E		M		E & M		L		∑ LP			
	Bones	%	Bones	%	Bones	%	Bones	%	Bones	%	Ind.	%
Cattle	1122	60.1	615	46.5	1949	55.2	677	72.6	3148	61.2	236	45.3
Ovicaprids	540	28.9	542	41.0	1150	32.6	92	9.9	1343	26.1	185	35.5
Pig	205	11.0	166	12.5	431	12.2	163	12.5	654	12.7	100	19.2
Total	1867		1323		3530		932		5145		521	

E–Early Linear Pottery; M–Mid Linear Pottery; E or M–Early or Mid Linear Pottery; E & M– Early and Mid Linear Pottery;
L–Late Linear Pottery; LP–Linear Pottery (phase unknown); ∑LP–Total Linear Pottery

Table No. 65

Cultivated Plants of the Linear Pottery Culture

	A	B	C	D	E	F	G	H	I	J	K	L
Rumania:												
Glvanestii Vechi	x											
Russia:												
Kotowania						x	x					
Nezwicka	x	x	x								x	
Torskie						?	?					
Austria:												
Wien-Vosendorf				x				x				
Poland:												
Chelmza						x	x		x			
Jurkowice						x						
Opatow						x	x					
Strzelce	x					x	x		x	x		
Zofipole								x				
Czechoslovakia:												
Bylany		x										
Mohelnice	x	x				?	?					
Tesetice	?	x										
Germany:												
Derenburg						?	?					
Doschwitz						x						
Eisenberg						x					x	
Erfurt-Steiger	x						x					
Ettersburg						?	?					
Herkheim		x										
Köln-Lindenthal	?					x	x					x
Lauingen	x					x		x				
Merzien						?	?					
Nahermemmingen	x						?					
Tröbsdorf	x	x									x	
Zilgendorf	x	x										
Zorbig						?	?					

A—Einkorn; B—Emmer; C—Bread wheat; D—Hard wheat; E—Club wheat;
F—Wheat (unspecified); G—Barley (unspecified); H—Millet; I—Rye; J—Oat
K—Pea; L—Flax

Table No. 66

Czechoslovakian Plants (Neolithic)

	A	B	C	D	E	F
Mohelnice	28 (51)	52 (79)	11	7 (10)	(3)	(2–3)
Tesetice	1	(1)	–	–	–	–
Sarovce	1	(1)	–	–	–	–
Brno Lisen	21	(11)	4	2 (3)	(2)	–

Numbers in brackets denote probable identifications of the grain.

A—Emmer; B—Einkorn; C—Emmer or einkorn; D—Wheat (unspecified); E—Barley; F—Millet

Table No. 67

Domestic Animals of the Boian Culture

	Cattle	Ovicaprids	Pig	Dog
Bulgaria:				
Loveč	x	x		x
Rumania:				
Aldeni	x			x
Bogata	x	x		x
Boian-Varaşti	x	x	x	
Crusovu	x	x		
Malul Rosu	x	x	x	
Ocna Sibiului	x	x	x	
Slobozia	x	x		
Spantov	x	x	x	x
Tangîru	x	x	x	x

Table No. 68

Bogata (Boian)	I				II			
Animals	Bones	%	Ind.	%	Bones	%	Ind.	%
Domestic:								
Cattle	140	86.5	47	68.2	4		2	
Ovicaprids	14	8.6	14	20.3	1		1	
Dog	3	1.9	3	4.4	1		1	
Wild:								
Red deer	1	0.6	1	1.4	—		—	
Horse	1	0.6	1	1.4	—		—	
Fox	2	1.2	2	2.9	1		1	
Hare	1	0.6	1	1.4	—		—	
Mustelidae	—	—	—	—	1		1	
Total	162		69		8		6	
Domestic	157	97.0	64	92.9	6		4	
Wild	5	3.0	5	7.1	2		2	

Table No. 68 (contd.)

Bogata		Total		
Animals	Bones	%	Ind.	%
Domestic:				
Cattle	160	78.8	60	58.8
Ovicaprids	26	12.8	25	24.5
Dog	7	3.4	7	6.9
Wild:				
Red deer	1	0.5	1	1.0
Horse	1	0.5	1	1.0
Fox	4	2.0	4	3.9
Hare	3	1.5	3	2.9
Mustelidae	1	0.5	1	1.0
Total	203		102	
Domestic	193	95.0	92	90.2
Wild	10	5.0	10	9.8

Domestic	Bones	%	Ind.	%
Cattle	160	82.9	60	65.2
Ovicaprids	26	13.5	25	27.2
Dog	7	3.6	7	7.6

	III				IV		
ones	%	Ind.	%	Bones	%	Ind.	%
2		2		14		9	
8		7		3		3	
1		1		2		2	
—		—		—		—	
—		—		—		—	
1		1		—		—	
2		2		—		—	
—		—		—		—	
14		13		19		14	
11		10		19		14	
3		3		—		—	

Table No. 69(a)

Tangîru (Boian and Gumelniţa)

Domestic Animals

Period		Cattle		Ovicaprids		Pig		Dog	
		Bones	Ind.	Bones	Ind.	Bones	Ind.	Bones	Ind.
B	I	53.2	48.5	23.4	26.6	18.2	18.6	5.2	6.3
B	II	60.7	56.4	16.4	19.3	20.2	20.9	2.4	3.2
B	III	54.1	48.7	18.7	20.5	18.7	20.5	8.3	10.3
B	IV	57.7	47.4	13.7	19.3	20.2	24.5	8.3	8.7
G	I	50.0	38.8	36.9	44.4	10.9	13.9	2.2	2.8
G	II	47.5	44.2	32.6	31.7	17.7	21.1	2.1	2.8
G	III	46.4	40.9	23.3	29.5	23.3	29.5	—	—
B—Boian; G—Gumelniţa									
Boian		57.0	49.8	16.9	21.1	19.6	21.9	6.5	7.2
Gumelniţa		47.7	42.4	32.9	33.7	17.7	21.7	1.7	2.2

Table No. 69 (b)

Tangîru

Animals		Wild		Domestic		Total	
Period		B.%	I.%	B.%	I.%	Bones	Ind.
B	I	2.5	3.0	97.5	97.0	81	70
B	II	21.0	17.3	79.0	82.7	102	77
B	III	12.7	15.2	87.3	84.8	55	46
B	IV	5.0	7.3	95.0	92.7	183	129
G	I	2.1	2.6	97.9	97.4	48	38
G	II	1.4	1.8	98.6	98.2	149	114
G	III	5.0	6.4	95.0	93.6	59	44
Boian		9.5	9.9	90.5	90.1	421	322
Gumelniţa		2.4	3.1	97.2	96.3	256	196

Table No. 70 (a)

Domestic Animals of the Hamangia culture

	Cattle	Ovicaprids	Pig	Dog
La Adam	x	x	x	
Ceamurlia de Jos	x	x	x	x
Cernavoda	x	x	?	
Techirghiol	x	x	x	x

Table No. 70 (b)

Techirghiol (Hamangia)

Animals	Bones	%	Ind.	%	Domestic % Bones	Ind.
Domestic:						
Cattle	550	50.3	166	44.6	53.2	50.0
Ovicaprids	456	41.7	148	39.8	44.1	44.4
Pig	22	2.1	13	3.5	2.1	3.9
Dog	7	0.6	6	1.6	0.6	1.7
Wild:						
Roe deer	2	0.2	2	0.5		
Pig	3	0.3	2	0.5		
Donkey	13	1.2	8	2.2		
Small equoid	9	0.8	8	2.2		
Fox	14	1.2	7	1.9		
Hare	10	0.9	7	1.9		
Dolphin	8	0.7	5	1.3		
Total	1094		372			

Table No. 71

Wild Animals of the Russian Neolithic

a) Pontic Region

	A	B	C	D
Red deer	x	x	x	x
Roe deer	x	x		x
Aurochs	x		x	
Pig	x	x	x	x
Horse		x	x	x
Wolf	x	x	x	
Beaver	x	x		x
Hare	x	x	x	
Fox	x	x	x	x
Badger	x			
Cat		x		
Polecat				x
Hamster	x			
Small rodents				x
Marsh turtle				x
Tortoise	x	x	x	
Birds	x	x	x	x
Fish	x	x	x	x

A—Igren 8; B—Shulaev; C—Surskii;
D—Kaneva and Pekaryame

Table No. 71

b) Northern Russia

	A.		B.		C.		D.
	B.	I.	B.	I.	B.	I.	B.
Cattle	—	—	—	—	—	—	—
Ovicaprids	—	—	—	—	—	—	—
Dog	36	15	54	9	311	39	726
Wild:							
Reindeer	—	—	—	—	—	—	—
Red deer	7	6	47	9	143	21	10
Roe deer	4	3	14	6	24	11	32
Elk	4512	144	310	14	7166	198	2022
Aurochs	60	12	26	5	1065	50	1354
Bison	—	—	—	—	—	—	—
Pig	54	13	211	16	3214	135	1715
Horse	30	7	—	—	282	21	—
Bear	74	10	34	7	613	59	139
Lynx	1	1	—	—	5	4	1
Wild Cat	—	—	—	—	2	2	—
Polecat	—	—	—	—	2	1	1
Otter	36	13	4	3	139	36	18
Badger	2	1	—	—	167	19	3
Beaver	1822	117	289	24	3920	296	250
Wolverine	—	—	—	—	—	—	1
Marten	5	3	9	5	460	68	97
Mink	—	—	—	—	3	2	1
Fox	—	—	1	1	3	1	20
Wolf	15	7	1	1	23	9	—
Guinea pig	—	—	—	—	—	—	4
Vole	—	—	—	—	—	—	21
Squirrel	—	—	—	—	3	2	—
Hare	1	1	2	2	26	11	4
Hedgehog	—	—	—	—	1	1	1
Seal	73	12	20	6	—	—	973
Turtle	—	—	3	—	19	—	—
Birds	204	—	112	—	421	—	2495
Fish	108	—	314	—	148	—	303
Total	6732	365	1022	103	17572	1016	7353

A — Kunda (Estonia); B—Narva I—III (Estonia); C—Kiääpä (Estonia);
G—Piestina (Latvia); H—Kreici (Latvia); I—Budyanka (Latvia); J—Akali

E. I.	F. B.	G. B	G. I.	H. B	H. I.	I. B.	J. B.	J. I.	K.	L.	M.
−	−	−	−	−	−	−	1	1	?	−	−
−	−	−	−	3	3	−	−	−	−	−	−
3	6	5	2	17	5	4	12	6	x	x	x
−	−	−	−	−	−	−	−	−	x	x	x
1	6	21	3	6	5	11	3	1	−	−	-
3	7	5	2	15	6	33	8	5	−	x	−
11	232	83	9	286	15	250	271	16	x	x	x
9	82	17	3	41	10	206	131	7	?	x	x
−	−	−	−	−	−	−	−	−	−	x	x
16	173	151	16	297	18	534	204	12	x	x	x
−	2	−	−	2	1	−	3	2	−	−	−
1	21	7	3	29	5	19	22	8	x	x	x
−	−	−	−	−	−	−	−	−	−	−	x
−	1	−	−	−	−	−	−	−	−	−	−
−	1	3	2	2	2	2	−	−	x	x	−
5	8	2	2	9	4	21	7	4	x	−	x
−	16	1	1	6	5	2	2	2	−	−	x
9	72	26	5	93	15	88	61	11	x	x	x
−	−	−	−	−	−	−	−	−	−	−	−
3	33	74	19	10	7	15	2	2	x	x	x
−	−	−	−	−	−	2	−	−	−	−	−
1	3	4	2	−	−	2	−	−	x	x	x
−	−	−	−	−	−	3	−	−	−	x	x
−	−	−	−	−	−	−	−	−	−	−	−
−	−	−	−	6	3	6	−	−	x	x	x
−	−	−	−	2	2	−	−	−	x	−	−
1	3	17	3	6	5	2	−	−	x	x	x
−	−	−	−	−	−	1	−	−	−	−	−
2	−	−	−	−	−	−	−	−	−	x	−
−	−	1	−	−	−	−	−	−	−	−	−
−	24	58	−	−	−	−	9	1	−	−	−
−	26	20	−	−	−	−	274	1	−	−	−
65	666	416	72	830	111	1201	728	78			

−Rigikyula I–III (Estonia); E–Valma (Estonia); F–Malmuta (Latvia);
.stonia); K–Bologoe; L–Ladogasee; M–Volosovo.

Table No. 72

Domestic Animals of the Central European Neolithic Period

	Cattle	Ovicaprids	Pig	Dog
Yugoslavia:				
Csoka (Vinča & Tisza)	x	x	x	
Gornja Tuzla (Vinča)	x	x	?	x
Butmir (Butmir)	x	x	x	
Crvena Stijena (Butmir)		x		
Danilo (Butmir)	x	x	x	x
Grapceva Spilja (Butmir)	x	x	x	
Lisicici (Butmir)	x			
Nebo (Butmir)	x	x	x	x
Smilcic (Butmir)	x	x		
Rumania:				
Dealu Ruschi (Vinča-Tordos)	x	x		x
Dudeşti (Vinča-Tordos)	x		?	
Nandor (Vinča-Tordos)	x	x		
Tordos (Vinča-Tordos)		x		
Hungary:				
Aggtelek (Bükk)	x	x	x	x
Borod-Derekegyházi-dülö (Bükk)	x	x	x	
Berettyószentmárton (Herpály)	x	x	x	x
Herpály (Herpály)	x	x	x	x
Hódmezövásárhely (Tisza)	x	x		x
Hódmezövásárhely-Gorzsa-Cukortanya (Tisza)	x	x	x	x
Polgár-Csoszhalom (Tisza)	x	x	x	x
Szegvár-Tuzköves (Tisza)	x	x	x	x
Lebo (Tisza & Szilmeg)	x	x	x	x
Polgár-Basatanya (Szilmeg)	x	x	x	x
Szilmeg (Szilmeg)	x	x	x	x
Pécsvárad-Aranyhegy (Lengyel)	x	x	x	x
Zengövarkony (Lengyel)	x	x	x	x
Kenezlo-Fazekaszug (Neolithic)	x			
Zalavar (Neolithic)	x	x	x	
Austria:				
Kufstein (Neolithic)	x	x	x	x
Eggendorf a. Walde (Lengyel)				x
Wien XXI-Aspern (Neolithic)				x
Wien XIII (Neolithic)				x
Ziegelofen Kargl (Neolithic)				x
Czechoslovakia:				
Chyza				x
Oborin				x
Sarkanova-dira		x	?	

Table No. 73

Borod-Derekegyházi dülö (Bukk)

Animals	Bones	%	Ind.	%	Domestic % Bones	Ind.
Domestic:						
Cattle	56	60.3	17	46.0	73.9	58.6
Ovicaprids	11	11.7	5	13.5	14.3	17.3
Pig	10	10.8	7	18.9	12.8	24.1
Wild:						
Red deer	11	11.7	4	10.8		
Roe deer	1	1.1	1	2.7		
Aurochs	2	2.2	1	2.7		
Fox	1	1.1	1	2.7		
Hare	1	1.1	1	2.7		
Total	93		37			
Domestic	77	82.8	29	78.4		
Wild	16	17.2	8	21.6		

Table No. 74

Hódmezövásárhely-Gorzsa-Cukortanya (Tisza)

Animals	Bones	%	Ind.	%	Domestic % Bones	Ind.
Domestic:						
Cattle	101	44.1	51	35.4	73.1	66.2
Ovicaprids	7	3.1	5	3.5	5.1	6.5
Pig	15	6.5	14	9.7	10.9	18.2
Dog	15	6.5	7	4.9	10.9	9.1
Wild:						
Red deer	20	8.7	13	9.0		
Roe deer	8	3.5	6	4.2		
Aurochs	25	10.9	20	13.9		
Pig	17	7.4	13	9.0		
Fox	1	0.5	1	0.7		
Turtle	8	3.5	4	2.8		
Fish	12	5.3	10	6.9		
Total	229		144			
Domestic	138	60.2	77	53.5		
Wild	91	39.8	67	46.5		

Table No. 75

Polgár-Basatanya

Animals	Szilmeg B.	Szilmeg I.	Tisza-Polgár B.	Tisza-Polgár I.	Bodrogkeresztur B.	Bodrogkeresztur I.	Baden B.	Baden I.
Domestic:								
Cattle	77	9	13	7	3	3	21	16
Ovicaprids	2	2	156	16	216	14	17	9
Pig	4	4	156	28	170	11	103	7
Dog	2	1	150	5	—	—	—	—
? Horse	—	—	—	—	1	1	—	—
Wild:								
Red deer	—	—	3	3	—	—	5	4
Roe deer	—	—	2	2	—	—	1	1
Aurochs	—	—	10	10	—	—	—	—
Pig	—	—	4	4	—	—	—	—
Equoid	2	2	—	—	—	—	—	—
Turtle	—	—	—	—	2	1	—	—
Fish	—	—	1	1	13	1	—	—
Birds	—	—	—	—	—	—	1	1
Total	87	18	495	76	405	31	148	38
Domestic %								
Cattle	90.5	56.3	2.7	12.5	0.8	10.4	14.9	50.0
Ovicaprids	2.4	12.5	32.8	28.6	55.4	48.3	12.1	28.1
Pig	4.7	25.0	32.8	50.0	43.5	37.9	73.0	21.9
Dog	2.4	6.2	31.7	8.9	—	—	—	—
Horse	—	—	—	—	0.3	3.4	—	—

Table No. 76

Szilmeg (Szilmeg)

Animals	Bones	%	Ind.	%	Domestic % Bones	Domestic % Ind.
Domestic:						
Cattle	53	33.6	27	40.3	44.2	51.9
Ovicaprids	9	5.7	4	6.0	7.5	7.7
Pig	51	32.3	17	25.3	42.5	32.7
Dog	7	4.4	4	6.0	5.8	7.7
Wild:						
Red deer	9	5.7	3	4.5		
Roe deer	10	6.3	3	4.5		
Aurochs	1	0.6	1	1.5		
Pig	14	8.9	5	7.4		
Cat	2	1.3	1	1.5		
Wolf	1	0.6	1	1.5		
Fish	1	0.6	1	1.5		
Total	158		67			
Domestic	120	76.0	52	77.6		
Wild	38	24.0	15	22.4		

Table No. 77

Berettyöszentmárton (Herpály)

Animals	Bones	%	Ind.	%	Domestic % Bones	Domestic % Ind.
Domestic:						
Cattle	392	14.2	207	16.9	62.7	56.8
Ovicaprids	43	1.5	36	2.9	6.9	9.9
Pig	180	6.5	111	9.0	28.8	30.5
Dog	10	0.3	10	0.8	1.6	2.8
Wild:						
Red deer	461	16.7	241	19.6		
Roe deer	35	1.2	27	2.2		
Aurochs	1485	53.7	477	38.8		
Pig	117	4.2	82	6.7		
Cat	3	0.1	3	0.2		
Lynx	1	0.1	1	0.1		
Badger	1	0.1	1	0.1		
Otter	1	0.1	1	0.1		
Wolf	2	0.1	2	0.2		
Fox	5	0.2	4	0.3		
Beaver	18	0.6	16	1.3		
Hare	2	0.1	2	0.2		
Turtle	5	0.2	5	0.4		
Birds	2	0.1	2	0.2		
Total	2763		1128			
Domestic	625	22.5	364	29.6		
Wild	2138	77.5	764	70.4		

Table No. 78

Herpály (Herpály)

Animals	Bones	%	Ind.	%	Domestic % Bones	Domestic % Ind.
Domestic:						
Cattle	70	13.0	27	12.7	54.2	41.6
Ovicaprids	21	3.9	12	5.6	16.3	18.4
Pig	32	5.9	22	10.3	24.8	33.8
Dog	6	1.1	4	1.9	4.7	6.2
Wild:						
Red deer	82	5.2	39	18.3		
Roe deer	4	0.7	4	1.9		
Aurochs	287	53.3	82	38.5		
Pig	36	6.7	22	10.3		
Fish	1	0.2	1	0.5		
Total	539		213			
Domestic	129	23.9	65	30.5		
Wild	410	76.1	148	69.5		

Table No. 79

Pécsvárad-Aranyhegy (Lengyel)

Animals	Bones	%	Ind.	%	Domestic % Bones	Ind.
Domestic:						
Cattle	42	33.9	29	30.2	76.5	70.7
Goat	2	1.6	2	2.1	3.6	4.9
Pig	9	7.3	8	8.4	17.3	19.5
Dog	2	1.6	2	2.1	3.6	4.9
Wild:						
Red deer	31	25.0	25	26.1		
Roe deer	3	2.4	3	3.1		
Aurochs	27	21.8	20	20.8		
Pig	5	4.0	4	4.2		
Cat	1	0.8	1	1.0		
Beaver	1	0.8	1	1.0		
Fish	1	0.8	1	1.0		
Total	124		96			
Domestic	55	44.4	41	42.8		
Wild	69	55.6	55	57.2		

Table No. 80

Zengővarkony (Lengyel)

Animals	Pre—1947 B.	Ind.	1947 Bones	%	Ind.	%	Domestic % 1947 Bones	Ind.
Domestic:								
Cattle	15	8	736	51.6	277	42.0	85.3	77.4
Ovicaprids	6	3	9	0.6	7	1.1	1.0	2.0
Pig	41	12	101	7.1	66	10.0	11.7	18.4
Dog	1	1	17	1.2	8	1.2	2.0	2.2
Wild:								
Red deer	34	21	258	18.1	119	18.0		
Roe deer	6	4	37	2.6	25	3.8		
Aurochs	13	10	219	15.4	122	18.5		
Pig	11	11	45	3.1	34	5.2		
Beaver	—	—	1	0.1	1	0.1		
Hare	4	1	3	0.2	1	0.1		
Fish	1	1	—	—	—	—		
Total	132	72	1426		660			
Domestic	63	24	863	60.5	358	54.3		
Wild	69	48	563	39.5	302	45.7		

Table No. 81

Central European Cultivated Plants

	A	B	C	D	E	F	G	H	I	J	K
Yugoslavia:											
Vinča (Vinča-Pločnik)					x						
Butmir (Butmir)	x	x				x					
Danilo (Butmir)	?	?					x				
Lisicici (Butmir)	x	x				x					
Lug (Butmir)	x	x				x					
Hungary:											
Aggtelek (Bükk)	x		x			?	x		P,B		
Lengyel (Lengyel)							x		B	x	x
Zengővarkony (Lengyel)				x		x					
Austria:											
Eggendorf (Lengyel)	x	x									
Kuhnring (Neolithic)	x	x									
Roggendorf (Neolithic)	x	x									
Stillfried (Neolithic)					?	?					
Wien/Gumpendorf (Neolithic)					x						
Wien/Ober St. Viet (Neolithic)						x					
Wien/Vosendorf (? Lengyel)				x				x			
Czechoslovakia:											
Byçiscala							x		x		
Lobositz							?				

A—Einkorn; B—Emmer; C—Club wheat and bread wheat; D—Spelt;
E—Wheat (unspecified); F—Barley; G—Millet; H—Rye; I—Legumes;
J—Oats; K—Flax
P—Pea; B—Bean.

Table No. 82

Cultivated Grain at Lisicici and Lug in Yugoslavia

	Impressions		Carbonised Grain
	Lisicici	Lug	Lug
Einkorn	7	7	—
Emmer	1	8	—
Wheat (unspecified)	6	7	—
Barley	2	3	120

Table No. 83

Wild Animals of the Cortaillod Culture

	A	B	C	D	E	F	G	H	I	J	K	L	M	N	O
Red deer	x	x	x	x	x	x	x	x	x	x	x	x·	x	x	x
Roe deer	x	x	x	x	x	x	x	x	x	x	x		x	x	x
Elk			x	x		x				x	x		x	x	
Chamois						x				x			x	x	
Aurochs		x	x	x		x	x	x			x		x		
Bison		x		x		x					x				
Pig	x	x	x	x	x	x	x	x	?	x	x	x	x	x	
Horse			x				x				x	x			
Wolf		x	x	x						x	x		x		
Fox		x	x	x	x	x			x	x	x		x	x	
Badger		x	x	x	x	x				x	x		x	x	
Otter		x		x									x		
Marten		x		x		x				x			x	x	
Polecat		x											x		
Beaver		x	x	x		x	x		x	x	x		x	x	x
Bear		x	x	x		x	x			x	x		x	x	?
Lynx				x									x		
Cat		x		x		x					x		x		
Weasel													x		
Hare		x											x		
Hedgehog		x		x									x	x	
Mouse													x		
Squirrel		x								x			x	x	
Fish	x										x		x		x
Birds	x		x			x							x		

A—Auvernier; B—Burgaschisee-sud; C—Burgaschisee sud-ouest; D—Egozwil II;
E—Inkwil; F—Lattringen. G—Luscherz; H—Lobsigersee; I—Moosseedorf;
J—Neuville; K—Obermeilen; L—Port; M—St, Aubin; N—Schaffis; O—St, Leona
P—Thun; Q—Wauwil; R—Neiderwil; S—Pfyn.

278

Table No. 84

Domestic Animals of the Cortaillod Culture

R	S		Cattle	Ovicaprids	Pig	Dog
x	x	Auvernier	x	x	x	x
x	x	Burgaschisee sud	x	x	x	x
x	x	Burgaschisee sud-ouest	x	x	x	x
		Cortaillod	x	x	x	x
x	x	Egozwil II	x	x	x	x
x		Egozwil III	x	x	x	
x	x	Inkwil	x	x		x
		Lattringen	x	x	x	x
		Lobsigersee	x	x	x	x
x		Luscherz	x	x	x	x
x		Moosseedorf	x	x	x	x
		Neuville	x	x	x	x
		Obermeilen	x	x	x	x
		Port	x	x	x	x
x		Saint Aubin	x	x	x	x
		Schaffis	x	x	x	x
		Seematte-Gelfingen	x	x	x	x
		Saint Leonard	x	x	x	x
		Thun	x	x		x
		Wauwil	x	x	x	x
x		Niederwil	x	x	x	x
		Pfyn	x	x	x	x

x

Table No. 85

Burgaschisee sud (Cortaillod)

Animals	Bones	%	Ind.	%	Domestic % Bones	Domestic % Ind.
Domestic:						
Cattle	352	1.8	8	1.9	35.0	12.5
Ovicaprids	222	1.2	20	4.7	22.1	31.3
Pig	234	1.2	23	5.4	23.3	35.9
Dog	197	1.0	13	3.0	19.6	20.3
Wild:						
Red deer	9013	47.0	119	27.7		
Roe deer	1626	8.5	39	9.1		
Aurochs	1899	9.9	18	4.2		
Bison	108	0.6	5	1.2		
Uncertain						
bos	1714	9.0	3	0.7		
Pig	1824	9.5	62	14.4		
Pig (? wild)	701	3.7	10	2.3		
Bear	72	0.4	7	1.6		
Badger	235	1.2	21	4.9		
Beaver	595	3.1	29	6.8		
Wolf	61	0.3	4	0.9		
Fox	131	0.7	15	3.5		
Cat	42	0.2	6	1.4		
Otter	38	0.2	6	1.4		
Marten	43	0.2	7	1.6		
Squirrel	8	0.05	2	0.5		
Polecat	21	0.1	6	1.4		
Hare	1	0.05	1	0.2		
Hedgehog	13	0.1	5	1.2		
Total	19150		429			
Domestic	1005	5.2	64	15.0		
Wild	18145	94.8	365	85.0		

Table No. 86

Burgaschisee sud-ouest (Cortaillod)

Animals	Bones	%	Ind.	%	Domestic % Bones	Ind.
Domestic:						
Cattle	1015	31.0	49	22.6	64.0	42.6
Ovicaprids	190	5.8	23	10.6	12.0	20.0
Pig	302	9.2	34	15.7	19.1	29.6
Dog	77	2.3	9	4.1	4.9	7.8
Wild:						
Red deer	745	22.7	34	15.7		
Roe deer	206	6.3	15	6.9		
Elk	9	0.3	3	1.4		
Aurochs	396	12.1	14	6.4		
Horse	2	0.1	1	0.5		
Pig	238	7.2	16	7.4		
Bear	39	1.2	5	2.3		
Wolf	7	0.2	1	0.5		
Fox	2	0.1	2	0.9		
Badger	28	0.8	4	1.8		
Beaver	21	0.6	5	2.3		
Birds	2	0.1	2	0.9		
Total	3279		217			
Domestic	1584	48.3	115	53.0		
Wild	1695	51.7	102	47.0		

Table No. 87

Egozwil II (Cortaillod)

Animals	III	II	I	Total	%	Domestic %
		Individuals				
Domestic:						
Cattle	29	80	13	122	13.4	40.1
Ovicaprids	16	55	5	76	8.3	25.0
Pig	23	50	6	79	8.7	26.0
Dog	4	17	6	27	3.0	8.9
Wild:						
Red deer	61	162	27	250	27.5	
Roe deer	16	51	6	73	8.0	
Elk	12	25	3	40	4.4	
Aurochs	19	34	5	58	6.4	
Bison	3	8	2	13	1.4	
Pig	13	42	5	60	6.6	
Lynx	2	2	1	5	0.6	
Cat	1	3	–	4	0.4	
Fox	–	5	–	5	0.6	
Wolf	2	2	1	5	0.6	
Otter	2	3	1	6	0.7	
Pine martin	1	1	–	2	0.2	
Badger	7	17	2	26	2.8	
Bear	6	14	3	23	2.5	
Beaver	12	21	1	34	3.7	
Hedgehog	1	1	–	2	0.2	
Total	230	593	87	910		
Domestic	72	202	30	304	33.4	
Wild	158	391	57	606	66.6	

Table No. 88

Seematte-Gelfingen (Cortaillod)

Animals	Upper	Lower	Total	%	Domestic %
		Individuals			
Domestic:					
Cattle	84	7	91	21.0	43.7
Ovicaprids	35	4	39	9.0	18.8
Pig	55	3	58	13.4	27.9
Dog	18	2	20	4.6	9.6
Wild:					
Red deer	109	16	125	28.8	
Roe deer	16	3	19	4.4	
Aurochs	20	1	21	4.9	
Elk	3	—	3	0.7	
Pig	18	3	21	4.9	
Cat	2	—	2	0.5	
Fox	2	1	3	0.7	
Wolf	1	—	1	0.2	
Otter	1	1	2	0.5	
? Marten	1	—	1	0.2	
Polecat	2	1	3	0.7	
Badger	4	—	4	0.9	
Bear	4	2	6	1.4	
Beaver	10	2	12	2.8	
Squirrel	1	—	1	0.2	
Hedgehog	—	1	1	0.2	
Total	386	47	433		
Domestic	192	16	208	48.0	
Wild	194	31	225	52.0	

Table No. 89

Luscherz (Cortaillod)

Animals	Bones	%	Ind.	%	Domestic % Bones	Ind.
Domestic:						
Cattle	523	50.5	38	36.5	74.3	55.9
Sheep	62	5.9	7	6.7	8.8	10.3
Pig	59	5.7	9	8.6	8.4	13.2
Dog	60	5.8	14	13.4	8.5	20.6
Wild:						
Red deer	136	13.1	10	9.6		
Roe deer	24	2.3	2	1.9		
Aurochs	144	13.9	16	15.4		
Horse	4	0.4	1	1.0		
Pig	16	1.6	3	2.9		
Bear	2	0.2	1	1.0		
Fox	1	0.1	1	1.0		
Beaver	4	0.4	1	1.0		
Birds	1	0.1	1	1.0		
Total	1036		104			
Wild	332	32.1	36	34.8		
Domestic	704	67.9	68	65.2		

Table No. 90

Lobsigersee (Cortaillod)

Animals	Bones	%	Ind.	%	Domestic % Bones	Ind.
Domestic:						
Cattle	57	35.4	9	26.5	62.0	45.0
Ovicaprids	12	7.4	5	14.7	13.1	25.0
Pig	18	11.3	5	14.7	19.5	25.0
Dog	5	3.1	1	2.9	5.4	5.0
Wild:						
Red deer	28	17.4	3	8.8		
Roe deer	4	2.5	2	5.9		
Aurochs	13	8.1	3	8.8		
Pig	24	14.8	6	17.7		
Total	161		34			
Domestic	92	57.2	20	58.8		
Wild	69	42.8	14	41.2		

Table No. 91

Obermeilen (Cortaillod)

Animals	Bones	%	Ind.	%	Domestic % Bones	Ind.
Domestic:						
Cattle	245	29.3	21	22.3	52.8	40.4
Ovicaprids	28	3.3	7	7.5	6.1	13.4
Pig	149	17.8	16	17.1	32.1	30.8
Dog	42	5.1	8	8.5	9.0	15.4
Wild:						
Red deer	321	38.3	16	17.1		
Roe deer	12	1.4	5	5.3		
Elk	3	0.4	2	2.1		
Aurochs	2	0.2	2	2.1		
Bison	4	0.5	2	2.1		
Pig	13	1.6	2	2.1		
Horse	5	0.6	2	2.1		
Beaver	2	0.2	2	2.1		
Cat	2	0.2	1	1.1		
Fox	2	0.2	1	1.1		
Wolf	1	0.1	1	1.1		
Badger	2	0.2	2	2.1		
Bear	3	0.4	2	2.1		
Fish	2	0.2	2	2.1		
Total	838		94			
Domestic	464	55.5	52	55.4		
Wild	374	44.5	42	44.6		

Table No. 92

St. Aubin (Port Conty) (Cortaillod)

Animals	1921 Ind.	1926 B.	1926 Ind.	Level IV 1928–30 B.	1928–30 Ind.	Total B.	Total In
Domestic:							
Cattle	75	370	10	893	52	1263	1
Ovicaprids	16	218	14	582	78	800	1
Pig	27	244	15	419	38	663	
Dog	32	70	8	173	26	243	
Wild:							
Red deer	10	111	5	450	20	561	
Roe deer	4	1	1	97	11	98	
Elk	3	1	1	9	3	10	
Aurochs	2	—	—	22	3	22	
Chamois	—	—	—	1	1	1	
Pig	1	17	2	62	7	79	
Wolf	1	1	1	2	2	3	
Fox	4	5	2	23	5	28	
Badger	2	—	—	9	3	9	
Otter	2	—	—	1	1	1	
Pine marten	2	—	—	5	1	5	
Polecat	—	—	—	1	1	1	
Beaver	3	15	4	25	7	40	
Bear	2	1	1	3	2	4	
Lynx	—	—	—	1	1	1	
Cat	2	1	1	7	2	8	
Weasel	—	—	—	1	1	1	
Hare	1	2	1	6	2	8	
Hedgehog	2	2	2	10	6	12	
Field mouse	1	—	—	2	1	2	
Squirrel	—	2	1	6	2	8	
Total	192	1061	69	2810	276	3871	5
Domestic	150	902	47	2067	194	2969	3
Wild	42	159	22	743	82	902	1

	Domestic % Bones	Ind.
Cattle	42.6	35.1
Ovicaprids	26.9	27.6
Pig	22.3	20.5
Dog	8.2	16.8

Table No. 93

Wauwil (Cortaillod)

		Animals	Ind. (1)	%	Ind. (2)	%	Domestic % (1)	Domestic % (2)
%								
B.	Ind.	*Domestic:*						
		Cattle	22	32.8	30	21.4	68.7	40.0
32.6	25.5	Ovicaprids	3	4.5	12	8.6	9.4	16.0
20.7	20.1	Pig	6	8.9	30	21.4	18.8	40.0
17.2	14.9	Dog	1	1.5	3	2.1	3.1	4.0
6.3	12.3	*Wild:*						
		Red deer	19	28.3	19	13.6		
14.5	6.5	Roe deer	2	3.0	6	4.3		
2.5	3.0	Elk	1	1.5	3	2.1		
0.2	1.3	Aurochs	3	4.5	3	2.1		
0.5	0.9	Bison	3	4.5	3	2.1		
0.05	0.2	Pig	3	4.5	10	7.2		
2.0	1.9	Horse	1	1.5	2	1.5		
0.1	0.7	Bear	1	1.5	3	2.1		
0.7	2.0	Others	2	3.0	16	11.5		
0.2	0.9	Total	67		140			
0.05	0.6	Domestic	32	47.7	75	53.5		
0.1	0.6	Wild	35	52.3	65	46.5		
0.05	0.2							
1.0	2.6							
0.1	0.9							
0.05	0.2							
0.2	0.9							
0.05	0.2							
0.2	0.7							
0.3	1.9							
0.05	0.4							
0.3	0.6							
76.8	72.8							
23.2	27.2							

Individuals (1)—on basis of shoulder blades
Individuals (2)—on basis of bones

Table No. 94

Niederwil (Pfyn/Cortaillod)

Animals	Bones	Ind.	Domestic % Bones	Ind.
Domestic:				
Cattle	660	45	55.6	32.3
Ovicaprids	64	13	5.4	9.4
Pig	453	76	38.2	54.7
Probably dom. pig	186			
Dog	9	5	0.8	3.6
Wild:				
Red deer	188	10		
Roe deer	15	4		
Elk	?			
Cattle or red deer	47			
Aurochs	4	1		
Bison	?			
Pig	50	8		
Probably wild pig	7			
Domestic or wild pig	195			
Domestic or wild horse	1	1		
Fox	3	1		
Badger	1	1		
Beaver	14	4		
Hedgehog	1	1		
Total	1898	170		
Domestic	1372	139		
Wild	526	31		

Clason (1964) gives Domestic : Wild 81.8 : 18.2 (Bones) and
87.4 : 12.6 (Ind.).

Table No. 95

Pfyn (Pfyn/Cortaillod)

Animals	Bones	Ind.
Domestic:		
Cattle	40 (?13)	4
Pig	3	1
Ovicaprids	1	1
Dog	1	1
Wild:		
Red deer	130 (? 9)	
Roe deer	5	
Elk	1 (? 3)	
Aurochs	? 1	
Cattle/red deer	18	
Wild or domestic pig	2 (? 2)	
Wild pig	3	
Total	204 (?28)	
Domestic	45 (?13)	
Wild	159 (?15)	

Clason (1964) gives Domestic : Wild 36.1 : 63.8 (Bones) and
43.5 : 56.3 (Ind.).

Table No. 96

Cultivated Plants of the Cortaillod culture

	Wheat									
	A	B	C	D	E	F	G	H	I	J
Auvernier							?			
Burgaschi			x			x		x	x	
Burgaschisee sud-ouest				x				x	x	
Egozwil I			x			x				
Egozwil II		x	x		x			x	x	
Egozwil III			x					x	x	
Meyriez					x					
Moosseedorf			x	x		x		x	x	P
Neuville									x	
Niederwil			x			x	x	x	x	
Port	x	x	x			x				P
St. Blaise			x	x		x		x	x	P,L
Thun	x	x	x			x			x	P

A–Einkorn; B–Emmer; C–Club; D–Bread; E–Uncertain;
F–Barley; G–Millet; H–Poppy; I–Flax; J–Legumes;
P–Pea; L–Lentil.

Table No. 97

Wild Animals of the Later Swiss Neolithic

	A	B	C	D	E	F	G	H	I	J	K	L	M	N
Red deer	x			x	x	x	x	x	x	x		x	x	x
Roe deer	x			x		x			x	x		x		x
Elk	x									x			x	
Aurochs	x			x		x				x	?	x	?	
Bison										x	?			
Pig	x			x			x	x	x	x				x
Horse	x					x				x		x		
Bear	x		x			x		x		x		x		x
Wolf										x				
Fox	x	x	x							x		x		
Marten	x											x		x
Lynx			x											
Cat	x	x	x									x		
Otter		x								x				
Beaver	x					x	x		x	x		x		
Badger										x		x		x
Hare	x	x								x		x	x	
Squirrel												x		
Birds		x	x								x			
Fish														
Turtle											x			

A—Auvernier; B—Caverne du Bossey; C—Caverne de la Grande Poule;
D—Haltnau; E—Herblingen; F—Hof; G—Horgen; H—Litzelstetten;
I—Männedorf; J—Ossingen; K—Raunegg; L—Schweizerbild; M—Steckborn
N—Storren-Wildsberg; O—Wangen.

290

Table No. 98

Domestic Animals of Later Swiss Neolithic Period

	Cattle	Ovicaprids	Pig	Dog
Horgen Culture:				
Auvernier III	x	x	x	x
Horgen	x		x	x
Saint Aubin III	x	x	x	x
Michelsberg Culture:				
Luscherz	x	x	x	x
Männedorf	x	x	x	
Obermeilen	x	x	x	x
Ossingen	x		x	x
Steckborn	x			
Storren-Wildsberg	x		x	
Thayngen-Weiher	x	x	x	
Neolithic:				
Caverne du Bossey	x	x	x	
Caverne de la grande Poule	x	x	x	
Haltnau			x	x
Herblingen	x	x	x	x
Hof	x			x
Litzelstetten		x		
Raunegg	x			
Schweizerbild	x	x		
Wangen	x	x		x

Table No. 99

Auvernier (Horgen and Corded Ware)

a) 1932

Animals	Level III B.	Level III %	Level III Ind.	Level III %	Level II B.	Level II %	Level II Ind.	Level II %	Domestic % Level III B.	Domestic % Level III Ind.	Domestic % Level II B.	Domestic % Level II Ind.
Domestic:												
Cattle	87	19.6	5	10.6	58	26.5	5	17.2	39.7	22.7	29.3	23.8
Ovicaprids	35	7.9	5	10.6	78	35.6	7	24.1	16.0	22.7	39.4	33.3
Pig	91	20.4	10	21.3	52	23.7	7	24.1	41.6	45.5	26.2	33.3
Dog	6	1.3	2	4.3	10	4.6	2	6.9	2.7	9.1	5.1	9.6
Wild:												
Red deer	133	29.9	7	14.9	7	3.2	2	6.9				
Roe deer	5	1.1	1	2.1	5	2.3	2	6.9				
Elk	1	0.2	1	2.1	–	–	–	–				
Aurochs	14	3.2	1	2.1	4	1.8	1	3.5				
Pig	2	0.4	1	2.1	–	–	–	–				
Horse	6	1.4	1	2.1	–	–	–	–				
Bear	2	0.4	1	2.1	–	–	–	–				
Fox	52	11.8	6	12.9	1	0.5	1	3.5				
Marten	6	1.4	2	4.3	–	–	–	–				
Cat	2	0.4	1	2.1	–	–	–	–				
Beaver	2	0.4	2	4.3	4	1.8	2	6.9				
Hare	1	0.2	1	2.1	–	–	–	–				
Total	445		47		219		29					
Domestic	219	49.2	22	46.8	198	90.4	21	72.3				
Wild	226	50.8	25	53.2	21	9.6	8	27.7				

b) Post 1948

Animals	Level IV		Level III		Level II		Level I		Domestic %			
	B.	%	B.	%	B.	%	B.	%	IV	III	II	I
Domestic:												
Cattle	8	21.0	9	20.0	14	16.7	20	20.0	36.4	37.5	29.2	32.8
Ovicaprids	7	18.4	6	13.3	15	17.85	20	20.0	31.8	25.0	31.4	32.8
Pig	5	13.2	6	13.3	18	21.4	18	18.0	22.7	25.0	37.5	29.5
Dog	2	5.3	3	6.7	1	1.2	3	3.0	9.1	12.5	2.1	4.9
Wild:												
Red deer	7	18.4	8	17.8	12	14.3	18	18.0				
Roe deer	4	10.5	3	6.7	8	9.5	9	9.0				
Pig	3	7.9	–	–	1	1.2	5	5.0				
Others	2	5.3	10	22.2	15	17.85	9	9.0				
Total	38		45		84							
Domestic	22	57.9	24	53.3	48	57.15	61	61.0				
Wild	16	42.1	21	46.7	36	42.85	39	39.0				

Table No. 100

St. Aubin (Horgen)

Animals	1921 Ind.	1926 B.	1926 Ind.	1928–30 B.	1928–30 Ind.	Total B.	Total Ind.	% B.	% Ind.
Domestic:									
Cattle	20	55	5	87	6	142	31	16.0	17.9
Ovicaprids	6	13	3	47	6	60	15	6.8	8.7
Pig	16	73	6	156	22	229	44	25.8	25.4
Dog	3	6	1	13	3	19	7	2.1	4.0
Wild:									
Red deer	9	88	4	213	10	301	23	33.9	13.3
Roe deer	1	—	—	—	—	—	1	—	0.6
Elk	1	4	1	10	2	14	4	1.6	2.3
Aurochs	—	3	1	3	1	6	2	0.7	1.1
Chamois	—	—	—	1	1	1	1	0.1	0.6
Pig	2	4	1	25	2	29	5	3.3	2.9
Fox	2	4	2	7	3	11	7	1.2	4.0
Badger	3	—	—	25	4	25	7	2.8	4.0
Pine marten	—	—	—	26	5	26	5	2.9	2.9
Marten	—	—	—	3	1	3	1	0.3	0.6
Polecat	1	—	—	—	—	—	1	—	0.6
Beaver	4	5	2	8	4	13	10	1.5	5.8
Bear	2	2	1	5	1	7	4	0.8	2.3
Cat	1	—	—	1	1	1	2	0.1	0.1
Hare	1	—	—	—	—	—	1	—	0.6
Hedgehog	1	—	—	1	1	1	2	0.1	1.2
Total	73	257	27	631	73	888	173		
Domestic	45	147	15	303	37	450	97	50.7	56.0
Wild	28	110	12	328	36	438	76	49.3	44.0

Table No. 101

Ossingen (Michelsberg)

	estic %						
	Ind.	Animals	Bones	%	Ind.	%	Domestic % Bones / Ind.

Animals	Bones	%	Ind.	%	Domestic % Bones	Domestic % Ind.
Domestic:						
Cattle	398	49.7	21	29.6	70.1	58.3
Ovicaprids	–	–	–	–	–	–
Pig	166	20.7	13	18.3	29.2	36.1
Dog	4	0.5	2	2.8	0.7	5.6
Wild:						
Red deer	146	18.2	17	24.0		
Roe deer	1	0.1	1	1.4		
Elk	–	–	–	–		
Aurochs	14	1.7	1	1.4		
Bison	–	–	–	–		
Pig	33	4.1	4	5.6		
Horse	4	0.5	1	1.4		
Beaver	28	3.5	7	9.9		
Hare	–	–	–	–		
Wolf	1	0.1	1	1.4		
Fox	–	–	–	–		
Otter	–	–	–	–		
Badger	2	0.3	1	1.4		
Bear	5	0.6	2	2.8		
Total	802		71			
Domestic	568	70.9	36	50.7		
Wild	234	29.1	35	49.3		

(Left margin, partially cut off)

estic % Ind.
32.0
15.5
45.3
7.2

Table No. 102

Cultivated Plants of the Later Swiss Neolithic Period

	A	B	C	D	E	F	G	H	I
Horgen Culture:									
Horgen				x			x		x
Utoquai				x			x	x	x
Mürtensee						x			
Zug							x		
Michelsberg Culture:									
Obermeilen							x		x
Storren-Wildsberg		x							
Thayngen-Weiher	x	x	x		x	x	x	x	x
Neolithic:									
Irgenhausen						x			
Litzelstetten						x	x		
Morat					x				
Nidau-Steinberg				x		x			
Oberkirch-Sempachersee									x
Riedikon					x				
Walm III	x	x	x			x			
Wangen						x	x	x	
Wollishofen				x		x			

A—Einkorn; B—Emmer; C—Club wheat; D—Wheat (unspecified);
E—Barley; F—Millet; G—Flax; H—Peas; I—Poppy.

Table No. 103

Wild Animals of the Italian Neolithic

	A	B	C	D	E	F	G	H	I	J	K	L	M	N	O	P	Q	R	S	T	U	V	W	X	Y
Red deer	x	?	x	x	x	x					x	x	x	x	x	x	x	x	x	x	x	x	x	x	x
Roe deer		?	x	x	x	x						x		x		x		x	x	x		x	x		x
Elk											x														
Aurochs	?																					?	?		
Bison	?										x														
Pig	?				x						x	x	x			x	x				x	x		x	x
Horse	?						?					x	x			x	x				x			x	x
Donkey										x															
Fox		x														x									
Wolf												x	x												
Cat		x	x								x									x	x				
Lynx		x																							
Badger			x					x								x	x								
Beaver				x													x				x				
Otter																			x						
Marmot														x	x	x									
Hyena									x																
Hare		x	x										x			x	x							x	
Porcupine																x									
Bear		x												x			x	x							
Birds																					x				

A—Alba; B—Arene Candide; C—Armorari; D—Calerno; E—Capanne del M. Loffa; F—Caverna dell'Acqua; G—Caverna di S. Angelo; H—Caverna di Pipistrelli. I—Caverna Pocala; J—Caverna dell'Orso; K—Grotta del Alca; L—Grotta Azzura; M—Grotta del Diavolo; N—Grotta dei Gotti; O—Grotta della Guerra; P—Grotta all'Onda; Q—Grotta di Talamone; R—Il Tamannio; S—Molina alle Scalucce; T—Norcia; U—Reggiano; V—Murgecchia; W—Vaio Campostrini; X—Vayes; Y—Vibrata.

Table No. 104

Domestic Animals of the Italian Neolithic Period

	Cattle	Ovicaprids	Pig	Dog
Molfetta Culture:				
Monte dell'Uccellina	x	x	x	
Murgecchia	x	x	x	
Timone		x	x	x
Setti Ponti				x
Bocca Quadrata Culture:				
Arene Candide		x	x	x
Lagozza Culture:				
Arene Candide		x		
Neolithic:				
Alba	x	x	x	
Albinea	x			
Armorari	x	x		
Calerno	x	x		
Campeggine	x	x	x	
Capanne del M. Loffa	x	x	x	x
Caverna dell'Acqua	x	x	x	
Caverna di S. Angelo	x		x	
Caverna di Pipistrelli	x	x	x	
Caverna Pocala	x	x	x	
Caverna dell'Orso	x	x	x	
Grotta dell'Alca	x			
Grotta Azzura	x	x	x	
Grotta del Diavolo	x	x	x	
Grotta dei Gotti	x			
Grotta della Guerra	x	x	x	
Grotta all'Onda	x	x		
Grotta di Talamone	x	x		
II Tamaccio	x	x	x	
Jesi	x		x	
Molina alle Scalucce	x	x	x	x
Marghotto				x
Nariere				x
Norcia	x	x	x	x
Parrano	x			
Reggiano	x	x	x	
Rivole				x
Servirola				x
Vaio Campostrini			x	
Vayes	x	x		
Vibrata	x	x	x	

ld Animals of the Chassey-Chalain Cultures

	A	B	C	D	E	F	G	H	I	J	K	L	M	N	O	P	Q
d deer	x			x	x	x		x	x	x	?		?	?	x	x	x
e deer				x	x					x	?		?	?	x	x	x
rochs							x										x
son																	x
g				x		x	x	?	x	?	x	x	x	x	x		x
rse		x	x												x		x
nkey																x	
lf						x									x	x	
rten								x				x			x	?	
x				x			x	x					x				
ar															x		x
dger												x			x		x
t													?	x			
nx															x		x
dgehog							x										x
bbit				x			x	x	?								
re				x		x			?				x	x			x
asel																	x
le																	x
ad																	x
use															x		
ds					x	x											x
h							x										

-L'Abri d'Eglise; B—Campigny; C—Chassey; D—Châteauneuf-les-Martigues;
-Fort Harrouard; F—Genissait; G—Lumbres; H—La Madeleine. I—Mas d'Azil;
Monte Vaudois; K—Nermont; L—Pertus II; M—Peu Richard; N—Recoux;
-Roucadour; P—St. Benoit; Q—Les Matignons.

Table No. 106

Domestic Animals of the Chassey-Chalain Culture

	Cattle	Ovicaprids	Pig	Dog
L'Abri d'Eglise	x	x	x	
Biard	x	x	x	
Campigny	x			
Catenoy	x			
Chassey	x	x	x	
Châteauneuf	x	x		x
Fort Harrouard	x	x	x	x
Genissait	x	x	x	x
Lumbres	x	x	x	x
La Madeleine	?	?	?	
Les Matignons	x	x	x	x
Mas d'Azil	x	x		
Montes Gassicourt	x			
Mont Vaudois	x		?	
Nermont	x			
Pertus II	?	?		
Peu Richard	x	x		
Recoux	x	x	x	x
Roucadour	x	x	?	?
Saint Benoit	x	x	x	x
Unang	x			
Chalain				x
Clairvaux				x

Table No. 107a

Fort Harrouard

Animals	Bones	%
Cattle	737	66.1
Ovicaprids	161	14.5
Pig	216	19.4
Total	1114	

Table No. 107b

Genissait

Animals	Ind.	%	Domestic %
Domestic:			
Cattle	13	34.2	44.8
Ovicaprids	9	23.7	31.0
Pig	6	15.8	20.7
Dog	1	2.6	3.5
Wild:			
Red deer	2	5.3	
Roe deer	2	5.3	
Pig	2	5.3	
Wolf	1	2.6	
Hare	1	2.6	
Birds	1	2.6	
Total	38		
Domestic	29	76.3	
Wild	9	23.7	

300

Les Matignons (Chassey & Peu Richard)

	Chassey						Peu Richard					
	B.	%	I.	%	B.	I.	B.	%	I.	%	B.	I.
Domestic:												
Cattle	1515	42.7	124	28.5	49.7	39.7	221	55.8	31	34.0	65.0	44.9
Ovicaprids	751	21.3	91	20.9	24.8	29.2	54	13.7	16	17.6	15.9	23.2
Pig	431	12.2	89	20.5	14.2	28.5	44	11.1	20	22.0	12.9	29.0
Dog	343	9.7	8	1.8	11.3	2.6	21	5.3	2	2.2	6.2	2.9
Wild:												
Red deer	153	4.3	33	7.6			8	2.0	4	4.4		
Roe deer	35	1.0	14	3.3			3	0.8	2	2.2		
Aurochs	91	2.6	17	3.9			31	7.9	9	9.9		
Bison	6	0.2	1	0.2			–		–			
Pig	153	4.3	33	7.6			9	2.3	3	3.3		
Bear	1	0.1	1	0.2			–		–			
Lynx	1	0.1	1	0.2			–		–			
Badger	4	0.1	1	0.2			–		–			
Hare	1	0.1	1	0.2			–		–			
Hedgehog	3	0.1	3	0.7			–		–			
Weasel	1	0.1	1	0.2			–		–			
Horse	2	0.1	2	0.5			–		–			
Vole	5	0.1	4	0.9			1	0.3	1	1.1		
Birds	6	0.2	6	1.4			–		–			
Toad	26	0.7	5	1.2			–		–			
Fox							3	0.8	3	3.3		
Total	3528		435				395		91			
Domestic	3040	85.9	312	71.7			340	85.9	69	75.8		
Wild	488	14.1	123	28.3			55	14.1	22	24.2		

Table No. 109

St. Benoit

Animals	Bones	%	Domestic %
Domestic			
Cattle	70	13.7	15.5
Ovicaprids	335	65.7	74.1
Pig	25	4.9	5.5
Dog	22	4.3	4.9
Wild:			
Donkey			
? domestic	7	1.4	
Red deer	12	2.3	
Roe deer	2	0.4	
Cat	7	1.4	
Others	30	5.9	
Total	510		
Domestic	452	90.0	
Wild	58	10.0	

Table No. 110

Cultivated Plants of the Chassey-Chalain Culture

	A	B	C	D	E	F	G	H	I
Campigny						x			
Chalain	x	x				x		x	x
Chassey			x				x	x	
Genissait	x	x		x					
La Madeleine					x				
La Condamine					?	x			
Trou Arnaud			x	x					
St. Martin la Riviere					?	?			
Pinacle									Be

A—Einkorn; B—Emmer; C—Bread wheat; D—Spelt; E—Wheat (unspecified);
F—Barley; G—Millet; H—Flax; I—Poppy; J—Legumes.

Table No. 111

Wild Animals of the French Neolithic

	A	B	C	D	E	F	G
Red deer	x		x		x		x
Roe deer					x		
Pig	x		x				
Horse				x	x		
Fox		x	?				
Wolf			?				x
Rabbit	x	x					x
Hare	x					x	
Birds		x	x			x	

A—Châteauneuf-Les-Martigues; B—Devezas; C—Gaude;
D—Pas-de-Clavel; E—Roucadour; F—Sotch de la Gardie;
G—Unang.

Table No. 112

Domestic Animals of the French Neolithic Period

	Cattle	Ovicaprids	Pig	Dog
Lagozza Culture:				
Châteauneuf	x	x		?
Gaude	x	x		
Unang	x	x	x	
Michelsberg Culture:				
Kertzfeld	x			
Horgen/S.O.M.:				
Roucadour	x	x	x	
Neolithic:				
Devezas		x		
Mauvelle	x	x	?	
Mimet		x		
Pas-de-Clavel	?	?		
Pilon du Roy		x		
Sotch de la Gardie		x	x	

Table No. 113

Wild Animals of the T.R.B. Culture

	A	B	C	D	E	F	G	H	I	J	K	L
Red deer	x			x			x	x			x	x
Roe deer							x					x
Aurochs							x					
Pig		x					x					x
Bear							x					
Horse				?	?	x	x			x		
Badger												x
Fox			x									
Beaver							x		x			x
Otter							x				x	x
Cat												x
Marten							x					
Seal								x			x	x
Polecat							x					
Birds							x		x		x	
Fish									x		x	

A—Halle-Mötzlich; B—Ichstedt; C—Latdorf; D—Tangermünde;
E—Calbe; F—Weissenfels; G—Heklingen; H—Havnelev;
I—Jordløse; J—Øgaarde; K—Ørnekul; L—Mollehüsen.

Table No. 114

Domestic Animals of the T.R.B. culture

	Cattle	Ovicaprids	Pig	Dog	Horse
Poland:					
Ćmielow	x	x	x	x	
Grodek	x	x	x	x	
Klementowice	x	x	x		
Lasek	x	x	x		
Ustowie	x	x	x	x	x
Jordanow	x	x	x	x	
Czechoslovakia:					
Stolmir	x		?		

[continued

Table No.114 [continued]

	Cattle	Ovicaprids	Pig	Dog	Horse
Germany:					
Ammendorf	x	x	x		
Barleben	x	x			
Biendorf	x				
Braunsdorf	x	x	x	x	
Fuchsberg-Sudensee	x	x	x	x	
Gehofen	x	x	x	x	
Halle-Mötzlich	x	x		x	
Ichstedt	x	x			
Jaucha			x	x	
Latdorf				x	
Mittelhausen			?		
Plotha	x			x	
Rheingewann	x			x	
Schwabsburg	x		x	x	
Stöben		x			
Tangermünde	x				?
Calbe	?				?
Weissenfels	x	x	x	x	
Reuden				?	
Salzmunder				x	
Holland:					
Heklingen	x	x	x	?	
Vlaardingen	x	x	x	x	
Zandwerven	x	x	x		
Denmark:					
Gammellung	x	x	x		
Hallebygaard	x				
Havnelev	x	x			
Hundesøen	x				
Jordløse	x				
Øgaarde	x	x			
Ørnekul	x	x	x		
Ørting	x				
Østrup	x				
Salpetermøsen	x	x			
Sweden:					
Mollehüsen	x	x	x	x	

Table No. 115

Ćmielow (TRB)

	Bones 1948	1950	Total	%	Domestic %
Domestic:					
Cattle	1171	407	1578	57.7	62.3
Ovicaprids	184	92	276	10.1	10.9
Pig	389	177	566	20.7	22.4
Dog	42	69	111	4.1	4.4
Wild:					
Red deer	26	10	36	1.3	
Roe deer	27	18	45	1.6	
Elk	4	—	4	0.1	
Pig	22	21	43	1.6	
Bear	4	—	4	0.1	
Horse	35	23	58	2.1	
Badger	2	3	5	0.2	
Fox	3	—	3	0.1	
Beaver	5	—	5	0.2	
Wolf	2	—	2	0.1	
Total			2736		
Domestic			2531	92.6	
Wild			205	7.4	

Table No. 116

Grodek (TRB)

Animals	Bones 1952	1954	Total	%	Domestic %
Domestic:					
Cattle	276	989	1265	60.8	62.9
Ovicaprids	77	175	252	12.1	12.5
Pig	141	312	453	21.8	22.6
Dog	13	28	41	2.0	2.0
Wild:					
Red deer	3	17	20	1.0	
Roe deer	3	8	11	0.5	
Elk	6	—	6	0.3	
Bear	—	3	3	0.1	
Horse	4	12	16	0.8	
Badger	—	1	1	0.05	
Fox	1	2	3	0.1	
Hare	2	4	6	0.3	
Otter	—	1	1	0.05	
Turtle	—	3	3	0.1	
Total			2081		
Domestic			2011	96.7	
Wild			70	3.3	

Table No. 117

Klementowice (TRB)

Animals	Bones	%	Domestic %
Domestic:			
Cattle	63	48.1	50.4
Ovicaprids	8	6.1	6.4
Pig	54	41.2	43.2
Wild:			
Red deer	3	2.3	
Roe deer	1	0.8	
Horse	2	1.5	
Total	131		
Domestic	125	95.4	
Wild	6	4.6	

Table No. 118

Ustowie (TRB)

Animals	Bones	%	Domestic %
Domestic:			
Cattle	393	30.3	46.9
Ovicaprids	77	5.9	9.2
Pig	276	21.3	32.9
Dog	37	2.8	4.4
Horse	55	4.2	6.6
Wild:			
Red deer	192	14.8	
Roe deer	60	4.6	
Aurochs	62	4.8	
Pig	17	1.3	
Bear	4	0.3	
Wolf	1	0.1	
Fox	2	0.2	
Cat	1	0.1	
Marten	2	0.2	
Beaver	117	9.0	
Seal	1	0.1	
Total	1297		
Domestic	838	64.5	
Wild	459	35.5	

307

Table No. 119

| *Fuchsberg-Südensee* (TRB) | | | | | Domestic % | |
Animals	Bones	%	Ind.	%	Bones	Ind.
Domestic:						
Cattle	624	67.5	24	41.4	79.3	63.1
Ovicaprids	51	5.5	5	8.6	6.5	13.2
Pig	94	10.2	6	10.4	11.9	15.8
Dog	18	1.9	3	5.2	2.3	7.9
Wild:						
Red deer	45	4.9	5	8.6		
Roe deer	18	1.9	2	3.4		
Aurochs	20	2.2	3	5.2		
Pig	46	5.0	6	10.4		
Horse	5	0.5	2	3.4		
Beaver	3	0.3	1	1.7		
Cat	1	0.1	1	1.7		
Total	925		58			
Domestic	787	85.1	38	65.6		
Wild	138	14.9	20	34.4		

Table No. 120

Berlin & Weissenfels

| | Weissenfels | | Berlin | |
Animals	No. Bones	%	No. Bones	%
Cattle	230	65.7	96	39.5
Ovicaprids	31	8.9	34	14.0
Pig	13	3.7	108	44.4
Dog	76	21.7	4	1.7
Horse	—	—	1	0.4
Total	350		243	

Table No. 121

Cultivated Plants of the TRB culture

	A	B	C	D	E	F	G	H	I	J
Poland:										
Cmielow		x					x		x	P
Ksiaznica Wielkie	x	x	x	x	x		x			
Lasek					x					
Pietrzykow							x			P
Zberzykow					x					
Złota		x								
Germany:										
Derenburg		x								
Hohlenstedt						?	?			
Lietfeld	x	x					x		x	
Salzmunder						?	?			
Schraplau	x									
Weissenfels		?					x	x		
Denmark:										
Aamosen		?	x				x			
Barkaer		x					x			
Havnelev	?	x	?				x			
Stora Valby	x	x	x				x			
Sweden:										
Fredriksborg							x			
Limhamn	x									
Linved	x									
Maglarp-Albäcksborg							x			
Mogetorp	x	x	x				x			PB
Östra Vrå	x	x					x			
Oxie	x	?					x			
Rosenlund-Hjulberg							x			
Simris						x				
Toltorp		x								
Vätteryd	?	?					x			

A—Einkorn; B—Emmer; C—Club wheat; D—Bread wheat; E—Spelt;
F—Wheat (unspecified); G—Barley; H—Millet; I—Flax; J—Legumes.
P—Pea; B—Bean.

Table No. 122

Cultivated grain found at Lietfeld (TRB)

	Weight (gm.)	%
Einkorn	180.5	63.3
Emmer	98.2	33.5
Barley	8.5	2.4
Flax	3.0	0.8

Table No. 123

Domestic Animals of the Polish Neolithic Period

	Cattle	Ovicaprids	Pig	Dog
Gdansk	x			
Krakow				x
Krzeszowice	x			
Maszycha	x	x	x	
Mnikow	x	x	x	
Pamiatkowo	x			
Prosna	x			
Wiechow		x		
Wieruszow	x			
Wyszkowce		x		
Wlostow	x			

Table No. 124

Wild Animals of the Later German Neolithic

	A	B	C	D	E	F	G	H	I	J	K	L	M	N	O	P	Q	R	S	T
Red deer	x	x	?	?	?	x	x			x	x	x	x	x	x	x	x	x		
Roe deer	x	x	?	?	?	x	x			x	x	x	x	x	x	x	x	x		
Elk		x																		
Aurochs	x	x	x	?	x					x	x	x	x	x	?	x	x			x
Pig	x	x	?	?	x	x	x	x	?	x	x		x	x	?	x	x			
Bear	x	x								x							x			
Horse	x	x		x	x					x		x	x	?		x	?	x	x	x
Donkey											x									
Badger	x	x								x	x	x								
Otter	x										x						x			
Beaver	x										x	x	x		x					
Marten	x									x										
Wild Cat	x	x											x					?		
Lynx	x																			
Wolf	x											x	x			x				
Fox	x	x				x				x		x	x	x		x	x			
Hedgehog												x								
Hare	x					x				x	x	x								
Turtle	x																			
Fish	x										x		x	x			x			
Birds	x								x				x							

A–Ehrenstein; B–Einhornhöhle; C–Goldberg; D–Hausen; E–Heilbronn; F–Hohenneck; G–Hutberg; H–Isteiner Koltz; I–Jechtingen; J–Jungfernhöhle; K–Mon Repos; L–Nauendorf; M–Rauberhöhle; N–Regensburg-Kumpfmühl; O–Reusten; P–Reute OA Waldsee; Q–Riedschachen; R–Schwörstadt; S–Strüth; T–Volpke.

Table No. 125

Domestic Animals of the Later German Neolithic Period

	Cattle	Ovicaprids	Pig	Dog	Horse
Rössen Culture:					
Heilbronn	x	x	x		
Nauendorf	x	x	x		
Regensburg-Kumpfmühl	x	x	x		
Bissinger Pfad				x	
Michelsberg Culture:					
Cannstatt	x	x	x		
Ehrenstein	x	x	x	x	
Goldberg	x	x	x		
Hutberg	x	x	x		
Jechtingen		x	?		
Riedschachen	x	x	x	x	?
Vaihingen	x				
Unter-Grombach	x	x	x	x	
Neolithic:					
Berlin	x	x	x	x	x
Einhornhöhle	x	x	x	x	
Feuerbach	x	x	x		
Gluchstadt	x				
Hausen	?		?		
Hohenneck	x	x	x	x	
Hohenzahden	x				
Isteiner Klotz			?		
Jungfernhöhle				x	
Kornwestheim		x			
Mon Repos	x	x	x		
Monsheim	x	x	x		
Neuenheim	x	x	x	x	
Niederwitz	x		?		
Osthofen	x				
Rauberhöhle	x	x	x	x	
Reusten	x	x	x		
Reute OA Waldsee	x	x	x	x	
Schelmengraben	x	x	x	x	
Roseninsel			x		
Schwörstadt		x		x	

Table No.125 [continued]

	Cattle	Ovicaprids	Pig	Dog	Horse
Strüth	x			x	
Triebsee			x		
Volpke	x	x	x	x	
Wurmsee			x		
Hildesheim				x	
Klein Wanzleben				x	
Nickelsdorf				x	
Westerregeln				x	
Altendorf				x	
Düsedau	x				
Engers	?				?
Goddula	x			x	

Table No. 126

*Einhornh*öhle

	% Bones	Domestic %
Domestic:		
Cattle	12.5	23.8
Ovicaprids	30.0	55.3
Pig	8.0	15.2
Dog	3.0	5.7
Wild:		
Red deer	18.0	
Roe deer	5.0	
Aurochs	2.5	
Pig	17.0	
Horse	1.0	
Bear	4.0	
Domestic	53.5	
Wild	47.5	

Table No. 127

Cultivated Plants of the Later German Neolithic Period

	A	B	C	D	E	F	Others
Rössen Culture:							
Heilbronn	x	?	x			x	
Ur-Fulerum		x				x	
Wahlitz	x		x			x	
Winzinger St.	x	x	x			x	Pea
Michelsberg Culture:							
Ehrenstein	x	x	?	x		x	Dog wood
Riedschachen	x	x	x			x	Flax
Taubried	x	x	x			x	Flax
Reute O.A.							
Waldsee	x	x	x			x	Flax, pea
Neolithic:							
Bockingen	x	x	x			x	
Bremer						x	
Dötlingen	x	x	x			x	
Heidelberg		x					
Kleinbardorf	x	?					
Linsenbühl						x	
Ohringen	x	x					
Riekofen	x	x				x	
Steinsburg	x						
Tauber-bishofsheim	x						
Stuttgenhof						x	
Worms		x					

A—Einkorn; B—Emmer; C—Club wheat; D—Bread or club wheat;
E—Unspecified wheat; F—Barley.

Table No. 128

Wild Animals of the Scandinavian Middle Neolithic Period

	A	B	C	D	E	F	G	H	I
Red deer	x	x		x	x	x	x		x
Roe deer	x	x		x			x	x	x
Elk		x							
Aurochs		x						?	
Pig		x						?	
Seal		x	x				x		
Horse	x								
Otter		x					x	x	
Badger							x		
Marten		x					x		
Bear		x					x		
Wolf							x		
Fox				x			x		
Cat							x		
Polecat		x							
Squirrel							x		
Hedgehog				x	x				
Hare				x					
Turtle	x								
Birds	x	x							x
Fish		x							x

Table No. 129

Domestic Animals of the Scandinavian Middle Neolithic

	Cattle	Ovicaprids	Pig	Dog	Horse
Blandebjerg	x	x	x		
Bundsø	x	x	x	x	
Gundsølille		x			
Hesselø		x	x		
Lejre Aa	x	x	x	x	
Lindø	x	x	x	x	?
Lindskov	x	x			?
Ørum Aa	x	x	x	x	
Svendborg	x	?	?		
Signalbakken	x	x	x		
Troldebjerg	x	x	x		
Trelleborg	x				
Verup Møse	x				

Table No. 130

Cultivated Plants of the Scandinavian Middle Neolithic

	A	B	C	D	E	F
Denmark:						
Aarby					x	x
Bistrup					x	
Blandebjerg	x					x
Bundsø	x	x	x	x		x
Ejby					x	
Flintige Byskov					x	x
Folleslev					x	
Fredsgaarde						x
Gundestrup					x	
Gundsølille					x	
Hammer					x	
Hegum		x			x	
Hjelm					x	
Hjortegaardene		x			x	
Himmelev					x	
Killerup					x	
Kulby					x	
Lejre Aa		x		x	x	x
Lindeskov					x	x
Lindø		x			x	x
Lindskov	x	x		x	x	
Lundvorlund					x	
Ørum Aa					x	
Øster Krusegaarde						x
Skørbaek	x				x	
Sodervidinge					x	
Stenstrup					x	
Stenvad						x
Strandholm					x	
Tjaerby					x	
Troldebjerg					x	x
Udskolpe						x
Uggerslev					x	
Vedskølle	x				x	
Vellerup					x	

[continued

Table No. 130 [continued

	A	B	C	D	E	F
Sweden:						
Akarp		x				
Berg						x
Bjellerup						x
Gillhög	x	x				x
Hammar						x
Hogsmolla	x	x				
Ivetofta						x
Kungsdosen	x	x				x
Lacklanga	x	x				
Maglø						x
Nosaby	x	x				x
Orenas	x	x				x
Ramsbjer		x				
Sodervidinge	x	x				
Storegarden	x	x				x
Svenstorp						x
Västra Torp	x	x				
Västra Koby	x	x		x		x
Viktorshog	x	x				x

A—Einkorn; B—Emmer; C—Club wheat; D—Bread or club wheat
E—Unspecified wheat; F—Barley.

Table No. 131

Bundsø (Scandinavian Middle Neolithic)

	Finds	%
Einkorn	88	15.5
Emmer	46	8.1
Einkorn/Emmer	370	65.4
Wheat	11	1.9
Barley	51	9.1
Total	566	

Table No. 132

Wild Animals of the Scandinavian Neolithic

	A	B	C	D	E	F	G	H	I
Red deer	x		x			x	x		
Roe deer	x			x		x	x		
Elk			x				x		
Aurochs			x						
Pig	x		x		x				
Seal	x	x		x	x	x		x	x
Horse									x
Bear							x		
Otter							x		
Beaver							x		
Badger			x				x		
Marten			x	x		x			
Wolf								x	
Fox				x				x	x
Lynx	x								
Wild cat						x			
Hare						x			x
Fish			x			x			x
Birds						x			x
Porpoise			x						

A—Aalborg; B—Munkholm; C—Alvastra; D—Frennemark; E—Hemmor; F—Siretorp; G—Sjöholmen; H—Stora Karslö; I—Västerbjers.

Table No. 133

Domestic Animals of the Scandinavian Neolithic

	Cattle	Ovicaprids	Pig	Dog	Horse
Pitted Ware Culture:					
Alvastra	x	x	x	x	
Danielslund			?		
Gullrum			x		
Hemmor			x	x	
Jonstorp	x				
Siretorp	x	x	x		
Sjöholmen	x		x	x	
Stora Karslö	x	x	x	x	
Västerbjers	x	x	x	x	
Visby	x	x	x		
Humlekärrshult	x	x	x		
Rolfsaker	x	x	x		
Glumslöv	?	?	?		

Table No.133[continued]

	Cattle	Ovicaprids	Pig	Dog	Horse
Late Neolithic Period:					
Kiaby			x		
Ullstorpsbach					?
Neolithic Period:					
Aalborg	x	x.	x	x	
Christainsholm				x	
Munkholm	x	x	x		
Dyrehavegaard				x	
Hasmark				x	
Stigtehave				x	
Voldtofte				x	
Sweden:					
Frennemark	x		x		
Malmø	x		?		
Norway:					
Ruskennesset	x				

Table No. 134

Västerbjers (Pitted Ware)

Animals	Bones	%	Domestic %
Domestic:			
Cattle	54	3.1	3.6
Ovicaprids	57	3.1	3.8
Pig	1262	72.7	84.7
Dog	117	6.7	7.9
Wild:			
Horse	12	0.7	
Fox	13	0.8	
Seal	189	10.9	
Hare	3	0.2	
Birds	20	1.2	
Fish	11	0.6	
Total	1738		
Domestic	1490	85.6	
Wild	248	14.4	

Table No. 135

Cultivated Plants of the Scandinavian Neolithic

	A	B	C	D	E	F
Pitted Ware Culture:						
Alvastra					x	
Fägervik				x	x	x
Jonstorp	x	x	x		x	
Norrshog					x	
Sater II					x	
Stora Karslö					x	
Torslunda		x			x	
Siretorp					x	
Neolithic:						
Denmark:						
Aalborg				x	x	
Emmedsbo				x	x	
Sweden:						
Nosaby				x	x	
Norway:						
Ruskennesset					x	
Late Neolithic:						
Denmark:						
Borreby		x			x	
Herslev				x		
Langø				x		
Frihedslund					x	
Ty			x			
Sweden:						
St. Bosgarden	x					
Kvarnby					x	
L. Lund		x				
Nolgarden					?	
Torpet		x				
Utbogarden					x	

A—Einkorn; B—Emmer; C—Bread or club wheat;
D—Unspecified wheat; E—Barley; F—Pea.

Table No. 136

Wild Animals of the Windmill Hill Culture

	A	B	C	D	E
Red deer	x	x	x	x	x
Roe deer	x	x	x		x
Aurochs		x	x	x	
Horse			x	x	x
Pig		?			
Badger				x	x
Fox			x	x	x
Cat				x	
Hare				x	

A—Maiden Castle; B—Nutbane; C—Thickthorn
Down; D—Windmill Hill; E—Wor Barrow.

Table No. 137

Domestic Animals of the Windmill Hill Culture

	Cattle	Ovicaprids	Pig	Dog
Amesbury 42	x			
Badshot	x			
Fussell's Lodge	x	x		
Hembury	x	x	x	
Heytesbury I	x			
Knap Hill	x			
Maiden Castle	x	x	x	x
Nutbane	x	x	?	
Rudston	x			
Thickthorn Down	x	x	x	
The Trundle	x	x	x	
Whitehawk	x	x	x	
Tilshead 5	x			
Whitesheet Hill	x			
Windmill Hill	x	x	x	x
Wor Barrow	x	x	x	x

Table No. 138

Windmill Hill

Animals	a) Pre-enclosure occupation			b) Primary levels of enclosure ditch		
	Bones	%	Dom. %	Bones	%	Dom. %
Domestic:						
Cattle	90	66.2	68.7	292	40.2	45.2
Ovicaprids	16	11.7	12.2	121	16.6	18.7
Pig	22	16.2	16.8	74	10.2	11.5
Dog	3	2.2	2.3	159	21.9	24.6
Wild:						
Red deer	5	3.7		9	1.2	
Horse				2	0.25	
Cat				50	6.9	
Fox				8	1.1	
Badger				2	0.25	
Hare				10	1.4	
Total	136			727		
Domestic	131	96.3		646	88.9	
Wild	5	3.7		81	11.1	

Table No. 139

Cultivated Plants of the Windmill Hill Culture

	A	B	C	D	E	F	G	H
Haldon					x			
Hembury	?	x	x					
Maiden Castle	?	x		?		x		
Whitehawk						x		
Windmill Hill	x	x				x	x	x

A—Einkorn; B—Emmer; C—Bread wheat; D—Bread or club wheat;
E—Wheat (unspecified); F—Barley; G—Flax; H—Apple pips.

Table No. 140a

Wheat and Barley in Great Britain and Denmark

Locality	Wheat	Barley	Proportion in %	Apple	Flax
Windmill Hill	109	10	91.6 — 8.4	6	2
Troldeberg	172	8	95.6 — 4.4	1	—
Blandebjerg	334	19	94.6 — 5.4	2	—
Lindø	387	80	78.2 — 21.8	4	—

Table No. 140(b)

Windmill Hill Cultivated grain	No. impressions		%	
Einkorn	2 ⎫		1.7 ⎫	
Emmer	46 ⎬	109	38.7 ⎬	91.6
Einkorn/Emmer	61 ⎭		51.2 ⎭	
Naked Barley	7 ⎫	10	5.9 ⎫	8.4
Hulled Barley	3 ⎭		2.5 ⎭	

Table No. 141

Wild Animals of the Later British Neolithic

	A	B	C	D	E	F	G	H	I	J	K	L	M
Red deer	?		x		x	x	x	x	x	x	x		
Roe deer	?		x		x			x					
Aurochs					x								
Pig				?			x		x				
Bear			x										
Horse		x									x		
Fox					x	x		x				x	
Otter								x					
Pine marten								x					
Wild cat					x							x	
Weasel					x								
Vole					x			x					
Hare								x					x
Birds					x						x		x
Fish						x				x		x	x
Whale										x			
Porpoise												x	

A—Abingdon; B—Durrington Walls; C—Ratfyn; D—The Sanctuary;
E—Woodhenge; F—Woodlands; G—Colonsay; H—Oban; I—Oronsay;
J—Skara Brae; K—Lough Gur; L—Rockmarshall; M—Sutton.

Table No. 142

Domestic Animals of the Later British Neolithic

	Cattle	Ovicaprids	Pig	Dog
Abingdon:				
Abingdon	x	x	x	
Ronaldsway:				
Ronaldsway	x	x		
Rinyo-Clacton:				
Durrington Walls	x	x	x	
Ratfyn	x		x	
Woodhenge	x	x	x	x
Woodlands	x	x	x	x
Knockadoon:				
Lough Gur	x	x	x	x
Neolithic:				
Durrington	x			
The Sanctuary			?	
Rockmarshall				x
Sutton			?	x
Colonsay	x	x		
Oban	x	x	x	x
Oronsay		x		
Skara Brae	x	x	?	

Table No. 143

Durrington Walls (Rinyo-Clacton)

Animals	Bones	%
Domestic:		
Cattle	220	34.9
Ovicaprids	24	3.8
Pig	385	61.0
Wild or domestic:		
Horse	2	0.3
Total	631	

Table No. 144

Cultivated Plants of the Later British Neolithic

	A	B	C
Abingdon:			
Abingdon	x		
Neolithic:			
Easterton of Roseisle			x
Townhead		?	
Whitepark			x

A—Emmer; B—Wheat (unspecified); C—Naked barley

Table No. 145

Wild Animals of the British Chambered Tombs

	A	B	C	D	E	F	G	H	I	J	K	L	M	N
Red deer	x				x			x			x			
Roe deer								x	x		x			
Aurochs							x							
Pig	x		?	?		?	?	x	x	x	x		x	
Horse	x					x		x	x			x	x	x
Fox		x				?								
Cat		x												
Wolf												?		
Squirrel														
Otter														
Vole														
Birds														
Fish														

A—Brown Hill; B—Burn Ground; C—Ffostyll; D—Eyford; E—Luckington;
J—Tinkinswood; K—Ty Isaf; L—West Kennet; M—Willersey; N—Ringham Lo
T—Holm of Papa Westray; U—Isbister; V—Kenny's Cairn; W—Knowe of Ran
B'—Ormiegill; C'—Quoyness; D'—Unstan; E'—Wideford Hill.

P	Q	R	S	T	U	V	W	X	Y	Z	A'	B'	C'	D'	E'
?	x	?	?		x	x	x	?	x		?	x	?	?	
?		?	?					?				?		?	?
x		x	x	x		x						x		x	
x	x	x	x			x				x	x			x	x
								x							
								x							
								x	x						
x	x		x	x		x	x	x	x		x		x		
	x					x		x	x						

Table No. 146

Domestic Animals of the British Chambered Tombs

	Cattle	Ovicaprids	Pig	Dog
Severn-Cotswold:				
Brown Hill	x			x
Burn Ground	x	x	x	
Ffostyll	x	x	?	
Eyford	x	x	?	x
Gatcombe	x			
Heston Brake	x			
Luckington	x	x		
Notgrove	x	x	?	x
Nympsfield	x	x	?	x
Poles Wood East	x	x	x	
Poles Wood South	x	x	x	
Rodmarton	x			
Tinkinswood	x	x		
Ty Isaf	x	x		x
West Kennet	x	x	x	x
Waylands Smithy				x
Willersey	x			
Derbyshire:				
Ringham Low	x			x
Clyde-Carlingford:				
Ballyalton	x	x	x	x
Goward	x			
Loughcrew	x			
Boyne:				
Bryn Celli Ddu	x			
Carrowkeel	x			
Caithness-Zetland & allied tombs:				
Blackhammer	x	x		
Burray		?		x
Camster	x			
Cuween Hill	x			x
Embo	x	x		
Garrywhin	x	x		x
Holm of Papa Westray	x	x		

[continued

Table No. 146 [continued]

	Cattle	Ovicaprids	Pig	Dog
Isbister	x	x		
Hill of Bruan	x	x		
Kenny's Cairn	x	x		x
Knowe of Ramsay	x	x		
Knowe of Rowiegar	x	x		
Knowe of Yarso	x	x		x
Loch Stennis	x	x		x
Lower Dounreay	x	x		x
Midhowe	x	x	x	
Muckle Heog	x			
Ormiegill	x			x
Quoyness	x	x		
Unstan	x	x		x
Wideford Hill	x	x	x	

Table No. 147

Cultivated Plants of the British Chambered Tombs

	A	B	C	D
Severn-Cotswold:				
West Kennet				x
Clyde-Carlingford:				
Dunloy Cairn	x	x		
Mull Hill			x	
Boyne:				
Baltinglass Hill			x	
Caithness-Zetland & Allied Tombs:				
Calf of Eday				x
Unstan				x

A—Einkorn; B—Emmer; C—Wheat (unspecified); D—Barley

Table No. 148a

Wild Animals of the Gumelniţa and Salcuţa Cultures

	A	B	C	D	E	F	G	H	I	J	K	L	M	N	O	P	Q
Red deer	x		x	x	x	x	x	?	x	x		x	x	x	x	x	x
Roe deer	x		x	x	x	x	x	?	x	x		x	x	x	x	x	x
Aurochs		?	x	x		?	x	?	x							x	
Pig	x		x	x	x	?	x	?	x					x		x	
Bear	x		x	x	x		x	?	x					x			
Horse				x						x							
Halfass																x	x
Chamois														x		x	
Marten	x																
Badger	x					x								x			
Wild cat															x		
Lynx	x																
Beaver	x									x							
Wolf	x																
Fox	x		x			x					x			x			
Hare	x					x					x						
Tortoise											x						
Others									x		x						
Birds			x				x			x				x			
Fish			x	x	x		x			x			x		x	x	x
Turtle																	x

A–Denev; B–Deve Bargan; C–Devetaki; D–Hissarlik; E–Karanovo; F–Kodza Dermen; G–Loveć; H–Morovica; I–Okol Glava; J–Ruse; K–La Adam; L–Adam III–IV; M–Luncaviţa; N–Salcuţa O–Vadřasta; P–Vulcaneşti; Q–Bolgrad.

Table No. 148b

Domestic Animals of the Gumelniţa and Salcuţa Cultures

	Cattle	Ovicaprids	Pig	Dog	Horse
Bulgaria:					
Denev	?	x		x	
Deve Bargan	?	x			
Devetaki	x	x	x	x	
Hissarlik			?	x	
Janka Kubrat	?				
Karanovo	x	x	x	x	
Kodza Dermen	?	x	?	x	
Loveč	x	x	x	x	
Madara	x	x	x	x	?
Morovica		x	?		
Okol Glava	x	x	?	x	
Pod-Grada	x	x	x	x	?
Provertenkata			?	x	
Rusě		x	?	x	
Sveta Kyrillovo	x		?		
Rumania:					
La Adam	x	x	x	x	
Adam III & IV	x	x	x		
Aldeni	x	x	x	x	
Cernavoda	x	x	x	x	x
Luncaviţa	x	x	x	x	
Malul Rosu	x	x	x		
Tangîru	x	x	x	x	
Salcuţa	x	x	x	x	
Vadrăsta	x	x	x	x	
Vulcaneşti	x	x	x	x	
Russia:					
Bolgrad	x	x	x	x	

Table No. 149

Vulcaneşti (Proto-Gumelniţa) & *Bolgrad* (Gumelniţa)

Animals	Vulcaneşti						Bolgrad					
	B.	%	I.	%	B.	I.	B.	%	I.	%	B.	I.
Domestic:												
Cattle	247	59.6	14	34.3	60.7	38.8	304	54.8	18	29.1	63.1	40.0
Ovicaprids	119	28.7	15	36.7	29.3	41.7	130	23.4	16	25.8	27.0	35.6
Pig	40	9.7	6	14.6	9.8	16.7	41	7.4	9	14.5	8.5	20.0
Dog	1	0.2	1	2.4	0.2	2.8	7	1.3	2	3.2	1.4	4.4
Wild:												
Roe deer	2	0.5	1	2.4			–		–			
Pig	1	0.2	1	2.4			–		–			
Horse	1	0.2	1	2.4			47	8.5	10	16.1		
Half ass	3	0.7	1	2.4			16	2.9	3	4.9		
Deer							1	0.2	1	1.6		
Hare							1	0.2	1	1.6		
Turtle							1	0.2	1	1.6		
Fish	1	0.2	1	2.4			7	1.3	1	1.6		
Total	415		41				555		62			
Domestic	407	98.2	36	88.0			482	86.9	45	72.6		
Wild	8	1.8	5	12.0			73	13.1	17	27.4		

Table No. 150

Cultivated Plants of the Gumelniţa and Salcuţa Cultures

	A	B	C	D	E	F
Bulgaria:						
Banyata	x	x			x	
Karanovo	x	x			x	
Karnobat				x		
Kodza Dermen			x			
Janka Kubrat				x		
Rasev				x		
Rusé				x		
Sveta Kyrillovo			x			
Meckur				x		
Yasa Tepe	x	x				
Yunatsita				x		
Rumania:						
Aldeni				x		
Brailita				x		
Cascioarele				x		
Vidra				x		
Salcuţa				x	x	x

A—Einkorn; B—Emmer; C—Bread wheat;
D—Wheat (unspecified); E—Barley; F—Millet.

Table No. 151

Wild Animals of the Cucuteni Culture

	A	B	C
Red deer			x
Roe deer	x		x
Aurochs			x
Pig	x	x	x
Bear			x
Beaver			x
Wolf			x
Otter			x

A—Hăbăseşti; B—Izvore; C—Traian.

Table No. 152

Domestic Animals of the Cucuteni Culture

	Cattle	Ovicaprids	Pig	Dog	Horse
Hăbăseşti	x	x	x	x	
Izvore	x	x			
Mindrisca	x	x	x		
Petreni	x				
Ruptura-Floresţi	x	x	x		x
Traian	x	x	x	x	?
Trusesţi	x	x	x		
Valea Lupului	x	x -			

Table No. 153

Cultivated Plants of the Cucuteni Culture

	Wheat	Others	T. comp.	T. vulg.	T. sp.
Bontesţi	x				x
Casolt-Boita	x				x
Hăbăseşti	x	Vetch	x	x	
Frumusica	x		x	x	
Izvore	x				x

Table No. 154

Wild Animals of the Tripolye culture

	A	B	C	D	E	F	G	H	I	J	K	L	M	N	O	P	Q	R	S	T	U	V	W	X	Y
Red deer	x		x	x	x	x	x	x		x	x	x	x	x	x	x	x	x	x		x	x	x	x	x
Roe deer	x		x	x	x	x	x	x		x	x	x	x	x	x	x	x		x		x	x	x	x	
Elk						x		x		x	x	x	x	x	x	x	x			x	x	x	x	x	
Antelope																						x			
Aurochs	x			x	x		x			x	x	x	x	x	x	x	x							x	
Pig	x			x	x	x	x	x		x	x	x	x	x	x	x	x	x			x	x	x	x	
Horse	x			x	x	x	x	x	x	?	x	?	x	x	x	x	x		x		x	x	x		x
Ass																						x			
Bear	x			x	x	x	x			x	x	x	x	x	x	x	x							x	
Beaver	x			x	x	x	x	x		x	x	x			x	x	x					x	x		
Badger	x					x	x	x		x	x				x	x	x					x	x	x	
Otter				x						x	x					x								x	
Wolverine										x															
Wolf										x	x			x	x	x	x					x	x		
Fox					x		x			x	x		x	x	x	x						x	x		
Cat														x											
Polecat										x															
Marten							x			x	x			x	x	x				x					
Lynx										x															

[continued

Table No. 154 [continued]

	A	B	C	D	E	F	G	H	I	J	K	L	M	N	O	P	Q	R	S	T	U	V	W	X	Y
Hare	x			x			x		x	x	x			x	x		x			x	x	x	x		x
Rodents			x		x					x											x			x	
Turtle		x		x			x		x			x			x	x		x		x	x	x	x	x	x
Tortoise			x	x																		x			
Hedgehog													x												
Spalax pod.						x		x													x	x			
Cricetus															x	x					x				
Citellus				x																	x				
Frog						x	x																		
Fish	x	x	x	x			x	x			x	x	x	x		x	x		x	x	x	x	x	x	x
Birds	x	x	x	x			x	x	x		x	x		x	x		x	x		x		x	x	x	x

A—Bernova-Luka; B—Kiev City; C—Kriposnoma; D—Lenkovtse; E—Pavloc; F—Norcia Čortoria; G—Sandraki; H—Vladimirovka; I—Bilogrudivka; J—Luka-Vrublevetskaia; K—Stena; L—Podgortse; M—Soloncene I; N—Polivanov Jar; O—Troyanov; P—Sabatinovka; Q—Molyukhov Bugor; R—Kunisivtse; S—Kosilovtse; T—Kiev (Sirtsi); U—Khalepje; V—Kolomiischina; W—Usatovo; X—Gorodsk; Y—Raiki.

Table No. 155

Domestic Animals of the Tripolye culture

	Cattle	Ovicaprids	Pig	Dog	Horse	Camel
Andrejevka	x	x	x	x		
Bernova-Luka	x	x	x	x		
Bilogrudivka	x	x	x	x		
Gorodsk	x	x	x		x	x
Grenovka	x	x		x		
Khalepye	x	x	x	x		
Kiev	x	x	x	x		
Kiev City	x	x	x			
Kiev (Sirtsi)	x	x	x		?	
Kolomiischina	x	x	x	x		
Koretnoye	x					
Kosilovtse	x	x	x	x		
Krinicki	x	x	x	x		
Kriposnoma	x					
Kunisivste	x	x	x			
Lenkovtse	x	x	x	x		
Ljubushka Posad	x	x	x	x		
Luka Vrublevetskaia	x	x	x	x	x	
Molyukov Bugor	x				x	
Norcia Čortoria	x	x		x		
Novi Ruseşti	x	x	x	x		
Ozarintse	x	x	x			
Pavloc	x	x	x	x		
Pliskov	x	x	x	x		
Podgortse	x	x	x	x	x	
Podolsk	x	x	x	x		
Polivanov Jar	x	x	x	x		
Raiki	x	x	x	x		
Sabatinovka I & II	x	x	x	x		
Sandraki	x	x	x	x		
Scerbatovo	x	x		x		
Solocheny I	x	x	x	x		
Stenya	x	x	x	x		
Sushkovka	x	x	x	x		
Troyanov	x	x	x	x		
Usatovo	x	x	x	x	x	
Vladimirovka	x	x	x	x		

Table No. 156

Luka-Vrublevetskaia (Tripolye A)

	Bones	1945—1950 %	Ind.	%
Domestic:				
Cattle	1317	30.7	42	22.2
Goat	463	10.7	33	17.4
Sheep	67	1.5	5	2.8
Pig	2364	54.9	93	49.2
Dog	75	1.7	12	6.3
Horse	22	0.5	4	2.1
Wild:				
Roe deer	641		31	
Red deer	2091		57	
Elk	103		9	
Pig	537		33	
Bear	41		8	
Badger	20		7	
Wolverine	4		2	
Otter	2		1	
Marten	30		8	
Polecat	1		1	
Wolf	15		4	
Fox	79		14	
Cat	8		4	
Lynx	2		1	
Hare	49		9	
Squirrel	27		9	
Beaver	24		6	
Hedgehog	4		4	
Total	7986		397	
Domestic	4308	54.0	189	47.6
Wild	3678	46.0	208	52.4

Table No. 157a

Sabatinovka (Tripolye B; after Hancar 1956) 1938

Animals	B.	%	I.	%
Domestic:				
Cattle	481	75.9	12	42.9
Ovicaprids	80	12.6	6	21.4
Pig	47	7.4	7	25.0
Dog	26	4.1	3	10.7
Wild:				
Horse	104		4	
Others	127		18	
Total	865		50	
Domestic	634	73.3	28	56.0
Wild	231	26.7	22	44.0

Table No. 157b

Sabatinovka (I → Tripolye B; II – Tripolye A)

Animals	I (1948)			Domestic %		II (1948 – Bibikova 1963; Pidoplicko 1956)					
	B.	%	I.	B.	I.	B.	%	I.	%	B.	I.
Domestic:											
Cattle	47	58.7	4	68.1	44.5	763	58.2	22	23.7	74.0	48.9
Ovicaprids	11	13.8	2	15.9	22.2	115	8.6	12	12.9	10.9	26.7
Pig	9	11.2	2	13.1	22.2	158	11.7	10.	10.8	14.9	22.2
Dog	2	2.5	1	2.9	11.1	2	0.1	1	1.1	0.2	2.2
Wild:											
Red deer						145	10.8	8	8.6		
Roe deer						13	1.0	4	4.3		
Aurochs						1	0.1	1	1.1		
Pig						7	0.5	3	3.2		
Horse	11	13.8	1	10.0		87	6.5	9	9.7		
Marten						3	0.2	3	3.2		
Bear						5	0.4	3	3.2		
Wolf						1	0.1	1	1.1		
Fox						4	0.3	3	3.2		
Beaver						4	0.3	2	2.1		
Badger						1	0.1	1	1.1		
Hare						6	0.4	4	4.3		
Hamster						2	0.1	1	1.1		
Birds						2	0.1	2	2.1		
Turtle						6	0.4	2	2.1		
Fish						2	0.1	1	1.1		
Total	80		10			1347		93			
Domestic	69	86.2	9	90.0		1058	78.6	45	48.5		
Wild	11	13.8	1	10.0		289	21.4	48	51.5		

Table No. 158a (after Pidoplicko 1956)

Khalepye (Tripolye B)

Animals	1936 B.	1936 I.	1937 B.	1937 I.	Total (1936–7) B.	Total (1936–7) %	Total (1936–7) I.	Total (1936–7) %	Domestic % B.	Domestic % I.
Domestic:										
Cattle	63	5	522	6	585	71.3	11	18.1	75.8	29.8
Ovicaprids	23	3	109	14	132	16.1	17	27.9	17.1	45.9
Pig	3	2	51	6	54	6.6	8	13.1	7.0	21.6
Dog	—	—	1	1	1	0.1	1	1.6	0.1	2.7
Wild:										
Red deer	3	1	2	1	5	0.6	2	3.3		
Elk	6	1	1	1	7	0.9	2	3.3		
Pig	—	—	1	1	1	0.1	1	1.6		
Horse	2	1	7	1	9	1.1	2	3.3		
Squirrel	1	1	1	1	2	0.2	2	3.3		
Mole	3	3	10	2	13	1.7	5	8.2		
Hamster	—	—	2	1	2	0.2	1	1.6		
Vole	—	—	1	1	1	0.1	1	1.6		
Hare	1	1	1	1	2	0.2	2	3.3		
Turtle	—	—	1	1	1	0.1	1	1.6		
Fish	2	2	4	3	6	0.7	5	8.2		
Total					821		61			
Domestic					772	94.1	37	60.7		
Wild					49	5.9	24	39.3		

Table No. 158b

Khalepye (Tripolye Bii; after Hančar 1956)

Animals	B.	%	I.	%
Domestic:				
Cattle	338	75.1	11	37.9
Sheep	65	14.5	7	24.2
Pig	47	10.4	11	37.9
Wild:				
Horse	7		2	
Others	20		9	
Total	477		40	
Domestic	450	94.5	29	72.5
Wild	27	5.5	11	27.5

Table No. 159

Krinicki & Podolsk (Tripolye B; after Hančar 1956)

Animals	Krinicki				Podolsk	
	B.	%	I.	%	I.	%
Domestic:						
Cattle	79	73.8	13	44.8	31	46.3
Ovicaprids	8	7.5	5	17.2	13	19.4
Pig	18	16.8	9	31.1	19	28.3
Dog	2	1.9	2	6.9	4	6.0
Wild:						
Horse	3		2		5	
Others	8		5		12	
Total	118		36		84	
Domestic	107	90.7	29	80.5	67	79.8
Wild	11	9.3	7	19.5	17	20.2

Table No. 160

Bilogrudivka (Tripolye)

Animals	B	%
Domestic:		
Cattle	349	45.8
Ovicaprids	220	28.9
Pig	186	24.5
Dog	6	0.8
Wild:		
Horse	77	
Hare	1	
Turtle	1	
Total	840	
Domestic	761	90.6
Wild	79	9.4

Table No. 161 (after Hančar 1956)

Suskovka (Tripolye Ci)

Animals	B.	%	I.	%
Domestic:				
Cattle	37	59.6	7	43.8
Ovicaprids	12	19.4	3	18.7
Pig	13	21.0	6	37.5
Wild:				
Horse	1		1	
Others	13		3	
Total	76		20	
Domestic	62	81.6	16	80.0
Wild	14	18.4	4	20.0

Table No. 162 (after Hančar 1956)

Andrejevka (Tripolye Ci)

Animals	B.	%	I.	%
Domestic				
Cattle	21	42.9	3	30.0
Ovicaprids	21	42.9	4	40.0
Pig	5	10.2	2	20.0
Dog	2	4.0	1	10.0
Wild:				
Horse	7		1	
Others	8		7	
Donkey	1		1	
Total	65		19	
Domestic	49	75.5	10	52.5
Wild	16	24.5	9	47.5

Table No. 163a (after Bibikova 1963)

Usatovo (Tripolye Cii)

Animals	B.	%	I.	%	Domestic B.	Domestic %
Domestic:						
Cattle	2218	26.6	228	28.4	27.3	31.7
Ovicaprids	4731	56.6	334	41.6	58.2	46.4
Pig	38	0.4	19	2.4	0.5	2.6
Dog	25	0.3	12	1.5	0.3	1.7
Horse	1112	13.4	127	15.8	13.7	17.6
Wild:						
Red deer	25	0.3	13	1.6		
Roe deer	4	0.05	3	0.4		
Pig	6	0.05	4	0.5		
Ass	66	0.8	22	2.7		
Antelope	4	0.05	3	0.4		
Wolf	3	0.05	3	0.4		
Fox	38	0.4	18	2.2		
Badger	1	0.05	1	0.1		
Turtle	6	0.05	1	0.1		
Beaver	1	0.05	1	0.1		
Hare	3	0.05	2	0.2		
Fish	65	0.75	12	1.5		
Birds	1	0.05	1	0.1		
Total	8347		804			
Domestic	8124	97.3	720	89.7		
Wild	223	2.7	84	10.3		

Table No. 163b (after Hančar 1956)

Usatovo (Tripolye Cii)

Animals	B.	%	I.	%
Cattle	1551	32.3	186	30.0
Ovicaprids	2425	50.5	323	52.1
Pig	24	0.5	13	2.1
Dog	11	0.2	7	1.1
Horse	790	16.5	91	14.7
Wild	111		56	
Total	4912		576	

Table No. 164 (a) (after Hančar 1956)

Gorodsk (Tripolye Cii)

Animals	B.	%	I.	%
Cattle	107	29.5	9	40.9
Ovicaprids	20	5.5	3	13.6
Pig	5	1.4	2	9.1
Horse	230	63.3	7	31.8
Camel	1	0.3	1	4.6
Wild	28		13	
Total	391		35	

Table No. 164b

Gorodsk (Tripolye Cii)

Animals	I.		II.		Total				Domestic %	
	B.	I.	B.	I.	B.	%	I.	%	B.	I.
Domestic:										
Cattle	26	2	31	1	57	27.6	3	12.0	30.8	25.0
Ovicaprids	3	1	18	2	21	10.1	3	12.0	11.4	25.0
Pig	1	1	1	1	2	1.0	2	8.0	1.1	16.7
Horse	38	2	67	2	105	50.8	4	16.0	56.7	33.3
Wild:										
Red deer	2	1	2	1	4	1.9	2	8.0		
Elk	1	1	2	1	3	1.4	2	8.0		
Bear	1	1	1	1	2	1.0	2	8.0		
Pig	–	–	3	1	3	1.4	1	4.0		
Aurochs	–	–	1	1	1	0.5	1	4.0		
Roe deer	–	–	3	1	3	1.4	1	4.0		
Otter	–	–	1	1	1	0.5	1	4.0		
Turtle	–	–	3	1	3	1.4	1	4.0		
Birds	–	–	2	2	2	1.0	2	8.0		
Total					207		25			
Domestic					185	89.5	12	48.0		
Wild					22	10.5	13	52.0		

Table No. 165a (after Bibikova 1963)

Bernova-Luka (Tripolye A)

Animals	B.	%	I.	%	Domestic % B.	I.
Domestic:						
Cattle	690	30.4	23	18.6	81.1	52.2
Ovicaprids	44	1.9	9	7.3	5.2	20.5
Pig	111	4.9	11	8.9	13.1	25.0
Dog	5	0.2	1	0.8	0.6	2.3
Wild:						
Red deer	866	38.0	25	20.2		
Roe deer	180	7.9	17	13.7		
Aurochs	14	0.6	2	1.6		
Pig	297	13.1	17	13.7		
Bear	4	0.2	1	0.8		
Horse	4	0.2	2	1.6		
Badger	14	0.6	6	4.8		
Hare	1	0.1	1	0.8		
Beaver	7	0.3	2	1.6		
Birds	8	0.4	4	3.2		
Fish	28	1.2	3	2.4		
Total	2273		124			
Domestic	850	37.4	44	35.6		
Wild	1423	62.6	80	64.4		

Table No. 165b (after Bibikova 1963)

Lenkovtse (Tripolye A)

Animals	B.	%	I.	%	B.	I.
Domestic:						
Cattle	937	47.5	30	25.0	84.0	49.1
Ovicaprids	44	2.2	10	8.3	3.9	16.4
Pig	129	6.5	19	15.8	11.6	31.2
Dog	5	0.2	2	1.7	0.5	3.3
Wild:						
Red deer	650	32.9	25	20.9		
Roe deer	80	4.0	9	7.5		
Aurochs	1	0.1	1	0.8		
Pig	90	4.6	9	7.5		
Horse	17	0.9	5	4.2		
Bear	1	0.1	1	0.8		
Otter	2	0.1	1	0.8		
Hare	3	0.1	2	1.7		
Beaver	3	0.1	2	1.7		
Birds	1	0.1	1	0.8		
Fish	12	0.6	3	2.5		
Total	1975		120			
Domestic	1115	56.4	61	50.8		
Wild	860	43.6	59	49.2		

Table No. 166 (after Bibikova 1963)

Soloncene I (Tripolye A)

Animals	B.	%	I.	%	Domestic % B.	I.
Domestic:						
Cattle	176	20.2	9	13.6	51.8	27.3
Ovicaprids	28	3.2	10	15.2	8.3	30.3
Pig	128	14.7	13	19.7	37.8	39.4
Dog	7	0.8	1	1.5	2.1	3.0
Wild:						
Red deer	261	29.8	13	19.7		
Roe deer	137	15.7	5	7.6		
Aurochs	4	0.5	2	3.0		
Pig	127	14.6	9	13.7		
Bear	2	0.2	2	3.0		
Fox	1	0.1	1	1.5		
Fish	2	0.2	1	1.5		
Total	873		66			
Domestic	339	38.9	33	50.0		
Wild	534	61.1	33	50.0		

Table No. 167 (after Pidoplicka 1956)

Kolomiischina (Tripolye B)

Animals	I (1938) B.	I.	II (1939) house 2 B.	I.	II (1939) house 3 B.	I.	II (1939) pit B.	I.	Total B.	%	I.	%	Domestic % B.	I.
Domestic:														
Cattle	343	12	24	3	9	1	77	4	453	59.2	20	26.7	68.6	44.5
Ovicaprids	118	8	12	1	8	1	15	3	153	19.9	13	17.3	23.2	28.9
Pig	33	7	2	1	–	–	11	2	46	6.0	10	13.3	7.0	22.2
Dog	–	–	6	1	–	–	2	1	8	1.0	2	2.7	1.2	4.4
Wild:														
Red deer	–	–	–	–	–	–	1	1	1	0.1	1	1.3		
Elk	–	–	–	–	–	–	3	1	3	0.4	1	1.3		
Pig	–	–	–	–	–	–	9	2	9	1.2	2	2.7		
Horse	13	3	4	1	–	–	3	1	20	2.6	5	6.7		
Mole	9	3	–	–	2	1	2	1	13	1.7	5	6.7		
Beaver	8	3	–	–	–	–	–	–	8	1.0	3	4.0		
Hare	1	1	–	–	–	–	–	–	1	0.1	1	1.3		
Turtle	–	–	–	–	–	–	12	2	12	1.6	2	2.7		
Birds	1	1	–	–	–	–	2	1	3	0.4	2	2.7		
Fish	–	–	–	–	–	–	37	8	37	4.8	8	10.6		
Total									767		75			
Domestic									660	86.1	45	60.0		
Wild									107	13.9	30	40.0		

Table No. 168 (after Bibikova 1963)

Polivanov-Jar (Tripolye B)

Animals	B.	%	I.	%	Domestic % B.	I.
Domestic:						
Cattle	1367	24.2	33	12.7	29.6	19.1
Ovicaprids	963	17.1	39	15.0	20.8	22.6
Pig	2256	39.9	92	35.3	48.8	53.1
Dog	35	0.6	9	3.5	0.8	5.2
Wild:						
Red deer	658	11.6	24	9.2		
Roe deer	123	2.2	14	5.4		
Elk	29	0.5	2	0.8		
Pig	118	2.1	16	6.2		
Bear	4	0.1	3	1.1		
Horse	30	0.5	3	1.1		
Fox	12	0.2	7	2.7		
Wolf	1	0.05	1	0.4		
Marten	1	0.05	1	0.4		
Cat	1	0.05	1	0.4		
Hare	33	0.6	9	3.5		
Hedgehog	1	0.05	1	0.4		
Birds	4	0.1	4	1.5		
Fish	2	0.1	1	0.4		
Total	5638		260			
Domestic	4621	81.8	173	66.5		
Wild	1017	18.2	87	33.5		

Table No. 169a (after Pidoplicko 1956)

Vladimirovka (Tripolye B)

Animals	B.	%	I.	%	Domestic % B.	I.
Domestic:						
Cattle	125	67.3	2	16.75	73.5	25.0
Ovicaprids	34	18.3	3	25.0	20.0	37.5
Pig	10	5.4	2	16.75	5.9	25.0
Dog	1	0.5	1	8.3	0.6	12.5
Wild:						
Red deer	11	5.9	1	8.3		
Roe deer	1	0.5	1	8.3		
Elk	3	1.6	1	8.3		
Horse	1	0.5	1	8.3		
Total	186		12			
Domestic	170	91.5	8	66.8		
Wild	16	8.5	4	33.2		

Table No. 169b (after Pidoplicko 1956)

Sandraki (Tripolye C)

Animals	B.	%	I.	%	Domestic % B.	I.
Domestic:						
Cattle	105	22.7	4	9.0	50.0	26.7
Ovicaprids	63	13.6	5	11.1	30.0	33.3
Pig	32	6.9	3	6.7	15.2	20.0
Dog	10	2.2	3	6.7	4.8	20.0
Wild:						
Red deer	51	11.0	3	6.7		
Roe deer	17	3.7	3	6.7		
Elk	4	0.9	1	2.2		
Aurochs	12	2.6	1	2.2		
Pig	42	9.1	5	11.1		
Horse	40	8.6	3	6.7		
Bear	3	0.6	1	2.3		
Fox	11	2.4	3	6.7		
Badger	2	0.4	1	2.2		
Marten	7	1.5	2	4.4		
Mole	5	1.1	2	4.4		
Turtle	1	0.2	1	2.2		
Frog	25	5.4	1	2.2		
Birds	31	6.7	2	4.4		
Fish	2	0.4	1	2.2		
Total	463		45			
Domestic	210	45.4	15	33.5		
Wild	253	54.6	30	66.5		

Table No. 170 (after Bibikova 1963)

Pavoloc (Tripolye C)

Animals	B.	%	I.	%	Domestic % B.	Domestic % I.
Domestic:						
Cattle	342	64.6	6	15.8	72.0	37.5
Ovicaprids	100	18.9	6	15.8	21.1	37.5
Pig	32	6.1	3	7.9	6.7	18.8
Dog	1	0.2	1	2.6	0.2	6.2
Wild:						
Red deer	14	2.6	3	7.9		
Roe deer	4	0.8	1	2.6		
Aurochs	2	0.4	1	2.6		
Pig	1	0.2	1	2.6		
Bear	2	0.4	1	2.6		
Fox	5	0.9	2	5.3		
Hare	5	0.9	2	5.3		
Beaver	3	0.6	1	2.6		
Vole	3	0.6	2	5.3		
Horse	1	0.2	1	2.6		
Turtle	8	1.5	2	5.3		
Squirrel	1	0.2	1	2.6		
Fish	5	0.9	4	10.6		
Total	529		38			
Domestic	475	89.8	16	42.1		
Wild	54	10.2	22	57.9		

Table No. 171a (after Bibikova 1963)

Stena (Tripolye C)

Animals	B.	%	I.	%	Domestic % B.	I.
Domestic:						
Cattle	370	38.3	13	16.7	69.4	33.3
Ovicaprids	59	6.1	9	11.5	11.1	23.1
Pig	94	9.7	14	18.0	17.6	35.9
Dog	10	1.0	3	3.8	1.9	7.7
Wild:						
Red deer	74	7.7	6	7.7		
Roe deer	43	4.5	4	5.1		
Pig	106	10.9	5	6.4		
Horse	185	19.1	9	11.5		
Bear	7	0.7	3	3.8		
Wolf	2	0.2	1	1.3		
Fox	6	0.6	3	3.8		
Badger	2	0.2	1	1.3		
Otter	1	0.1	1	1.3		
Marten	1	0.1	1	1.3		
Hare	1	0.1	1	1.3		
Beaver	5	0.5	2	2.6		
Birds	2	0.2	2	2.6		
Total	968		78			
Domestic	533	55.1	39	50.0		
Wild	435	44.9	39	50.0		

Table No. 171b (after Bibikova 1963)

Troyanov (Tripolye C)

Animals	B.	%	I.	%	Domestic % B.	Domestic % I.
Domestic:						
Cattle	465	71.0	13	22.4	84.3	44.8
Ovicaprids	68	10.4	7	12.1	12.4	24.2
Pig	11	1.7	6	10.3	2.0	20.7
Dog	7	1.1	3	5.2	1.3	10.3
Wild:						
Red deer	21	3.2	4	6.9		
Roe deer	4	0.6	2	3.5		
Elk	2	0.3	2	3.5		
Pig	19	2.9	4	6.9		
Bear	1	0.2	1	1.7		
Fox	1	0.2	1	1.7		
Hare	7	1.1	3	5.2		
Beaver	3	0.4	2	3.5		
Marten	1	0.2	1	1.7		
Horse	37	5.6	5	8.5		
Turtle	5	0.8	3	5.2		
Hamster	2	0.3	1	1.7		
Total	654		58			
Domestic	551	84.2	29	50.0		
Wild	103	15.8	29	50.0		

Table No. 172a (after Pidoplicko 1956)

Kunisivtse (Tripolye G) and *Kosilovste* (Tripolye C)

Animals	Kunisivtse						Kosilovste					
	B.	%	I.	%	B.	I.	B.	%	I.	%	B.	I.
Domestic:												
Cattle	190	78.2	5	33.3	88.0	45.4	166	85.2	5	38.4	86.9	45.4
Ovicaprids	19	7.8	3	20.0	8.8	27.3	3	1.5	2	15.4	1.6	18.2
Pig	7	2.9	3	20.0	3.2	27.3	21	10.8	3	23.1	11.0	27.3
Dog	–						1	0.5	1	7.7	0.5	9.1
Wild:												
Red deer	24	9.9	2	13.3			–		–			
Roe deer	–		–				2	1.0	1	7.7		
Pig	2	0.8	1	6.7			–		–			
Horse	–		–				2	1.0	1	7.7		
Hare	1	0.4	1	6.7			–		–			
Total	243		15				195		13			
Domestic	216	88.9	11	73.3			191	98.0	11	74.6		
Wild	27	11.1	4	26.7			4	2.0	2	15.4		

Table No. 172b (after Pidoplicko 1956)

Kiev (Sirtsi) (Tripolye G)

Animals	B.	%	I.	%	Domestic % B.	Domestic % I.
Domestic:						
Cattle	68	12.3	5	9.4	22.9	26.3
Ovicaprids	174	31.4	12	22.7	58.6	63.1
Pig	54	9.7	1	1.9	18.2	5.3
Horse	1	0.2	1	1.9	0.3	5.3
Wild:						
Roe deer	34	6.1	3	5.6		
Marten	1	0.2	1	1.9		
Hare	3	0.5	1	1.9		
Fish	208	37.6	25	47.2		
Birds	2	0.4	1	1.9		
Turtle	9	1.6	3	5.6		
Total	554		53			
Domestic	297	53.6	19	35.9		
Wild	257	46.4	34	64.1		

Table No. 173 (after Bibikova 1963)

Molyukhov Bugor (Tripolye)

Animals	Pit B.	Pit I.	Transitional B.	Transitional I.	Tripolye G B.	Tripolye G %	Tripolye G I.	Tripolye G %	Domestic % B.	Domestic % I.
Domestic:										
Cattle	27	2	?1	1	23	4.4	2	4.8	16.0	40.0
?Pig	5	2	–	–	–		–			
Horse	45	2	2	1	121	23.1	3	7.1	84.0	60.0
Wild:										
Red deer	48	3	3	2	78	14.9	3	7.1		
Roe deer	22	3	4	1	30	5.7	4	9.5		
Aurochs	?1	1	–	–	15	2.9	2	4.8		
Elk	8	2	4	1	18	3.4	1	2.4		
Pig	81	4	8	2	121	23.1	4	9.5		
Bear	4	1	–	–	4	0.8	1	2.4		
Wolf	1	1	–	–	–		–			
Otter	1	1	–	–	–		–			
Marten	1	1	–	–	–		–			
Badger	4	2	2	1	1	0.2	1	2.4		
Beaver	–	–	–	–	6	1.1	2	4.8		
Birds	89	20	6	3	20	3.8	7	16.6		
Turtle	130	19	26	3	87	16.6	12	28.6		
Total					524		42			
Domestic					144	27.5	5	11.9		
Wild					380	72.5	37	88.1		

Table No. 174 (after Bibikova 1963)

Podgortse (Tripolye G)

Animals	I B.	I I.	II B.	II I.	Total B.	Total %	Total I.	Total %	Domestic % B.	Domestic % I.
Domestic:										
Cattle	135	7	188	11	323	43.0	18	21.9	56.6	35.3
Ovicaprids	4	2	34	6	38	5.0	8	9.8	6.6	15.7
Pig	4	1	77	16	81	10.8	17	20.7	14.2	33.3
Dog	2	1	–	–	2	0.3	1	1.2	0.3	2.0
Horse	14	1	113	6	127	16.9	7	8.6	22.3	13.7
Wild:										
Red deer	62	4	3	1	65	8.6	5	6.1		
Roe deer	1	1	–	–	1	0.1	1	1.2		
Pig	29	3	–	–	29	3.8	3	3.7		
Bear	2	1	–	–	2	0.3	1	1.2		
Elk	16	2	2	1	18	2.4	3	3.7		
Turtle	19	8	29	4	48	6.4	12	14.6		
Beaver	2	2	–	–	2	0.3	2	2.4		
Fish	11	2	4	1	15	2.0	3	3.7		
Birds	–	–	1	1	1	0.1	1	1.2		
Total					752		82			
Domestic					571	76.0	51	62.2		
Wild					181	24.0	31	37.8		

Table No. 175a (after Hančar 1956)

Animals	Grenovka B.	Ind.	Ljubushka-Posad B.	Ind.	Kolomiischina B.	Ind.	Korytnoye B.	Ind.	Scerbatovo B.	Ind.
Cattle	16	2	22	4	21	3	3	1	13	6
Ovicaprids	4	1	7	3	11	1	–	–	4	2
Pig	–	–	5	4	1	1	–	–	–	–
Dog	1	1	3	2	6	1	–	–	–	1
Horse	5	1	1	1	3	1	–	–	1	1
Wild	9	2	–	–	–	–	4	3	2	1

Table No. 175b (after Pidoplicko 1956)

Animals	A B.	l.	B B.	I.	C B.	I.	D B.	I.
Domestic:								
Cattle	76	18	8	2	9	2	22	2
Ovicaprids	1	1	1	1	6	2	26	3
Pig	–	–	3	1	5	2	13	2
Dog	1	1	–	–	1	1	3	1
Wild:								
Red deer	27	1	–	–	1	1	5	1
Pig	–	–	–	–	1	1	–	–
Horse	–	–	–	–	2	1	5	2
Hare	–	–	–	–	–	–	3	1
Hamster	1	1	–	–	–	–	–	–
Birds	–	–	–	–	–	–	1	1
Total	106	22	12	4	25	10	78	13

A—Norcia Čortoria; B—Ozarintse; C—Pliskov; D—Raiki

359

Table No. 176

Cultivated Plants of the Tripolye Culture

	Wheat	Barley	Millet	A	B	C	D	E
Bernova-Luka	x	x	x					x
Chalep'je	x							x
Chernyachenye	x							x
Kolodistoye	x	x	x					
Kolomiischina	x	x	x	x				
Koretnoye	x							x
Krinicki	x							x
Krutoborodintse	x	x	x					x
Luka-Vrublevetskaia	x	x	x	x	x	x	x	
Novoselkach	x							x
Semeniv	x	x						x
Schervaneka	x		x		x			
Stayikach	x		x		x			
Sushkovka	x	x	x					x
Tripolye	x		x		x			x
Verem'je	x	x	x		x			
Vladimirovka	x	x	x	x				
Zhukovste	x							x

A—Hard wheat *(Triticum durum)*; B—Bread wheat *(Triticum vulgare)*; C—Club wheat *(Triticum compactum)*; D—Emmer *(Triticum dicoccum)*; E—Unspecified wheat *(Triticum sp.)*.

Table No. 177

Wild Animals of the Hungarian Copper Age

	A	B	C	D	E	F	G
Red deer	x		x	x	x	x	
Roe deer	x			x		x	
Aurochs	x	x	x	x	x	x	x
Pig	x	x		x		x	x
Horse							x
Hare						x	
Cat	x						
Turtle	x			x			
Fish	x			x		x	
Birds			x	x			

A—Budapest-Andor utca; B—Derecske-Téglagyár; C—Hódmezóvásárhely-Tartársánc-Zalay-Téglagyár; D—Polgár-Basatanya; E—Pusztaföldvár-Baki malom; F—Tarnabod; G—Tiszaigar.

Table No. 178

Domestic Animals of the Hungarian Copper Age

	Cattle	Ovicaprids	Pig	Dog	Horse
Tisza-Polgar culture:					
Hajduszoboszlo	x				
Hódmezövásárhely-Tartársánc-					
Zalay-Téglagyár	x	x	x	x	
Polgár-Basatanya	x	x	x	x	
Pusztaföldvár-Bakimalom	x	x	x		
Tiszaiger	x		x		
Bodrogkeresztur culture:					
Derecske-Téglagyár	x	x	x		
Polgár-Basatanya	x	x	x		
Székely-Zöldteltk	x	x	x		
Tarnabod	x	x	x	x	
Baden culture:					
Alsonmedi	x				
Budapest-Andor utca	x	x	x	x	
Polgár-Basatanya	x	x	x		
Székely-Zöldteltk	x	x	x		
Üllö	x				
Copper Age:					
Deszk B					x

Table No. 179

(Tisza-Polgár)

Animals	Tiszaigar		Hódmezövásárhely-Tartársánc-Zalay-Téglagyár		Pusztaföldvár-Bakimalom	
	B.	Ind.	B.	Ind.	B.	Ind.
Domestic:						
Cattle	24	4	9	4	7	2
Ovicaprids	–	–	5	4	9	4
Pig	1	1	1	1	11	5
Dog	–	–	2	2	–	–
Wild:						
Red deer	–	–	1	1	9	4
Aurochs	4	3	1	1	9	2
Pig	3	1	–	–	–	–
Horse	1	1	–	–	–	–
Birds	–	–	–	–	1	1
Total	33	10	19	13	46	18

Table No. 180

Derecske-Téglagyàr (Bodrogkeresztur)

Animals	B.	%	Ind.	%	Domestic % B.	Domestic % Ind.
Domestic:						
Cattle	158	75.5	23	50.0	84.1	63.9
Ovicaprids	10	4.8	6	13.1	5.3	16.7
Pig	20	9.6	7	15.2	10.6	19.4
Wild:						
Aurochs	20	9.6	9	19.5		
Pig	1	0.5	1	2.2		
Total	209		46			
Domestic	188	89.9	36	78.3		
Wild	21	10.1	10	21.7		

Table No. 181

Tarnabod (Bodrogkeresztur)

Animals	B.	%	Ind.	%	Domestic % B.	Domestic % Ind.
Domestic:						
Cattle	562	61.3	42	30.9	75.6	45.2
Ovicaprids	69	7.5	26	19.1	9.3	27.9
Pig	109	11.9	22	16.2	14.7	23.7
Dog	3	0.3	3	2.2	0.4	3.2
Wild:						
Red deer	43	4.7	13	9.5		
Roe deer	12	1.3	6	4.4		
Aurochs	83	9.1	11	8.1		
Pig	31	3.4	9	6.6		
Hare	2	0.2	2	1.5		
Fish	3	0.3	2	1.5		
Total	917		136			
Domestic	743	81.0	93	68.4		
Wild	174	19.0	43	31.6		

Table No. 182

Székely-Zöldteltk (Bodrogkeresztur & Baden)

	Bodrogkeresztur				Baden	
Animals	B.	%	Ind.	%	B.	%
Domestic:						
Cattle	31	34.8	7	33.3	21	25.9
Ovicaprids	39	43.8	9	42.9	53	65.5
Pig	19	21.4	5	23.8	7	8.6
Total	89		21		81	

Table No. 183

Budapest-Andor utca (Baden)

					Domestic %	
Animals	B.	%	Ind.	%	B.	Ind.
Domestic:						
Cattle	160	32.1	63	32.8	34.4	36.6
Ovicaprids	194	38.9	69	35.9	41.7	40.2
Pig	105	21.0	36	19.3	22.6	20.9
Dog	6	1.2	4	2.1	1.3	2.3
Wild:						
Red deer	13	2.6	8	4.2		
Roe deer	4	0.8	1	0.5		
Aurochs	4	0.8	3	1.6		
Pig	4	0.8	3	1.6		
Cat	2	0.4	2	1.0		
Turtle	6	1.2	1	0.5		
Fish	1	0.2	1	0.5		
Total	499		191			
Domestic	465	93.2	172	90.1		
Wild	34	6.8	19	9.9		

Table No. 184

Wild Animals of the Austrian Copper Age

	A	B	C	D
Red deer	x		x	x
Roe deer	x		x	x
Pig		?		x
Chamois				x
Cat				x
Bear			x	x
Lynx				x
Fox				x
Beaver				x
Wolf				x
Fish				x

A—Attersee; B—Merkstein-Felsensitz; C—Ossarn; D—Priesterhügel.

Table No. 185

Domestic Animals of the Italian Copper Age

	Cattle	Ovicaprids	Pig	Dog
Cantalupo	x		x	x
Caverna di Sapendol	x		x	
Pescale	x	x	x	x
La Starza	x	x	x	x

Table No. 186

La Starza (Copper Age)

Animals	% Bones
Cattle	25.5
Pig	11.0
Sheep	60.5
Dog	3.0
Total	487

Table No. 187

Domestic Animals of the Swiss Copper Age

	Cattle	Ovicaprids	Pig	Dog
Concise	x	x	x	x
Niederwil	x	x	x	
Roseaux		x	x	
Uerikon	x	x	x	x

Table No. 188

Uerikon (Copper Age)

Animals	Ind.	%	Domestic %
Domestic:			
Cattle	22	30.2	46.7
Ovicaprids	7	9.6	14.9
Pig	16	21.9	34.1
Dog	2	2.7	4.3
Wild:			
Red deer	10	13.7	
Roe deer	5	6.8	
Elk	2	2.7	
Aurochs	3	4.1	
Ibex	1	1.4	
Pig	3	4.1	
Bear	1	1.4	
Beaver	1	1.4	
Total	73		
Domestic	47	64.4	
Wild	26	35.6	

Table No. 189

Cultivated Plants of the Swiss Copper Age

	A	B	C	D	E	F
Niederwil					x	x
Nidau				x		
St. Blaise	x	x	x		x	x
Montiller		x	x	x		
Uerikon		x	x		x	x

A—Emmer; B—Club wheat; C—Barley;
D—Millet; E—Flax; F—Poppy.

Table No. 190

Wild Animals of the French Copper Age

	A	B	C	D	E	F	G	H	I	J	K	L	M
Red deer		x				x			?	?			x
Roe deer									?	?			x
Aurochs	x												x
Pig		?	x	x	x	x	x	x				x	x
Horse						x							
Fox				x	x							x	x
Badger		x							x			x	
Hare									x		x	x	
Rabbit	x	x			x		x						
Squirrel												x	
Hedgehog												x	
Wolf						?							
Vole													x

A—Anis-Deux-Hortus; B—Bergerie Neuve; C—Biard; D—Garde de Barzan;
E—Gimel; F—Monna; G—La Paillade; H—Pertus II; I—Peu Richard;
J—St. Paul-de-Varces; K—Terrevaine; L—Trache 2; M—Les Matignons.

Table No. 191

Domestic Animals of the French Copper Age

	Cattle	Ovicaprids	Pig	Dog
Peu Richard Culture:				
Biard	x	x	?	
Garde de Barzan	x	x		
Les Matignons	x	x	x	x
Peu Richard	x	x		
Copper Age:				
Anis-Deux-Hortus	x	x	x	
Bergerie Neuve	x	x	x	
La Couronne	x	x		
Gimel	x	x	x	x
Mas Rougous		x		
Monna		x		x
Nimose	x	x		
La Paillade	x	x	x	
Pertus II	?	x		
Saint Paul-de-Varces		x		
Terrevaine	x	x		
Trache Deux		x	x	x
Ferussac				x
Liquisse				x

Table No. 192

Anis-Deux-Hortus (French Copper Age)

Animals	B.	%	Ind.	%	Domestic % B.	Ind.
Domestic:						
Cattle	24	35.3	5	33.3	39.3	41.7
Ovicaprids	33	48.5	5	33.3	54.1	41.7
Pig	4	5.9	2	13.35	6.6	16.6
Wild:						
Aurochs	2	2.9	1	6.7		
Rabbit	5	7.4	2	13.35		
Total	68		15			
Domestic	61	89.7	12	79.95		
Wild	7	10.3	3	20.05		

Table No. 193

Bergerie Neuve (French Copper Age)

Animals	B.	%	Ind.	%	Domestic % B.	Ind.
Domestic:						
Cattle	23	16.2	6	20.0	20.4	23.1
Sheep	82	57.8	16	53.4	72.5	61.5
Pig	8	5.6	4	13.3	7.1	15.4
Wild:						
Deer	2	1.4	1	3.3		
Badger	22	15.5	2	6.7		
Rabbit	5	3.5	1	3.3		
Total	142		30			
Domestic	113		26			
Wild	29		4			

Table No. 194

Gimel (French Copper Age)

Animals	B.	%	Ind.	%	Domestic % B.	Ind.
Domestic:						
Cattle	9	13.4	2	12.5	15.8	15.4
Ovicaprids	46	68.7	9	56.25	80.8	69.2
Pig	1	1.5	1	6.25	1.7	7.7
Dog	1	1.5	1	6.25	1.7	7.7
Wild:						
Pig	6	8.9	1	6.25		
Fox	1	1.5	1	6.25		
Rabbit	3	4.5	1	6.25		
Total	67		16			
Domestic	57	85.1	13	81.25		
Wild	10	14.9	3	18.75		

Table No. 195

La Paillade (French Copper Age)

Animals	B.	%	Ind.	%	Domestic % B.	Ind.
Domestic:						
Cattle	7	16.7	3	30.0	18.4	37.5
Ovicaprids	27	64.3	3	30.0	71.1	37.5
Pig	4	9.5	2	20.0	10.5	25.0
Dog	–	–	–	–	–	–
Wild:						
Pig	1	2.4	1	10.0		
Fox	–	–	–	–		
Rabbit	3	7.1	1	10.0		
Total	42		10			
Domestic	38	90.5	8	80.0		
Wild	4	9.5	2	20.0		

Table No. 196

Trache 2 (French Copper Age)

Animals	B.	%	Ind.	%	Domestic % B.	Domestic % Ind.
Domestic:						
Pig	47	11.6	6	18.2	36.4	42.8
Sheep	57	14.0	7	21.2	44.2	50.0
Dog	25	6.2	1	3.3	19.4	7.2
Wild:						
Pig	15	3.7	2	6.1		
Fox	149	36.7	5	15.3		
Badger	41	10.1	3	9.1		
Hare	70	17.3	7	21.2		
Squirrel	1	0.2	1	3.3		
Hedgehog	1	0.2	1	3.3		
Total	406		33			
Domestic	129	31.8	14	42.7		
Wild	277	68.2	19	58.3		

Table No. 197

Plants of the Iberian Copper Age

	A	B	C	D	E	F	G
Assentas		x		x	x		
Almizaraque	x	x	x	x	x	x	x
Baleal		x		x	x		x
Campos				x			x
Fuente Vermeja				x			
Lugarico Viejo			x	x	x		x
Monte della Bersella		?	?	x			
Zambujul							x

A—Emmer; B—Club wheat; C—Bread wheat; D—Wheat (unspecified);
E—Barley; F—Flax; G—Legumes.

Table No. 198

Wild fauna of German Neolithic/Copper Age sites

	A	B	C	D	E	F	G	H	I	J
Red deer	x	x	?	x	x	x	x	x	x	x
Roe deer	x	x	?	x	x	x	x	x	x	x
Elk	x	x							x	x
Aurochs	x	x		x	x	?			x	x
Bison		x			x				x	
Pig	x	x		x	x	x	x	x	x	x
Bear	x	x		x	x	x	x	x	x	x
Horse			x	x	x				x	
Beaver	x	x		x	x				x	x
Otter		x			x				x	
Badger	x	x			x					x
Wolf										x
Fox	x	x			x				x	
Cat		x			x				x	
Turtle								x		
Birds		x						x	x	x
Fish		x			x					

A–Bodman; B–Dullenried; C–Hall; D–Unterrühldingen;
E–Nussdorf; F–Altenerdingen; G–Altheim; H–Pesternacker;
I–Sipplingen; J–Pölling.

Table No. 199

Domestic Animals of German Late Neolithic/Copper Age sites

	Cattle	Ovicaprids	Pig	Dog	Horse
Altheim Culture:					
Altenerdingen	x	x	x	x	x
Altheim	x	x	x	x	
Hall	x	x	x		
Heroldingen	?		?		
Hohenaltheim	?		?		
Nähermemmingen	?		?		
Pesternacker	x	x	x	x	x
Pölling	x	x	x	x	
Horgen Culture:					
Dullenried	x	x		x	x
Ravensburg	x			x	
Sipplingen	x	x	x	x	
Other sites:					
Bodman	x	x	x	x	
Nussdorf	x	x	x	x	
Reinlingen	?		?		
Unterrühldingen	x	?	x	x	

Table No. 200

Altenerdingen (Altheim)

Animals	B.	%	Ind.	%	Domestic % B.	Ind.
Domestic:						
Cattle	333	54.4	14	27.0	66.7	36.8
Ovicaprids	20	3.3	5	9.6	4.1	13.2
Pig	76	12.4	9	17.3	15.2	23.7
Dog	1	0.1	1	1.9	0.2	2.6
Horse	69	11.3	9	17.3	13.8	23.7
Wild or domestic:						
Cattle	12	2.0	2	3.9		
Pig	22	3.6	1	1.9		
Wild:						
Red deer	49	8.0	5	9.6		
Roe deer	6	1.0	1	1.9		
Pig	22	3.6	4	7.7		
Bear	2	0.3	1	1.9		
Total	612		52			
Domestic	499	81.5	38	73.1		
Wild	113	18.5	14	26.9		

Table No. 201

Altheim (Altheim)

Animals	1914 B.	1938 B.	%	Ind.	%	Domestic % B.	Ind.
Domestic:							
Cattle	9	220	62.3	8	26.6	67.1	36.4
Ovicaprids	5	37	10.5	6	20.0	11.3	27.3
Pig	3	68	19.3	5	16.7	20.7	22.7
Dog	–	3	0.8	3	10.0	0.9	13.6
Wild:							
Red deer	26	10	2.8	3	10.0		
Roe deer	7	8	2.3	3	10.0		
Pig	1	7	2.0	2	6.7		
Bear	1	–	–	–	–		
Total	52	353		30			
Domestic	17	328	92.9	22	73.3		
Wild	35	25	7.1	8	26.7		

Table No. 202

Pesternacker (Altheim)

Animals	B.	%	Ind.	Domestic % B.	Ind.
Domestic:					
Cattle	19	16.4	6	31.7	30.0
Ovicaprids	14	12.1	4	23.3	20.0
Pig	10	8.6	4	16.7	20.0
Dog	2	1.7	1	3.3	5.0
Horse	15	12.9	5	25.0	25.0
Wild or domestic:					
Pig	2	1.7			
Wild:					
Red deer	36	31.0	?		
Roe deer	10	8.6	3		
Pig	3	2.6	2		
Bear	1	0.9	1		
Turtle	3	2.6	2		
Crane	1	0.9	1		
Total	116				
Domestic	60				
Wild	56				

Table No. 203

Sipplingen (German Copper Age)

Animals	B.	%	Ind.	%	Domestic % B.	Ind.
Domestic:						
Cattle	469	30.1	40	19.3	35.3	24.8
Ovicaprids	149	9.6	33	15.9	11.2	20.5
Pig	601	38.6	70	33.8	45.2	43.5
Dog	110	7.1	18	8.7	8.3	11.2
Wild:						
Red deer	98	6.3	8	3.8		
Roe deer	45	2.9	8	3.8		
Elk	3	0.2	1	0.5		
Aurochs	5	0.3	2	1.0		
Bison	1	0.1	1	0.5		
Pig	54	3.5	11	5.3		
Horse	1	0.1	1	0.5		
Bear	10	0.6	4	1.9		
Beaver	2	0.1	2	1.0		
Otter	2	0.1	2	1.0		
Fox	2	0.1	2	1.0		
Cat	1	0.1	1	0.5		
Bird	2	0.1	2	1.0		
Fish	1	0.1	1	0.5		
Total	1556		207			
Domestic	1329	85.4	161	77.7		
Wild	227	14.6	46	22.3		

Table No. 204

Pölling (Altheim)

Animals	Bones	%	Ind.	%
Cattle (Wild and domestic)	98	11.3	16	10.9
Red deer	360	41.7	41	27.9
Roe deer	15	1.7	7	4.7
Elk	2	0.2	2	1.4
Cattle or deer	7	0.8	1	0.7
Ovicaprids	20	2.3	9	6.1
Ovicaprids or roe deer	4	0.5	4	2.7
Domestic pig	37	4.3	9	6.1
Wild pig	164	19.0	25	17.0
Wild or domestic pig	88	10.2	10	6.8
Turbary dog	28	3.2	4	2.7
Wolf	?1	0.1	?1	0.7
Bear	7	0.8	5	3.4
Beaver	31	3.6	10	6.8
Badger	1	0.1	1	0.7
Birds	2	0.2	2	1.4
Total	865		147	

Table No. 205

Wild fauna of the Single Grave and Globular Amphorae Complex

	A	B	C	D	E	F	G	H	I	J	K	L	M	N	O
Red deer	x	x			x	x	x	x	?	x	x	x	x		x
Roe deer	x				x				?	x		x		x	x
Elk				x	x	x		x				x			
Aurochs	x				x	x									
Bison															x
Pig	x			x	x				x	x	x	?	x	x	?
Horse													x		
Beaver	x				x		x	x							
Badger					x									x	
Otter					x										
Bear	x				x										
Wolf		x													
Fox	x				x							x			
Marten					x										
Wolverine					x										
Cat	x														
Hare			x		x										
Seal	x				x										
Porpoise	x														
Tortoise				x											
Fish	x	x	x												
Birds	x	x					x								

A—Rzucewo; B—Succase; C—Tolkemit; D—Zota; E—Rinnekalns; F—Dümmersee; G—Bedinge; H—Bergsvägen; I—Kirche; J—Klagstorp; K—Vagnshed; L—Strzelce (Globular Amphorae); M—Fleith (Globular Amphorae); N—Majdan Mokwinski; O—Proszowice.

Table No. 206

Domestic Animals of the Single Grave Complex

	Cattle	Ovicaprids	Pig	Dog	Horse
Poland:					
Majdan Mokwinski	x	x	x		
Nowy Daromin	x	x	?	x	
Potyry			x		
Proszowice	x	x	?		
Rzucewo	x	x	x	x	
Strzyzow	x			x	
Succase	?		?	x	
Tolkemit	x		x	x	
Zaklodzie				x	
Złota	x	x	x	x	?
Baltic States:					
Barenkopf	x		x	x	
Nidden	x			x	
Rinnekalns				x	
Czechoslovakia:					
Lovosice				x	
Marefy				x	
Germany:					
Dobris		x		x	
Gutenberg	x	x			
Köthen				?	
Schafstadt	x			?	
Schelditz	x				
Sittichenbach				?	
Uthleben				x	
Zeitzer Forst				x	
Switzerland:					
Amberg	x	x	x	x	
Auvernier	x	x	x	x	
Baldegg	x	x	x	x	x
Greng		x		x	
Luscherz	x	x	x	x	
Meyer	x	x	x	x	
Robenhausen	x	x	x	x	
Sutz	x		x		
Utoquai	x	x	x	x	
Vinelz	x	x	x	x	
Austria:					
Föllik	x	x		x	x

[continued

Table No. 206 (Contd.)

	Cattle	Ovicaprids	Pig	Dog	Horse
Sweden:					
Åvaslov		?			
Bedinge		x			
Bergsvägen		x		x	
Bodarp		x			
Kirche		?			
Klagstorp		?			
Linkoping				x	
Vagnshed		x			
Vanneberga		?			
Vilby		x			
Hvellinge					?
Globular Amphorae					
Poland:					
Adolfin	x				
Biskupin			x		
Brzesc Kujawski	x		x	x	
Debiče	x				
Dobre	x				
Mierzanowice	x	x	x	x	
Parchatka	x				
Pitutkowo	x				
Raciborowice	x	x			
Stok	x	x	x		
Strżelce	x	x	?		
Zdrojówka	x	x	x		
Germany:					
Alltoplitz	x				
Dölkau	x				
Dümmersee	x		x	x	x
Fleith	x		x	x	
Frohndorf				x	
Gretesch				x	
Gross-Osterhausen			x		
Ketzin	x		x		
Langendorf	?				?
Mittelhausen	x				
Osterburg	x				
Schönebeck	x				
Stobra	x		x		
Trebus	x		?		
Weick-Luisenthal					?

Table No. 207

Baldegg (Single Grave Complex)

Animals	1938 Ind.	1939 Ind.	Total Ind.	%	Domestic %
Domestic:					
Cattle	20	10	30	20.7	28.8
Ovicaprids	35	12	47	32.4	45.2
Pig	15	6	21	14.4	20.2
Dog	1	2	3	2.1	2.9
Horse	1	2	3	2.1	2.9
Wild:					
Red deer	10	11	21	14.4	
Roe deer	1	1	2	1.4	
Aurochs	2	–	2	1.4	
Pig	5	3	8	5.5	
Wolf	–	1	1	0.7	
Marten	1	–	1	0.7	
Bear	1	2	3	2.1	
Beaver	2	1	3	2.1	
Total	94	51	145		
Domestic	72	32	104	71.7	
Wild	22	19	41	28.3	

Table No.208

Utoquai (Single Grave Complex)

Animals	B.	%	Ind.	%	Domestic % B.	Domestic % Ind.
Domestic:						
Cattle	342	45.9	16	23.9	57.2	34.0
Ovicaprids	39	5.2	8	11.9	6.5	17.0
Pig	185	24.9	17	25.4	30.9	36.2
Dog	32	4.3	6	8.9	5.4	12.8
Wild:						
Red deer	77	10.4	6	8.9		
Roe deer	42	5.6	5	7.5		
Pig	16	2.2	2	3.0		
Bear	1	0.1	1	1.5		
Badger	1	0.1	1	1.5		
Fox	2	0.3	1	1.5		
Beaver	5	0.7	3	4.5		
Hare	2	0.3	1	1.5		
Total	744		67			
Domestic	598	80.3	47	70.1		
Wild	146	39.7	20	29.9		

Table No. 209

Dümmersee (Megalithic Village)

Animals	Nobis 1955 No. bones	Luttschwäger 1954 No. bones	Ind.
Domestic:			
Cattle	1	11	4
Pig	1	—	—
Dog	5	—	—
Horse (? dom.)	186	2	1
Wild:			
Aurochs	—	41	6
Red deer	—	52	7
Elk	—	10	5
Total	193	116	23

Table No. 210

Cultivated Plants of the Single Grave Complex

	A	B	C	D	E	F	G	H	I
Poland:									
Proszowice	x	x	x		x				
Złota		x		x					
Baltic States:									
Lindenberg		x		x					
Nidden					x				
Germany:									
Schafstadt		?		x					
Schelditz				x					
Switzerland:									
Auvernier					x				
Amberg				x			x		
Luscherz									P
Meyer	x	x	x		x	x	x	x	
Robenhausen			x		x	x	x	x	P
Sutz						x			
Utoquai		x	x		x		x		P
Denmark:									
Gaarslev					x				
Hammer					x				
Hornslev		x		x					
Klelund					x				
Kettrup			?	x					
Tyregodlund					x				
Sweden:									
Hyltarp					x				
Maglø					x				
Rotved					x				
Sannehed					x				
Svedela					x				

A—Einkorn; B—Emmer; C—Club wheat; D—Wheat (unspecified);
E—Barley; F—Millet; G—Flax; H—Poppy; I—Legumes
(P—Pea).